Banking Resilience and Global Financial Stability

Transformations in Banking, Finance and Regulation

Print ISSN: 2752-5821
Online ISSN: 2752-583X

Series Editors: Sabri Boubaker
(*EM Normandie Business School, France*)
Duc Khuong Nguyen
(*EMLV Business School, France*)

Presently, the banking and finance sectors evolve within a globalized and highly uncertain environment. Each business and financial decision requires careful consideration of country-specific and international factors due to high levels of shock transmission and volatility spillovers. Furthermore, it would be remiss to omit the COVID-19 health crisis, which caused harmful effects to all areas of the real economy and made profound changes in the way our firms, economies, and markets used to function.

Many other already well-known aspects, including the repercussions of quantitative easing policies, disruptive technologies in finance (e.g., FinTech, Big Data, Data Analytics, Artificial Intelligence, and Blockchains), as well as innovative financing instruments for startups (e.g., ICOs and crowdfunding) are currently revolutionizing banking and finance and posing numerous challenges to regulatory bodies and policymakers. Climate change emergencies also put pressure on governments and firms worldwide to improve policy on governance, corporate social responsibility, and sustainability practices.

This book series "Transformations in Banking, Finance and Regulation" attempts to address these issues by focusing on transformative perspectives in banking and finance. Accordingly, it provides evidence-based guidance, recommendations, and pathways to assist businesses and policy decision-makers through an interdisciplinary and in-depth understanding of ongoing changes in the behavior of economic agents.

Published

For the complete list of volumes in this series, please visit
www.worldscientific.com/series/tbfr

Transformations in Banking, Finance and Regulation

Volume 10

Banking Resilience and Global Financial Stability

Editors

Sabri Boubaker

EM Normandie Business School, France

Marwa Elnahass

Newcastle University Business School, UK

World Scientific

NEW JERSEY • LONDON • SINGAPORE • BEIJING • SHANGHAI • HONG KONG • TAIPEI • CHENNAI • TOKYO

Published by

World Scientific Publishing Europe Ltd.
57 Shelton Street, Covent Garden, London WC2H 9HE
Head office: 5 Toh Tuck Link, Singapore 596224
USA office: 27 Warren Street, Suite 401-402, Hackensack, NJ 07601

Library of Congress Cataloging-in-Publication Data
Names: Boubaker, Sabri, editor. | Elnahass, Marwa, editor.
Title: Banking resilience and global financial stability / edited Sabri Boubaker, EM Normandie Business School, France, Marwa Elnahass, Newcastle University Business School, UK.
Description: New Jersey : World Scientitfic, [2024] | Series: Transformations in banking, finance and regulation, 2752-5821 ; vol. 10 | Includes bibliographical references and index.
Identifiers: LCCN 2023016695 | ISBN 9781800614314 (hardcover) | ISBN 9781800614321 (ebook) | ISBN 9781800614338 (ebook other)
Subjects: LCSH: Banks and banking, International. | International finance. | Financial crises.
Classification: LCC HG3881 .B35135 2024 | DDC 332.1/5--dc23/eng/20230413
LC record available at https://lccn.loc.gov/2023016695

British Library Cataloguing-in-Publication Data
A catalogue record for this book is available from the British Library.

For any available supplementary material, please visit
https://www.worldscientific.com/worldscibooks/10.1142/Q0422#t=suppl

Desk Editors: Aanand Jayaraman/Ana Ovey/Shi Ying Koe

Typeset by Stallion Press
Email: enquiries@stallionpress.com

https://doi.org/10.1142/9781800614321_fmatter

Preface

The banking industry underwent significant transformations in the last decade due to new regulations aimed at mitigating the risk of failure and promoting enhanced stock market valuations. These regulations were aimed at ensuring that the industry operates in a more stable and secure environment and that it is better equipped to weather economic downturns and financial crises. This has led to an increased focus on risk management, compliance, and a renewed emphasis on transparency and accountability. Moreover, the industry has had to adapt to the rapidly changing technological landscape and the rise of FinTech, which has brought new opportunities and challenges. In parallel, the complexity and diversity of banking financial instruments and transactions have led to substantial information asymmetries and agency conflicts. There is so far a lack of conclusive evidence on the impact of institutional characteristics of banking, the role of bank type (e.g., Islamic vs. conventional), and systematic risk on global banking stability. Moreover, evidence addressing the implications of the COVID pandemic on alternative banking systems is still burgeoning.

This is the first book on global banking stability and resilience, which collectively addresses several contemporary issues across the industry. It provides a comprehensive understanding of the challenges and opportunities facing the global banking industry and how these may be addressed through banking business models, effective policies, and regulations. It covers a wide range of topics, such as corporate governance, asset–liability management, risk management, financial performance, and regulatory frameworks, providing a comprehensive understanding of the global banking sector. This book also highlights the potential benefits of alternative banking models, such as Islamic banking, and their potential contributions to global financial stability and resilience.

This book offers new insights, recent findings, and future perspectives on the global banking industry concerning bank stability and resilience through contributions from international scholars using quantitative and qualitative methods. This book also provides updated evidence and debates regarding the impact of recent regulations and governance structures on the banking industry. It notes that the industry underwent significant changes in response to financial turmoil and new laws and regulations to improve bank resiliency, protect against systematic risks, and promote fair and ethical banking practices.

This book serves as a valuable reference for researchers, policymakers, and industry professionals in banking, finance, economics, and international business. It is a timely and insightful collection of theoretical, empirical, and policy contributions from renowned international scholars and practitioners.

This book is divided into three parts and contains ***15*** chapters. The first part deals with the effect(s) of financial and institutional characteristics. In ***Chapter 1***, the study concludes that the capital buffer concept is ineffective in promoting financial stability and develops an alternative concept. The new concept consists of only two components: a resilience buffer and a sustainability buffer. This alternative concept is more effective in generating sufficient financial stability and is not about banks' higher capital buffers. It is important to note that simple and transparent handling is highly beneficial to banks and supervisors. However, this requires comprehensive analyses of systemic risks, and stress tests play an essential role in this process. ***Chapter 2*** examines the stability of banks in Asia under two different accounting regimes: Local GAAP-compliant and mixed accounting standards. The study determines whether adopting Local GAAP and IAS/IFRS contributes to bank stability in 10 Asian countries. The findings suggest that Local GAAP had a detrimental effect on bank stability, but the transition to IAS/IFRS improves bank stability. ***Chapter 3*** shows that the stability of the banking system does not significantly impact economic growth in the 24 countries studied during 2011–2020. Other factors, such as the investment rate of the economy, financial development, and human resources quality, were found to have a positive impact on economic growth. However, foreign direct investment, trade openness, and population do not seem to impact economic growth. The study in ***Chapter 4*** concludes that intellectual capital efficiency (ICE) has a positive and statistically significant effect on the financial stability of Islamic banks in Asia. The specific components of ICE, namely, structural capital efficiency and relational capital efficiency, were found to have the greatest impact on stability. The study suggests that policymakers and bank management should focus on improving ICE resources as a way to improve efficiency and stability and to help banks remain competitive during crisis times. ***Chapter 5*** investigates the impact of regulatory pressure on the behavior of Tunisian banks over 2005–2020. The results indicate that regulatory capital pressure improves bank profitability and stability, but this effect depends on a certain threshold.

The second part of this book presents several studies addressing systematic risk and risk management. ***Chapter 6*** examines the relationship between financial institutions' heterogeneity and systemic risk using a sample of US bank holding companies (BHCs) over a period spanning from 2000 to 2021. The results suggest that BHC-level heterogeneity negatively correlates with systemic risk. The study also constructs a sector-heterogeneity index and shows the presence of a reduction of heterogeneity in the US financial sector prior to the Great Recession and the COVID-19 Recession. The findings suggest that the heterogeneity measures proposed in this study are useful early indicators of where and when systemic risk is building up. In ***Chapter 7***, researchers examine the effects of the foreign exchange (FX) debt level of Turkish banks on the riskiness of the banking sector between January 2008 and December 2021. It suggests that the impact of FX debt on the riskiness of the banking sector is more pronounced during periods of economic and financial stress. Overall, the study provides valuable insights for policymakers and regulators in case of high levels of FX debt in their banking sectors, highlighting the need for effective risk management strategies to mitigate the potential negative impacts of FX debt on the stability of the banking sector. ***Chapter 8*** examines the effectiveness of a proposed integrated competency development approach in addressing the challenges faced by a bank's risk management function during the COVID-19 pandemic. It argues that the regulatory reforms implemented after the 2008 Global Financial Crisis were insufficient to address long-term challenges. The findings suggest that these requirements align with the proposed integrated approach, and it is proposed that this approach is relevant in helping banks build resilience for future pandemics and challenges. ***Chapter 9*** reviews prior literature to support the policymaking processes of the European Commission in reforming the financial sector. It discusses how new prudential requirements, resolution, and supervision tools have helped reduce the risk of systemic crises in the aftermath of the Global Financial Crisis. This chapter also examines the potential benefits of completing the Banking Union, including the introduction of a European Deposit Insurance Scheme and a European Safe Asset, as well as further harmonization of resolution and insolvency frameworks.

The third part of this book contains several insightful studies that offer important implications from macroeconomic factors. ***Chapter 10*** shows that stock market illiquidity has a stronger negative impact on bank lending than bond market illiquidity. This suggests that a lack of liquidity in equity markets can impede banks' ability to raise capital and increase their lending capacity, ultimately reducing the effectiveness of the monetary policy transmission mechanism. Overall, the results highlight the importance of maintaining market liquidity for the effective transmission of monetary policy through the bank lending channel. The authors of ***Chapter 11*** argue that there is a trade-off between stabilizing the monetary union, maintaining free capital mobility, and exiting expansionary monetary policy in the euro area. The empirical analysis is used to support the existence of this trilemma and the importance of resolving it without compromising the euro and financial stability in the European Union. ***Chapter 12*** focuses on using the countercyclical capital buffer (CCyB) as an instrument of macroprudential policy and using the credit-to-GDP gap as a leading indicator for CCyB decision-making. It highlights the lack of research and practical applications regarding the stability of the credit-to-GDP gap, particularly during crises, such as the COVID-19 pandemic. This chapter proposes several practical approaches to correcting the credit-to-GDP gap in real time, aiming to reduce volatility and provide stable signals for decision-makers. The study in ***Chapter 13*** evaluates the ability of Altman's Z-score model to predict the economic distress of 12 Kazakh banks over the period 2008–2014. The results imply the relevance of Altman's Z-score model in detecting economically distressed banks. ***Chapter 14*** aims to help readers understand the impact of the COVID-19 pandemic on the microfinance industry by analyzing global data of 2,995 microfinance institutions (MFIs) from 2000 to 2018 and comparing it to the impact of the 2007–2009 Global Financial Crisis (GFC). The study finds that the GFC had a negative impact on the dual goals of MFIs and triggered a transformation of the legal status of MFIs from Non-Governmental Organizations (NGOs) to other types. Finally, ***Chapter 15*** concludes that uncertainty has a significant impact on banks' liquidity hoarding behavior in Qatar and that Islamic banks appear to respond differently to uncertainty compared to conventional banks, primarily in terms of their asset-side liquidity hoarding.

In summary, this book represents contributions from leading experts in the field, presenting a diverse range of perspectives and research and providing valuable resources for scholars, practitioners, and policymakers. This book addresses the challenges and opportunities facing the global banking industry in the current economic and political climate and offers insights and recommendations for future developments in the field. This book highlights that the banking industry is unique in its strict regulatory and governance structures, high leverage, and potential for contagion. It also mentions that potential agency conflicts within banks are more difficult to monitor and manage than in non-financial firms, impacting bank stability and risk management.

Finally, this book concludes that given the intermediation and financing role of the banking industry, it is crucial to have a sound, stable, and healthy financial system to efficiently allocate resources and distribute risks across the economy. For global banking resilience and stability, corporate risk-taking, risk monitoring, and promoting financial performance should be the focus of researchers, practitioners, and policymakers.

Sabri Boubaker and Marwa Elnahass

https://doi.org/10.1142/9781800614321_fmatter

About the Editors

Sabri Boubaker is a Professor of Finance at EM Normandie Business School (Paris, France) and the University of Swansea (Swansea, Wales, United Kingdom). Sabri holds a Ph.D. in Finance from the University of Paris Est (2006) and an HDR degree (Habilitation for Supervising Doctoral Research) (2010) from the same university. Professor Boubaker is the editor-in-chief of the *Journal of International Financial Management and Accounting.* Sabri Boubaker has recently published many academic papers (+100 papers) in international refereed journals, including the *Journal of Corporate Finance, Journal of Banking and Finance, Journal of International Money and Finance, Financial Management, Journal of Business Ethics, Journal of Economic Dynamics and Control, Auditing: A Journal of Theory & Practice, British Journal of Management,* and *Journal of Financial Research.* Professor Boubaker has also edited many books on corporate finance and financial markets and serves on the editorial boards of several peer-reviewed finance journals. He is the co-founder and co-chair of the annual Paris Financial Management Conference (2013–), the Vietnam Symposium in Banking and Finance (2016–), and the Annual Meeting of the International Society for the Advancement of Financial Economics (2022–).

Marwa Elnahass is a Professor in Accounting and Finance at Newcastle University, United Kingdom. She has a fairly long and successful record on editorial boards as associate editor of the *International Journal of Finance and Economics, Emerging Markets Review, Journal of Financial Reporting and Accounting*, and *International Journal of Financial Studies*, managing guest editor for a special issue of the *International Journal of Accounting*, guest editor for special issue of the *Journal of Risk and Financial Management*, and also two edited books for World Scientific Publishing. Professor Elnahass is a peer reviewer/panellist and a referee for several highly ranked and high-impact journals and UK/international research councils (e.g., AHRC, ESRC, Innovate UK, and QNRF). Professor Elnahass has published numerous articles in top-tier peer-reviewed, ABS listed 3 & 4 academic journals on governance, green finance, and financial reporting quality, such as the *British Journal of Management*, *European Journal of Finance*, and *Journal of International Financial Markets, Institutions and Money*. All publications are listed in the top 25 downloadable papers, as reported by Science Direct. Professor Elnahass is ranked in the top 10% of authors on SSRN by total new downloads within the last 12 months, while her recent publications in banking and CSR (2020–2022) are among the top 8 citations/downloads within many ranked journals. Her work on green finance and climate change has been utilized by policymakers (e.g., British High Commission, Central Bank of Qatar, and Ministry of Higher Education of Egypt and others) and published by the UK Government on GOV.UK. She secured several external (large) and international grants. She has been featured in the Top 500 List of the Most Influential Women in Islamic Business and Finance for 2021/2022 (and shortlisted for 2022/2023). She has published technical and industry reports/articles (e.g., ACCA and Frontiers in Digital Health Journal) and has regularly been invited as a keynote speaker in UK policy roundtables, international conferences, workshops, and webinars.

https://doi.org/10.1142/9781800614321_fmatter

About the Contributors

Abdulla Ahmed Albinali is currently holding the position of Assistant Executive Director in the Financial Stability and Statistics Sector, Qatar Central Bank, Doha, Qatar. Mr. Abdulla holds a Master of Science degree in Islamic Finance from Hamad bin Khalifa University, Qatar. He has more than 25 years of work experience in policymaking. His current work profile entails supervising and coordinating various units within the sector, including overseeing publication of various reports as well as ensuring timely data dissemination. His position also requires him to actively participate in high-level policy meetings, such as with the IMF, rating agencies, and underwriters of sovereign bond issuances. As a member of the Task Force on Prudential and Structural Islamic Financial Indicators of Islamic Financial Services Board (IFSB), Mr. Abdulla is actively involved in various research activities focusing on the growth and development of these institutions. His current research interests include macroprudential supervision, FinTech, and climate risk issues. Mr. Abdullah is presently pursuing his Ph.D. degree at the Hamad bin Khalifa University, Doha, Qatar.

Aigul P. Salina is a Professor of Finance at Satbayev University, Almaty, Kazakhstan. Aigul holds a Ph.D. in Finance from Robert Gordon University, Scotland (2017). She was a visiting professor at Narxoz University, Kazakh-British Technical University, Almaty, Kazakhstan. Aigul Salina has taught various finance courses for undergraduates, graduates, and executives at many universities and she has also supervised many Ph.D. students. Aigul Salina has published numerous academic papers in international refereed and local Kazakhstani journals.

Aishath Shahudha Abdulla is a final year Ph.D. candidate in Economics at the School of Business and Economics, Universiti Brunei Darussalam (UBD), Brunei. She has completed her Bachelor's degree with a double major in Economics and Accounting and Finance from the UBD. Her research interests include risk management, interconnectedness, financial stability, and the economic effects of accounting. She has also taught modules on applied econometrics, principles of economics, business statistics, and monetary economics.

Anam Iqbal is an Assistant Professor of Islamic Banking and Finance at the School of Islamic Economics, Banking & Finance Minhaj University, Lahore, Pakistan. She holds a Ph.D. in Islamic Banking and Finance from International Islamic University Malaysia, Kuala Lumpur, Malaysia, and a Master of Philosophy degree from the University of Management and Technology, Lahore, Pakistan. She has taught various Islamic finance courses for undergraduates, graduates, and executives in several institutions. Anam has published many academic papers in international refereed journals, including *Borsa Istanbul Review, Corporate Governance, Asian Journal of Accounting Research, International Journal of Business Excellence, Journal of King Abdulaziz University, Islamic Economics, Journal of Islamic Marketing, Islamic Economic Studies, Business & Economic Review*, and *Journal of Islamic Thought and Civilization*. She has participated in several national and international conferences, workshops, and webinars.

Aziz ur Rehman is Assistant Vice President, Shari'ah Controller, Noor Takaful Family, General, and Dar Al Takaful, UAE. Aziz is a Ph.D. scholar at IIUM Institute of Islamic Banking and Finance, International Islamic University Malaysia, Malaysia. He holds master's degrees with specialization in Islamic Jurisprudence, Islamic Law, and AAOIFI profession certification CSSA and CIPA. Aziz is a Shari'ah Scholar in Islamic economics, banking, finance, Halal and Takaful consultant, auditor, and trainer with a unique blend of in-depth formal academic training and rich professional industry experience of 27 years. He is also an internationally acclaimed

Professional Shari'ah Technician with extensive experience having engineered/structured multi-billion-dollar worth Islamic financial transactions across banking, non-banking, Takaful, and Halal industries globally. He is a Shariah arbitrator with vast experience in investigation, research, providing advice, counseling, and resolving disputes. Aziz has also published several research papers in reputed journals and book chapters with renowned publishers.

Begoña Torre-Olmo is an Associate Professor in Banking and Finance and Director of Santander Financial Institute (SANFI), a research center at the University of Cantabria, Spain. She is the manager of the program supported by Banco Santander focused on Financial Education (named the best Spanish initiative in 2018 by the Bank of Spain). She is an independent member of the Board of ICAF (Institute of Finance in Cantabria) and OPE (European Projects Office), both state-owned financing entities in the region of Cantabria. Her research interests include banking and corporate finance, topics in which she has published numerous articles in prestigious scientific journals and has collaborated on several books. She has directed and supervised several doctoral theses and she has participated in national and international conferences. She has managed the international course "Business, Banking and Finance" conducted by the University of Cantabria and UNCC Charlotte University (USA) from the beginning of the agreement between both universities in 2014. She has served as the Dean of the Business and Economics School of the University of Cantabria (2010–2014) and as a member of the Board of a private owned fabricator of nuclear equipment (2017–2020).

Carlos León is the Director of Financial Market Infrastructures and Digital Currencies Solutions at Financial Network Analytics (FNA), co-editor of the *Latin American Journal of Central Banking*, associate editor of the *Journal of Financial Market Infrastructures*, guest researcher of Tilburg School of Economics and Management, and part-time professor at Universidad del Rosario. His prior experience includes positions as a senior researcher at the Central Bank of Colombia's Financial Market Infrastructure Oversight Department, short-term expert at the International Monetary Fund, and part-time professor at Externado de Colombia University. His current research interests include digital currencies, network analysis, payment systems, and financial markets. Carlos received his Ph.D. from Tilburg University (the Netherlands) and holds an M.Sc. in Banking and Finance from HEC-Université de Lausanne (Switzerland), an M.A. in International Economics, and a B.A. in Finance and International Relations from Externado de Colombia University (Colombia).

Dorra Mezzez Hmaied is a Professor of Finance at the Institut des Hautes Etudes Commerciales of Carthage, Tunisia. She has been the head of the department of finance and the director of the Master of Research in Finance program for many years in the same institution. She holds a Ph.D. with a finance specialization from the Paris Dauphine University, Paris, France. Her research interests include corporate governance, mergers and acquisitions, and market microstructure. She has published many papers in international peer-reviewed academic journals, such as *The Journal of Private Equity, Journal of Financial Regulation and Compliance, Review of Quantitative Finance and Accounting, Managerial Finance, Research in International Business and Finance*, and *Journal of Asset Management*. She is also a senior researcher and team leader in the EMNES research network "Euro-Mediterranean Network for Economic Studies."

Ejaz Aslam is an Assistant Professor of Islamic Banking and Finance at the School of Islamic Economics, Banking & Finance, Minhaj University, Lahore, Pakistan. He holds a Ph.D. in Islamic Banking and Finance from International Islamic University Malaysia, Kuala Lumpur, Malaysia, and a Master of Philosophy degree in Finance from the University of Management and Technology, Lahore, Pakistan. He has taught various Islamic finance courses for undergraduates, graduates, and executives in several institutions around the world. He has published many academic papers (+25 papers) in international refereed journals, including *Borsa Istanbul Review, Environmental Science and Pollution Research, Corporate Governance: The International Journal of Business in Society, Global Business Review, Asian Journal of Accounting Research, International Journal of Business Excellence, Journal of King Abdulaziz University, Islamic Economics, Journal of Islamic Marketing, Islamic Economic Studies, Business & Economic Review*, and *Journal of Islamic Thought and Civilization*. Dr. Ejaz has participated as a speaker, session chair, and presenter in many national and international conferences, workshops, and webinars.

Eric H. Y. Koh is an Associate Professor at the Department of Finance, Faculty of Business and Economics, Universiti Malaya, Kuala Lumpur, Malaysia. He offers a unique blend of practical experience and academic credentials. Eric began his professional life in external auditing and subsequently joined the banking industry during which he held senior management positions and led business performance analysis assignments. He has published in various peer-reviewed journals, such as *Asian Journal of Business and Accountancy*, *Banking Insight*, *Chinese Management Journal*, *International Journal of Banking, Accountancy and Finance*, *International Journal of China Studies*, *International Review of Economics and Finance*, *Journal of Education in Business*, *Journal of Southeast Asian Economies*, and *Service Business*. Eric has authored a book entitled *Risk Management Competency Development in Banks* (Palgrave Macmillan) and co-authored *Corporate Finance: An Asian Perspective* (Oxford Publishing, Malaysia, a then subsidiary of Oxford University Press). He has also authored a study manual and developed question banks for a regulatory body. Besides his Ph.D. from the University of Nottingham (United Kingdom), Eric is also a CFA charterholder and a Fellow of CPA Australia. He facilitates various undergraduate and postgraduate academic and professional courses in the areas of Bank Management, Risk Management, and Corporate Finance. Eric also serves as an Examination Committee member of the Asian Institute of Chartered Bankers.

Erica Francesca Di Girolamo works at the European Commission, Joint Research Centre. She is coordinating activities in the field of finance and financial stability. She joined the Joint Research Centre in 2009 and she has been actively involved in the work of the European Commission to create a safer and sounder financial system. From 2018 to 2019, she joined the Single Resolution Board before coming back to the European Commission in 2019. Her more recent research focuses are on climate risk and sustainability in the financial sector, as well as digital finance. Earlier, she contributed to EC proposals on higher capital requirements for banks, harmonized deposit protection schemes, and the EU framework for bank recovery and resolution. Erica holds a Ph.D. in financial modeling from Katholieke Universiteit of Leuven, Belgium, and a Degree in Mathematical Engineering from Politecnico di Milano, Italy.

Gamini Premaratne holds a Master's degree in Policy Economics and a Ph.D. in Economics with a specialization in Econometrics from the University of Illinois at Urbana-Champaign, United States. He also holds a Bachelor's degree in Mathematics and a postgraduate diploma in Statistics. He has served as an Assistant Professor in the Department of Economics at the National University of Singapore and also as a Statistician at the Department of Census and Statistics, Sri Lanka. Currently, he is a faculty member at the UBD School of Business and Economics, Brunei. His research interests include behavioral finance, volatility models, applied economics, and risk management. He has published extensively in local and international refereed journals, including the *Journal of Financial Econometrics*, *Journal of Statistical Planning and Inference*, *Communication in Statistics*, and *Handbook of Asian Finance*. Dr. Premaratne has supervised several master's and Ph.D. students. In addition, he has vast experience as a trainer for statistical software and is also an expert on sample surveys and data analysis.

Hong Thu Nguyen is a graduate of doctoral study at the Banking University of Ho Chi Minh City, Vietnam. She works for Thu Dau Mot University (Vietnam) and specializes in macroeconomics, banking, and financial inclusions. She has published several peer-reviewed academic papers in international refereed journals and participated in many international conferences on macroeconomics, banking, and financial inclusions as well as economic development in Vietnam and the ASEAN countries.

İlkay Şendeniz-Yüncü is an Assistant Professor of Finance at Middle East Technical University, Department of Business Administration, Ankara, Turkey. She obtained B.S. and M.S. degrees in Civil Engineering as well as an MBA from Middle East Technical University. She received her Ph.D. in Finance from Bilkent University, Ankara, Turkey, and subsequently conducted postdoctoral research at the University of California, Berkeley, United States, and Tilburg University, the Netherlands. She previously held positions of Instructor at Bilkent University, Lecturer at Tilburg University, Assistant Professor of Finance at IÉSEG School of Management, and Assistant Professor of Finance at MEF University. Her research interests are banking, finance–economic growth relationships, and financial markets. She has published in many international refereed journals, such as the *Journal of Banking and Finance, Journal of Corporate Finance, Finance Research Letters, Applied Economics*, and *Emerging Markets Finance and Trade.*

Luc Renneboog is a Professor of Corporate Finance at Tilburg University, the Netherlands. His research interests span corporate social responsibility, ethical investing, corporate finance, corporate governance, remuneration contracting, law and economics, shareholder activism, and the economics of art. He has graduated with degrees in management engineering (B.Sc. and M.Sc.) and philosophy (BA) from the Catholic University of Leuven, Belgium, with an MBA from the University of Chicago, United States, and with a Ph.D. in Financial Economics from the London Business School, United Kingdom. Prior to joining Tilburg, he was on the faculty at the Universities of Leuven, Belgium, and Oxford, United Kingdom. He held visiting positions at Cambridge University, HEC Paris, Cunef (Madrid), EUI (Florence), and University Paris Dauphine (France). He currently also has a part-time affiliation at Ghent University (Belgium). He has many academic papers published in top-tier economic and finance journals, such as the *Journal of Finance, Journal of Financial Economics, Review of Financial Studies, Review of Finance, American Economic Review, Management Science, Organization Science, Strategic Management Journal, Journal of International Business Studies, Journal of Law and Economics, Journal of Corporate Finance*, and *Journal of Financial Intermediation.* His research has been cited more than 20,000 times.

Lucia Alessi is Team Leader at the European Commission, Joint Research Centre. She is responsible for research in support of EU policymaking in the field of finance, including banking and financial stability, corporate finance, and digital and sustainable finance. From 2007 to 2015, she worked at the European Central Bank, where she served in various DGs, including research, economics, and macroprudential policy and financial stability. Her more recent research focuses on sustainable finance, in particular the assessment of the greenness of financial assets, climate risk and sustainability in financial markets, and the development of carbon stress tests for financial institutions. On systemic risk more generally, she has worked on early warning systems for financial crises, including sovereign crises. Earlier in her career, she worked on econometric models for big data, with a focus on dynamic factor models. She has published papers in journals, such as *Journal of Business and Economic Statistics, Economic Policy, Journal of Financial Stability*, and *Journal of Financial Econometrics*. She was awarded the CEPR/ESI "Best Central Bank Research Paper" prize in 2009. Lucia holds a Ph.D. in Economics and Management from Sant'Anna School for Advanced Studies, Pisa, Italy, and a Degree in Economics from Bocconi University, Milan, Italy.

Marco Petracco-Giudici is currently a Senior Economist in the Finance and Economy Unit of the Directorate General Joint Research Centre (JRC) of the European Commission, working on new developments in finance and financial stability issues. He has been involved in science for policy and research support work on several post-crisis reforms. His present main research interests focus on sustainable finance, digitalization of finance (FinTech), and the use of simulation and non-traditional analysis techniques for economics and finance. Previously, he worked in the Econometrics and Applied statistics unit of the JRC and as an economist for the British Government Economic Service and Caribbean Development Bank. He has published many articles and working papers on simulation methods for financial crises, the impacts of post-crisis regulatory reforms, and the use of text analysis in financial research.

María Cantero-Saiz is an Associate Professor in Finance at the University of Cantabria, Spain, teaching in undergraduate and postgraduate programs. After earning a B.S. in Business Management (2010) and a Master in Business Administration (MBA) (2011), she completed her Ph.D. in finance at the University of Cantabria (2015). Her research interests focus on banking, monetary policy, sovereign risk, and corporate finance. She has published many articles in prestigious scientific journals and has collaborated on several books. She has also presented numerous papers at national and international conferences and has received several awards for her research. She has taken part in numerous national and international research projects. She has been a visiting researcher at Norwich Business School (University of East Anglia, United Kingdom) (2013–2014), Berlin School of Economics and Law (2017), Germany, and Università degli Studi di Palermo (2022–2023), Italy, and has been in charge of the University of Cantabria Classroom Debate since 2015.

Md Aslam Mia holds a Ph.D. in development economics (research area: microfinance) from the University of Malaya, Malaysia. He is currently a Senior Lecturer at the School of Management (SOM), Universiti Sains Malaysia (USM). Dr. Mia has published around 35 articles related to productivity and efficiency of financial institutions, market structure, microfinance, and urban economics in internationally reputed peer-reviewed journals such as *The European Journal of Development Research, Business History, Finance Research Letters, Economics Letters, Journal of the Asia Pacific Economy, Journal of Cleaner Production, Social Indicators Research, International Journal of Social Economics, Cities, Economic Analysis and Policy*, and *Strategic Change*. Recently, his sole-authored book, *Social Purpose, Commercialization, and Innovations in Microfinance*, has been published by Springer. He has also presented his research findings in over 20 national and international conferences/seminars during the last five years. Due to his significant contribution to research and publication, Dr. Mia received the *Ph.D. Candidate with Highest Impact Publications* award from the University of Malaya in 2018. Dr. Mia also conducted over 20 workshops/seminars on various research issues/techniques/tools both in and outside Malaysia.

Mert Malkoç is an Assistant Specialist in the market department at the Turkish Mercantile Exchange, Turkey. He graduated with a degree in Business Administration from Middle East Technical University in 2019. Currently, he is a graduate student enrolled in the Financial Mathematics Program at Applied Mathematics Institute at Middle East Technical University, Ankara, Turkey. His job definition includes reporting daily and monthly data to the Ministry of Trade of the Republic of Türkiye. He also takes part in forming the Tawarruq market on the Turkish Mercantile Exchange.

Omaima A. G. Hassan is a Senior Lecturer in accounting and finance and the Research Degrees Coordinator (RDC) at Aberdeen Business School (ABS) of Robert Gordon University, Aberdeen, United Kingdom. She is the Research Degrees Coordinator for MRes and Ph.D. students at the ABS. Before joining the ABS, she was a lecturer in financial accounting at the School of Social Sciences at Brunel University, London. Her research interests are in corporate reporting and market-based accounting research.

Rim Zakraoui is a Ph.D. student in Finance. She graduated from the Institut de Financement du Développement du Maghreb Arabe, El Manar, Tunisia, and works at the Central Bank of Tunisia, Tunis, Tunisia.

Sebastian Lang is a Professor of Finance, Investments, and Accounting at Berufliche Hochschule Hamburg in Hamburg, Germany, and was a Visiting Fellow at Harvard University's Graduate School of Arts and Sciences and Harvard Business School, United States, as well as at the Wharton School of the University of Pennsylvania, United States. He holds a Ph.D. from the University of St. Gallen, Switzerland, where he is affiliated as a researcher. Sebastian Lang researches and teaches in the areas of banking and corporate finance, as well as portfolio management and capital markets.

Sergio Sanfilippo-Azofra is an Associate Professor in Finance at the University of Cantabria, Spain, teaching in undergraduate and postgraduate programs. After receiving his B.S. in economics, he completed his Ph.D. in finance at the University of Cantabria, Spain. His research interests focus on banking, monetary policy, mergers and acquisitions, and corporate finance. He has published more than 30 articles in prestigious scientific journals and has collaborated on several books. He has also presented numerous papers at national and international conferences and has received several best paper awards. He has supervised two doctoral theses and taken part in numerous national and international research projects. He was also a visiting researcher at Cass Business School, City University of London, United Kingdom, and was in charge of the University of Cantabria Summer School in Laredo.

Silvio Andrae is an Economist. Most of his professional experience has been in the financial sector. Since 2000, he has worked as a senior consultant in various financial regulation projects in Europe, Latin America, Africa, and Asia. He is currently a senior adviser with the German Savings Banks Association. Silvio Andrae studied and received his Ph.D. at the Free University Berlin, Germany.

Sunil Sangwan is presently an Assistant Professor (Finance) at the Institute of Rural Management Anand (IRMA), Gujarat, India. He holds a Ph.D. degree from Indian Institute of Technology Kharagpur, West Bengal, India, in Entrepreneurial Finance (Microfinance). His teaching and research interests include entrepreneurship, entrepreneurial finance, microfinance, development finance, financial inclusion, financial accounting, and financial management. Dr. Sangwan has published research articles in international peer-reviewed journals, such as *Applied Economics, Journal of Financial Economic Policy, Managerial and Decision Economics, Journal of Public Affairs, Journal of Human Behavior in the Social Environment*, and *Journal of Social and Economic Development.*

Tihana Škrinjarić, Ph.D., is an Advisor at the Department for Financial Stability at Croatian National Bank, Zagreb, Croatia. Tihana holds a Ph.D. in Economics from the University of Zagreb, Croatia (2018). Before her current position, she was an assistant professor at the Faculty of Economics and Business, at the Department for Mathematics at the University of Manchester, United Kingdom, where she was also a visiting researcher in 2015. Her area of work and research includes quantitative models and methods in macroprudential policymaking and quantitative finance. Tihana Škrinjarić taught various quantitative courses for undergraduate and graduate levels when she was working at the university from 2013 to 2021. She has published many academic papers (+140 papers) in international refereed journals, including the *Journal of Cleaner Production, Expert Systems with Applications, Post-Communist Economies, Sustainability, Mathematics, Economic Systems, Economic Modeling*, and *International Journal of Finance & Economics*. Dr. Škrinjarić has edited two books on quantitative finance (IGI Publishing) and several special issues in MDPI Journals. She is a member of editorial and reviewer boards for the following journals: *Journal of Risk and Financial Management, Journal of Financial Studies, The Journal of Eastern European and Central Asian Research, The University Without Borders Journal of Economics and Business, Izvestiya Journal of University of Economics — Varna, The European Journal of Applied Economics, The International Economic Policy, Statistics of*

Ukraine, Econometric Research in Finance, Financial Studies, CEA Journal of Economics, and *Croatian Review of Economic, Business and Social Statistics.*

Tong Jiao is a Lecturer in Finance at Aberdeen Business School, Robert Gordon University, United Kingdom. Tong holds a Ph.D. in Management (finance concentration) from Aberystwyth University, United Kingdom, and is also a Chartered Financial Analyst (CFA) and a member of CFA Society of the UK. Tong has taught various finance and banking modules for undergraduate and postgraduate courses and his research interests lie primarily in the fields of corporate finance and credit rating.

Van Chien Nguyen is a graduate of doctoral study at the Department of Economics at the University of Colombo, Sri Lanka. He works for Thu Dau Mot University (Vietnam) and his research interests are macroeconomics and finance. He has published in several international refereed journals, such as *Heliyon, Cogent Business and Management*, and *Cogent of Economics and Finance.* He has also participated in many national and international conferences on macroeconomics and finance, especially covering the topics of financial development, financial inclusions, and economic performance.

Wolfgang Schadner is an Early Career Researcher and Ph.D. candidate at the University of St. Gallen, Switzerland. His research articles have been published in various high-impact journals in the areas of financial economics, empirical finance, quantitative finance, and sociophysics. He recently became a Visiting Fellow at Harvard Business School, United States.

Xin Zhang is a Lecture in Finance at Robert Gordon University, Aberdeen, United Kingdom. Xin was working at CITIC Industrial Bank before starting his Ph.D. journey. Xin earned a Ph.D. in Finance from Aberystwyth University in 2013. Dr. Zhang has taught various accounting and finance modules for undergraduates and postgraduates across universities and business schools. He also acts as an external examiner for undergraduate and postgraduate programs in various universities. Xin supervises many Ph.D. students from different nationalities. Xin Zhang has recently published a few academic papers in international refereed journals including *Journal of Small Business and Enterprise Development, International Journal* *of Computational Economics and Econometrics*, and *Asian Journal of Accounting Research*.

Zihao Liu is a Ph.D. candidate in Finance at Tilburg University, the Netherlands. His research interests span empirical corporate finance and artificial intelligence, financial intermediaries, corporate social responsibility, and corporate governance. He graduated with a bachelor's degree in Finance from the Ocean University of China, with an M.Sc. in Finance and Accounting and a CEMS double degree in International Management from Stockholm School of Economics, Sweden, and Copenhagen Business School, Denmark. Before joining Tilburg, he was a research assistant at the Swedish House of Finance, Stockholm, Sweden. During his Ph.D. studies, he also visited the research department at Sveriges Riksbank.

https://doi.org/10.1142/9781800614321_fmatter

Contents

PART I

The Effect(s) of Financial and Institutional Characteristics

https://doi.org/10.1142/9781800614321_0001

Chapter 1

Revision of Capital Buffer Framework

Silvio Andrae

Senior Advisor and Author

andrae@zedat.fu-berlin.de

Abstract

The capital buffer concept for banks misses its target: The capital buffers do not harm financial stability. However, they do not make a positive contribution either. Based on sobering practical experience, an alternative capital buffer concept has been developed. What is striking is that capital buffers for a bank no longer consist of seven components. Instead, the capital buffer consists of only two components: a resilience buffer and a sustainability buffer. The alternative capital buffer concept is effective in generating sufficient financial stability. It is not *per se* about higher capital buffers for banks. Instead, simple and transparent handling is highly beneficial to both banks and supervisors. However, this simple handling requires comprehensive analyses of systemic risks. Stress tests have an essential role to play here.

Keywords: Bank capital, capital buffers, financial stability, macroprudential regulation, systemic risks

1. Introduction

The 2007–2008 financial crisis has massively changed the view of financial stability. Before the crisis, the prevailing view was that microprudential measures were sufficient to ensure financial stability. To this was added a rule-based monetary policy designed to keep inflation low. Such an approach proved irrelevant during the financial crisis. A new approach to financial stability was proclaimed. As a result, a variety of macroprudential measures were introduced. They aim to stabilize the monetary and financial system at the macro level.

On the one hand, systemic risk comes from the procyclicality of economic behavior. On the other hand, it can propagate at a given time because of the interconnectedness of financial institutions and the concentration of risk. Therefore, macroprudential measures aim to reduce the likelihood of systemic financial crises and limit their intensity and externalities when they occur.

The main macroprudential tools are as follows (Cerutti *et al.*, 2017):

- countercyclical capital buffer,
- the leverage ratio for banks,
- dynamic provisioning rules,
- caps on loan-to-value ratio or leverage ratio,
- caps on foreign currency loans,
- caps on risk concentration, and
- capital surcharges for systemically important banking institutions.

Financial markets have become increasingly interconnected over the past ten years. Externalities have continued to rise, calling into question the macroprudential toolkit that has been in place for more than ten years. Jackson and Pernoud (2021) state the following:

> "At a most basic level, insolvencies involve substantial costs which are then passed on via defaults and drops in equity values, especially if left to cascade. The externalities are clear: if one organization has poor judgment in its investments, poorly managed business practices, or even just unusually bad luck, this ends up affecting the values of its partners, and their partners; and in discontinuous ways. There are also many other forms of externalities in financial networks including bank runs, changes in asset values due to fire sales, inferences that investors make

> about one institution based on the health of another, and credit freezes. Although some of these risks can be hedged, there are no markets for insurance against many of them. The externalities mean that the system as a whole can experience crises that are much broader and costlier than the independent failures that ignite them — hence the term 'systemic risk.'" (p. 172)

Surprisingly, the introduction of macroprudential tools is based on the finding that existing microprudential rules are procyclical and failed to prevent a systemic financial crisis. In contrast, many of the previous tools are merely an extension of the previous microprudential rules. Therefore, post-crisis macroprudential policies do not represent a paradigm shift in the assessment of risks in both their temporal and cross-sectional dimensions (Quan and Scialom, 2022).

The promotion of countercyclical microprudential rules to fulfill a macroprudential objective is widely accepted because of the now well-known procyclicality of prudential rules. These countercyclical rules aim to counter the well-known paradox whereby any balance sheet item[1] no longer fulfils this function as soon as regulatory pressure — by setting minimum requirements — is exerted on it. Only equity that exceeds these minimum requirements is a sound absorber of unforeseen losses. When capital reaches the minimum requirements, additional losses lead to a depletion of regulatory capital and credit rationing or other procyclical balance sheet adjustments, such as distress sales. From shock absorbers, regulatory minima consequently become shock amplifiers. From a macroprudential perspective, the countercyclicality of prudential rules contradicts the time invariance of liquidity and capital ratios (Kleinnijenhuis *et al.*, 2020). For this reason, capital buffers introduced countercyclical components in the Basel III framework in 2012.

However, the COVID crisis calls for a radical rethink of macroprudential policy. After all, it should be noted that the future will be characterized by uncertainty. For example, a precise assessment of climate-related financial risks is impossible. Instead, this uncertainty relates to quantifying their impact on the economy and finance. In addition, there is the "inaction bias" inherent in macroprudential

---

[1]Each balance sheet item is a shock absorber (liquid assets or equity) against adverse and unpredictable shocks.

policy: the temptation to wait for a better analytical understanding and assessment of certain systemic risks and their dynamics leads to inaction.[2] The consequence of this sequential approach is that macroprudential policy is not implemented until substantial improvements in information have been achieved. The resulting delays in action are inconsistent with the irreversibility effects and tipping points emanating from climate risks, for example (Quang and Scialom, 2021).

It would be better to break with the sequential approach and implement macroprudential policy while building knowledge about systemic financial risks' nature and dynamics (Quang and Scialom, 2021). One contribution lies in the fundamental revision of the capital buffer concept as a critical tool of macroprudential regulation.

An alternative buffer concept is presented in the following. It leaves the microprudential framework and focuses on the macroprudential dimension. It is striking that the capital buffer for a bank no longer consists of seven components. Instead, the capital buffer consists of only two components: a resilience buffer and a sustainability buffer. The alternative capital buffer concept is effective in generating sufficient financial stability. It is not *per se* about higher capital buffers for banks. Instead, the simple and transparent way of handling it benefits both banks and supervisors.

2. Macroprudential Policies

The current macroprudential policy has not fundamentally changed the basics of banking regulation from before the financial crisis. The existing macroprudential tools should be interpreted as extensions of the existing microprudential regulatory corpus (ESRB, 2018). This microprudential framework provides the definition of risk. The multitude of capital buffers builds on this, but they do not have the desired effect. Concerning financial stability, the supervisor pursues the traditional goal that higher capital buffers *per se* lead to higher financial stability, especially in the banking market.

[2]Bengtsson (2020) examines institutional governance structures in the European Union (EU). He finds that the inertia of policymakers is best addressed by having a single macroprudential authority.

Chari *et al.* (2022) show that macroprudential regulation reduces the volume and volatility of bank credit. At the same time, regulation leads to risk shifting, so vulnerabilities in other parts of the financial system are amplified. Mirzaei and Samet (2022) use a panel dataset of 4,109 banks from 91 countries and find for the period 2001–2013 that the effectiveness of macroprudential measures is more pronounced in countries with stricter bank supervision and more robust private monitoring.

Macroprudential instruments constrain the credit growth of small, less capitalized, and less liquid banks when they are accompanied by stringent bank regulation. In particular, capital-constrained and less liquid banks reduce their lending more than their capital-rich and highly liquid counterparts after macroprudential measures are activated. Thus, Mirzaei and Samet (2022) conclude that the quality of bank regulation and supervision affects the effectiveness of macroprudential measures.

Given these empirical observations, the following section will examine whether the current definition of risk and the design of capital buffers are still justified in today's world.

2.1. *Definition of risk*

The main instrument of prudential regulation continues to be the risk-weighted capital ratio. The problem with this ratio is that its calculation is based on a risk definition that does not allow either fat-tailed risks or risks without historical records to be captured.[3] However, they are significant sources of systemic risk. Such a definition relies entirely on mathematical models that define emerging risk as a mere reflection of risk as it has occurred in the past. Implicitly, the capital constraints to which banks are subject are calculated based on a risk that is not radically different from how it materialized in the past.[4] Such a hypothesis is entirely irrelevant if the risks

[3]Boom–bust cycles in asset markets and systemic banking crises are driven primarily when tail risks are ignored (Roy, 2022).

[4]"[T]raditional approaches to risk management consisting in extrapolating historical data based on assumptions of normal distributions are largely irrelevant to assess future climate-related risks. Indeed, both physical and transition risks are characterised by deep uncertainty, nonlinearity and fat-tailed distributions." (Bolton *et al.*, 2020, p. 10).

are too rare to be statistically significant and thus to be considered in probabilistic models.

It leads to whether a risk is considered exogenous or endogenous. Risk is treated as an exogenous variable in both microprudential and macroprudential regulations of banks.[5] Risk is assumed regardless of a bank's behavior or other market participants' actions. "The economy is prone to instability regardless of the level of aggregate risk because leverage and risk-taking are endogenous" (Brunnermeier and Sannikov, 2014, p. 419).

The fact that risks are endogenous comes to light precisely when unstable markets or crises erupt (Danielsson *et al.*, 2013). The financial actors' actions then influence the occurrence of losses.[6] It is where the assessment of systemic risk comes in. Therefore, standardized risk measurement according to regulatory and supervisory requirements poses significant financial stability risks. In this way, banks are forced to form uniform expectations, which can foster crises.

A distinction can be made between two types of systemic risks (Jackson and Pernoud, 2021):

- contagion through various channels that generate externalities between banks and other financial institutions (e.g., defaults, correlated portfolios, and sales), and
- self-fulfilling prophecies and feedback effects (e.g., bank runs, credit freezes, and equilibrium multiplication).

Usually, such systemic risks are to be considered in the context of macroprudential regulation. However, a systematic analysis of, for example, network effects does not take place. Thus, the capital buffers presented in the following do not address such systemic risks, although they were created for this purpose. Of course, it should be noted that capital buffers are not a panacea for the above-mentioned systemic risks. They can at least be seen as a

[5]The exogenous view applies to the standard risk treatment in financial valuation models and asset pricing.

[6]For example, climate risk is endogenous because current perceptions of climate risk influence investments, directly affecting future risk (see Avril *et al.*, 2022).

precautionary instrument. *Ex ante* regulation ensures that inappropriately risky investments are avoided.[7]

2.2. *Capital buffers*

After the financial crisis, the Basel Committee introduced several capital buffers (BCBS, 2011). The European Commission eventually added to them. The following seven buffers can be found in European banking regulation today:

1. capital conservation buffer (CCoB),
2. countercyclical capital buffer (CCyB),
3. specific capital surcharge for global systemically important banks (G-SII),
4. capital buffer for other systemically important banks (O-SII),
5. systemic risk buffer (SyRB),
6. capital surcharge (P2R), and
7. bank-specific recommendation (P2G) indicates the amount of capital the regulator expects banks to hold in addition to their mandatory capital requirements.

The seven total capital buffers pile above the minimum requirements (Figure 1). These are briefly presented and evaluated in the following:

2.2.1. *Capital conservation buffer*

The capital conservation buffer (CCoB) is designed to ensure that banks have an additional layer of usable capital that can be drawn down in the event of losses. The capital conservation buffer has been in place since 2019 and is set at 2.5% of total risk-weighted assets. It may only be covered by Common Equity Tier 1 (CET1) and is set above the regulatory minimum capital requirements. Apart from

[7]An alternative option is to allow arbitrary investment but then intervene and inject capital when there is a risk of cascading failures to minimize contagion. It then depends on the financial centrality of the bank in question as to whether to intervene. Suppose a bank is so central that it poses a significant systemic risk. In that case, whether it is better to regulate it *ex ante* or bail it out *ex post* depends on the relative opportunity cost of foregone excess returns, from forcing the bank to hold safer assets compared with the actual cost of a bailout.

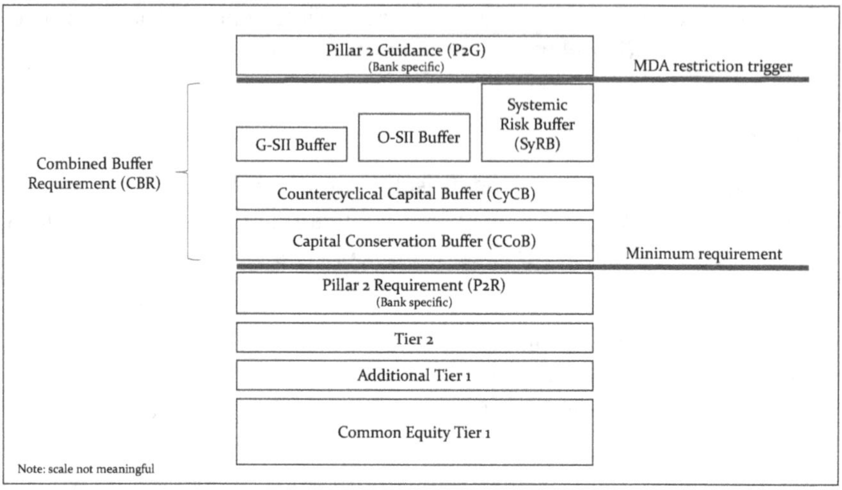

Figure 1. Capital stack.

the distribution restrictions mentioned in the following, a bank can continue to conduct its business as usual if it draws down its capital conservation buffer.

2.2.2. *Countercyclical capital buffer*

The countercyclical capital buffer (CCyB), which has been fully effective since 2019, is designed to protect the banking sector from periods of excess aggregate credit growth, which are often associated with the build-up of system-wide risk. Supervisors activate and increase the CCyB when they assess aggregate credit growth as excessive and associated with building system-wide risk.[8] The buffer would then be scaled down in a downturn to ensure that banks maintain the

[8]Auer *et al.* (2022) show that activating a CCyB does not necessarily lead to the desired effects. In 2013, a CCyB for housing loans was set up in Switzerland. The additional capital requirements resulting from CCyB activation were associated with higher growth in commercial lending among Swiss banks. Banks lend more to all firms, whereas the new macroprudential policy mainly benefits smaller and riskier firms. In contrast, Cappelletti *et al.* (2022) show that capital surcharges depend on the level of required capital and the borrower's industry. In the authors' empirical study, tightening the requirements leads to a more substantial decline in lending compared with other credit institutions.

flow of credit in the economy. The CCyB varies between 0 and 2.5% of total risk-weighted assets and must be backed by CET1 capital.[9] Because banks need time to adjust to an increase in buffer requirements, a country must give up to 12 months notice of its decision to increase the CCyB. On the other hand, a country's decision to lower the CCyB value takes effect immediately.

2.2.3. *G-SII buffer*

The main objective of the G-SII buffer is to make significant, highly interconnected, and internationally active banks more resilient by requiring them to hold additional capital reserves. The institutions qualifying as G-SIIs are identified yearly based on international criteria.[10] The more systemically important an institution is, the higher its requirement for the additional capital buffer within a range of 1–3.5%.

2.2.4. *O-SII buffer*

The objective of the capital buffer for O-SII is very similar to that for G-SII. The focus here is on banks that are important for their country's economy and therefore have national systemic importance. The Basel Committee deliberately allows national authorities discretion in their methodology to determine O-SII.[11]

2.2.5. *Systemic risk buffer*

The systemic risk buffer (SyRB) is designed to counter systemic risks that could lead to disruption with severe effects on the domestic financial sector or the real domestic economy. The SyRB is not imposed on individual institutions but on specific groups of institutions or even all groups of institutions. The buffer can be imposed

[9] An estimate for large banks shows that the upper limit for CCyB in times of stress should not be less than 1.7% of total assets. Typically, the value is 0.8% of total assets (van Ooordt, 2022).

[10] The current list of designated banks can be found on the Financial Stability Board's website.

[11] If an institution is considered systemically crucial at the national and global level, it only needs to apply the higher of the two buffers (G-SII or O-SII).

not only on domestic exposures, exposures in an EU member state, or exposures in a third country but also on sector-specific risk exposures or sub-groups thereof (e.g., currently in Germany for loans in the residential real estate sector at 2%). Therefore, it is possible to use several systemic risk buffers for different risk positions simultaneously. The buffer rate is not capped but is at least 0.5%.

2.2.6. *Pillar 2 requirements*

The Pillar 2 requirement (P2R) is a capital requirement set individually for each bank. It applies in addition to the minimum capital requirement (Pillar 1) and covers the risks underestimated in the minimum capital requirement or not covered by it. A bank's P2R is derived from the Supervisory Review and Evaluation Process (SREP). The P2R is a legally binding requirement. Non-compliance can result in supervisory measures (including sanctions) being imposed on institutions. In addition to CET1, banks can also use instruments of additional Tier 1 capital (AT1) and Tier 2 capital (T2) to meet their P2R, provided that at least 56.25% of the P2R capital is Common Equity Tier 1 capital and at least 75% is Additional Tier 1 capital.

2.2.7. *Pillar 2 guidance*

Pillar 2 guidance (P2G) is a bank-specific recommendation that indicates the amount of capital the European Central Bank expects banks to hold in addition to their mandatory capital requirements. It serves as a buffer for banks to withstand stressful situations. The P2G is also set as part of the SREP. Unlike the P2R, the P2G is not legally binding as it only reflects supervisory expectations. The European Central Bank's banking supervision uses a two-step approach to determine banks' P2G levels. The basis for determining banks' P2G levels is their performance in regular EU-wide stress tests, which examine how an economic shock would affect banks' capital ratios (i.e., their capital level relative to their risk-weighted assets).[12]

[12]For banks that do not participate in the stress test, ECB supervisors set the P2G based on a forward-looking assessment of the bank's resilience and the potential impact of adverse scenarios on the bank's solvency.

There is a lively debate among regulators about how capital buffers are used. During the corona crisis, supervisors and regulators urged banks to use their capital buffers when necessary. In other words, supervisors and regulators released the capital buffers. It was to ensure that banks were able to act and provide the economy with sufficient credit during these difficult times. As is well known, banks have primarily refrained from drawing on their capital buffers. There are many reasons why this is so. For example, EU countries and the European Central Bank (ECB) have adopted many monetary and fiscal policy measures that have made it unnecessary to draw on capital buffers (Abad and Pascual, 2022).

The main reasons why capital buffers have not been used are technical. These include interaction with other regulatory requirements, lack of parameters for replenishment, market expectations, supervisors' communicated stance, and the risk approach of a bank's management. This short, rough list alone illustrates how closely the macroprudential framework is interwoven with other requirements and expectations.

The framework theoretically clarifies which capital buffer should be used for which risk. However, there is an inherent overlap between the requirements. Furthermore, there is an apparent overlap between P2R and P2G. Whether and to what extent an activated capital buffer helps reduce the targeted risk has not yet been demonstrated. In this respect, the usefulness of a capital buffer requirement broken down into various, increasingly refined individual capital buffers whose calculation is hugely complex and time-consuming must be questioned. The result is a combined capital buffer requirement that must be met. As soon as this requirement is breached, restrictions on capital distribution (e.g., dividends, share buybacks, and discretionary bonus payments) are automatically introduced to replenish the capital buffers.[13]

2.3. *Capital and financial stability*

Bank capital has been a critical element of banking regulation for at least two centuries to promote financial stability. Memmel and

[13]As a general rule, the maximum distributable amount (MDA) restrictions increase as the bank's capital ratio approaches the minimum capital requirement.

Raupach (2010, p. 509), for example, note that bank capital ratios are a "natural indicator of soundness." However, the banks that failed during the financial crisis generally had more capital than required by regulators. It is true not only for the pre-crisis period but also concerning the regulations issued after the crisis (Flannery and Giacomini, 2015). It casts doubt on the assumption that bank capital would be stability's key (or even practical) aspect.

However, academic studies show contradictory statements on the relationship between capital and stability. On the one hand, studies show that more capital is associated with higher bank stability (Holmstrom and Tirole, 1997; Thakor, 2012). On the other hand, there are a large number of studies that point to the opposite effect. According to these studies, more capital would lead to higher risk-taking by banks (Koehn and Santomero, 1980; Jokipii and Milne, 2011). It could be because raising capital is expensive, and banks try to offset these additional costs by investing in more profitable assets, which are also the riskiest ones.

The different results are due to the different samples or methods used in these studies. These possibilities can be explained — at least in part — by the endogenous relationship between bank capital and stability. The observed relationship between bank capital and stability may be co-determined by other factors that could be the underlying cause of changes in capital and stability. Bank managers' decisions about the amount of capital held (typically higher than the regulatory minimum) may be strongly related to other decisions that affect bank stability.

The relationship between capital and risk could also reflect a relationship from the latter to the former. It is an effect in the opposite direction of that implied in the regulatory rationale for capital controls. Regulatory pressure on banks near the minimum level to increase their risk-taking when investment opportunities are good would encourage these banks to increase their capital to avoid regulatory sanctions in the event of losses that could push their capital below the required threshold. Higher capital levels could also be a response by banks to increased risk in order to reduce bankruptcy costs. In addition, bank managers' risk aversion could lead them to increase their capital to compensate for the high risks they took to avoid personal losses resulting from their institution's insolvency. We find that in these cases, the narrative shifts from taking risks to determining the amount of capital.

This question boils down to whether bank capital itself can help promote stability. It is a question of causality, not just correlation. However, causality is usually assumed only implicitly. We know that assumptions (and intuitions) can be entirely wrong, even if they sound plausible. Moreira (2022) notes that the correlation between capital and bank stability is likely due to other factors affecting these two variables. However, this implies that a change in the capital does not lead to a change in stability. It contradicts the general assumption that capital *per se* would be necessary for improving stability. Moreover, none of the additional factors assessed appear to contribute to increased stability. The analysis focuses on capital held by banks rather than the capital required by regulators.[14] Although regulatory requirements partly determine the adequate level of capital, it is only capped at the bottom. The excess capital is discretionary. If the requirements of the supervisors increase due to any buffers, the scope naturally becomes smaller. This active management of capital underscores the importance of studying the impact of capital on stability, as such a practice raises the possibility that banks could influence their resilience through changes in capital allocation (should capital be a relevant cause of stability). Another critical aspect of the study is that bank regulation, which focuses heavily on capital, implies the idea of intervention. Therefore, causal inference is significant in this case, as policy evaluations aim to quantify changes in impact following changes in potential causes. It is worthwhile to note the empirical results as evidence that bank capital does not affect stability. Instead, one should look for the factors that can improve stability.

Moreira (2022) combines four methods to address endogeneity to capture the effect of unobserved confounders and reverse causality (fixed effects, 2SLS-IV, structural equation modeling, and generalized moment methods). As a result, it can be stated that there is no fixed relationship between the main variables (risk and stability). It holds for both directions of the relationship (i.e., from the capital to probability of default or vice versa). Proven correlations are due to the influence of unobserved common causes. This conclusion is strengthened by using the four methods that treat endogeneity differently. Indeed, it can be shown that focusing on other aspects typically

[14]The analyses are based on a sample of 2,350 listed banks headquartered in 51 countries. Their period ranges from 1990 to 2018.

considered by regulators and supervisors (asset quality, management quality, earnings, liquidity risk, and market risk sensitivity) does not lead to higher stability.

These conclusions may sound implausible, as they counter the status quo in this area. However, they align with other studies that find no significant link between bank capital and risk or argue that capital may not be an essential prerequisite for achieving financial stability. While capital is relevant, it is insufficient to ensure resilient banking systems. One may even go so far as to argue that higher bank capital is not associated with a lower risk of a banking crisis.

Thus, there must be other factors at play in the relationship. For instance, since equity is more expensive than debt, it would be natural to expect banks that increase their capital ratios to seek more profitable opportunities (which tend to be riskier) to increase their earnings and pay the dividends expected by shareholders. The increase in risk-taking would offset the banks' higher loss-absorbing capacity due to the additional capital raised. In other words, these banks would be better prepared to absorb higher losses, but the probability of such losses would also increase. These offsetting effects could keep the probability of bank failure virtually unchanged. Consequently, (relatively constant) stability would be independent of capital (which would change). Thus, many of these regulatory initiatives might be ineffective, even though unobserved factors provided some stability.[15] A natural next step in this area would be to look for factors and aspects that improve bank stability (and not just go hand in hand with stability). It is not a trivial task, as endogenous relationships can influence the results in empirical analyses, but it is essential in the search for stability.

3. Political Initiatives for the Further Development of Capital Buffers

Macroprudential policies are not an "elixir" (*Forbes*, 2021). They do not protect economies from volatility. However, they lead to leakages

[15]Banking regulation generally reacts significantly differently in the imperfect competition model than in the perfect competition model (Corbae and D'Erasmo, 2021). Thus, it is not only internationally imperative to pay attention to how the interaction of supposedly stability-promoting policies and market structures works.

into the non-bank financial system and spillovers through international bonds, loans, and other cross-border exposures (Karamysheva and Seregina, 2022). Some of these unintended consequences may weaken the effectiveness of macroprudential measures and lead to new vulnerabilities and risks. Finally, the instruments mentioned above have different effects in the respective (financial) economic context. Araujo *et al.* (2020) conducted a meta-analysis covering 58 of the most relevant research articles on the impact of macroprudential policies. Most results suggest that instruments that restrict lending standards (such as caps on loan-to-value or debt service-to-income ratios) have a more substantial dampening effect on credit and house price dynamics than, for instance, capital and liquidity requirements for banks.

The post-COVID period provides an excellent opportunity to assess the effectiveness of current macroprudential regulations during extreme market volatility and economic stress.[16] It is therefore logical that the macroprudential framework and its implementation are currently under scrutiny. For the European legislator, this is an opportunity to take the macroprudential framework out of its infancy and adapt it to meet future challenges. The review of the macroprudential framework must also recognize the limits of macroprudential supervision. The banking sector is not a transmission channel that macroprudential supervision can use to correct actual or perceived monetary policy slippages or compensate for missing fiscal policy measures.

The most important initiatives will be summarized in the following:

The European Commission (2021) launched a consultation process in November 2021. The questions asked concern the following:

- the evaluation of the capital buffer framework,
- its possible improvements,
- missing or obsolete instruments,
- the reduction of complexity,
- activities in the internal market, and
- global and emerging risks.

[16]Cao and Chou (2022) find that banks with higher regulatory capital ratios before the COVID-19 shock are more resilient in lending to the real economy during the crisis than banks with lower regulatory capital ratios *ex ante*.

In its report, the ESRB (2021) addresses the overlap between capital buffers and minimum capital requirements. The ESRB proposes courses of action that essentially lead to increased capital requirements. Finally, the ESRB is concerned with information sharing and disclosure, mainly related to banks or exchanges between authorities.

The European Banking Authority (2022) positions itself as follows concerning the revision: In its view, regulatory capital buffers should be restored to a sufficient level so that they can be released if needed. The authority urges a comprehensive assessment of the interaction of macroprudential measures with other capital requirements, such as leverage ratio, own funds, and eligible liabilities (MREL). It highlights establishing a supervisory and oversight system for non-bank lenders and extension of the scope of the macroprudential framework to non-bank lenders.

Although work on the revision of macroprudential instruments has not yet been completed, the following trends can be identified concerning capital buffers:

1. The number of buffers will be maintained.
2. Policymakers are looking for solutions to ensure that capital buffers remain permanently activated and "breathe" depending on the stress situation.
3. When buffers are activated, more attention will be paid to the interaction with other capital requirements.
4. Cooperation between the respective national supervisory authorities is to be improved. This improvement is to be achieved through greater transparency.

4. Alternative Capital Buffer Concept

While capital regulation is fiendishly complex, its underlying economic objectives are pretty simple: to ensure that the banking sector has sufficient capital to absorb losses, maintain financial stability, and support the economy in times of stress.

As discussed in Section 3, the overhaul of capital buffer rules appears to be leading to increased complexity. A radical concept has recently been presented by Sam Woods (2022). His simple "Bufferati"

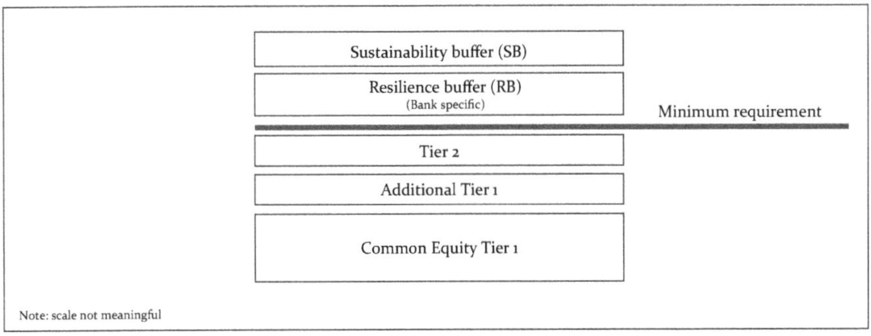

Figure 2. New capital stack with new capital buffer.

concept "revolves around a single, releasable buffer of common equity, sitting above a low minimum requirement."

In the following, we will present another concept consisting of two capital buffers (Figure 2). They aim to capture actual systemic risks.

4.1. *Design features*

The following principle applies: any element of the framework that is not necessary to achieve these fundamental objectives should be abandoned. The capital buffer concept should be as simple as possible but not more straightforward. The proposed approach has two releasable buffers. Compared to the current framework, there are no more CCoBs, CCyBs, O-SII buffers, G-SII buffers, and Pillar 2 capital charges.

4.1.1. *Number of buffers*

At the heart of this concept are two capital buffers. They are calibrated to reflect systemic risks in the financial system adequately.

1. **Resilience buffer (RB)**: In the case of the RB, the issue is the resilience of banks to systemic risks within the banking market (e.g., corporate insolvencies due to a shock and risky developments in asset markets).
2. **Sustainability buffer (SB)**: In the case of SB, the issue is the resilience of banks that may result from risks outside the banking market (e.g., climate risks, corona risks, and cyber risks).

The decisive factor is that the two capital buffers are reserved for macroprudential risks. The minimum capital requirements address the bank's microprudential risks. In this way, microprudential and macroprudential risks are prevented from overlapping.[17] So as not to be misunderstood, both microprudential and macroprudential regulations have the same fundamental goal: a financial system that serves the real economy, even when tensions arise. They aim to avoid banking crises, disorderly collapses, or adverse credit supply shocks that can amplify downturns and turn recessions into depressions.[18]

More qualitative and analytical approaches should compensate for the lack of reliable quantitative indicators to calibrate macroprudential policy. It is not inconsistent with the need to improve information transparency, quality, and standardization in parallel. However, this information cannot be used to assess systemic financial risks under current risk assessment methodologies. For example, climate-related financial risks have a longer time horizon than traditional financial risks and cannot be derived from past data. They are nonlinear and subject to tipping points. Their occurrence has irreversible consequences, and their cost is potentially infinite. The usual division between the temporal dimension (procyclicality) and the cross-cutting dimension of systemic risk (joint exposures and interconnectedness) is irrelevant for avoiding, for example, climate-related systemic financial risks. More precisely, the issue of procyclicality is irrelevant (Quang and Scialom, 2021).

Conversely, the cross-cutting dimension of systemic risk must focus on macroprudential policy design. This part of the financial stability policy focuses on the interactions between different markets and among different financial institutions to account for common exposures, risk concentrations, and credit relationships at a given point in time. For example, given the need to understand transition

[17]It also leads to conflicts between the institutions entrusted with these tasks. The most frequently cited hypothetical example is the risk that microprudential authorities would not allow banks to use their buffers in a stressful situation, which would be good for the resilience of these individual institutions but would harm the system as a whole. In the corona crisis, the behavior was exactly the opposite.

[18]In this context, the nonlinear interactions between the financial market and the real economy must be emphasized above all (Brunnermeier and Sannikov, 2014).

risk through cascades of failures due to the upstream and downstream interdependencies of the fossil fuel extraction and consumption industry, it is indeed the cross-cutting dimension of systemic risk that is relevant to structuring macroprudential "climate" policy (Quang and Scialom, 2021).

1. *Resilience buffer*: Macroeconomic analysis is used to analyze for the RB what systemic risks exist in the banking market. Such analyses include direct and indirect network interdependencies such as the following:

- credit growth and excessive leverage of individual market participants,
- maturity mismatches and liquidity shortages in the markets,
- direct and indirect risk concentrations,
- cascades of insolvencies,
- panics and runs,
- self-fulfilling defaults,
- distressed sales and contract renegotiations, or
- financial infrastructure resilience.

These different types of externalities and linkages interact. A bank may be vulnerable in one network (e.g., by deriving from another failure) and then trigger a cascade in another (e.g., by defaulting). Therefore, an appropriate assessment of systemic risk requires a holistic view of the different types of interdependencies among banks (Jackson and Pernoud, 2021).

The system evolution must be studied and not only a sequence of synchronous iterations. With such an approach, it is even more possible to assess the system's final global state and closely explore the complete and fine-grained dynamics of each agent or market participant. Moreover, one can observe the causal chain of events and reactions that determined the particular behavior of the agent within the system execution. Effective handling of large financial systems, which exhibit a higher degree of agent heterogeneity, is achievable through highly scalable analysis. On this basis, very flexible stress tests can be developed to experiment with many hypothetical scenarios in a test-oriented style quickly.

Agent-based modeling

For the analysis and simulation of emergent phenomena, methods or techniques are required that do justice to the underlying complexity. Agent-based modeling (ABM) provides such an innovative or contemporary approach. This computer-based approach allows complex natural and economic/social systems to be modeled in detail and studied experimentally over an individually designable period. It is achieved by the central ability of ABM to transfer the comprehensive interaction of a large number of heterogeneous agents (e.g., credit institutions) with each other and with their environment (e.g., central banks) quite uncomplicatedly into the digital world. Among other things, the agents can influence each other (e.g., formation of speculative bubbles) or react individually to changes in their environment, which can change through their actions (e.g., adjustment of crucial interest rates). Due to a largely realistic representation of the system to be analyzed and its components' individual properties and behaviors, very different circumstances can be explained, sustainable solutions to problems can be developed, or widely reliable forecasts can be made. The simulation can run in a very dynamic way. Among other things, the agents can move freely in their environment according to previously defined rules of behavior and jointly perform different (interlocking) activities. These rules or the resulting behavior, in turn, can be modified by learning processes. The epistemic possibilities of the ABM method are thus almost inexhaustible or subject only to the limits of imagination or, much more trivial, to data availability (Haldane and Turrell, 2018).

Determining which banks contribute most to systemic risk can be measured using the concept of financial centrality. Various centrality measures can be used to assess a particular bank's exposure to systemic risk or its contribution to systemic risk.[19]

Based on a cost-benefit analysis, the overall level of capital requirements for the system is determined, which would move up or down depending on the build-up and reduction of systemic risk. To illustrate, the regulator conducts macroeconomic analysis of the

[19]The measure of financial centrality does have some similarities with existing G-SII buffers (see EBA, 2020). Such indicator analyses can be improved, for example, by using agent-based modeling (ABM) tools (Teply and Klinger, 2019; Crafa, 2021).

banking and financial markets. The analysis concludes that the average capital level should be 13%. The supervisor then reviews the capital requirement for each bank. If that bank is firmly positioned based on its characteristics, then the authority may set the capital requirement at 15%. Conversely, a bank with lower risk would have to comply with a capital requirement of 11%, and so on.

2. *Sustainability buffer*: The setting of the SB is also subject to macroeconomic analysis. However, it is recognized that systemic risks cannot be quantified with pinpoint accuracy. These could include climate risks or cyber risks.

In this respect, the SB would not relate to the risk-weighted assets of an institution. Instead, the assessment basis for the SB — analogous to the leverage ratio — is the bank's business volume.

The supervisory authority conducts a macroeconomic analysis of further systemic risks that do not directly result endogenously from the banking system. The analysis concludes that banks must maintain a leverage ratio of at least 6%. Given the systemic nature, these capital requirements would have to be equally met by all banks.

Overall, the capital buffer design proposed here would have a risk-based (RB) and a leverage-based (SB) assessment basis.[20]

4.1.2. *Thresholds*

The next main feature concerns the existing thresholds. Today, there are a large number of thresholds that must be observed when drawing on the capital buffer.[21] These thresholds are replaced by a judgment-based "ladder of intervention." Automatic thresholds come at an actual cost to supervisory intervention. For example, banks will do whatever it takes to stay above their MDA threshold, including

[20] If only a leverage-based assessment basis were used, the entire system would likely have to operate at a much higher level of capital.

[21] For example, the requirements for recovery planning stipulate that specific indicators and the falling below predefined thresholds (early warning threshold and recovery threshold) require the bank to take specific measures (escalation process and options for action). One important indicator is CET1 capital. The early warning threshold is significantly higher than P2G in the rules. Using capital buffers would mean that the early warning and recovery thresholds are undercut.

restricting lending to the real economy. It defeats a significant part of the purpose of capital regulation.

Utilization of the RB would have no automatic consequences. The bank would only be expected to implement a plan to restore its capital resources. What must be included in this plan would vary widely. The content would depend on the company-specific or macroeconomic circumstances that led to the company drawing on its capital buffer. It also relates to whether the authorities have already released a portion of the RB. At both the micro and macro levels, supervisors have various tools that could be used on an intervention ladder as needed. However, these tools would never be triggered automatically by the company reaching a predefined threshold.

Below the two capital buffers, there is a designed minimum capital requirement (risk and leverage based). The minimum requirement should be set so low that the two buffers can fulfill their task. Their violation should not have automatic consequences (e.g., insolvency).

4.1.3. *Usability of bank capital buffers*

The two capital buffers are intended to be potentially releasable in a stressful situation. Banks should build up capital in good times to be in a solid position to use capital to support lending in a downturn. It is essential to distinguish what is meant by the "usability" of a buffer.

There can be two manifestations. If a bank suffers losses during a crisis or its risk-weighted assets increase, it will have no choice but to "use" its capital buffers. However, this is an automatic process and not a voluntary use of capital so that one could speak of a "passive use" of capital buffers. In contrast, management could actively decide not to reduce a bank's risk-weighted assets or expand them further, i.e., to continue lending. It could be called "active use" of capital buffers. "Active" release of capital requirements in a downturn allows banks to do so more efficiently and smoothly. They do not have to worry about running into buffers and triggering restrictions or other supervisory actions. If systemic risks emerge, authorities could lower the average capital requirement for the entire system to the level they deem necessary to avoid an unwarranted deterioration in credit conditions and give firms room to maneuver during the stress period.

Even if the two buffers were reduced to zero, there is a risk that the market will pressure banks to maintain their capital ratios in a stressful situation. Below the so-called market-driven capital requirements, banks will have difficulty funding themselves. However, in cases where the regulatory cap is above the market-driven requirement, the release of buffers gives banks more room to maneuver.

4.1.4. *Composition of capital buffers*

All two capital requirements must be met by common equity. Common Equity is the loss-absorbing instrument par excellence and is easy to understand. Other capital instruments such as AT1 have no place in this reduced capital buffer concept.

4.2. *Stress testing*

Stress testing is an essential analytical contribution that holds the system together. Conceptually, stress tests can be seen as an expression of risk appetite: They indicate the degree to which an optimally capitalized banking system is likely to be exposed to stress. In addition, individual portfolios are scrutinized (Budnik *et al.*, 2022). This way, which banks are exposed to more significant risks is determined. Crucially, the two capital buffers are also subject to different stress tests in each case.

The stress tests will generally be performed in a decentralized manner. The primary input for many stress tests is balance sheet data describing the amount of each type of financial asset and liability held by each bank. Depending on the country, balance sheet data do not always provide complete or even partial information on counterparties and hence on the network structure. Such "local" data may completely miss which banks are most likely to trigger or be involved in a default cascade (Jackson and Pernoud, 2021). Therefore, the non-trivial parts of the network should be included in the stress tests (Farmer *et al.*, 2020; di Iasio, 2022).[22]

The regular exercises for banks today are essentially based on a single stress test for an annual economic scenario. There, the ability of banks to maintain their capital levels above a predefined threshold in a severe but plausible economic downturn is tested.

[22]Agent-based modeling (ABM) and actor-based reactive system (ARS) can be applied as methods to perform such stress testing — see also box in the text (Teply and Klinger, 2019; Crafa, 2021).

Stress testing is an extensive exercise for both regulators and banks. Similar approaches, sometimes with a small handful of scenarios instead of just one, exist in individual countries (de Guindos, 2021).

With the revision of capital buffers, stress tests need to be robust but more straightforward and frequent. The tests should cover a much broader range of economic outcomes. It could be reflected in a wide range of scenarios. One can imagine a world in which a hundred scenarios are created based on the distribution of possible shocks to the sector, and a risk appetite is set for those scenarios. Instead of selecting just one point on the distribution of scenarios, the overall level of capital would be set by the macroprudential assessment mentioned above (applies primarily to RB).

The stress tests would show how much of the distribution of scenarios banks can withstand. It would be helpful to cross-check the top-down macroprudential decision on capital levels. The exercise would identify outliers and could also be a way to allow authorities to assume a higher risk appetite for smaller banks by requiring systemically important banks to be robust to a broader range of scenarios.

4.3. *Institutional setting*

Macroprudential policy faces several challenges related to the institutional context. These include resistance from policymakers and interest groups, weaknesses in the governance framework, and limited institutional memory among policymakers (Bengtsson, 2020). In this context, the determination of the various capital buffers embeds itself. It has so far been the responsibility of the respective nation-states. The ESRB has so far only had a coordinating role. Given the endogeneity of risks and the systemic nature of many risks, it seems necessary to provide the ESRB with competencies beyond a coordinating role.[23] The ESRB must be endowed with specific power or

[23]The ESRB does not see itself taking such a leading role. It advocates closer cooperation among national authorities with different mandates (resolution, supervisory, macroprudential, financial stability, and fiscal). Such cooperation could include discussion of systemic stress scenarios and using macroprudential analytical tools (e.g., macroprudential stress tests or cross-border and cross-sectoral interconnectedness analysis) to support crisis management processes (ESRB, 2022).

authority that allows it to obtain, directly or indirectly, all the necessary information and data from banks and other market actors to adequately identify the emergence of systemic risks at an early stage and assess them accordingly. For this reason, the ESRB must no longer be merely a board of the ECB. Instead, the ESRB should be institutionally upgraded and established as an independent authority. It is proposed to rename the ESRB the European Systemic Risk Authority (ESRA).

The work should not focus only on networks of financial organizations. ESRA should be interested in the implications for the economy as a whole. Indeed, contagion is not specific to financial markets. For example, the structure of input–output networks and supply chains can cause small shocks to amplify in much the same way that a financial network can amplify shocks in returns and affect asset prices. Interactions among banks include direct mutual holdings and indirect interdependencies through holding common assets outside the banking system (Barnett *et al.*, 2022). Determining the optimal supply of capital then requires a good understanding of the interplay between financial networks and supply chains, a topic that has not received much attention.

Finally, attention should be paid to how a financial network's structure responds to regulation changes. Anderson *et al.* (2019) analyze the impact of the National Banking Acts (NBAs) of 1863–1864 on the topology of the U.S. banking system. The NBAs established reserve and capital requirements and created a reserved hierarchy. It led to a greater concentration of the banking system in a few core banks located in specific reserve cities. It allowed for better diversification but also increased the risk of contagion if one of the core banks failed.

An essential and problematic feature of financial networks is their complexity, which can make them opaque. Financial markets involve many market participants trading different types of financial assets, leading to complex and multidimensional interconnections. Moreover, some of this complexity is a response to a regulation, with financial innovations and new products introduced to circumvent regulatory restrictions. Notably, a significant portion of these trades are conducted in over-the-counter markets and, therefore, may only be known to the two parties directly involved in the exchange if they are not required to be disclosed.

These examples show that the analysis of systemic risks should not be left to the respective national supervisory authorities. Even if ESRA has detailed data on all financial institutions, monitoring the financial network is complicated by the ever more significant part of the financial system that operates outside the purview of financial regulation, making it even more difficult for regulators to get a complete picture of the market. Moreover, the shadow banking system is endogenous and may expand in response to tighter restrictions in the regulated system.

5. Conclusion

It can be observed that the macroprudential regulatory corpus introduced after the financial crisis is strongly imbued with the microprudential conception of banking regulation. Risk is still defined as an asset-specific characteristic that can be determined using probabilistic models based on historical data. To be sure, new instruments such as the various capital buffers have been introduced. However, they should instead be interpreted as extensions of a set of rules. However, the instruments remain blind to any risks whose origin lies outside the market. The recent COVID crisis highlights the extent to which risks can materialize outside the market in a hyper-connected world and beyond on the brink of a climate crisis.

Defining a macroprudential policy that considers the specifics of systemic risks requires the development of tools that go beyond the restrictive risk approach of current prudential regulations and, in particular, the risk-weighted capital ratio. "As should be clear from our discussion above, regulation is far from one-size-fits-all, and optimal intervention depends on many factors, including network positions and centralities that are constantly shifting. Unfortunately, regulations are slow to adjust and often constrained by politics, since intervention can benefit some parties more than others" (Jackson and Pernoud, 2021, p. 191).

A new capital buffer concept is presented. To sum up:

1. Two capital buffers are calibrated to reflect primarily macroprudential risks.

2. There is a low minimum capital requirement to maximize the buffer size.
3. There is an "intervention ladder" based on the assessment of banks included in the buffer. The approach does not include mechanical triggers and thresholds.
4. Both RB and SB are potentially triggerable in the event of stress.
5. All requirements are met with hard equity.
6. Comprehensive stress testing is at the core of capital sizing.

It should be noted that the proposed capital buffer framework differs significantly from current international standards. However, any capital framework — complex or simple — will only succeed if it is based on strong, common international standards. There is no reason why a global standard needs to be complex or overloaded with buffers and thresholds. These decisions would need to be made within a clear international framework (e.g., through the Basel Committee on Banking Supervision) to maintain a global playing field.

Specifically, this is about a macroeconomic anchor point for total equity in regular times, guidance on the definition of stress situations, approaches to stress testing and the speed of buffer rebuilding, and how much loss-absorbing capacity is needed in a resolution. It requires that the G20 agree on common objectives and a standard analytical approach so that individual countries can make their decisions within a common framework. It also inevitably depends on a degree of international trust and goodwill. "But this will mean changing from a myopic fixation on extracting the maximum from each part of the system in the short term, developing a better understanding of the structure of the underlying links in the system, and exploiting its capacity for self-organization to make it more resilient" (Hynes *et al.*, 2022, p. 383).

References

Abad, J. and Pascual, A. G. (2022). Usability of bank capital buffers: The role of market expectations. *IMF WP/22/21*. Available from: https://www.imf.org/en/Publications/WP/Issues/2022/01/28/Usability-of-Bank-Capital-Buffers-The-Role-of-Market-Expectations-511947. Accessed: 14 February 2022.

Anderson, H., Paddrik, M. and Wang, J. J. (2019). Bank networks and systemic risk: Evidence from the national banking acts. *American Economic Review, 109*(9), 125–161.

Araujo, J. D., Patnam, M., Popescu, M. A., Valencia, M. F. and Yao, W. (2020). Effects of macroprudential policy: Evidence from over 6,000 estimates. *IMF Working Papers, 2020/067.* Available from: https://www.imf.org/en/Publications/WP/Issues/2020/05/22/Effects-of-Macroprudential-Policy-Evidence-from-Over-6-000-Estimates-49440. Accessed: 21 November 2020.

Auer, R., Matyunina, A. and Ongena, S. (2022). The countercyclical capital buffer and the composition of bank lending. *Journal of Financial Intermediation, 52*, 100965.

Avril, P., Levieuge, G. and Turcu, C. (2022). Natural disasters and financial stress: Can macroprudential regulation tame green swans? *Banque de France Working Paper No. 874.* Available from: https://www.banque-france.fr/sites/default/files/media/2021/06/10/gdre_avril.pdf. Accessed: 2 June 2022.

Basel Committee on Banking Supervision (2011). Basel III: A global regulatory framework for more resilient banks and banking systems. Available from: https://www.bis.org/publ/bcbs189.pdf. Accessed: 8 April 2020.

Barnett, W. A., Wang, X., Xu, H. C. and Zhou, W. X. (2022). Hierarchical contagions in the interdependent financial network. *Journal of Financial Stability, 61*, 101037.

Bengtsson, E. (2020). Macroprudential policy in the EU: A political economy perspective. *Global Finance Journal, 46*, 100490.

Bolton, P., Despres, M., Da Silva, L. A. P., Samama, F. and Svartzman, R. (2020). Central banking and financial stability in the age of climate change. *BIS Working Paper No. 31.* Available from: https://www.bis.org/publ/othp31.pdf. Accessed: 14 January 2021.

Brunnermeier, M. and Sannikov, Y. (2014). A macroeconomic model with a financial sector. *American Economic Review, 104*(2), 379–421.

Budnik, K., Dimitrov, I., Groß, J. and Caccia, A. (2022). Using the ECB macroprudential stress testing framework for policy assessment — lessons learned from the COVID-19 pandemic. *ECB Macroprudential Bulletin, 17.* Available from: https://www.ecb.europa.eu/pub/financial-stability/macroprudential-bulletin/html/ecb.mpbu202206_3 37629fc857.en.html. Accessed: 21 May 2022.

Cao, Y. and Chou, J. (2022). Bank resilience over the COVID-19 crisis: The role of regulatory capital. *Finance Research Letters, 48*, 102891.

Cappelletti, G., Reghezza, A., d'Acri, C. R. and Spaggiari, M. (2022). Compositional effects of bank capital buffers and interactions with monetary policy. *Journal of Banking & Finance, 140*, 106530.

Cerutti, E., Claessens, S. and Laeven, L. (2017). The use and effectiveness of macroprudential policies: New evidence. *Journal of Financial Stability*, *28*, 203–224.

Chari, A., Dilts-Stedman, K. and Forbes, K. (2022). Spillovers at the extremes: The macroprudential stance and vulnerability to the global financial cycle. *Journal of International Economics*, *136*, 103582.

Corbae, D. and D'Erasmo, P. (2021). Capital buffers in a quantitative model of banking industry. *Econometrica*, *89*(6), 2975–3023.

Crafa, S. (2021). From agent-based modeling to actor-based reactive systems in the analysis of financial networks. *Journal of Economic Interaction and Coordination*, *16*(3), 649–673.

Danielsson, J., Shin, H. S. and Zigrand, J.-P. (2013). Endogenous and systemic risk. In J. G. Haubrich and A. W. Lo (eds.) *Quantifying Systemic Risk*. National Bureau of Economic Research.

de Guindos, L. (2021). Macroprudential stress testing under great uncertainty. *Financial Stability Review* (Banque de France), *24*, 17–28. Available from: https://publications.banque-france.fr/sites/default/files/medias/documents/820101_fsr_2020_en.pdf. Accessed: 16 February 2022.

di Iasio, G., Kördel, S., Nicoletti, G. and Salakhova, D. (2022). Stressing the financial system with multiple sectors in an equilibrium approach. *ECB Macroprudential Bulletin*, *17*. Available from: https://www.ecb.europa.eu/pub/financial-stability/macroprudential-bulletin/focus/2022/html/ecb.mpbu202206_focus1.en.html. Accessed: 21 May 2022.

European Banking Authority (EBA). (2020). Guidelines on the specification and disclosure of systemic importance indicators (EBA/GL/2020/14). Available from: https://www.eba.europa.eu/regulation-and-policy/own-funds/guidelines-for-the-identification-of-global-systemically-important-institutions-g-siis-. Accessed: 12 January 2021.

European Commission (2021). Targeted consultation on improving the EU's macroprudential framework for the banking sector. Available from: https://ec.europa.eu/info/consultations/finance-2021-banking-macroprudential-framework_en. Accessed: 4 January 2022.

European Systemic Risk Board (2018). *The ESRB Handbook on Operationalising Macroprudential Policy in the Banking Sector*. Available from: https://www.esrb.europa.eu/pub/pdf/reports/esrb.report180115_handbook~c9160ed5b1.en.pdf. Accessed: 10 January 2019.

European Systemic Risk Board (2021). Report of the analytical task force on the overlap between capital buffers and minimum requirements. December 2021. Available from: https://www.esrb.europa.eu/pub/pdf/reports/esrb.ATFreport211217_capitalbuffers a1d4725ab0.en.pdf. Accessed: 8 February 2021.

European Systemic Risk Board (2022). Review of the EU macroprudential framework for the banking sector. *A Concept Note*. March 2022. Available from: https://www.esrb.europa.eu/pub/pdf/reports/esrb.reviewmacropruframework.220331 65e86a81aa.en.pdf?bfc4a41f94ce2a016dbdfb6958eff83e. Accessed: 12 April 2022.

Farmer, J. D., Kleinnijenhuis, A. M., Nahai-Williamson, P. and Wetzer, T. (2020). Foundations of system-wide financial stress testing with heterogeneous institutions. *Bank of England Working Paper No. 861*. Available from: https://www.bankofengland.co.uk/-/media/boe/files/working-paper/2020/foundations-of-system-wide-financial-stress-testing-with-heterogeneous-institutions.pdf. Accessed: 25 July 2020.

Flannery, M. and Giacomini, E. (2015). Maintaining adequate bank capital: An empirical analysis of the supervision of European banks. *Journal of Banking & Finance*, *59*, 236–249.

Forbes, K. J. (2021). The international aspects of macroprudential policy. *Annual Review of Economics*, *13*, 203–228.

Haldane, A. and Turrell, A. (2018). An interdiscplinary model for macroeconomics. *Oxford Review of Economic Policy*, *34*(1–2), 219–251.

Holmstrom, B. and Tirole, J. (1997). Financial intermediation, loanable funds, and the real sector. *The Quarterly Journal of Economics*, *112*(3), 663–691.

Hynes, W., Trump, B. D., Kirman, A., Haldane, A. and Linkov, I. (2022). Systemic resilience in economics. *Nature Physics*, *18*, 381–384.

Jackson, M. O. and Pernoud, A. (2021). Systemic risk in financial networks: A survey. *Annual Review of Economics*, *13*, 171–202.

Jokipii, T. and Milne, A. (2011). Bank capital buffer and risk adjustment decisions. *Journal of Financial Stability*, *7*(3), 165–178.

Karamysheva, M. and Seregina, E. (2022). Prudential policies and systemic risk: The role of interconnections. *Journal of International Money and Finance*, *127*, 102696.

Kleinnijenhuis, A., Kodres, K. and Wetzer, T. (2020). Useable bank capital. VoxEU.org. Available from: https://voxeu.org/article/usable-bank-capital. Accessed: 23 September 2020.

Koehn, M. and Santomero, A. (1980). Regulation of bank capital and portfolio risk. *Journal of Finance*, *35*(5), 1235–1244.

Memmel, C. and Raupach, P. (2010). How do banks adjust their capital ratios? *Journal of Financial Intermediation*, *19*, 509–528.

Mirzaei, A. and Samet, A. (2022). Effectiveness of macroprudential policies: Do stringent bank regulation and supervision matter? *International Review of Economics & Finance*, *80*, 342–360.

Moreira, F. (2022). Are we living in an illusion? A fresh look at the importance of bank capital in the quest for stability. *Journal of International Financial Markets, Institutions and Money, 76*, 101468.

Quang, G. L. and Scialom, L. (2021). Better safe than sorry: Macroprudential policy, Covid 19 and climate change. *International Economics, 172*, 403–413.

Roy, S. (2022). What drives the systemic banking crises in advanced economies? *Global Finance Journal, 54*, 100746.

Teply, P. and Klinger, T. (2019). Agent-based modeling of systemic risk in the European banking sector. *Journal of Economic Interaction and Coordination, 14*(4), 811–833.

Thakor, A. (2012). Incentives to innovate and financial crises. *Journal of Financial Economics, 103*(1), 130–148.

van Ooordt, M. R. C. (2022). Calibrating the magnitude of the countercyclical capital buffer using market-based stress tests. *Journal of Money, Credit and Banking, 55*(2–3), 465–501.

Woods, S. (2022). Bufferati. *Speech at City Week 2022*. Available from: https://www.bankofengland.co.uk/speech/2022/april/sam-woods-speaking-at-city-week-2022-developments-in-prudential-regulation-in-the-uk. Accessed: 26 April 2022.

https://doi.org/10.1142/9781800614321_0002

Chapter 2

Do Accounting Standards Contribute to Bank Stability?

Aishath Shahudha Abdulla* **and Gamini Premaratne**†

Universiti Brunei Darussalam, Jalan Tungku Link,
Gadong BE1410, Brunei
**aishath.shahudha@gmail.com*
†*gamini.premaratne@ubd.edu.bn*

Abstract

This chapter examines the bank stability indicators under two different accounting regimes: Local GAAP-compliant and mixed accounting standards. The objective is to determine whether adopting Local GAAP and IAS/IFRS contributes to bank stability in Asia, focusing on China, Japan, South Korea, Hong Kong, Taiwan, Indonesia, Malaysia, Thailand, Singapore, and the Philippines from 2005 Q1 to 2021 Q4. The findings indicate Local GAAP may have had a detrimental effect on banks' stability, but the transition to IAS/IFRS improves bank stability. The results also suggest the procyclicality of bank stability for Local GAAP-compliant and mixed accounting banks, increased risk-taking, and bank capitalization during economic/financial upturns. Further, Local GAAP-compliant banks are more susceptible to changes in excessive credit growth, and mixed accounting banks are more vulnerable to changes in economic activities. In addition, the rise in risk appetite is greater than the rise of regulatory buffers for economic and financial upturns for Local GAAP-compliant banks.

Keywords: Accounting standards, bank stability, local GAAP, IAS/IFRS, lending risk, bank capitalization, Asian banks

1. Introduction

The Global Financial Crisis of 2007–2008 was precipitated by several factors including imprudent regulation of the banking and mortgage industries, aggressive accounting practices that obscured risks, rating agencies that failed to properly assess the risks associated with complex financial instruments, inadequate capital buffers, and poor governance. These corporate failures during the crisis contributed to the loss of confidence in the banking system, which led to decreased lending and increased borrowing costs. The resulting economic downturn had far-reaching consequences, including high unemployment and foreclosures. This has led to increased regulation and oversight and calls for greater transparency and accountability.

On the other hand, the globalization of business and capital markets brought different economies into ever-closer contact, making capital markets more homogenous. Nobes and Parker (2008) stated that the growing need for information and harmonized, high-quality, globally accepted accounting standards among foreign investors has risen because of the globalization of the capital market. Subsequently, global accounting standards also contributed to the gradual transition globally.

In response to globalization and the Global Financial Crisis, policymakers worldwide have taken steps to improve bank stability, reduce financial reporting differences, and strengthen banks' resilience by strengthening prudential regulations and enhancing supervisory standards. The growing recognition that accounting standards need revisions to reflect the risks they face improves transparency and ensures that banks have adequate capital and liquidity to withstand shocks. One key area that has come under scrutiny and renewed interest is the role of accounting standards, bank stability, and the efficacy of these standards.

In response, various initiatives were launched to improve the quality of financial reporting and its enforcement. As a result, a standardized set of principles and policies known as "accounting standards" has been developed to serve as the foundation for consistent financial reporting across institutions and over time. These standards apply to all aspects of a company's financial health, including its assets,

Table 1. Example of income statement subject to accounting standards.

Income	Expenses
Operating Income	**Operating Expenses**
Sale of Goods for Resale	Purchases of Goods for Resale
Productions Sold (Goods and Services)	Taxes and Similar Payments
Operating Grants	Wages and Salaries
Operating Profit	Fixed Assets: Appropriations to Depreciation
Financial Income	Fixed Assets: Appropriation to Provisions
Financial Fixed Asset Securities and Debt Receivable	Current Assets: Appropriation to Provisions
Interest Income and Similar Income	Liabilities and Charges: Appropriation to Provisions
Non-interest Income and Similar Income	
Currency Exchange Gains	
	Financial Expenses
	Appropriations to Depreciation and Provisions
	Interest Expenses and Similar Expenses
	Non-interest Expense
	Currency Exchange Losses
Total Income	**Total Expense**

liabilities, revenues, expenses, and shareholders' equity. Table 1 is an example of a bank income statement comprising operating and financial income and expenses subject to accounting standards.

Table 2 is an example of a bank balance sheet composition comprising current assets, fixed assets that are tangible, intangible, and financial, capital and reserves, and debt payable subject to accounting standards.

The two primary sets of accounting standards are as follows: International Financial Reporting Standards (IAS/IFRS), issued by the International Accounting Standards Board (IASB), and Local Generally Accepted Accounting Principles (GAAP) (IFRS Foundation, 2010). Local GAAP refers to generally accepted accounting principles specific to a particular country, region, or

Table 2. Example of balance sheet subject to accounting standards.

Assets	Liabilities
Current Assets	**Capital and Reserves**
Stocks and Work in Progress	Capital
Debt Receivables	Premiums on Shares Issues
Short-term Investment Securities	Reserves
Own Shares	Investment Grants
Short-term Financial Instruments	Profit or Loss Carried Forward
Liquid Assets	
Prepayments	**Debt Payable**
	Convertible and Other Debenture Loans
Fixed Assets	Loans and Debts Payable
Intangible Fixed Assets	Trade Creditors and Related Accounts
Establishment Costs	Short-term Financial Instruments
Goodwill	Deferred Income
Research and Development Costs	
Tangible Fixed Assets	
Land	
Construction	
Property, Plant, and Equipment	
Financial Fixed Assets	
Portfolio and Other Long-term Investment Securities	
Total Loans	
Total Assets	**Total Liabilities**

jurisdiction. IAS/IFRS is the global accounting standard that allows harmonization to ensure that financial statements are comparable and transparent across borders (McLeay and Riccaboni, 2000). Thus, IAS/IFRS has become the predominant reference for financial reporting.

There are various reasons why the globalization of accounting standards and procedures has become vital, replacing the outdated restricted perspectives of national financial reporting. First, economic globalization includes financial liberalization, increasing foreign commerce and investment, and the flow of products and services, as well as people, technology, and information. According to the journal *Foreign Policy*'s Globalization Index, "Singapore is among the most globalized countries" (Nobes and Parker, 2008). Second, global financial markets connect domestic and global financial markets with high financial integration, innovation, and technical breakthroughs.[1] Thus, it leads to the emergence of international corporations, while also changing share ownership patterns.[2] Third is the increased global influence of specific countries. These trends are related to one another and have impacted financial reporting. Given these considerations, there is a compelling case for investigating the effect of financial reporting and accounting standards on bank stability.

There may be considerable differences in financial reporting between IAS/IFRS and Local GAAP, depending on the differences between the accounting standards and the set of rules that accompany them, as well as the choices allowed within those regulations (Norbes and Parker, 2008).[3] Therefore, it has always been essential to comprehend the causes of such differences in financial reporting.

[1]Although domestic variables are still crucial, globalization of the financial markets has led to financial integration, in which securities are priced based on global factors rather than domestic considerations (Froot and Dabora, 1999).

[2]Share ownership patterns and investor behavior differ significantly from one country to the other, despite the fact that the globalization of financial markets has facilitated greater communication and trade across these economies. As a result, there is a corresponding impact on the financial reporting styles. There is a higher requirement for publicly disclosed and independently audited financial accounts when there is a larger split between owners and managers (Nobes and Parker, 2008).

[3]Financial reporting differences persist across countries despite widespread adoption or transition to IAS/IFRS. This is because IAS/IFRS is typically used only for consolidated statements and Local GAAP for unconsolidated statements in many countries. This is partly because many countries' Local GAAP incorporate certain practices of IAS/IFRS.

1.1. *Banking sector in Asia*

The Asian banking sector has undergone dramatic changes in the wake of the Global Financial Crisis of 2007–2009. The industry was highly fragmented, with numerous small, primarily locally owned banks. Over the past decade, there has been a dramatic transformation of the banking sector, mainly due to the rise of a new breed of banks known as the "universal banks". Universal banks are large, full-service banks offering a wide range of banking products and services to corporate and retail customers. They typically have a strong presence in both the domestic and international markets.

The number of banks in Asia has increased from 8,000 in 1997 to 10,000 in 2005. The rise of the universal banks has been a significant driver of consolidation in the Asian banking sector, resulting in a much lesser number of registered banks, from 12,000 in 2007 to over 5,000 by 2015. The top 10 banks in Asia now control over 60% of the region's total banking assets, even though most were small, with less than US$1 billion in assets, in 2007. The share of assets held by the largest banks increased from 60% in 1997 to 70% in 2007 due to the acquisition of smaller banks. Between 2005 and 2015, the banking industry's total assets in Asia grew from US$3 trillion to US$14 trillion, representing an annual growth rate of 17%.

The rapid expansion of the banking sector, multiplied by the growth of bank consumers, shift in their risk profile, and a growing interest in Asia, highlights the relevance of analyzing bank stability in Asia. The changing legal, corporate, and economic climates in Asia signify the importance of accounting standards to understanding banking functions. Banks, as both borrowers and lenders, make extensive use of financial statements. As the most dynamic financial service institutions in the world, banks are required by stakeholders to maintain their regulatory and prudential reporting obligations and set examples for peripheral institutions. Thus, adopting IAS/IFRS has become crucial for banks, given their roles as global institutions, as leaders in risk management, and as yardsticks of institutional and economic stability.

Nonetheless, there have been concerns about the appropriateness of the accounting standards for developing economies (Perera, 1989). For example, the complexity of the standards and the extensive disclosure may involve costs that exceed the benefits for countries with few listed banks. IAS/IFRS face criticisms as being less flexible while considering a country's cultural norms, political climate, and economic situation. To further emphasize, these factors are significantly different among developing and developed economies, leading to deviations from the Local GAAP practiced in the US and UK (Mir and Rahaman, 2005). Limited knowledge and inadequate legal framework often encumber developing countries' transition from Local GAAP to IAS/IFRS (Tyrrall *et al.*, 2007). The effect of economic consequences on accounting standards varies from country to country. Thus, a hurdle to the global harmonization of accounting standards is the extent to which these consequences are considered by these accounting standards (Norbes and Parker, 2008).

This chapter will attempt to address the research gap by examining the relationship between banking stability under Local GAAP and that under mixed accounting standards during Q1 2005–Q4 2021. Further, it investigates the predictive ability of bank stability for banks adopting mixed accounting standards relative to Local GAAP-compliant banks in Asia, specifically China, Japan, South Korea, Hong Kong, Taiwan, Indonesia, Malaysia, Thailand, Singapore, and the Philippines, for the period Q1 2005–Q4 2021. First, this study examines the bank stability measures, specifically lending and capital measures, to determine whether adopting Local GAAP and IAS/IFRS contributes to or threatens bank stability. Second, the study examines the influence of cyclical changes on lending and capital measures under Local GAAP and mixed accounting standards.

This chapter contributes to the literature in two ways. First, this study contributes to the accounting standards' literature, examining the impact of the Local GAAP and IAS/IFRS on bank stability. Second, this study measures the impact of the accounting standards from cyclicality — resulting from business and financial cycles — on the measures of bank stability. The findings are useful to analysts, investors, and other users in Asia to help them reassess how using specific accounting standards in financial reports can contribute to banks' stability. The study also adds to the global debate on implementing IAS/IFRS accounting standards. It supports the argument that IAS/IFRS accounting standards positively impact bank stability.

This chapter proceeds as follows: Section 2 provides an overview of the existing literature on accounting standards and bank stability;

Section 3 presents the data sample selection methodology; Section 4 discusses the findings; and Section 5 concludes.

2. Literature Review

2.1. *Financial reporting and accounting standards*

The primary function of financial reporting is to provide accurate information to market participants on a timely basis and assist banks and their regulators in identifying early warning signals of potential threats to the macroeconomy, financial market conditions, or commonality in banks' exposures that trigger losses or liquidity needs for banks.

The usefulness of banking functions and accounting in the economy may be explained by the development of the asymmetric information paradigm.[4] Bank supervision and deposit-taking duties are complicated by the asymmetric knowledge between borrowers and depositors (Freixas and Rochet, 2008).

The central proposition is that many risk exposures may be imperfectly observable (see Diamond and Dybvig, 1983) due to cyclical influences. Nonetheless, these risks can be mitigated, and market discipline can be strengthened, through solid accounting standards

[4]The cultural context of the economy has an impact on financial reporting. According to Hofstede (1984), societies with high levels of uncertainty avoidance cultures retain rigid rules of thought and behavior and are intolerant of unconventional people and ideas. As a result, people begin to hold onto notions of assuring certainty and organizations that uphold uniformity. According to Gray (1988), cultural differences can account for regional variations in financial reporting and the nature of accounting methods. Conservative measurements and a preference to restrict disclosure to those directly involved in the business will be more likely to be displayed by cultures with high uncertainty avoidance and low individualism. According to him, differences can be caused more specifically by differences in accounting values, which depend on culture. These values include those related to authority (professionalism vs. statutory control), enforcement (uniformity vs. flexibility), measurement (conservatism vs. optimism), and disclosure (secrecy vs. transparency). However, compared to measurement differences resulting from external accounting environment factors like legal systems, corporate financing, tax systems, and financial markets, the effect of cultural attributes is ambiguous and indirect.

and the reporting of banks' capitalization and risk exposures. Empirical evidence suggests that stronger banks are less prone to cyclical decision-making and use better financial reporting (Acharya and Ryan, 2016). Thus, this poses the question of whether banks need to transition from Local GAAP to IAS/IFRS resulting in more stable and less cyclical decisions.

Financial statement information is useful as a foundation for capital regulation, assessing banks' oversight of borrowers, and alleviating agency costs between managers and shareholders exacerbated by information asymmetry (Beatty and Liao, 2014). Thus, information asymmetry is addressed through accounting standards that improve transparency and comparability of financial statements through timely, authentic, and fair information.[5] This leads to better-informed decision-making by investors and creditors to assess the financial health of banks, allocate capital efficiently, and thus smoothen the functions of the financial system (Ball *et al.*, 2000; Beatty and Liao, 2014). This is particularly important in times of distress when banks may seek to raise capital but cannot do so because investors lack confidence in the quality of their financial information.

[5] "Fair" refers to the requirement that shareholders and outside investors have unbiased information about a bank's performance and financial situation, to compare periods and one business to another, which calls for expert and auditor judgment on the accuracy of these financial statements (Nobes and Parker, 2008). Shareholders are interested in unbiased estimates of prospects, while creditors are concerned whether they will receive their investment back in the most extreme circumstances. By classifying economies into two main groups — equity/outsider, or those with significant equity markets and numerous outside shareholders, and credit-based financing/insider, or those with credit-based financing systems and relatively minor outside shareholders — these distinctions are more pronounced (Zysman, 1983). The most direct cause of financial reporting differences is separation of regulatory reporting (tax) and accounting regulations, and a significant auditing profession is the result of economies with equity/outsider systems (Nobes and Parker, 2008). In addition, Zeghal and Mhedhbi (2006) discovered that in developing nations, capital market-based economies are the ones that implement IAS/IFRS more frequently. There are, however, two more justifications for adopting a particular style of financial reporting based on advantages, other than the contrast between equity/outsider and credit-based/outsider. The legal system has an impact on how financial reporting is regulated and how regulatory reporting (such as taxes) influences financial reporting.

Table 3. Role of accounting standards in enhancing financial reporting quality, transparency, and timeliness to facilitate bank stability.

Role of Accounting Standards to Facilitate Bank Stability			
Providing Accurate, 'True and Fair', and Timely Information to Market Participants			
Bank Characteristics	**Macroeconomic Conditions**	**Financial Market Conditions**	**Other Characteristics**
Profitability Earnings Management	Investment Interest Rate Cyclicality	Stock Market Debt Market	**Internal Controls** Contracting Bank Regulations Internal and External Audit Corporate Governance
Capital Risk Balance Sheet Composition Regulatory Capital			
Liquidity and Leverage Risk Leverage Behavior Liquidity Behavior			
Credit Risk Lending Behavior Loan Composition Loan Loss Provision			

Financial reporting for banks produced in line with accounting standards includes several constituents. Thus, financial reporting comprises banks' characteristics, macroeconomics, financial market conditions, and other characteristics (refer to Table 3) to provide accurate, true, fair, and timely information to market participants, to facilitate bank stability. In order to aid bank stability, accounting standards' information-facilitating objectives can thus range from assisting the macroeconomic to the microeconomic frameworks (Table 4).

Table 4. Objectives of accounting standards to facilitate microeconomic and macroeconomic frameworks and their related market participants.

	Objective of Accounting Standards to Facilitate Bank Stability				
	Microeconomic Framework			Macroeconomic Framework	
Objectives	Investment Decisions	Performance and Management	Social Management	Sectoral Planning, Control, and Surveillance	National Planning, Control, and Surveillance
Market Participants	Creditors Shareholders	Managers Creditors Shareholders	Managers Creditors Stakeholders	Interbank Market Banking Sector Financial Market	Government Interbank Market Banking Sector Financial Market Global Market Global Supervisory Bodies

2.2. *Accounting standards and bank stability*

There has been an increasing consensus that early action should be taken to preserve bank stability, restore public trust, and mitigate losses. Several studies highlight the need for a prompt response during incidents threatening bank stability (Laeven and Valencia, 2018). Access to information and information sharing are among the many desired features of the legal, administrative, and regulatory framework that the Financial Stability Board (2014) has outlined as necessary for the successful resolution of banking distress and key to maintaining bank stability.

Deutsche Bundesbank (2003) defines bank system stability as a "steady state in which the financial system efficiently performs its key economic functions, such as allocating resources and spreading risk as well as settling payments". Kick and Jahn (2014) define bank instability as a situation resulting from either idiosyncratic or systematic shocks or a mixture of both. Idiosyncratic risks such as poor banking practices can harm an individual bank's solvency, while systematic risks are triggered by common shocks, resulting in financial stress on the banking system. Li *et al.* (2022) define banking stability as banks' willingness and capacity to refrain from aggressive or excessive risk-taking, avoiding insolvencies and distresses in lending and financing decisions.

Two key aspects can be taken away from these definitions. First, banks are essential to stability since they are the primary sources of liquidity in the economy and the issuers of deposits to households that assist in allocating resources, spreading risks, and settling payments. Second, stability is improved by restraining and monitoring idiosyncratic components that compromise bank solvency and reducing the impact of aggregate shocks (e.g., common exposures) from financial strains. For example, when banks are restrained from imprudent investments (poor banking practices) when there is high credit availability during economic upturns (good times), it helps mitigate the occurrence and intensity of disinvestment when credit is scarce during economic downturns (bad times). Preventing disinvestments during economic downturns can be achieved by discouraging banks from building up excessive leverage (debt overhangs) and ownership of potentially illiquid assets (risk overhangs) during economic upturns (Acharya and Ryan, 2016). On the other hand, debt and risk overhang discourages banks from making new investments and encourages them to remain undercapitalized. Thus, debt and risk overhangs are highly correlated among banks (Acharya and Ryan, 2016), leading to common exposures and threatening stability by limiting the spreading of risks and reintermediation in the banking sector.

2.3. *Accounting standards: Local GAAP and IAS/IFRS*

A critical difference between Local GAAP and IAS/IFRS relates to how different types of transactions are measured. For example, under Local GAAP, companies can choose between different measurements, for instance, amortized cost accounting, historical cost accounting, or fair value accounting, when valuing financial instruments. In contrast, under IAS/IFRS, fair value accounting is obligatory to value financial instruments. This difference can lead to different outcomes when comparing banks under different accounting regimes.

Fair value accounting (IAS/IFRS) and amortized or historical cost accounting (Local GAAP) have varying sensitivity to market illiquidity and bank discretion for the financial instruments. Fair value accounting allows banks to use "mark-to-myth" measures to underprice risks or create price distortions in the market due to central banks' lender of last resort supplying liquidity against troubled assets (Acharya and Ryan, 2016). In contrast, Daske *et al.* (2008) find that IAS/IFRS eliminates accounting alternatives that managers use, removing these opportunistic substitutes that would improve the quality of financial reporting.

On the other hand, a bank reporting using amortized or historical cost accounting under Local GAAP may appear more profitable than a bank reporting under IAS/IFRS. In amortized cost accounting, banks may delay write-downs[6] of impaired assets while generating profits from selling nonproblem assets that have appreciated, thus reducing the quality of their asset mix (Acharya and Ryan, 2016).

Furthermore, the varying sensitivity to choices in financial reporting under different accounting standards is more present over the cycle. This is done by reducing banks' accounting volatility or transparency on the impact of changing economic circumstances. Although it is less disruptive during normal business cycles, it diminishes the potential of financial reporting to serve as an early warning of economic shifts, making banks and regulators complacent during economic upturns and hiding signs of threats during economic downturns (Acharya and Ryan, 2016).

Nonetheless, there are limits to what accounting standards can achieve. Accounting standards are designed to provide accurate and timely information, not intended to prevent financial crises. This leads to two proponents of research on accounting standards compliance and bank stability, namely, (a) strong accounting standards reducing threats to bank stability and (b) accounting standards improving transparency, enhancing market discipline, and thus improving bank stability.

The first proponent argues that countries with robust accounting standards are less likely to experience threats to bank stability and

[6]There are two definitions of conservatism used in accounting literature. First, it is defined by Nobes and Parker (2008) as the practice of underreporting income or assets in order to reduce taxable income or dividend payments to creditors. In addition, according to Ball *et al.* (2000), it is the timeliness of loan loss reporting. Whereas "conservatism" is used in the US, "prudence" is used in IAS/IFRS, instead of "conservatism".

banking crises. Barth and Landsman (2010) show that countries with higher-quality accounting standards are more likely to experience fewer threats to banking stability during periods of economic turmoil. On the other hand, Berger and Hann (2007) found that banks that adopted IAS/IFRS were more likely to experience distress during the Global Financial Crisis of 2007–2009 than those that did not adopt IAS/IFRS. However, they also found that banks that followed Local GAAP were no more likely to experience distress than those following IAS/IFRS. These studies suggest that while IAS/IFRS may not provide as much protection against banking distress as Local GAAP, it is still beneficial for banks to follow international accounting standards.

The second proponent shows that accounting standards improve transparency, accounting disclosure, accuracy, and comparability of financial statements and reduce information asymmetry, leading to increased bank stability. This increased transparency has helped improve market discipline, as investors are now better able to assess risk levels before making investment decisions. Barth *et al.* (2005) examined an increase in accounting quality resulting from adopting IAS/IFRS in 21 countries that previously used Local GAAP. They concluded that entities that prepare their financial statements under IAS/IFRS are exposed to fewer earnings management, more timely recognition of losses, and more value relevance of accounting amounts than those entities using only Local GAAP. They also concluded that the quality of accounting information is higher for banks that apply IAS/IFRS than those that do not.

Despite the gradual adoption of IAS/IFRS, compliance (and monitoring) and enforcement vary globally. If compliance is low in some countries, then the practice of IAS/IFRS may vary from IAS/IFRS requirements, thus impacting stability.

3. Data and Methodology

3.1. *Data*

The sample of this study is limited to 10 Asian economies, namely, South Korea, Hong Kong, China, Taiwan, Japan, Indonesia, Thailand, Malaysia, the Philippines, and Singapore, from Q1 2005 to

Q4 2021. The objective is to investigate the predictive ability of bank stability for banks adopting mixed accounting standards relative to Local GAAP. The sample is divided into two to measure compliance with accounting standards:

(1) banks reporting under Local GAAP,
(2) banks reporting under IAS/IFRS, i.e., mixed accounting banks (banks begin reporting with Local GAAP and transition into IAS/IFRS over the years).[7]

The impacts of Local GAAP and mixed accounting standards on bank stability will be examined in this study focusing on four key areas: cycles, asset quality, capital levels, and credit risk practices using relevant indicators. This study is restricted to 69 banks in Asia due to the limited information available in many banks in Asia.

3.2. *Bank stability measures*

In this section, relevant bank stability measures used in the empirical findings are discussed to examine the relationship between banking stability under Local GAAP and that under mixed accounting standards.

3.2.1. *Z-score (ZS)*

In line with the literature on bank stability (Demirgüç-Kunt and Huizinga, 2010; Stiroh, 2004, 2006; Stiroh and Rumble, 2006), *ZS* is used to measure bank stability, which is defined as the average return on asset plus the ratio of equity and total assets divided by

---

[7]Differentiating between adoption and convergence of IAS/IFRS is essential. A jurisdiction's adoption of IAS/IFRS means that either the national regulations are superseded by a mandate or permission to use IAS/IFRS directly, or the bank voluntarily makes the switch from using the national rules to using IAS/IFRS. For instance, depending on the state's regulations, unlisted banks may or may not use IAS/IFRS in their financial statements, while listed banks in some countries must use them. It is called "convergence" when economies make a concerted and gradual change from national rules to IAS/IFRS (Nobes and Parker, 2008). Thus, this chapter refers to banks that are converging to IAS/IFRS as the "mixed accounting banks".

the standard deviation of return on assets.

$$ZS_{i,t} = \frac{ROA_{i,t} + \frac{E}{TA}_{i,t}}{\sigma_{ROAi,t}} \tag{1}$$

ZS measures bank risk-taking and bank stability, defined as the number of standard deviations by which a bank's return on the asset falls for the bank to become insolvent. Roy (1952) introduced the *ZS*, which measures the distance from insolvency and is interpreted as the inverse of the probability of insolvency (i.e., a higher *ZS* indicates that the bank incurs less risks and is more stable). In other words, insolvency is defined as the state in which bank losses $(-\pi)$ exceed equity $(E)(= -\pi > E)$ or losses consume capital $(ROA + \frac{E}{TA} < 0)$. Therefore, the probability of insolvency can be expressed as $(ROA < -\frac{E}{TA})$, where the return on assets (ROA) is the ratio of total profit (π) over average total assets $(TA)(= \frac{\pi}{TA})$. Capital asset (shareholder's equity) ratio is the ratio of average equity (E) over the average total asset (TA) of the bank i in year t $(= \frac{E}{TA})$. As the main objective of this chapter is to analyze the overall bank stability in contrast to accounting standards, *ZS* is used as an indicator of bank risk-taking and stability.

ROA is the expected value of return on an asset (ROA) and σ_{ROA} denotes each bank's standard deviation of return on asset (ROA). σ_{ROA} following Bundesbank and Köhler (2012) is calculated over the whole sample period.

Averages of ZS and ROA for 83 banks are illustrated in Figure 1, which shows both indicators dropping significantly at the beginning of Q4 2006. The 83 banks consist of banks that are Local GAAP-compliant (52 banks), mixed accounting standards banks (17 banks), and IAS/IFRS-compliant banks (14 banks). IAS/IFRS-compliant banks are omitted from the full sample due to the lack of complete data.

The average of these 83 banks saw the full force of the Global Financial Crisis from Q4 2008 to Q3 2009, with ZS declining by 36.37 percent from Q1 2007 to Q3 2009. This trend was mirrored by a dip in the ROA average over the same period. Elnahass *et al.* (2021) found similar results during the COVID-19 pandemic, with banks experiencing low stability with higher insolvency risk and asset risk.

Figure 2 illustrates the average ZS and ROA for 52 Local GAAP-compliant banks. It shows a similar decline in ZS and ROA, as seen

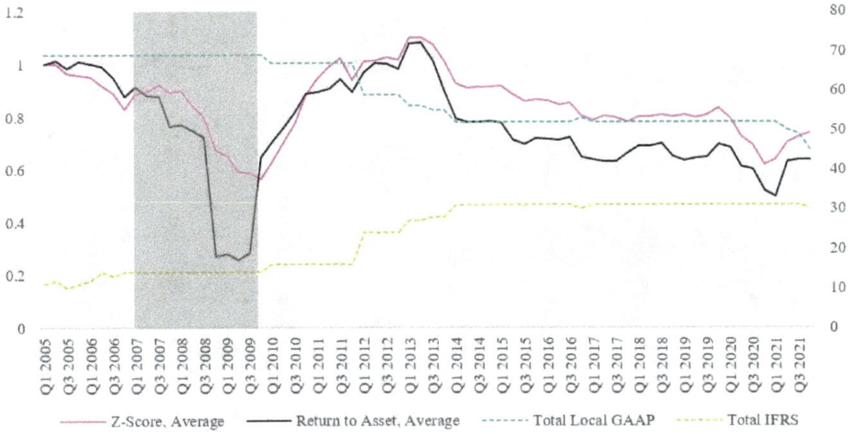

Figure 1. Average *ZS* and Average *ROA* and total number of banks implementing Local GAAP and IAS/IFRS (sample of banks = 83).

Figure 2. Average *ZS* and Average *ROA* and total number of banks implementing Local GAAP (sample of banks = 52).

in Figure 1. This figure suggests that banks reporting under Local GAAP experienced more severe financial distress than those reporting under IAS/IFRS. The Local GAAP-compliant banks had their *ZS* drop by 63.07 percent from Q3 2008 to Q3 2009.

Figure 3. Average ZS and Average ROA and total number of banks transitioning from Local GAAP to IAS/IFRS (sample of banks = 17).

Figure 3 shows that ZS of mixed accounting banks dropped by 18.6 percent from Q3 2008 to Q3 2009. During the Global Financial Crisis, mixed accounting banks began to transition from Local GAAP to IAS/IFRS in Q1 2010 and fully transitioned by Q1 2014. Despite Local GAAP-compliant banks experiencing a precipitous drop in ZS the mixed accounting banks had no such drop even before the transition and, as they transitioned, experienced a further improvement in ZS and ROA.

Accordingly, the IAS/IFRS was enacted as one of the changes made to accounting rules following the commencement of the Global Financial Crisis of 2007–2009. Since then, several banks have switched from Local GAAP to IAS/IFRS, with the number of Asian banks using IAS/IFRS increasing from 11 to 30 and the number of Local GAAP institutions decreasing from 69 to 45 (Figure 1).

3.2.2. *Lending measures*

Four measures are used to assess the impact of bank lending activities. First, to measure the effects of lending activities on bank stability, total loan to total asset ratio (LAR) is used. A greater LAR ratio indicates a riskier bank profile (Jokipii and Milne, 2008).

Second, to measure the loan composition of banks, consumer loans over total loans (*CSL*), commercial loans over total loans (*CML*), and real estate loans over total loans (*REL*) are used. This is to control the loan composition of banks' lending to different types of creditors.

The expectation is that *LAR* and *CML* (corporate credit) positively affect bank stability. On the other hand, *CSL* (consumer credit) and *REL* (real-estate credit) have a negative relationship with bank stability, following the findings of Jordà *et al.* (2011). They distinguish the influence of household credit, mortgage credit, and business credit on financial crises.

3.2.3. *Timeliness of loan loss provisions*

The timeliness of loan loss provision is determined by dividing the loan loss allowance by non-performing assets (*LLANA*). A dummy variable (*TIME*) is constructed using the lagged *LLANA*, equal to one if the lagged *LLANA* is greater than the median and zero otherwise, to quantify the delay in recognition of loan losses (Beatty and Liao, 2011).

The level of loan loss provisions tends to fluctuate with the economy and the cycle. Non-performing loans tend to emerge in times of economic stress and when borrowers have trouble completing their financial obligations. When this happens, banks increase their loan loss provisions to cover the increased cost of non-performing loans. However, the capacity of loan loss reserves to cover loan losses during economic downturns is influenced by the degree to which the recognition of predicted losses is delayed. This means increased loan loss provisioning is necessary but weakens bank capital adequacy when loan loss reserves are insufficient to absorb loan losses, thus worsening procyclicality (Beatty and Liao, 2011).

3.2.4. *Capital measures*

The effect of bank capital on bank stability is quantified using two measures. First, Tier 1 capital ratio (*T1R*) includes common equity, perpetual preferred stock, and minority interests. However, goodwill and other intangibles are subtracted, and loan loss allowance is not included. Second, the total regulatory capital ratio (*TRCR*) comprises Tier 1 and Tier 2 capital ratios.

The argument is that banks with higher capitalization are more stable, although their lending and profitability may drop. According to the van den Heuvel (2005) theory, optimally, banks may pass up potential lending possibilities to reduce future capital inadequacy risks. This suggests the relationship between lending and bank capitalization.

3.2.5. *Cycles*

Two measures are used to assess the impact of cyclicality on bank stability. First, the natural logarithm of GDP growth is used as a proxy for the business cycle (BC) (Shim, 2013). Second, the deviation of credit-to-GDP growth from its long-term trend identified using the Hodrick–Prescott filter is used as a proxy for the financial cycle. The financial cycle (FC) metric is based on the premise that a rise in credit-to-GDP growth is a precursor to bank instability (Borio *et al.*, 2018).

The objective of using business and financial cycles is to understand how the real economy and excessive credit growth affect bank risk-taking, respectively. The hypothesis is that if banks increase their risk-taking during economic upturns, bank stability will have a positive association with the cycle. If, on the other hand, banks are more willing to take higher risks when the economy is distressed, bank stability will have a negative association. As a result, bank stability would be procyclical.

3.2.6. *Bank size (BS)*

Bank size is calculated using the natural logarithm of total assets (Köhler, 2015). The expectation is that ZS shows a negative coefficient for bank size, suggesting that larger banks are less stable than their smaller counterparts.

3.2.7. *Non-interest income share (NIIS)*

Non-interest income, a component of the bank business model, includes fee and commission income associated with market-oriented and conventional banking activities. Non-interest income includes trading, market, and other operating revenues.

$$NIIS_{i,t} = \frac{\text{non-interest income}^*_{i,t}}{\text{non-interest income}_{i,t} + \text{interest income}_{i,t}} \times 100 \quad (2)$$

Note: * Non-interest $\text{income}_{i,t}$ = (fee $\text{income}_{i,t}$) + (trading $\text{income}_{i,t}$) + (other non-interest $\text{income}_{i,t}$).

Non-interest income is often riskier and more volatile than interest income (Stiroh and Rumble, 2006). On the other hand, Nisar *et al.* (2018) conclude that non-interest income improves bank profitability and stability, which is analogous to Köhler (2015). Since there is no consensus in the literature, it is expected that *NIIS* will either increase or decrease stability.

3.2.8. *Return on risk-weighted assets (RRWA)*

Return on risk-weighted assets is used to measure the banks' performance relative to bank risk-taking. The banking regulation mandates a certain level of capital to be held relative to the bank's risk-weighted assets to ensure stability. Since not all bank assets have the same level of risk, the required minimum capital is calculated using risk-weighted assets. Therefore, a robust *RRWA* will optimize the profits earned in relation to the level of bank risk-taking.

$$RRWA = \frac{\text{operating profit}_{i,t}}{\text{risk-weighted assets}_{i,t}} \times 100 \quad (3)$$

3.2.9. *Non-performing loans (NPL)*

A financial institution's on-balance-sheet credit exposures and assets can be approximated by its non-performing loans over total loan ratio (*NPLL*). An increase in non-performing loans not only decreases current profitability but it may also limit future credit lending because of heightened risk aversion and mandatory regulatory capital constraints, decreasing stability.

3.2.10. *Market-to-book ratio (MBR)*

Market-to-book ratio is a proxy for the market's assessment of an institution's aggregate exposure to financial distress. The primary factors influencing the indicator are current debt levels, potential earning expectations, and uncertainty (Fama and French, 1993).

Table 5. Summary statistics of local GAAP and mixed accounting standards.

		Summary Statistics							
		Local GAAP Sample				Mixed Accounting Sample			
	Variables	Min.	Max.	Mean	Std.	Min.	Max.	Mean	Std.
Insolvency	*ZS*	–5.08	7.96	1.32	1.76	–2.53	11.26	3.44	2.38
Capital	*T1R*	2.3	17.8	13.69	4.59	5.39	19.46	11.33	2.33
	TRCR	2.8	61.74	15.86	4.43	7.47	36.28	14.29	2.27
	LAR	2.933	115.9	62.48	11.43	11.5	117.89	60.33	7.21
Credit	*CSL*	0.087	16.58	62.35	12.58	3.58	29.08	43.78	13.95
	CML	0.026	46.49	37.64	27.15	1.652	40.88	39.89	15.12
	REL	0.014	21.03	32.46	13.47	0	26.25	32.69	12.54
Asset Quality	*NPLL*	0.04	12.93	3.26	3.66	0.07	16.11	1.63	2.07
Cycle	*BC*	14.29	22.15	18.91	2.26	10.83	20.05	12.89	2.13
	FC	1.5	190	105.9	62.34	1.5	358.2	175.6	74.84
Size	*BS*	3.52	14.06	4.291	3.62	5.47	14.19	11.01	1.31
Valuation	*MBR*	–20.79	32.7	1.16	1.64	0.32	4.19	1.382	0.56
Diversification	*NIIS*	0.44	27.5	20.97	20.84	0.52	48.33	31.08	34.48
Performance	*RRWA*	–2.64	4.84	0.45	0.51	–2.2	3.51	0.48	0.25
Macro	*INT*	0.161	218.9	11.65	37.13	0.01	218.9	9.2	35.68

Note: Summary statistics for the analysis of the variables.

For this reason, the expectation is that when the *MBR* ratio is low, bank stability is low.

Table 5 illustrates the descriptive statistics of the bank-specific and macroeconomic indicators. *ZS*, a proxy for bank stability, has a minimum of -5.08 and 2.53 for Local GAAP-compliant and mixed accounting banks, respectively. On the other hand, local GAAP-compliant and mixed accounting banks have a maximum *ZS* of 7.96 and 11.26, respectively. This implies that the magnitude of bank instability is significantly greater for Local GAAP-compliant banks. In contrast, the magnitude of bank stability is much greater for mixed accounting banks.

Local GAAP-compliant banks have an average *LAR* of 62.48 and a *T1R* of 13.69, while mixed accounting banks have an average *LAR* of 60.33 and a *T1R* of 11.33. This suggests that Local GAAP-compliant banks have more robust capitalization relative to lending than mixed accounting banks.

However, the *NPLL* is higher for Local GAAP-compliant banks, which also consist of smaller banks overall. This suggests that more borrowers have trouble completing their financial obligations and also implies that these banks would require higher loan loss provisioning in case of a loan default, reducing bank capitalization and so endangering bank stability. In addition, Local GAAP-compliant banks are

Table 6. Variable selection.

Mnemonics	Variables	Categories
AS	Accounting Standards	Accounting Standards
TIME	Timeliness of Loan Loss Provisions	
ZS	*Z*-score	Insolvency Risk
BC	Business Cycle	Cycles
FC	Financial Cycle	
LAR	Loan to Asset Ratio	Lending Risk
CSL	Consumer Loans to Total Loans	
CML	Commercial Loans to Total Loans	
REL	Real Estate Loans to Total Loans	
T1	Tier 1 Ratio	Capital Risk
TRCR	Total Risk-based Capital Ratio	
BS	Bank Size	Size
MBR	Market to Book Ratio	Market Valuation
RRWA	Return on Risk-weighted Assets	Bank Performance
NPLL	NPL to Total Loans	Asset Quality
NIIS	Non-interest Income Share	Revenue Diversification
INT	Interest Rate	Macroeconomic Risk

more likely to be affected by the business cycle, which is an indication that these banks are more influenced by economic activities. On the other hand, mixed accounting banks are more impacted by the financial cycle, which shows that these banks' stability is more likely affected by excessive credit growth.

3.3. *Empirical framework*

First, this study adopts a correlation network to identify the strength and intensity of the relationship between variables. Second, a panel estimation with bank fixed effects accounts for bank-specific differences in Asia to ensure that the reported significance levels are not driven by cross-sectional dependence in the residuals. The variable descriptions are reported in Table 6.

3.3.1. *Correlation network*

It is important to note that the dependence structure between variables is critical to bank stability. The main concern is identifying the linkages and clusters formed between these variables based on the attributes using a correlation network. Further, the network identifies the variation of these linkages between Local GAAP-compliant and mixed accounting banks and its implication on bank stability.

$K = (DG)$, with K being a graph, where S is the set of nodes and G is the set of edges $G \subseteq S \times S$, that is, unweighted $(u, s) \in G$. Furthermore, N is assumed to be a set of s's neighbors where all nodes are directly connected to s in K; $N = \{u : (u, s) \in G\}$. There are two vectors, x and y with length $|S|$, which can take any real value from positive, zero, or negative; $x \in S \times \mathbb{R}$.

The Pearson correlation coefficient between each variable is determined by $\rho_{x,y}$ to calculate the degree of linear correlation between two variables, x and y, given the data x_i and y_i, $i \in [1, n]$. On the other hand $\rho_{x,y,K}$ defines the function showing the correlation between x and y while considering the structure of K graph, which has the same domain as the Pearson correlation coefficient following that it is equal to 1 (perfectly positively correlated vectors), -1 (perfectly negatively correlated vectors), and 0 (non-correlated vectors).

Furthermore, considering the structure of K, each entry x_s in x relates not only to the corresponding y_s entry in y, similar to the Pearson correlation, but also to all the entries in y in N and the neighbors' neighbors.

The correlation coefficient is defined as

$$\rho_{x,y} = \frac{\mathrm{Cov}(x, y)}{\sigma_x \sigma_y} \tag{4}$$

where $\mathrm{Cov}(x, y)$ is called the covariance of x_i and y_i, $i \in [1, n]$. σ_x is the standard deviation of x_i and σ_y is the standard deviation of y_i. $\bar{x}$ is the arithmetic mean of $x.\bar{y}$ is the arithmetic mean of y. Thus, the Pearson correlation coefficient is

$$\boldsymbol{\rho}_{x,y} = \frac{\sum_{i=1}^{n}(x_i - \bar{x})(y_i - \bar{y})}{\sqrt{\sum_{i=1}^{n}(x_i - \bar{x})^2(y_i - \bar{y})^2}} \tag{5}$$

$\sigma_x = \sqrt{\sum_{i=1}^{n}(x_i - \bar{x})^2}$ is x's standard deviation and $\sigma_y = \sqrt{\sum_{i=1}^{n}(y_i - \bar{y})^2}$ is y's standard deviation.

The assumption is that two nodes are related proportionally to their shortest path distance in the network, calculated as l, as the matrix as pairwise distance and tp depicts the contribution of progressively far away nodes decays quickly as the distance grows, which is depicted with k. To sum up, the network correlation distance can be calculated as follows:

$$\boldsymbol{\rho_{x,y,K}} = \frac{\sum_{i=1}^{n}\sum_{j=1}^{n} e^{-kl_{ij}}(x_i - \bar{x})(y_i - \bar{y})}{\sqrt{\sum_{i=1}^{n}\sum_{j=1}^{n} e^{-kl_{ij}}(x_i - \bar{x})(x_j - \bar{x})} \times \sqrt{\sum_{i=1}^{n}\sum_{j=1}^{n} e^{-kl_{ij}}(y_i - \bar{y})(y_i - \bar{y})(y_j - \bar{y})}} \tag{6}$$

where l_{ij} is the i, jth element of l, length of the path between nodes i and j.

The Pearson correlation network is generated using bank indicators. The figure pertains to the timeframe from Q1 2005 to Q4 2021. The network line thickness is proportionate to each indicator's strength of correlation. The opacity of the edges is proportional to their weight (i.e., the intensity of correlation). The green lines represent positive correlations, whereas the pink lines represent negative correlations. This will assist in identifying the variation of dependence structure based on the accounting standard regime and, thus, its implications on bank stability.

3.3.2. *Regression framework*

This chapter uses a fixed effect panel data model to identify the differences in the direction of vulnerability of economies and addresses the drawback of using panel data, which is the issue of unobserved heterogeneity across individual economies and time. This chapter will follow a similar approach as Ben Bouheni and Hasnaoui (2017).

However, the model specification has been improved in four aspects. First, aside from the business cycle, the model also uses the financial cycle to measure the impact of excessive credit growth on bank stability, proxied by credit-to-GDP growth using the Hodrick–Prescott (HP) filter. Second, the timeliness of loan loss recognition is used to assess the variation of the timeliness of loan loss recognition under different accounting regimes and its effect on stability. Third, a dummy variable is used to measure the aftereffect of the Global Financial Crisis of 2007–2009 on bank stability. Fourth, the influence of different loan compositions, such as mortgage credit, business credit, and consumer credit, on stability is measured, as it varies in terms of intensity and strength for different loan types.

The panel regression models are specified as follows:

Model 1 (Baseline): Association of bank stability between bank lending and bank regulatory capital.

$$Z_{it} = \alpha + \beta_1 AS_{it} + \beta_2 L_{it} + \beta_3 K_{it} + \sum_{M=1}^{M} \delta_m X_{it}^m + \sum_{t=1}^{T} \lambda_t TF_t + \beta_4 Y_{it} + \beta_5 \Omega_{it} + \mu_i + \varepsilon_{it} \quad (7)$$

Subscript i denotes the bank ($i = 1, 2, \ldots, n$), whereas n is the total number of banks used in the sample, and subscript t indicates the period (t = Q1 2005, Q2 2005, …, Q4 2021). The full-sample period from Q1 2005 to Q4 2021 is used.

Z_{it} measures *ZS* of bank i's bank stability at time t. AS_{it} represents the accounting standards, L_{it}, the lending measures, and K_{it}, capital measures employed by the banks at time t. Y_{it} represents a matrix to control for bank-specific indicators, such as *NIIS*, *RRWA*, *BS*, *NPLL*, and *MBR* that impact bank stability in these economies over time. X_{it}^m represents a set of macroeconomic control variables, such as *INT*. TF_t measures the time-fixed effect, μ_i is the unobserved bank fixed effect, and ε_{it} is the remaining idiosyncratic error term. The coefficient α denotes the intercept of the regression.

Model 2: Association of bank stability between bank lending and bank regulatory capital and cycle proxies (i.e., business cycle and financial cycle).

$$\begin{aligned} Z_{it} = {} & \alpha + \beta_1 AS_{it} + \beta_2 L_{it} + \beta_3 K_{it} + \beta_4 \mathit{Cycle} \\ & + \beta_5 \mathit{Cycle} \times L_{it} + \beta_6 \mathit{Cycle} \times K_{it} \\ & + \sum_{M=1}^{M} \delta_m X_{it}^m + \sum_{t=1}^{T} \lambda_t TF_t + \beta_7 Y_{it} + \beta_8 \Omega_{it} + \mu_i + \varepsilon_{it} \end{aligned} \quad (8)$$

The prospect theory of Kahneman *et al.* (1979) claims that market players are more risk averse when presented with definite benefits and more risk seeking when presented with definite losses. That is to say, bank managers are more incentivized to boost risk-taking during economic downturns, i.e., difficult times. As a result, the business and financial cycles are utilized to evaluate deviations in risk-taking behavior between economic/financial upturns and downturns. Furthermore, the cycle proxies assist in determining whether the effect of real economic activities or excessive credit growth is responsible for the variation in risk-taking behavior and, thus, identifies its implications on stability.

The expectation is that bank stability is positively associated with business and financial cycles during economic/financial upturns if bank risk-taking decreases. Nevertheless, if bank risk-taking increases, bank stability is negatively affected during economic/financial downturns.

Model 3: Association of bank stability between bank lending and bank regulatory capital with the timeliness of loan loss recognition.

$$\begin{aligned} Z_{it} = \alpha &+ \beta_1 AS_{it} + \beta_2 L_{it} + \beta_3 K_{it} + \beta_4 Cycle \\ &+ \beta_5 Cycle \times L_{it} + \beta_6 Cycle \times K_{it} \beta_7 Time_{it} \\ &+ \sum_{M=1}^{M} \delta_m X_{it}^m + \sum_{t=1}^{T} \lambda_t TF_t + \beta_8 Y_{it} \\ &+ \beta_8 \Omega_{it} + \mu_i + \varepsilon_{it} \end{aligned} \tag{9}$$

Delay in loan loss recognition following the Global Financial Crisis of 2007–2009 aided weak banks in hiding their condition and may have exacerbated the drop in lending during recessions. Delaying the recognition of predicted loan losses produces a future overhang of unrecognized losses for the bank (BIS, 2021). Therefore, transparency in disclosing information on the timeliness of loan loss recognition is a channel that indirectly affects bank lending. In other words, market confidence in banks' asset quality and capital adequacy during crisis periods might decrease timeliness in loan loss recognition, making bank balance sheets more opaque (Haldane, 2011). Therefore, indicator *TIME* identifies the delay in loan loss recognition and is used to measure its influence on stability. The expectation is that a rise in *TIME* will decrease bank stability.

3.4. *Empirical results*

First, this section discusses the correlation network to identify the dependence structure of bank-specific and macroeconomic indicators.

Second, panel estimation with bank fixed effects measures the indicators influencing bank stability in Asia, with regard to different accounting standards regimes.

3.4.1. *Correlation network*

Figures 4 and 5 illustrate the Pearson correlation network of bank indicators for Local GAAP-compliant banks (Figure 4) and banks following mixed accounting standards (Figure 5). The correlation heatmap (Figure 6) depicts the correlation values of these two samples. The correlation network identifies the intensity and strength of correlation. There are several key takeaways from this analysis.

The correlation between bank capital and lending risk for mixed accounting banks and between lending risk and bank size for Local GAAP-compliant banks hints at the impact of bank size and bank capitalization on lending risk. According to Köhler (2015), the size and capitalization of banks are the most important elements in determining bank stability. Additionally, faster-growing banks are more likely to be risky (Altunbas, 2011; Deyoung and Roland, 2001; Köhler, 2015).

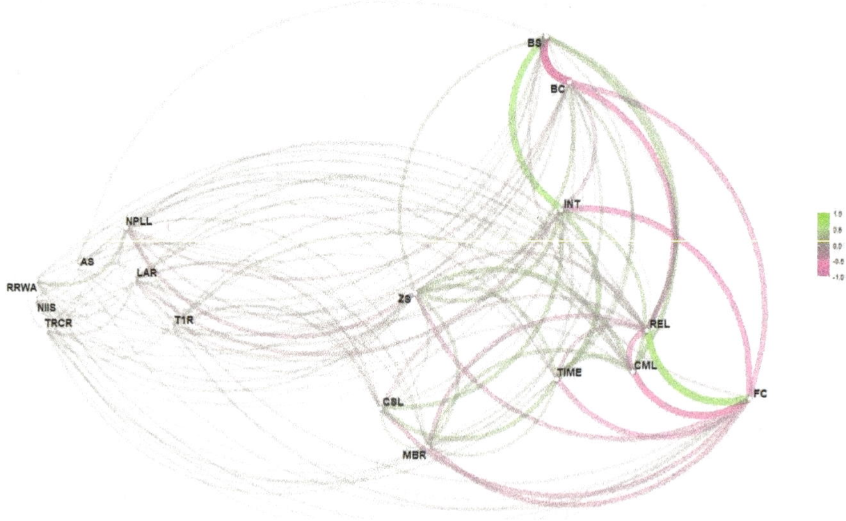

Figure 4. Correlation network of Local GAAP bank indicators.

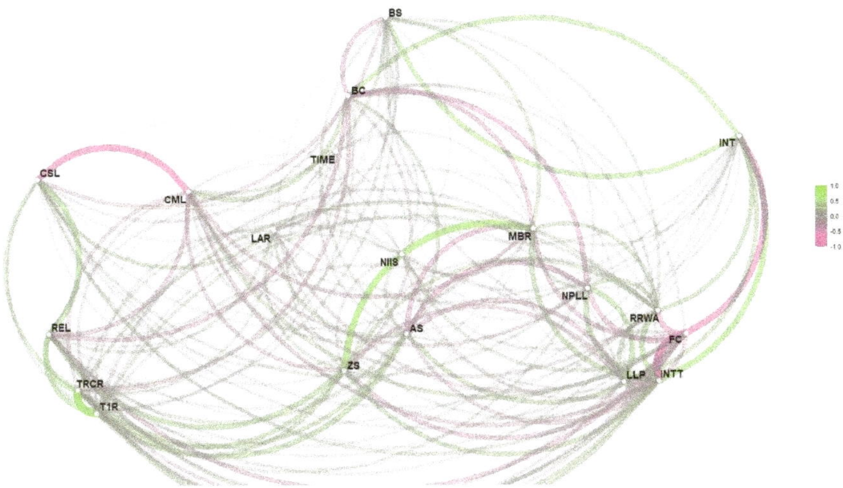

Figure 5. Correlation network of mixed accounting standards bank indicators.

Local GAAP Accounting Standard (above diagonal); **Mixed Accounting Standard** (below diagonal)

	BC	*INT*	*FC*	*AS*	*ZS*	*BS*	*T1R*	*NPLL*	*LAR*	*TIME*	*MBR*	*TRCR*	*RRWA*	*NIIS*	*CSL*	*CML*	*REL*
BC		-0.20	-0.38	-0.03	0.21	0.79	0.05	-0.13	-0.07	0.18	0.11	0.02	0.02	-0.01	0.02	0.01	-0.47
INT	0.38		-0.47	0.05	0.24	0.52	0.00	-0.09	-0.15	0.34	0.07	0.00	0.00	-0.01	0.26	0.25	-0.02
FC	0.08	-0.52		-0.03	-0.30	-0.10	-0.07	-0.05	0.01	-0.41	-0.33	-0.02	-0.04	0.02	-0.31	-0.57	0.63
AS	0.18	0.04	0.29		-0.01	0.03	0.00	0.03	0.01	-0.01	0.01	0.00	0.00	0.00	0.00	0.03	0.01
ZS	-0.14	0.03	-0.28	0.07		0.12	-0.03	-0.22	-0.12	0.19	0.17	-0.01	-0.04	0.06	0.06	0.27	-0.14
BS	-0.30	0.41	-0.12	0.10	0.03		-0.07	0.04	0.05	0.08	0.01	-0.02	-0.02	0.02	0.07	0.33	0.23
T1R	-0.07	-0.02	-0.09	0.33	0.23	0.09		0.01	0.02	-0.02	0.05	0.03	0.00	0.00	-0.08	0.12	-0.07
NPLL	-0.37	-0.04	-0.33	-0.37	-0.08	-0.08	-0.06		-0.01	-0.06	0.05	0.00	0.15	-0.01	0.01	-0.01	-0.09
LAR	-0.07	-0.08	-0.17	0.18	0.15	-0.10	-0.08	0.01		-0.08	-0.04	-0.06	-0.02	-0.05	-0.09	0.07	0.06
TIME	-0.03	-0.06	0.00	-0.11	0.06	-0.06	-0.01	0.00	0.00		0.12	0.05	0.00	-0.01	0.26	0.24	-0.24
MBR	-0.31	0.09	-0.30	-0.36	0.59	0.22	-0.12	0.18	0.05	0.07		0.04	0.02	-0.01	0.10	0.22	-0.26
TRCR	-0.22	-0.05	-0.18	0.27	0.28	0.10	0.81	0.10	0.10	0.01	-0.01		0.00	-0.01	0.02	0.01	-0.02
RRWA	-0.11	0.28	-0.42	-0.10	0.21	0.12	0.14	0.24	-0.02	0.00	0.23	0.16		0.00	-0.03	-0.03	-0.04
NIIS	0.07	-0.06	0.15	0.14	-0.09	-0.02	0.05	-0.04	-0.07	0.01	-0.10	0.09	0.06		-0.02	0.00	0.01
CSL	-0.11	-0.01	-0.08	0.05	0.04	-0.20	0.11	0.12	0.21	-0.03	-0.03	0.22	-0.05	0.00		-0.06	-0.14
CML	0.27	0.05	0.20	0.09	-0.24	0.17	-0.12	-0.19	-0.02	-0.02	-0.24	-0.19	-0.15	-0.05	-0.55		-0.44
REL	-0.28	-0.04	-0.28	0.14	0.34	0.03	0.36	-0.05	0.12	-0.03	0.03	0.39	0.07	-0.06	0.41	-0.25	

Mixed Accounting Standard

-1.00	-0.80	-0.60	-0.40	-0.20	0.00	0.20	0.40	0.60	0.80	1.00

Figure 6. Correlation heat map of bank indicators for Local GAAP and mixed accounting standards banks.

Financial cycle (FC) is closely correlated and clustered with credit risk with REL and CML for Local GAAP-compliant banks and is also clustered with INT, $RRWA$, and BS. This indicates that Local GAAP-compliant banks will be more influenced by the changes in the financial cycles than mixed accounting banks. On the other hand, the business cycle is correlated and clustered with BS

for both Local GAAP-compliant and mixed accounting banks, which may indicate that, in contrast to other characteristics, the size of the bank is more likely to affect how much a bank is impacted by economic upturns and downturns.

Furthermore, compared to Local GAAP-compliant banks, the link between mixed accounting banks and bank indicators is more clustered and with higher correlations. *NPLL* is highly correlated to *REL* compared to *RRWA* for Local GAAP-compliant banks, although, for mixed accounting banks, the inverse is true. This indicates that a significant portion of *NPLL* under Local GAAP may originate from *REL* (mortgage credit), which may be an unintended effect of Local GAAP-compliant banks promoting short-term thinking, excessive risk-taking, and the notion that any losses can be written off against future profits. However, the positive correlation between *NPLL*s and *RRWA* for mixed accounting banks indicates that the enhanced accounting requirements brought up by the switch to IAS/IFRS increased bank profitability by better reflecting risks in assets and earnings.

CSL (consumer credit) is negatively correlated with *CML* (corporate credit) across both accounting regimes. Jordà *et al.* (2020) used similar credit metrics for businesses and consumers. In their research, they discovered that a surge in consumer credit foreshadows a more severe economic downturn than an equivalent increase in corporate credit. *CSL* and *CML* for mixed accounting banks have a higher negative correlation of 0.54 than Local GAAP's 0.3.

Furthermore, the credit risk indicators for mixed accounting banks, *CSL*, *CML* and *REL*, are clustered together and connected to the cluster of capital measures *T1R* and *TRCR*. This suggests that banks transitioning to IAS/IFRS's lending behavior improve bank capitalization measures, improving the risk absorption capacity and, thus, cushioning against threats to bank stability. Local GAAP-compliant banks follow similar clustering traits of credit risk to that of mixed accounting banks; however, it is also related to *TIME* (timeliness of loan loss provisioning), *BS*, and *BC*. This indicates that credit risk for Local GAAP-compliant banks is subject to business cycle fluctuations and may experience these effects depending on the bank size.

3.4.2. *Panel regression models*

This section discusses the estimated panel models, which explain the influence of bank-specific and macroeconomic variables on bank stability under different accounting regimes using Tables 7 and 8, respectively.

Model 1(a) and (a'), as the baseline model of this chapter, examines the association between bank lending, capital, and stability in Tables 7 and 8. Models (a)–(f) in Table 7 demonstrate that the use of Local GAAP reduces bank stability from Q1 2005 to Q4 2021. Conversely, Models (a')–(f') in Table 8 show that transitioning from Local GAAP to IAS/IFRS increases bank stability by 0.889 at the 1% significance level. These findings are consistent with Barth and Landsman (2010). They found that jurisdictions that require or permit the use of IAS/IFRS tend to have lower banking sector losses during crises than those that do not allow IAS/IFRS. This could imply that transitioning to IAS/IFRS improves the accounting information quality, thus improving stability.

Model 1(a) also shows negative coefficients of 0.778–0.112 for *LAR* and *NPLL*, respectively. Similarly, Model 1(a') shows a negative coefficient of 0.187 for *NPLL* and a positive coefficient of 0.021 for *LAR*. Furthermore, a higher focus on lending activities may weaken stability for Local GAAP-compliant banks because of higher risk-taking and non-performing loans in contrast to mixed accounting banks (see Table 6). On the other hand, a rise in lending increases bank stability for mixed accounting banks. The riskiness of lending activities and problem loans is cushioned through regulatory capital, which improves stability by 0.285 for mixed accounting banks. This demonstrates how banks that transitioned to IAS/IFRS shifted their approach to assessing and managing credit risk. For instance, IAS/IFRS 9 mandates frequent and consistent credit risk reviews, with the impairment approach shifting from incurred loss (backward-looking) to expected loss (forward-looking). Thus, this allows a better assessment of potential risks and regulatory capital adjustments for better risk absorption.

Model 2($b-e$) and ($b'-e'$) analyzes the connection between lending, regulatory capital, and cyclicality. Therefore, Model 2(b) shows that Local GAAP-compliant banks tend to be more stable during

Table 7. Effect of accounting standards on bank stability for Local GAAP–compliant banks.

	Panel A: Local GAAP-Dependent Variable: *ZS*					
	Model 1	Model 2				Model 3
Variables	(*a*)	(*b*)	(*c*)	(*d*)	(*e*)	(*f*)
AS	−1.378*	−0.478	−0.838*	−0.842*	−0.7984*	−0.934*
	(0.609)	(0.407)	(0.408)	(0.406)	(0.592)	(0.417)
LAR	−0.778***	−1.270***	−1.756	−1.679	−3.135***	−0.021
	(0.176)	(0.155)	(0.877)	(2.874)	(0.624)	(0.022)
T1R	−0.046	−0.144*	−0.575***	−0.517***	−0.403***	−0.237***
	(0.095)	(0.083)	(0.429)	(0.428)	(0.154)	(0.059)
NPLL	−0.112***	−0.071***	−0.071***	−0.069***	−0.117***	
	(0.007)	(0.006)	(0.006)	(0.006)	(0.007)	
BS	0.033***	0.573***	0.580***	0.577***	0.061***	0.569***
	(0.007)	(0.017)	(0.017)	(0.017)	(0.009)	(0.019)
GFC	−0.017	−0.642				
	(0.090)	(0.065)				
INT	0.653***	−0.672***	−0.741***	−0.732***	−0.339**	−0.870***
	(0.040)	(0.053)	(0.057)	(0.057)	(0.135)	(0.068)
MBR	0.098***	0.090***	0.085***	0.085***	0.076***	0.082***
	(0.017)	(0.015)	(0.015)	(0.015)	(0.017)	(0.0157)
TRCR	−0.715***	−0.046				
	(0.161)	(0.1427)				
BC		0.930***	0.661**	0.666**		0.8204***
		(0.028)	(0.281)	(0.281)		(0.090)
*BC * LAR*			0.028	0.0254		0.0002
			(0.151)	(0.151)		(0.001)
*BC * T1R*			0.215***	0.212***		0.011***
			(0.069)	(0.069)		(0.002)
NIIS				0.0003**	0.0004***	
				(0.0001)	(0.0001)	
RRWA				−0.001	−0.001	
				(0.000)	(0.001)	
FC					−0.050***	
					(0.008)	
*FC * LAR*					0.015***	
					(0.004)	
*FC * T1R*					0.009***	
					(0.002)	
TIME						−0.006
						(0.091)
CSL						0.011***
						(0.002)
CML						0.006***
						(0.001)
REL						0.012***
						(0.002)

Table 7. (*Continued*)

	Panel A: Local GAAP-Dependent Variable: *ZS*					
	Model 1	Model 2				Model 3
Variables	(*a*)	(*b*)	(*c*)	(*d*)	(*e*)	(*f*)
Bank Fixed Effects	Yes	Yes	Yes	Yes	Yes	Yes
Time Fixed Effects	Yes	Yes	Yes	Yes	Yes	Yes
p-value (F-statistics)	0.000	0.000	0.000	0.000	0.000	0.000
Obs.	1,139	1,139	1,139	1,139	1,139	1,139

Notes: Fixed Effect Panel Regression with the dependent variable as *ZS* to examine the impact of transition from Local GAAP to IAS/IFRS accounting standards on bank stability for Mixed Accounting Standards banks. Significance Level signified using *10%, **5%, and ***1%.

economic upturns by 0.930, but they are more unstable during financial upturns by 0.050 as in Model 2(e). Similarly, Shim (2013) suggests that bank risk patterns tend to follow macroeconomic trends. On the other hand, mixed accounting standards are unstable during economic upturns (BC) by 0.064 in Model 2(b') and more stable during financial upturns (FC) by 0.0387 in Model 2(e'). This suggests that excessive credit growth (FC) destabilizes Local GAAP-compliant banks, which is in line with increase in lending activities (LAR) destabilizing these banks. Thus, it indicates the vulnerability of these banks to credit risks. Adrian and Shin (2014) posit that loosening value-at-risk by financial intermediaries might be a contributing factor to the substantial increase in risk appetite. This can be illustrated using financial cycle, considering the cyclical relationship between insight into valuation and risk, willingness to take risks, and access to capital (Borio *et al.*, 2018). Furthermore, the findings indicate that mixed accounting banks are more susceptible to changes in economic activities than excessive credit growth.

Model 2(c) and (c') further demonstrates that lending and regulatory capital rise during economic upturns, increasing stability. Model 2(c) indicates that, during economic upturns, the rise in lending and regulatory capital increases stability by 0.028 and 0.215, respectively. Similarly, in Model 2(c'), mixed accounting banks' increase in lending and capital improves stability by 0.040 and 0.070, respectively. Model 2(e) and Model 2(e') indicate a positive coefficient for the interaction terms $FC * LAR$ and $FC * T1R$. This shows the procyclical nature of lending and regulatory capital for Local GAAP-compliant and

Table 8. Effect of accounting standards on bank stability for mixed accounting standards banks.

	Panel B: Mixed Accounting Standard Dependent Variable: *ZS*					
	Model 1	Model 2				Model 3
Variables	(*a*′)	(*b*′)	(*c*′)	(*d*′)	(*e*′)	(*f*′)
AS	0.889***	0.947***	0.795***	0.821***	0.898***	0.814***
	(0.251)	(0.251)	(0.262)	(0.252)	(0.244)	(0.245)
LAR	0.021***	0.012**	−0.480***	−0.289***	−0.059***	−0.355***
	(0.008)	(0.007)	(0.054)	(0.067)	(0.019)	(0.067)
T1R	0.285***	0.161***	0.617***		0.175**	0.868***
	(0.035)	(0.041)	(0.312)		(0.073)	(0.310)
NPLL	−0.187***	−0.241***		−0.249***	−0.191***	
	(0.042)	(0.030)		(0.029)	(0.026)	
BS	−0.341***	−0.375***		−0.241***	−0.474***	−0.049
	(0.030)	(0.041)		(0.053)	(0.041)	(0.056)
GFC	−0.956***	−0.966***				
	(0.199)	(0.341)				
INT	0.178***	0.238***	0.043	0.193***	0.505***	0.053
	(0.049)	(0.054)	(0.051)	(0.057)	(0.102)	(0.050)
M2BR	3.162***	3.048***	3.236***	3.046***		3.129***
	(0.102)	(0.107)	(0.106)	(0.106)		(0.104)
TRCR		0.129***	1.521***	0.411**	3.416***	1.422***
		(0.039)	(0.414)	(0.204)	(0.104)	(0.404)
BC		−0.064***	−1.516***	−1.286***		−1.093***
		(0.029)	(0.372)	(0.421)		(0.398)
*BC * LAR*			0.040***	0.023***		0.030***
			(0.004)	(0.005)		(0.005)
*BC * T1R*			0.070***			0.084***
			(0.025)			(0.025)
*BC * TRCR*			0.119***	0.012		0.111***
			(0.034)	(0.016)		(0.033)
NIIS				−0.004***	−0.003**	
				(0.001)	(0.001)	
RRWA				0.603***	0.545**	
				(0.220)	(0.216)	
FC					0.0387***	
					(0.008)	
*FC * LAR*					0.0003***	
					(0.0001)	
*FC * T1R*					0.0005	
					(0.0004)	
TIME						0.393**
						(0.159)
CSL						−0.022***
						(0.004)
CML						−0.012***
						(0.004)
REL						0.055***
						(0.004)

Table 8. (*Continued*)

	Panel B: Mixed Accounting Standard Dependent Variable: *ZS*					
	Model 1	Model 2				Model 3
Variables	(a')	(b')	(c')	(d')	(e')	(f')
Bank Fixed Effects	Yes	Yes	Yes	Yes	Yes	Yes
Time Fixed Effects	Yes	Yes	Yes	Yes	Yes	Yes
p-value (F-statistics)	0.000	0.000	0.000	0.000	0.000	0.000
Obs.	3,515	3,515	3,515	3,515	3,515	3,515

Notes: Fixed Effect Panel Regression with the dependent variable as *ZS* to examine the impact of transition from Local GAAP to IAS/IFRS accounting standards on bank stability for Mixed Accounting Standards banks. Significance Level signified using *10%, **5%, and ***1%.

mixed accounting banks. Model 2(e) indicates that the rise in lending and bank capitalization for Local GAAP-compliant banks during financial upturns improves stability by 0.015 and 0.009, respectively. Likewise, a rise in lending and capitalization during financial upturns for mixed accounting banks is associated with increased stability. In other words, Local GAAP-compliant and mixed accounting banks' stability tends to be procyclical, with increased risk-taking during economic/financial upturns.

The findings in Model 2 contrast with Kahneman and Tversky's (1979) prospect theory. That is to say, the results suggest that bank managers are not incentivized to increase risk-taking during economic downturns but instead are more likely to do so during economic upturns. These findings indicate the fragmented structure of Asia's banking system, which may consist mainly of small- to medium-sized banks, especially Local GAAP-compliant banks (see Table 6). Hence, the results may be driven by these small banks' risk-taking behavior that contrasts with large banks' risk-taking behavior.

Similarly, bank size rise is associated with higher stability by 0.573 and lower stability by 0.375 for Local GAAP-compliant and mixed accounting standards, respectively. This indicates that mixed accounting banks' larger sizes are associated with less stable operations (see Table 6). This outcome is comparable to Ben Bouheni and Hasnaoui (2017). They compared the effects of cyclicality on lending and capital requirements at large and small banks. They concluded that the small banks were cycle followers, meaning that the lending patterns and capital needs tracked those of the economic activities.

Small banks' lending and capital needs rise during economic expansions and fall during recessions, unlike large banks, which are considered to be the drivers of the economy. This further suggests that Local GAAP-complaint and mixed accounting banks mostly consist of small banks, thus, cycle followers.

Model 3(f) and (f') investigates the loan risk composition and its effect on stability using *CSL* (consumer credit), *CML* (corporate credit), and *REL* (real estate credit). Local GAAP-compliant credit risk indicators, *CSL*, *CML*, and *REL*, have positive associations with bank stability of 0.011, 0.006, and 0.012, respectively. On the other hand, a rise in *CSL* and *CML*, however, decreased the stability of mixed accounting banks by 0.022 and 0.012, respectively. Contrarily, *REL* improves banks' stability by 0.055 for these banks. The results suggest that under mixed accounting standards, an increase in *CSL* (consumer credit) has a more significant effect on bank stability than an increase in *CML* (corporate credit), which has a smaller effect under Local GAAP-compliant banks. Similarly, Jordà *et al.* (2017) and Mian *et al.* (2017) measured the relationship between bank capital and the severity of the financial crisis and found similar results. Using data from 30 countries between 1960 and 2012, they discovered that rising consumer debt is a stronger predictor of falling credit-to-GDP ratio than increasing corporate debt.

Credit expansion may also reflect active risk-seeking by bankers due to misaligned incentives by shareholders (Baron and Xiong, 2016). This can be indicated by a varying magnitude of risk appetite and regulatory buffers between Local GAAP-compliant and mixed accounting banks. The magnitude of the rise in risk appetite is far more than the rise of regulatory buffers for economic and financial upturns for Local GAAP-compliant banks (Model 2). Thus, while a rise in credit risk (*CSL* and *CML*) can have a detrimental impact on a bank's stability, Model 3 (f') mixed accounting banks can mitigate this risk by increasing their regulatory capital ($T1R$) as well as by having stronger bank performance (*RRWA*) and market valuation (*MBR*). These findings corroborate Köhler's (2015) findings that well-capitalized banks are more resilient. That is to say, compared to Local GAAP-compliant banks, mixed accounting banks have a higher ratio of bank capitalization to lending operations, hence suggesting that they are more secure.

Repullo and Saurina (2011) state that during economic upturns, banks tend to underestimate risk, while during economic downturns, they tend to overestimate risk. Similarly, banks often account for the risks taken during the economic upturn only when credit losses start to materialize (Borio *et al.*, 2001). This is a common cause of prolonged periods of tight credit, which may contribute to or worsen a downturn in the real economy and a fragile financial system. Thus, Model 3(f) and (f') measures the impact of timeliness of loan loss recognition and its consequences on bank stability. As a result, even if capital measures are increased, the risks to a stability might be significantly magnified by delays in loan loss provision for both Local GAAP-compliant and mixed accounting banks.

On the other hand, the lack of statistical significance for Local GAAP-compliant banks indicates that there are no differences in lending practices related to the delays in loan loss recognition (Beatty and Liao, 2011). Lender of Last Resort (LOLR) liquidity on troubled assets also makes it easier for banks to keep non-performing loans and other assets on their books, delaying the moment when they report losses or reduce their leverage (Acharya and Ryan, 2016). In addition, a higher delayed loan loss provision is associated with a higher ZS for mixed accounting banks (Model $3f'$). This may suggest that when times are good, banks can afford to increase their capitalization due to lower costs, which may assist in averting the destabilization effects of delays in loan loss recognition. Furthermore, capital adequacy risks from larger current provisions are reduced as lending and economic growth rise with the upturns.

Banks with a high share of non-interest income are more stable, as reflected by the significantly positive coefficient for *NIIS* for Local GAAP-compliant banks. This is consistent with the view that non-interest income improves income diversification and makes a bank less dependent on overall business conditions (Stiroh and Rumble, 2006). On the other hand, mixed accounting banks are unstable with an increase in *NIIS*, which is consistent with Altunbas (2011) and Demirgüç-Kunt and Huizinga (2010). They conclude that banks that highly rely on non-interest income have lower bank stability. This may represent that these banks engage in high-risk trading activities compared to Local GAAP-compliant banks. It may also suggest that these banks are large and have a larger asset size (see Table 6).

Hence, they are more likely to participate in off-balance-sheet operations, which may help them enhance their financial leverage.

Furthermore, Deyoung and Roland (2001) suggest that if the transition toward higher non-interest-based activity is coupled with increased revenue volatility, the advantages of larger bank size and better risk diversification may diminish. This may be due to the fair value orientation of the IAS/IFRS, which may increase volatility in the financial statements by introducing both positive and poor information (Ball, 2006). Meanwhile, the fair value orientation of IAS/IFRSs is anticipated to increase volatility in book values and reported earnings (Hung and Subramanyam, 2007).

Therefore, in summary, Tables 7 and 8 indicate the procyclicality (*BC*) of bank stability for Local GAAP-compliant and mixed accounting banks, with increased risk-taking and bank capitalization during economic/financial upturns. Thus, bank managers increase risk-taking during economic/financial upturns and are likelier to decrease it during economic/financial downturns. The findings also suggest that Local GAAP-compliant banks are more susceptible to changes in excessive credit growth, and mixed accounting banks are more vulnerable to changes in economic activities.

On the other hand, the varying magnitude of the rise in risk appetite (*CSL*, *CML*, and *REL*) is far more than the rise of regulatory buffers for economic and financial upturns for Local GAAP-compliant banks. These findings corroborate Köhler's (2015) findings that well-capitalized mixed accounting banks are more resilient with higher *MBR* and *RRWA*, despite destabilizing effects of *NIIS*.

4. Conclusions

This study examines the bank stability indicators under two different accounting regimes: Local GAAP-compliant and mixed accounting standards. The objective is to determine whether adopting Local GAAP and IAS/IFRS contributes to bank stability in Asia. This study focuses on selected banks in China, Japan, South Korea, Hong Kong, Taiwan, Indonesia, Malaysia, Thailand, Singapore, and the Philippines from Q1 2005 to Q4 2021.

The findings indicate that Local GAAP may have had a detrimental effect on banks' stability. Following the Global Financial Crisis of 2007–2009, there is evidence of a negative and statistically significant link between banking stability and compliance with Local GAAP (Barth and Landsman, 2010). On the other hand, the results uncover a positive and statistically significant association between banks' stability and adherence to mixed accounting standards. This result follows the theory that IAS/IFRS may increase banks' resistance to shocks by encouraging more transparency, disclosure, and scrutiny from the market. Investors and creditors can better make educated decisions when financial statements are transparent and comparable, which assists in assessing banks' financial health, allocating capital efficiently, and thus smoothening the functions of the financial system (Ball *et al.*, 2000; Beatty and Liao, 2014). Nonetheless, IAS/IFRS accounting standards have a favorable but limited effect on bank stability. This may be because accounting regulations are only one of many variables contributing to or detracting from a country's bank stability.

Furthermore, the results indicate the procyclicality of bank stability for Local GAAP-compliant and mixed accounting banks, with increased risk-taking and bank capitalization during economic/financial upturns. Thus, the results contradict Kahneman and Tversky's (1979) prospect theory, which claims that market players are risk averse when presented with definite benefits and risk seeking when presented with definite losses. In other words, the findings indicate that bank managers increase risk-taking during economic/financial upturns and are more likely to decrease it during economic/financial downturns. The results also suggest that Local GAAP-compliant banks are more susceptible to changes in excessive credit growth, and mixed accounting banks are more vulnerable to changes in economic activities. These findings indicate the fragmented structure of Asia's banking system, which may consist mostly of small- to medium-sized banks. This outcome is comparable to Ben Bouheni and Hasnaoui (2017). They state that small banks' lending and capital needs rise during economic expansions and fall during recessions, unlike large banks, which are considered to be the drivers of the economy. This depicts that both Local GAAP-complaint and mixed accounting banks mostly consist of small banks, thus, cycle followers.

In addition, the rise in risk appetite is greater than the rise of regulatory buffers for economic and financial upturns for Local

GAAP-compliant banks. These findings corroborate Köhler's (2015) findings that well-capitalized banks are more resilient. That is to say, compared to Local GAAP-compliant banks, mixed accounting banks have a higher ratio of bank capitalization to lending operations. Additionally, these banks also have greater *RRWA* and *MBR*, which may suggest that mixed accounting banks are more secure. This would soften the consequences of *NIIS* and *NPLL*, which can be destabilizing. Mixed accounting banks are unstable with an increase in *NIIS*, which is consistent with Altunbas (2011) and Demirgüç-Kunt and Huizinga (2010). They conclude that banks that highly rely on non-interest income have lower bank stability. This may represent that these banks engage in high-risk trading activities compared to Local GAAP-compliant banks.

To sum up, there is no unanimous agreement on how accounting standards affect bank stability. However, based on our findings, accounting standards may influence bank stability, both positively and negatively. There are conflicting data on whether adhering to accounting standards contributes to a more secure economy (Norbes and Parker, 2008). Nonetheless, the findings suggest that the Asian banks transitioning from Local GAAP to IAS/IFRS experience higher and procyclical bank stability with rising lending behaviors and more robust bank capitalization cushioning against destabilizing bank-specific and macroeconomic risks.

The findings provide bank managers and regulators in Asia with valuable information that might assist them in re-evaluating how the application of accounting standards can contribute to the stability of banks. It also provides credence to the contention that IAS/IFRS accounting rules positively influence bank stability. The accessibility of bank data in greater detail limited the scope of this study. Future research may consider a more in-depth investigation of accounting standards for banks of varying sizes in Asia.

References

Acharya, V. V. and Ryan, S. G. (2016). Banks' financial reporting and financial system stability. *Journal of Accounting Research*, *54*(2), 277–340.

Adrian, T. and Shin, H. S. (2014). Procyclical leverage and value-at-risk. *Review of Financial Studies*, *27*(2), 373–403.

Altunbas, Y. (2011). Bank risk during the financial crisis do business models matter? *ECB Working Paper*.

Ball, R. (2006). International Financial Reporting Standards (IFRS): Pros and cons for investors. *Accounting and Business Research*, *36*(SPEC. ISS), 5–27.

Ball, R., Kothari, S. P. and Robin, A. (2000). The effect of international institutional factors on properties of accounting earnings. *Journal of Accounting and Economics*, *29*(1), 1–51.

Baron, M. and Xiong, W. (2016). Credit expansion and neglected crash risk. *National Bureau of Economic Research.*

Barth, M. E. and Landsman, W. R. (2010). How did financial reporting contribute to the financial crisis? *European Accounting Review*, *19*(3), 399–423.

Barth, M. E., Landsman, W. R., and Lang, M. H. (2005). International accounting standards and accounting quality. *Journal of Accounting Research*, *46*(3), 467–498.

Beatty, A. and Liao, S. (2011). Do delays in expected loss recognition affect banks' willingness to lend? *Journal of Accounting and Economics*, *52*(1), 1–20.

Beatty, A. and Liao, S. (2014). Financial accounting in the banking industry: A review of the empirical literature. *Journal of Accounting and Economics*, *58*(2–3), 339–383.

Ben Bouheni, F. and Hasnaoui, A. (2017). Cyclical behavior of the financial stability of eurozone commercial banks. *Economic Modelling*, *67*(March), 392–408.

Berger, P. G. and Hann, R. N. (2007). Segment profitability and the proprietary and agency costs of disclosure. *The Accounting Review*, *82*(3), 869–906.

BIS (2021). The procyclicality of loan loss provisions: A literature review. *BIS Working Papers* (May).

Borio, C., Drehmann, M. and Xia, D. (2018). The financial cycle and recession risk. *BIS Quarterly Review*, (December), 59–71.

Borio, C., Furfine, C., and Lowe, P. (2001). Procyclicality of the financial system and financial stability issues and policy options. *BIS Papers*, *1*(1), 1–57.

Bundesbank, D. and Köhler, M. (2012). Which banks are more risky? The impact of loan growth and business model on bank risk-taking. (33).

Daske, H., Hail, L., Leuz, C. and Verdi, R. S. (2008). Mandatory IFRS reporting around the world: Early evidence on the economic consequences. *Journal of Accounting Research*, *46*(5), 1085–1142.

Demirgüç-Kunt, A. and Huizinga, H. (2010). Bank activity and funding strategies: The impact on risk and returns. *Journal of Financial Economics*, *98*(3), 626–650.

Deutsche Bundesbank (2003). Report on the stability of the German financial system. Monthly Report, December.

Deyoung, R. and Roland, K. P. (2001). Product mix and earnings volatility at commercial banks: Evidence from a degree of total leverage model. *Journal of Financial Intermediation*, *10*(1), 54–84.

Diamond, D. W. and Dybvig, P. H. (1983). Bank runs, deposit insurance, and liquidity. *Journal of Political Economy*, *91*(3), 401–419.

Elnahass, M., Trinh, V. Q. and Li, T. (2021). Global banking stability in the shadow of COVID-19 outbreak. *Journal of International Financial Markets, Institutions and Money*, *72*, 101322.

Fama, E. and French, K. (1993). Common risk factors in the returns on stocks and bonds. *Journal of Financial Economics*, *33*(3), 3–56.

Financial Stability Board (2014). *Key Attributes of Effective Resolution Regimes for Financial Institutions.* (October), 1–85.

Freixas, X. and Rochet, J.-C. (2008). *Microeconomics of Banking.* Cambridge: The MIT Press (January 1997), p. 363.

Froot, K. and Dabora, E. (1999). How are stock prices affected by the location of trade. *Journal of Financial Economics*, *53*(2), 189–216.

Gray, S. (1988). Towards a theory of cultural influence on the development of accounting systems internationally. *Abacus*, *24*(I), 1–15.

Haldane, A. G. (2011). Andrew G Haldane: Accounting for bank uncertainty. *BIS Central Bankers Speeches*, (December).

Hofstede, G. (1984). Cultural dimensions in management and planning. *Asia Pacific Journal of Management*, *1*(2), 81–99.

Hung, M. and Subramanyam, K. R. (2007). Financial statement effects of adopting international accounting standards: The case of Germany. *Review of Accounting Studies*, *12*(3), 623–657.

IFRS Foundation (2010). *Annual Report 2010 Financial Reporting for the World's Interconnected Financial Markets.*

Jordà, Ò., Schularick, M. and Taylor, A. M. (2011). Financial crises, credit booms, and external imbalances: 140 years of lessons. *IMF Economic Review*, *59*(2), 340–378.

Jordà, Ò., Taylor, B., Moritz, R. and M., S. A. (2017). Bank capital redux: Solvency, liquidity, and crisis. *NBER Working Paper.*

Kahneman, D. and Tversky, A. (1979). Prospect theory: An analysis of decision under risk. *Econometrica*, *47*(2), 263–292.

Kick, T. and Jahn, N. (2014). Early warning indicators for the German banking system: A macroprudential analysis. *Credit and Capital Markets – Kredit Und Kapital*, *47*(1), 5–47.

Köhler, M. (2015). Which banks are more risky? The impact of business models on bank stability. *Journal of Financial Stability*, *16*, 195–212.

Laeven, L. and Valencia, F. (2018). *Systemic Banking Crises Revisited, WP/18/206, September 2018.*

Li, T., Trinh, V. Q. and Elnahass, M. (2022). Drivers of global banking stability in times of crisis: The role of corporate social responsibility. *British Journal of Management*, *32*(2), 1–28.

McLeay, S. and Riccaboni, A. (Eds) (2000). *Contemporary Issues in Accounting Regulation*, Boston: Kluwer Academic Publishers.

Mian, A., Sufi, A. and Verner, E. (2017). Household debt and business cycles worldwide. *Quarterly Journal of Economics*, *132*(3), 1755–1817.

Mir, M. Z. and Rahaman, A. S. (2005). The adoption of international accounting standards in Bangladesh: An exploration of rationale and process. *Accounting, Auditing and Accountability Journal*, *18*(6), 816–841.

Nisar, S., Peng, K., Wang, S. and Ashraf, B. (2018). The impact of revenue diversification on bank profitability and stability: Empirical evidence from South Asian countries. *International Journal of Financial Studies*, *6*(2), 40.

Nobes, C. and Parker, R. (2008). Comparative international accounting: Causes and examples of international differences. In *Comparative International Accounting.*

Òscar Jordà, Kornejew, M., Schularick, M. and Taylor, A. M. (2020). Zombies at large? Corporate debt overhang and the macroeconomy. *Federal Reserve Bank of San Francisco Working Paper.*

Perera, M. H. B. (1989). Accounting in developing countries: A case for localised uniformity. *The British Accounting Review*, *21*(2), 141–157.

Repullo, R. and Saurina, J. (2011). The countercyclical capital buffer of basel III: A critical assessment. *CEMFI Working Paper*, *534*(914), 290–551.

Roy, A. D. (1952). Safety first and the holding of assets. *Econometrica*, *20*(3), 431–449.

Shim, J. (2013). Bank capital buffer and portfolio risk: The influence of business cycle and revenue diversification. *Journal of Banking and Finance*, *37*(3), 761–772.

Stiroh, K. J. (2004). Diversification in banking: Is noninterest income the answer? *Journal of Money, Credit and Banking*, *36*(5), 853–882.

Stiroh, K. J. (2006). New evidence on the determinants of bank risk. *Journal of Financial Services Research*, *30*(3), 237–263.

Stiroh, K. J. and Rumble, A. (2006). The dark side of diversification: The case of US financial holding companies. *Journal of Banking and Finance*, *30*(8), 2131–2161.

Tyrrall, D., Woodward, D. and Rakhimbekova, A. (2007). The relevance of International Financial Reporting Standards to a developing country: Evidence from Kazakhstan. *International Journal of Accounting, 42*(1), 82–110.

Van den Heuvel, S. J. (2005). The Bank Capital Channel of Monetary Policy. *Federal Reserve Board Working Paper*, (May), 1–52.

Zeghal, D. and Mhedhbi, K. (2006). An analysis of the factors affecting the adoption of international accounting standards by developing countries. *International Journal of Accounting, 41*(4), 373–386.

Zysman, J. (1983). *Governments, Markets and Growth: Financial Systems and the Politics of Industrial Change.* Ithaca, London: Cornell University Press.

https://doi.org/10.1142/9781800614321_0003

Chapter 3

Impact of Stability on Economic Growth: A Case Study from the Financial Market

Hong Thu Nguyen* **and Van Chien Nguyen†**

Thu Dau Mot University, Binh Duong, Vietnam

**thunh@tdmu.edu.vn*

†chiennv@tdmu.edu.vn

Abstract

The banking system is expected to contribute many important aspects to the economic development in each country. The banking system is predominantly managed by the governments to ensure both system stability and economic development. The objective of this study is to assess the impact of the stability of the banking system on economic growth in 24 typical countries during the period 2011–2020. Using advanced quantitative research methods, analyzing the defects in the regression model as well as testing the robustness of the model, the research results show that the stability of the banking system has no impact on economic growth: although it has a positive effect, it is not statistically significant. The research also suggested that the investment rate of the economy, financial development, and quality of human resources have a positive impact on economic growth. However, foreign direct investment, trade openness, and population have no impact on economic growth.

Keywords: Stability, financial development, banking system, growth, regression, human resources, trade, population, emerging economies, human capital

1. Introduction

Economic development in each country cannot be without important contributions from the financial market, especially the banking system. Banks are responsible for acting as financial intermediaries, connecting idle capital sources in the economy and allocating capital to meet the needs of individuals, businesses, and the economy. According to previous studies, the authors believed that bank stability has the ability to increase the probability of success of investment projects; however, stability is often affected by the economic policy uncertainty of governments. More broadly, banking stability is often influenced by institutional quality (Shabir *et al.*, 2021).

The relationship between the banking sector stability and economic growth has been demonstrated by a number of recent case studies, and the results are quite mixed. The works of Monnin and Jokipii (2010), Ijza *et al.* (2020), and Eweke (2019) affirmed that the stability of the banking sector positively contributes to economic growth. During economic crisis, bank support has the ability to help a country quickly get out of the crisis. However, Boachie *et al.* (2021) also suggested that there may be the opposite effect of economic growth on bank stability because economic growth makes the bank more efficient, thus allowing the bank system to improve its charter capital, system monitoring, and system stabilization. Further, there is the view that competition between banks in the banking system has the potential to make banks stronger, and it is evident that the stability of the banking system is likely to provide an important driver for improving economic performance (Jayakumar *et al.*, 2018).

When the banking system is stable, it means that the banking system is able to withstand price shocks, economic crises, economic policy uncertainty, a pandemic, or disease, thereby making the bank more clearly demonstrate its role as a financial intermediary in the financial market, capable of providing capital at low cost to the economy and improving the quality of growth. Although previous studies have assessed the relationship between banking system stability and economic growth, all studies have either investigated this in high-income economies or provided a global analysis. To be more specific, Klein and Weill (2022) conducted a study between 1999 and 2013 and Stewart and Chowdhury (2021) conducted a study from 1995 to 2017 focused on a global sample, Bayar *et al.* (2021) analyzed the impact in transition countries in Europe between 1998 and 2016, and Jayakumar *et al.* (2018) analyzed the effects in 32 European countries in the period 1994–2014. The difference of this study is that we select 24 developing countries, especially focusing on Asia during the period 2011–2020. Nguyen *et al.* (2020) indicated that the world economy started to recover since 2011 and the banking system of countries witnessed key reforms with respect to monitoring system and authorized capital in order to prevent risks. In addition, the economies of most countries were highly affected by the COVID-19 pandemic, indicating that this research is necessary (Elnahass *et al.*, 2021; Trinh *et al.*, 2022).

This study is divided into five main sections. In addition to the introduction, Section 2 discusses previous studies and Section 3 discusses data sources and research methodology. Then, Sections 4 and 5 depict the results and conclusions, respectively.

2. Literature Review

The health of the financial system, especially the stability of banks, has attracted the attention of many scholars around the world. Basically, there are two dominant theories in the banking stability literature: the franchise value theory and the moral hazard theory (Toh and Zhang, 2022). In addition to internal factors of the bank, such as capital structure selection, liquidity, or bank size/age, the banking system is especially affected by external factors, such as the pandemic, the economic crisis, and the shocks of commodity prices that are able to affect the performance of the banking system.

The banking industry's development is always under competitive pressure. A bank with higher competition is positively correlated with higher economic development (Jayakumar *et al.*, 2018). Many studies also confirmed that banks are superior to other players in the financial market due to their active involvement in investments in light of economic development (Ueda, 2013). In addition, large banks often have the advantage of market power that is consistent with a higher level of stability, therefore banks often gain benefits for shareholders and ensure the safety of the system. In a study of 32 European countries in the period 1994–2014, using a panel vector error-correction model, Jayakumar *et al.* (2018) demonstrated that competition between banks is likely to make banks stronger, and at the same time, the stability of the banking system positively improves economic growth. Therefore, countries need to create a legal environment to promote competition in the financial market, and improve liquidity and policies in order to maintain the stability of the banking sector. In addition, the banking sector stability is often supported by banks with their market power; banks with a large market power often have a higher level of stability, as shown by Soedarmono *et al.* (2011) in a study of 12 commercial banks in Asian countries from 2001 to 2007.

In contrast, economic policy uncertainty (EPU) is likely to reduce the stability of the banking system; however, this effect can vary depending on specific banks and market structure (Shabir *et al.*, 2021). In particular, EPU has the ability to have a greater impact on banking stability during the economic crisis. Simultaneously, the interactive effect between institutional quality and EPU positively enhances a higher level of banking sector stability. More specifically, the effect of EPU on bank stability decreases in the case of countries with high institutional quality and increases in the case of countries with low institutional quality.

Research on the impact of banking system stability on economic growth has been carried out through a number of previous studies by Klein and Weill (2022) in 132 countries during the period 1999–2013, Stewart and Chowdhury (2021) in 140 countries between 1995 and 2017, Bayar *et al.* (2021) in Europe between 1998 and 2016, and Jayakumar *et al.* (2018) in 32 European countries in the period 1994–2014, with each study providing conflicting results. It mostly depends on the specific country and the period of study.

First, studies found a positive effect of banking system stability on economic growth. Research by Klein and Weill (2022) suggested that banks have a great role in economic growth and are correlated with bank stability. Using the GMM method, the authors believed that the development of the banking system has a positive impact on economic growth in both short and long terms, and the bank's profits can improve the stability of the system and thereby maintain economic growth. In addition, economic growth can lead to the banking system becoming more stable. Economic development can help a bank optimize its business operations, increase its retained earnings, and thus improve its internal financial resources and become more resilient to risks of the economy. Similarly, Dinger *et al.* (2022) argued that banks are the lifeblood of the economy, and governments often require banks and the banking system to operate stably, thereby helping to stabilize the financial markets. Usually, governments often support the operation of the banking system such as capital injections and liquidity support to the banking sector, and these policies often support the goal of economic growth. In addition, the refinancing policy has a positive effect on the liquidity of the system. A bank with better-capitalized characteristics and recapitalized systems has a higher opportunity to lend and will show a better economic performance.

Stewart and Chowdhury (2021) analyzed a sample of 140 countries during the period 1995–2017, using the GMM method in order to remove the endogeneity of the variables in the estimation model, and noted that a more stable banking system is able to reduce the crisis of the financial market and thereby improve the efficiency of the economy or especially increase the ability to recover the economy in times of crisis. The authors also emphasized that liquidity in the banking system helps economic recovery in high-income countries while charter capital in the banking system has a positive effect on economic resilience in low-income countries. Thereby, it can be seen that the banking system needs to improve in liquidity in high-income countries and in capital sources in low-income countries to achieve economic efficiency. Furthermore, regulatory capital plays a key role in accelerating economic growth and bank stability. It confirms that there is a positive correlation between bank stability and economic growth (Stewart *et al.*, 2021).

Second, there is sometimes no relationship between bank stability and economic growth, as shown in the study of Boachie *et al.* (2020) on 18 sub-Saharan African countries in the period 2008–2018. They argued that economic growth is capable of improving the stability of the banking system, but not vice versa, asserting only the positive impact of economic growth and stability of the banking system. As an explanation for this case, Boachie *et al.* (2021) argued that capital regulation has a negative impact on the stability of the banking system, and at the same time, the level of economic development in sub-Saharan African countries is still low; the banking system assumes the role of capital mobility in the strong economic development. Therefore, it is able to cope with market shocks and risks. In addition, the banking system is different across countries, so the banking system has the ability to promote economic growth or promote investment with different results (Senra Hodelin, 2022).

Third, some studies suggested that the relationship between bank stability and growth is relatively complex. Bayar *et al.* (2021) also argued that the banking sector stability is complex and dependent on a hierarchically structured multidimensional construct. By using the analysis of post-conversion countries in Europe for the period 1998–2016, they argued that there is a cross-dependent relationship between the banking systems and financial markets among countries. When the banking system is stable, it is able to prevent shocks and mitigate negative impacts, as well as stimulate economic growth. Specifically, the study also shows a positive impact of banking system stability on economic growth, that is, the higher the stability of the banking system, the higher the economic growth, and vice versa.

In the period of economic crisis, the stability of the banking system plays a more prominent role in the recovery of economic growth, as the support of banks can help the country quickly get out of the crisis (Ijza *et al.*, 2020). Eweke (2019) affirmed in the case of the Nigerian banking system that there is a positive relationship between banking system stability, financial depth, and Nigerian economic growth, thereby confirming an effective supervisory mechanism for the banking system on the basis of supervision of operations and capital sources, capable of improving the operational efficiency of the banking system and the economy. Furthermore, Monnin and Jokipii (2010) studied 18 leading developed countries in the world and found that there is a positive relationship between the stability of the banking system and economic growth. In particular, this relationship becomes more pronounced during the period of an unstable banking system. Moreover, the authors also asserted that the instability of the banking system is likely to increase uncertainty about future growth, thereby suggesting implications for governments to improve their operational capacity of the banking system. In addition to the function of circulating capital in the economy in the banking system and appropriate transaction costs, the banking system has high stability for improving economic growth in the long run.

Previous studies (Bist, 2018; Fatima *et al.*, 2020; Sengupta and Puri, 2018; Peterson, 2017) also suggested that there are some other factors that have an impact on economic growth. Specifically, Bist (2018) argued that there is a positive impact between financial development and growth. Fatima *et al.* (2020) asserted that trade openness has an impact on growth, and this relationship is negative if the country has low quality of human resources. In addition, capital investment is a vehicle for improving economic growth (Sengupta and Puri, 2018). In the study of the relationship between population size and growth, Peterson (2017) suggested that high population growth in developing countries is likely to reduce economic development, while population growth is low in developed countries and has the potential to help the country improve its social welfare.

3. Data Collection and Methodology

3.1. *Data collection*

In this study, the authors studied 24 emerging economies, including Bahrain, Bangladesh, China, Hong Kong SAR, India, Indonesia, Israel, Japan, Jordan, Kazakhstan, Korea, Lebanon, Malaysia, Oman, the Philippines, Qatar, Russian Federation, Saudi Arabia, Singapore, Sri Lanka, Thailand, Turkey, the United Arab Emirates, and Vietnam. Data were collected from the World Bank's World Development Indicators Report. After processing the missing data, this study selected the research period from 2010 to the end of 2020.

3.2. *Methodology*

This study used quantitative analysis to assess the impact of banking sector stability on economic growth. The methods used in this study include the pooled OLS method, fixed effects, and random effects method. This study also evaluated the phenomenon of heteroskedasticity and autocorrelation; if this phenomenon occurs, regression was performed to remove defects in the model.

In addition, to evaluate the robustness of the regression model, the study used PCSE as well as Driscoll–Kraay regression to assess whether the impact of banking system stability on economic growth is strong or not. If the results are consistent, it can be confirmed that the regression results are reliable.

As discussed above, the stability of the banking system plays an important role in maintaining the sustainable development of the financial market. Based on the previous studies by Klein and Weill (2022), Stewart and Chowdhury (2021), and Bayar *et al.* (2021), the proposed regression equation is as follows:

$$GDP_{it} = \beta_0 + \beta_1 STA_{it} + \beta_2 FD_{it} + \beta_3 HCI_{it} + \beta_4 FDI_{it} + \beta_5 TRADE_{it} + \beta_6 INVEST_{it} + \beta_7 POP_{it} + \mu \quad (1)$$

where GDP_{it} is the economic growth of time i and country t, STA_{it} is the stability in the financial market of time i and country t, FD_{it} is the financial development of time i and country t, HCI_{it} is the human capital index of time i and country t, and FDI_{it}, $TRADE_{it}$, $INVEST_{it}$, and POP_{it}, respectively, are foreign direct investment inflows, trade openness, investment (as % of GDP), and population of time i and country t. All data are described in Table 1.

Table 1. Describing variables.

Variable	Abbreviation	Previous Studies
Dependent variable		
Economic growth	GDP	Klein and Weill (2022), Stewart and Chowdhury (2021), Bayar *et al.* (2021)
Independent variables		
Stability	STA	Klein and Weill (2022), Stewart and Chowdhury (2021), Bayar *et al.* (2021)
Financial development	FD	Bist (2018)
Human capital	HCI	Fatima *et al.* (2020)
Foreign direct investment inflows	FDI	Sengupta và Puri (2018)
Trade openness	TRADE	Fatima *et al.* (2020)
Investment (as % of GDP)	INVEST	Sengupta và Puri (2018)
Population	POP	Peterson (2017)

4. Results

4.1. *Descriptive statistics*

Table 2 shows the descriptive statistical analysis, which indicates that the average growth rate of the group of countries in this study reached 4.39%, including countries with a high growth rate such as the case of Qatar reaching 13.37% in 2011 in the event of increasing oil prices. In contrast, the COVID-19 pandemic in 2020 has had a negative impact on global economic growth; most countries have had a sharp decline in economic growth as in the case of Lebanon which had a growth rate of −25.90%.

Table 2 shows the stability of the banking system in each country, as assessed by the Z-score analysis, showing that the average level of stability is 19.53. However, there is a huge difference in the degree of stability in the research group, such as the lowest stability level of 1.77 in the case of Kazakhstan with its banking system in the restructuring phase, in contrast to the highly appreciated stability of Jordanian banks. Regarding the financial development measured by M3 compared to GDP, or measured by liquid liabilities (M3) as % of GDP, the average level is 110.63% of GDP and the highest and lowest are 452.41% and 24.20%, respectively, showing that there is a huge difference in the level of financial development in selected countries.

Table 2. Descriptive statistics of research variables.

Variable	Obs.	Mean	Std.	Dev.	Min.
GDP	240	3.292099	3.878015	−25.90773	13.37518
STA	240	19.53883	11.76918	1.773499	66.86441
FD	240	110.631	79.69796	24.20433	452.4128
HCI	240	0.7771077	0.1038217	0.4640364	0.949
FDI	240	4.599216	8.179826	−2.760018	58.51875
TRADE	240	107.3181	90.33894	29.1438	442.6238
INVEST	240	27.99179	6.409286	9.548268	48.86907
POP	240	1.634767	1.640627	−0.4424635	9.231843

4.2. *Correlation and VIF analysis*

Table 3 presents the results of the correlation matrix; the results show that all the independent variables have correlation coefficients less than 0.85, so the possibility of multicollinearity in the regression model is unlikely. Previous studies have shown that when multicollinearity occurs, the estimation results will be biased and not guaranteed to be accurate. In addition, through the analysis of the VIF in Table 4, the mean VIF coefficient is less than 10, and the VIF indexes of each variable are also less than 10, which means that there is no multicollinearity phenomenon.

4.3. *Regression results and discussion*

The regression results are shown in Table 5.

By selecting the pooled OLS and REM model, the Breusch and Pagan Lagrangian multiplier test for random effects should be performed. According to the results, the coefficient p-value $= 1.000$ and more than 5%, so it can be confirmed that pooled OLS is more suitable than REM. According to the F test, the coefficient p-value $=$ 0.000 and less than 5%, so it can be confirmed that FEM is more suitable than pooled OLS. Thus, it can be confirmed that FEM is the best model. Table 6 depicts autocorrelation and heteroskedasticity of the model. Therefore, the analysis should be performed by feasible generalized least squares (FGLS).

Based on the regression results in Tables 5 and 7, the main results are as follows:

First, the regression coefficient of banking sector stability is positive but not statistically significant. Thereby, it can be confirmed that stabilizing the banking system has no impact on economic growth. This can be explained by the fact that banks have a great role in providing capital for the economy, especially the ability to connect saving needs and investment needs. Although there is a positive effect between bank stability and growth, this relationship is not statistically significant and not strong enough. This evidence may be explained by the fact that banking system stability has not

Table 3. Correlation matrix.

Item	GDP	STA	LIQ	HCI	FDI	TRADE	INVEST	POP
GDP	1.0000							
STA	−0.0138	1.0000						
FD	−0.2666	0.1114	1.0000					
HCI	0.0734	−0.0422	0.2691	1.0000				
FDI	−0.0968	0.0413	0.6060	0.3533	1.0000			
TRADE	−0.0433	0.0438	0.5186	0.4312	0.8349	1.0000		
INVEST	0.3861	−0.1926	−0.1432	−0.1641	−0.2341	−0.1923	1.0000	
POP	0.1521	0.2537	−0.1902	0.0485	−0.1110	0.0012	0.0595	1.0000

Table 4. Multicollinearity test table according to VIF.

Variable	VIF	1/VIF
FDI	3.95	0.252997
TRADE	3.66	0.273579
FD	1.72	0.579929
HCI	1.36	0.734827
POP	1.31	0.765076
STA	1.17	0.852697
INVEST	1.13	0.887816
Mean VIF		**1.95**

contributed to economic growth in the surveyed countries. Previous studies also gave different results on the impact of banking system stability and economic growth. The studies of Klein and Weill (2022), Dinger *et al.* (2022), and Stewart and Chowdhury (2021) assert a positive relationship, that is, high financial stability has an impact on promoting economic growth, thus requiring countries to improve financial markets through a supervisory mechanism to improve the stability of the banking system. However, Boachie *et al.* (2021) argued that there is no effect on stabilizing the banking system and on economic growth in 18 sub-Saharan African countries, in the period 2008–2018, which is a region with a low level of economic development and a weak banking system, quite similar to the countries selected in this study.

The study also indicated that a higher level of investment in the economy has the ability to increase economic growth, reflecting the importance of capital for economic development in countries. According to the Cobb–Douglas production function, capital is an important factor that can improve the productivity and efficiency of the economy, especially in developing countries with high capital needs for investment in infrastructure and doing business. In developing countries, the need for capital is very high; these countries need capital from home or abroad to create resources for development, as discussed by Nguyen and Nguyen (2022a, 2022b).

Table 5. Regression results of dependent variable GDP.

Variable	Regression Results		
	OLS	FEM	REM
STA	0.0316	0.0271*	0.0316
	(0.118)	(0.076)	(0.116)
FD	−0.0169***	−0.0116**	−0.0169***
	(0.000)	(0.000)	(0.000)
HCI	6.7215***	−5.2317**	6.7215***
	(0.005)	(0.012)	(0.005)
FDI	0.0558	−0.0293	0.0558
	(0.295)	(0.464)	(0.294)
TRADE	0.0016	−0.0048	0.0016
	(0.728)	(0.165)	(0.727)
INVEST	0.2520***	0.1967***	0.2520***
	(0.000)	(0.000)	(0.000)
POP	0.0964***	−0.1194	0.0964
	(0.000)	(0.287)	(0.508)
_Cons	−8.3121***	2.1485	−8.3121***
	(0.000)	(0.256)	(0.000)
R-squared	0.5590	0.5933	0.5590
Adj. R-squared	0.5366		
F test	F test = 21.57 Prob. > F = 0.0000		
Breusch and Pagan Lagrangian multiplier test for random effects			chibar2(01) = 0.00 Prob. > chibar2 = 1.000

Notes: *, **, and *** with significance level 10%, 5%, and 1%. Values in brackets are p-value.

As regards human capital, which represents the quality of human resources, the estimated coefficient is positive and statistically significant, meaning that a country with high human capital has many opportunities for economic growth, and conversely, a country with low human capital is unlikely to promote economic growth. It reflects that most of the countries often prioritize investment in education and healthcare in order to create a highly qualified workforce and achieve economic development, especially in the long term.

Table 6. Diagnostics test.

Autocorrelation	Wooldridge test for autocorrelation in panel data **Hypothesis 0:** no first-order autocorrelation F (1, 89) = 3.576; Prob. > F = 0.0912.
Heteroskedasticity	Modified Wald test for groupwise heteroskedasticity in fixed effect regression model **Hypothesis 0:** sigma(i)^2 = sigma^2 for all i chi2 (104) = 120.43; Prob. > chi2 = 0.0000.

Table 7. Regression results based on FGLS.

	Regression Results		
Variable	**FGLS**	**Driscoll–Kraal**	**PCSE**
STA	0.0316	0.0316	0.0316
	(0.110)	(0.180)	(0.322)
FD	−0.0169***	−0.0169***	−0.0169***
	(0.000)	(0.000)	(0.004)
HCI	6.7215***	6.7215*	6.7215*
	(0.004)	(0.098)	(0.093)
FDI	0.0558	0.0558	0.0558
	(0.286)	(0.428)	(0.427)
TRADE	0.0016	0.0016	0.0016
	(0.723)	(0.789)	(0.805)
INVEST	0.2520***	0.2520**	0.2520***
	(0.000)	(0.011)	(0.000)
POP	0.0964	0.0964	0.0964
	(0.501)	(0.645)	(0.644)
_Cons	−8.3121***	−8.3121*	−8.3121**
	(0.000)	(0.095)	(0.025)
Adj. R-squared		0.5590	0.5590
Prob. > Chi2/F	0.000	0.000	0.002

Notes: *, **, and *** with significance level 10%, 5%, and 1%.

5. Conclusions

Banks play an important role in the economic development of most countries. The banking system can be considered as the lifeblood of the economy, capable of connecting idle capital flows and investment needs of entities in the economy, such as businesses, individuals, the state, and foreign investment. Economies always face many challenges such as economic crises, pandemics, and price market shocks, which require countries to improve the effectiveness of the banking system so as to maintain its stability. The research was conducted in 24 countries from 2011 to 2022 to assess banking sector stability and economic growth, which carried out quantitative analysis through the pooled ordinary least squares method, random effects model, and fixed effect model and, at the same time, evaluated the defects in the research model. In addition, this study carries out a robustness test to assess the quality of the regression results. The research results confirm that banking sector stability has no impact on economic growth. Factors such as investment rate of the economy, financial development, and quality of human resources have a positive impact on growth. However, foreign direct investment, trade openness, and population size have no effect on growth.

This study has several recommendations. First, countries should continue to improve the effectiveness of the financial system, especially the banking system, which is considered as a channel that makes practical contributions to economic development in most countries. The banking system should be improved based on enhanced supervision and warning systems to minimize the negative impact on the financial market. Second, the banking system needs to improve its internal capital in combination with technological changes and digital transformation to best meet the needs of individuals, businesses, and economic development.

References

Bayar, Y., Borozan, D. and Gavriletea, M. D. (2021). Banking sector stability and economic growth in post-transition European Union countries. *International Journal of Finance & Economics*, *26*, 949–961.

Bist, J. P. (2018). Financial development and economic growth: Evidence from a panel of 16 African and non-African low-income countries. *Cogent Economics & Finance*, *6*(1), 1449780.

Boachie, R., Aawaar, G. and Domeher, D. (2021). Relationship between financial inclusion, banking stability and economic growth: A dynamic panel approach. *Journal of Economic and Administrative Sciences*.

Dinger, V., Erman, L. and te Kaat, D. M. (2022). Bank bailouts and economic growth: Evidence from cross-country, cross-industry data. *Journal of Financial Stability*, *60*, 100984.

Elnahass, M., Trinh, V. Q. and Li, T. (2021). Global banking stability in the shadow of COVID-19 outbreak. *Journal of International Financial Markets, Institutions and Money*, *72*, 101322.

Eweke, G. O. (2019). Banking system stability and economic growth in Nigeria: A bounds test to cointegration. *Euro Economica*, *38*(1), 1–14.

Fatima, S., Chen, B., Ramzan, M. and Abbas, Q. (2020). The nexus between trade openness and GDP growth: Analyzing the role of human capital accumulation. *SAGE Open*, *10*(4), 2158244020967377.

Ijaz, S., Hassan, A., Tarazi, A. and Fraz, A. (2020). Linking bank competition, financial stability, and economic growth. *Journal of Business Economics and Management*, *21*(1), 200–221.

Jayakumar, M., Pradhan, R. P., Dash, S., Maradana, R. P. and Gaurav, K. (2018). Banking competition, banking stability, and economic growth: Are feedback effects at work? *Journal of Economics and Business*, *96*, 15–41.

Klein, P.-O. and Weill, L. (2022). Bank profitability and economic growth. *The Quarterly Review of Economics and Finance*, *84*, 183–199.

Monnin, P. and Jokipii, T. (2010). The Impact of Banking Sector Stability on the Real Economy. Available at https://www.diw.de/documents/dokumentenarchiv/17/diw_01.c.373263.de/fin11_monnin_jokipii.pdf. Accessed on 20 June 2022.

Nguyen, T. T., Nguyen, V. C. and Tran, T. N. (2020). Oil price shocks against stock return of oil- and gas-related firms in the economic depression: A new evidence from a copula approach. *Cogent Economics and Finance*, 2020, *8*(1), 1799908.

Nguyen, V. C. and Nguyen, T. T. (2022a). The effect of COVID 19 pandemic on the financial market's performance: Evidence from top ASEAN stock markets. In Mansour, N. and Bujosa Vadell, L. M. (eds.) *Finance, Law, and the Crisis of COVID-19*. Contributions to Management Science, Cham: Springer.

Nguyen, V. C. and Nguyen, T. T. (2022b). Dependence and contagion between Vietnamese and major East Asian stock markets. *International Journal of Management Practice*, 2022, *15*(4), 445–459.

Peterson, E. W. F. (2017). The role of population in economic growth. *SAGE Open*, *7*(4), 2158244017736094.

Senra Hodelin, R. (2022). Public banking and economic growth: The experiences of 10 countries since the 1950s until 2017. *Economic Systems*, *46*(1), 100938.

Sengupta, P. and Puri, R. (2018). Exploration of relationship between FDI and GDP: A comparison between India and its neighbouring countries. *Global Business Review*, *21*(2), 473–489.

Shabir, M., Jiang, P., Bakhsh, S. and Zhao, Z. (2021). Economic policy uncertainty and bank stability: Threshold effect of institutional quality and competition. *Pacific-Basin Finance Journal*, *68*, 101610.

Soedarmono, W., Machrouh, F. and Tarazi, A. (2011). Bank market power, economic growth and financial stability: Evidence from Asian banks. *Journal of Asian Economics*, *22*(6), 460–470.

Stewart, R. and Chowdhury, M. (2021). Banking sector distress and economic growth resilience: Asymmetric effects. *The Journal of Economic Asymmetries*, *24*, e00218.

Stewart, R., Chowdhury, M. and Arjoon, V. (2021). Bank stability and economic growth: Trade-offs or opportunities? *Empirical Economics*, *61*, 827–853.

Toh, M. Y. and Zhang, Y. (2022). Bank capital and risk adjustment responses to economic uncertainty: Evidence from emerging Southeast Asian economies. *Research in International Business and Finance*, *60*, 101576.

Trinh, V. Q., Cao, N. D. and Elnahass, M. (2022). Financial stability: A 'vaccine' for tail risk of the global banking sector in the shadow of the pandemic. *The European Journal of Finance*, 1–28.

Ueda, K. (2013). Banks as coordinators of economic growth and stability: Microfoundation for macroeconomy with externality. *Journal of Economic Theory*, *148*(1), 322–352.

https://doi.org/10.1142/9781800614321_0004

Chapter 4

Intellectual Capital Efficiency and Islamic Banks' Stability: Evidence from Asian Countries

Ejaz Aslam[*,‡], **Aziz ur Rehman**[*,§], **and Anam Iqbal**[†,¶]

[*] *School of Islamic Economics, Banking & Finance, Minhaj University, Lahore, Punjab, Pakistan*

[†] *IIUM Institute of Islamic Banking and Finance (IIiBF), IIUM, Jalan Gombak, Malaysia*

[‡] *ejazaslam95@gmail.com*

[§] *mufti.aziz@hotmail.com*

[¶] *anamiqbal5050@gmail.com*

Abstract

This study aims to look into the effect of intellectual capital efficiency on Islamic banks' financial stability after controlling the bank-specific and macroeconomic variables. This study employed a hierarchical two-step system generalized method of moment (2SYS-GMM) estimation technique to analyze the data collected from 94 Islamic banks in 18 Asian Islamic countries during the period 2010–2020. The empirical findings show that ICE components, specifically SCE and RCE, have a positive and statistically significant effect on Islamic banks' financial stability. Our findings suggest that policymakers and top management at Islamic banks should pay closer attention to ICE resources, which have the potential to improve bank efficiency and stability while also keeping them competitive in times of distress.

Keywords: Financial stability, intellectual capital efficiency, human capital efficiency, structural capital efficiency, relational capital efficiency, resource-based theory, system generalized method of moments, competitive environment, Islamic banks, Asian countries

1. Introduction

Economic development and the stability of a nation largely depend on the performance of its financial sector (Festa *et al.*, 2021). Due to globalization, the banking sector has experienced a competitive and dynamic atmosphere that directs the banks to grow as a knowledge-intensive sector. This globalization process has increased the necessity of innovative industries, such as banking, finance, and information technology (Aslam and Haron, 2021). Hashim *et al.* (2015) state that knowledge is superior to land, labor, and capital as meaningful factors of production. Again, knowledge is regarded as a long-term strategic asset that may be used to achieve and preserve competitive advantages (Rehman *et al.*, 2021), and in a knowledge-based economy, intellectual capital (IC) is the most valuable asset a company can have (Aslam and Haron, 2020). Jetmiko (2018) mentions that knowledge is like light. It is delicate and intangible, and it can certainly travel the world, illuminating people's lives everywhere.

The significance of ICE has increased based on the growing demand for a knowledge economy (Poh *et al.*, 2018). ICE is the knowledge, experience, intellectual resource, and information that are used to generate wealth (Aslam and Haron, 2020b). The performance of the banking sector is important for the economy as banks serve as an instrument for economic growth (Shamsuddin *et al.*, 2017). It is very much essential to have better performance from ICE investments as the banks' long-term competitive advantages depend on it (Hashim *et al.*, 2015; Jetmiko, 2018), and in achieving sustainable growth, banks should emphasize their ICE resources (Edvinsson and Malone, 1997). Therefore, it is essential to focus more on the effect of ICE capability on bank performance to justify whether bank performance growth will increase or decrease in relation to the performance of ICE (Xu *et al.*, 2022). According to Dalwai *et al.* (2021), the percentages of intangible assets act as a proxy for future performance depending on the risky assets owned by the organization. The global financial crisis of 2007–2008, as well as the recent COVID-19 outbreak, shattered confidence and disrupted the region's capital flow. The impact of these crises and increased competition created a threat to Islamic banking and directed banking behavior toward stability (Elnahass *et al.*, 2021; Ullah *et al.*, 2021).

There are not many kinds of research on the ICE, such as those conducted by Xu *et al.* (2022), Rehman *et al.* (2021), Ting *et al.* (2021), and Xu and Liu (2021). Buallay *et al.* (2020), Siswanti and Sukoharsono (2019), Ousama *et al.* (2019), Nawaz (2019a), and Jetmiko (2018) are primarily concerned with performance as quantified by return on assets, return on equity, and return in the financial and non-financial sectors. Similarly, prior research claims that innovation is a knowledge-driven outcome influenced by strategic decisions (Aslam *et al.*, 2023) and technology adoption (Maji and Hussain, 2021). Innovation speed is closely associated with company performance in complex and fast-changing business contexts (Ur Rehman *et al.*, 2021). The faster a company innovates, the more likely it is to fulfill market demands and achieve its objectives. Staff-related variables, project support, and collaborations are also critical components in boosting a firm's innovation pace (Chahal and Bakshi, 2015). However, some of the studies focus on the ICE relationship with stability (Dalwai *et al.*, 2021; Festa *et al.*, 2021; Ullah *et al.*, 2021) but they ignore the Islamic financial sector, and there is an urgent need to fill this void. As a result, this study is to investigate the role of IC in bank stability in Asian countries. In financial stability, ICE includes three types of capital efficiencies: human, relational, and structural capital efficiencies.

A majority of Asian countries are facing challenges, and reforms are essential to boost long-term stable economic growth. Hence, continuous research needs to be done on how to overcome these issues to recover the economy. Besides, while ICE is a crucial issue in the banking sector in Asian countries, the regional impact differences in the inter-country context highlight the need for further investigation. As a part of ICE, human capital and structural capital help in achieving the stability and insolvency of banks in the complex competitive setting (Nawaz, 2019b), and as a driver for credit risk, investment in ICE can reduce credit risk that ultimately ensures growth and sustainability of banks and the economy. Value addition of the financial organization not only depends on physical capital but also depends on intangible assets (intellectual assets/capital). This study will focus on moderating the role of financial leverage on the relationship between ICE and financial stability in Asian countries. The findings may also aid investors to make investment decisions and actions, and financial experts devise strategies to enhance bank efficiency and prospective wealth generation. A very limited empirical study examines the relationship between ICE and bank stability in the Islamic banking sector as a whole. Given this context, the purpose of this study is to add to the body of knowledge on intellectual capital and financial stability in Asian countries. Hence, this study delves into the effects of IC efficiency on banks' stability in Asian Muslim countries, which are clearly missing in the previous outcomes of the study.

This study analyzes the ICE influence on banking stability using 2SYS-GMM estimation. The result shows that out of the three components of ICE, only structural capital efficiency and relational capital efficiency have a positive and significant impact on the financial stability of Islamic banks. Surprisingly, human capital efficiency has a negative impact on the financial stability of Islamic banks. This might be possible because people working in Islamic banks are not well trained or do not perform their duties well. Thus, the findings are relevant for the bank managers who should take advantage of the benefits of both SCE and RCE to improve their financial stability. SCE can be improved by implementing various internal control processes under corporate governance best practices. Moreover, better choice of employees and their proper training may be the recommended strategy for the other component.

The remaining part of this study is as follows: Section 2 debates the literature review. Section 3 delves into the methodology and data used in this study. Section 4 deals with the empirical findings and discussion and Section 5 closes this study with implications and limitations.

2. Literature Review

According to resource-based theory, an individual's ability to obtain and use resources is a valued and irreplaceable asset. According to the resource-based theory, businesses should look within themselves to identify areas where they may gain a competitive edge by better utilizing their own resources. The competitive advantage of a company is derived from the resources it has. The RBT discusses how resources can be leveraged to gain a competitive edge over the competition (Dalwai *et al.*, 2021; Rehman *et al.*, 2021; Ullah *et al.*, 2021).

2.1. *Relationship between ICE and stability*

Intellectual capital is broadly defined as any knowledge that can be converted into monetary value (Ullah *et al.*, 2021). ICE is associated with enhanced value and a company's ability to produce, enforce, and accurately measure intangible capital; in fact, this strengthens organizational effectiveness. Recently, intellectual property, expertise, facts, property rights, and encounter that can be used to produce wealth have all been identified as ICE (Xu and Liu, 2021). Referring to the resource-based theory of the organization (Rehman *et al.*, 2021), organizations gain a competitive advantage and improve performance when they acquire, hold, and then use strategic assets. ICE is undeniably a critical resource for the organization in today's knowledge economy, particularly for knowledge-intensive organizations like banks. Buallay (2017) argued that ICE plays a significant role in the process of company performance. Several empirical studies observed ICE and bank stability and performance (Alhassan and Asare, 2016; Hameed and Anwar, 2018; Rehman *et al.*, 2021; Ting *et al.*, 2021; Ullah *et al.*, 2021; Xu and Liu, 2021; Zukhri *et al.*, 2021).

Regardless of classification, there is agreement that ICE is a multidimensional concept comprising human, structural, and relational resources (Mention and Bontis, 2013). Human capital refers to employees' skills, knowledge, and experience, which are amplified through training and development. The study by Vo (2018) stated that human capital has a positive relationship with high-quality growth and plays an important role in achieving quality growth. Moreover, Onumah and Duho (2019) state that knowledge-based human capital is necessary for sustainable performance and is essential for competitive advantage. Structural capital is the organization's inseparable knowledge base, which includes structures, processes, systems, procedures, hardware, patents, and even the organization's strategy. Moreover, the study of Poh *et al.* (2018) structural capital refers to the information that a company retains even after a former employee leaves. Xu and Liu (2020) found positive effects of structural capital on banking performance. Further, they stated that structural capital is necessary for the stability of banks because organizations face risk when they establish and enter a new market. Lastly, relation relational capital refers to the organization's relationships with various stakeholders (Aslam and Haron, 2021). Relational capital efficiency is a core dimension of intellectual capital and has a significant direct relationship with organizational performance (Hameed and Anwar, 2018). Relational capital efficiency has a positive impact on an organization's performance and sustainable growth (Xu and Wang, 2019). Besides this, the study of Lukman and Tanuwijaya (2021) found that relational capital efficiency has a significant positive impact on a firm's value followed by the financial performance of the banks. This study is aimed at measuring the efficiency of IC and its components concerning Islamic banks. Thus, ICE is deemed an essential strategic tool for banking business; this study expects IC efficiency to be positively associated with the financial stability of Islamic banks. Therefore, in light of the above discussion and resource base theory, the following hypotheses are formulated:

Hypothesis 1: There is a positive relationship between intellectual capital efficiency and the financial stability of Islamic banks.
Hypothesis 1.1: Human capital efficiency has a positive association with Islamic banks' financial stability.
Hypothesis 1.2: Structural capital efficiency has a positive relationship with Islamic banks' financial stability.
Hypothesis 1.3: Relational capital efficiency has a positive relationship with Islamic banks' financial stability.

3. Methodology

3.1. *Data and their sources*

The research is based on secondary data collected from 112 Islamic banks between 2010 and 2020 from 18 Muslim Asian countries. We exclude 18 banks due to the complexity, lack of data availability, as well as their heterogeneity. The ICE and financial stability-related data were derived from Fitch Connect, with any missing data obtained from the corresponding IB's financial statements, balance sheets, and cash flow statements. From 2010 to 2020, all annual statements were accessible on the banks' respective portals. The data for macroeconomic variables are collected from the World Bank's database. Furthermore, all of the data are expressed in millions of US dollars.

3.2. *Research variables*

The key research variables in this study are categorized into three groups: dependent, independent, and control variables. Dependent variables focus on Islamic bank financial stability and are measured with ZEQTA and NFGF. The independent variables focus on intellectual capital efficiency that comprises HCE, SCE, and RCE, whereas the set of control variables comprises bank-specific (bank size and foreign ownership) and macroeconomic variables (GDP and INF). Table 1 summarizes the name, definitions, and codes of all selected variables in this study.

3.3. *System generalized method of moment (SYS-GMM)*

This study examines the relationship of intellectual capital efficiency with the stability of Islamic banks; for this purpose, two interrelated relationships are evaluated. The first is to assess the impact of ICE on bank stability by showing the effect of each aspect through a set of ICE mechanisms, and bank-specific and macroeconomic factors. Intellectual capital efficiency affects the stability of Islamic banks as shown in the following models:

$$ZEQTA_{it} = \alpha_0 + \sum_{k}^{3} B_1 ICE_{it} + \sum_{M}^{6} B_2 X_{it} + \varepsilon_{it} \tag{1}$$

$$NFGF_{it} = \alpha_0 + \sum_{k}^{3} B_1 ICE_{it} + \sum_{M}^{6} B_2 X_{it} + \varepsilon_{it} \tag{2}$$

In models 1 and 2, i represents the Islamic banks, t represents the years, *ZEQTA* and *NFGF* represent the proxy of financial stability, *ICE* represents the intellectual capital efficiency with three proxies (*HCE, SCE, RCE*), X represents the set of control variables with six proxies (*BS, LEV, MKS, FOWN, INF, GDP*), and ε represents the error term.

Table 1. Research variable and measurement.

Numbers	Variables	Codes	Definition
1	**Financial Stability**		
	Financial stability	ZEQTA	Ratio of ROA plus the equity asset ratio which is divided by the standard ROA
	Financial stability	NFGF	Ratio of non-performing financing to total gross financing
2	**Intellectual Capital (Independent)**		
	Human capital efficiency	HCE	Value-added = Gross income — operating expenses
	Structural capital efficiency	SCE	Value-added/total expenses for employees
	Relational capital efficiency	RCE	Value-added/expenditure related to research and development
3	**Bank Characteristics (Controls)**		
	Total debt to equity	DE	Proportion of total debt over equity
	Bank size	LNTA	Natural log of corporate total assets
	Market share	MKS	It is the share of assets of each bank to total banks assets
	Foreign ownership	FOWN	Dummy For is a binary variable that takes the value of one if foreign firms have ownership in the firm or zero otherwise
4	**Macroeconomic (Controls)**		
	Inflation	CPI	Natural log of consumer price index
	Country growth	GDP	Natural log of total gross domestic product

4. Empirical Results

4.1. *Descriptive statistics*

As presented in Table 2, the results of the descriptive statistics show the complete study sample based on 1,034 observations of financial stability, ICE components, and control variables. The results indicate that financial stability in the form of (ZEQTA) has the highest mean value followed by (NFGF). The high value of the standard

Table 2. Descriptive statistics of research variables.

Variable	Obs.	Mean	Std. Dev.	Min.	Max.
ZEQTA	1,034	0.1506	0.0581	0.2063	1.1270
NFGF	1,034	0.0942	0.3862	0.2235	3.3006
Human capital efficiency	1,034	1.0332	2.6749	−1.9140	23.4779
Structural capital efficiency	1,034	2.0976	5.2133	−3.4914	58.1782
Relational capital efficiency	1,034	0.5431	1.5474	−1.1717	14.7667
Bank size	1,034	6.8900	2.0174	3.5430	11.4241
Leverage	1,034	7.0611	5.5048	2.8670	24.7071
Market share	1,034	0.0594	0.0919	0.0076	0.6223
Foreign ownership	1,034	0.2093	0.4070	0.0000	1.0000
Inflation	1,034	4.7432	0.2620	4.3473	5.9789
Gross domestic product	1,034	27.9113	3.8150	22.8700	36.8326

deviation of ZEQTA indicates that equity varies significantly from other incomes among banks. Furthermore, the descriptive results of the indicators, namely, HCE, SCE, and RCE, demonstrate that SCE is perhaps the most essential facet in wealth accumulation, with the highest mean value of 2.097, compared to HCE and RCE, which have mean scores of 1.033 and 0.554, respectively. Regarding the control variables, we have the mean BS (6.89), mean LEV (7.061), mean MKS (0.059), and mean FOWN (0.209), respectively.

4.2. *Correlation analysis*

Table 3 shows the pairwise correlation matrix for the explanatory variables, which is used to gain more insight before testing the research hypotheses. The result directed that RCE is highly correlated with HCE with a coefficient of 0.512, and the lowest correlation exists between GDP and inflation with a coefficient of 0.045. Aside from that, all of the other correlation coefficients are less than 0.7. Thus, using the Kennedy (2008) rule of thumb of 0.7, the regression models will not be perverted by collinearity. Besides this, a variance inflation factor (VIF) test was performed. The results are less than three, well below the rule of thumb of ten, implying that multicollinearity does not exist.

Table 3. Correlation and multicollinearity.

Variables	HCE	SCE	RCE	BS	LEV	MKS	FOWN	INF	GDP
Human capital efficiency	1								
Structural capital efficiency	0.3616	1							
Relational capital efficiency	0.5126	0.4994	1						
Bank size	0.1175	−0.0005	0.0495	1					
leverage	0.1038	0.0892	0.0656	0.1525	1				
Market share	−0.0712	−0.0412	−0.0491	−0.0278	0.1189	1			
Foreign ownership	−0.0712	−0.0412	−0.0491	−0.0278	0.1189	0.0178	1		
inflation	0.1709	−0.0619	0.0244	0.1342	−0.0169	−0.1277	0.1243	1	
Gross domestic product	0.2183	0.0142	−0.0087	0.1363	0.1508	−0.1406	0.0188	0.045	1
Variance inflation factor	1.56	1.64	1.39	1.07	1.09	1.230	1.07	1.09	1.13

4.3. *Result and discussions*

Table 4 shows the findings of the relationship between ICE and financial stability. We used a hierarchical estimation technique with the 2SYS-GMM model, where the ICE components were added to the model sequentially. Thus, the need of ICE is not only for the shareholders but also for the employees. Columns 1–3 show the results, with one ICE measure shown in the first column and the outcomes with all ICE measures shown in the last column. In all models, the coefficient of lagged financial stability has a positive and statistical significant association with current financial stability in terms of ZEQTA and NFGF. The findings are consistent with those of Rehman *et al.* (2021), who found that current performance is heavily influenced by IB performance in the previous year. In the Hansen test, the null hypothesis is rejected for all models, indicating that the instruments used in the model are valid. Furthermore, AR (2) indicates that there are no autocorrelation issues in any of the models.

Concerning intellectual capital efficiency, the findings of this study indicated that HCE has positive and significant effects with financial stability. This supports our hypothesis 1 which stated that HCE drives the financial stability in IBs. The results are parallel to the findings of Ullah *et al.* (2021), who stated that HCE triggers financial stability. This highlights the significance of IC in increasing banks' innovative capabilities for improving financial stability. Column 4 outcomes, on the other hand, showed that HCE has a negative and significant relationship with FS of IBs in both models. This finding is consistent with the findings of Rehman *et al.* (2021), who contend that HCE has a detrimental impact on banking stability. This negative association may occur as a result of employees' inability to perform their duties due to the lack of skills and capabilities, which ultimately do not contribute to the financial stability of Islamic banks.

In the case of SCE, in both models, SCE has a positive and statistically significant impact on the FS of Islamic banks. This supports our hypothesis 2 which indicates that HCE spurs the financial stability in IBs. These findings are parallel to the findings of Ullah *et al.* (2021) and contradicted the study by Onumah and Duho (2019), who stated that SCE leads the financial stability in banks. These findings imply that IBs can play a significant role if they spend more

Table 4. 2SYS-GMM intellectual capital efficiency impact on financial stability (ZEQTA and NFGF).

	Model ZEQTQ				Model NFGF			
Variable	**1**	**2**	**3**	**4**	**1**	**2**	**3**	**4**
L1. Return on asset	0.1630***	0.1635***	0.1597***	0.1827***				
L1. Return on equity					0.9546***	0.9549***	1.0245***	1.0683***
Human capital efficiency	0.0120***			−0.0156***	0.0341***			−0.0492***
Structural capital efficiency		0.0151***		0.0241***		0.0518***		0.01243*
Relational capital efficiency			0.0125***	0.0221***			0.0002**	0.0003**
log of total assets	0.0035***	0.0036***	0.0035***	0.0036***	0.0035***	0.0298***	0.0299***	0.0298***
leverage	−0.0015***	−0.0018***	−0.0019***	−0.0014***	0	−0.0006	−0.0008	−0.0007
Market share	0.0070***	0.0070***	0.0077***	0.0074***	0.0070***	0.005	0.0029	0.0024
Foreign ownership	0.0105**	0.0103**	0.0105**	0.0102**	0.0105**	−0.0092	−0.0078	−0.0082
inflation	−0.0013***	0.0013***	−0.0011***	−0.0012***	−0.0013***	−0.0130***	−0.0130***	−0.0132***
Gross domestic product	0.0009*	0.0009*	0.0005	0.0009*	0.0009*	0.0095***	0.0094***	0.0099***
Year dummy	−0.0000***	−0.0000***	−0.0000***	−0.0001***	−0.0000**	0	0	0
Constant	0.00001	0.0012	0.00310	0.01123	−0.0093	−0.2044**	−0.2049**	−0.2179**
No. of observations	985	985	985	978	985	985	985	978
AR(1) test statistics (*p*-value)	0.2268	0.2304	0.22704	0.22872	0.0036	0.00272	0.00448	0.00504
AR(2) test statistics (*p*-value)	0.20936	0.27456	0.26056	0.22488	0.38224	0.41568	0.2732	0.27784
Hansen test (*p*-value)	0.1862	0.2104	0.2521	0.3218	0.3217	0.7649	0.03219	0.3201

in their hierarchical order and framework in ways that foster development and innovation that will promote financial stability in IBs. In addition, RCE has a positive and insignificant effect on the financial stability of IBs in column 3, but it has a significant relationship in column 4 in both models. This supports our hypothesis 3 and is parallel to the finding of Maji and Hussain (2021) and Rehman *et al.* (2021). Our findings suggest that RCE improves IB financial stability because banks are still in the early stages and it is essential to spend more on relational capital to foster strong relationships in the economy and society. As a direct consequence, individuals gain a better understanding of IBs and their Shariah compliance business, and they will be more likely to use them. As a result, RCE significantly contributes to retaining the financial stability in IBs.

As per control variables, results show that bank size positively and significantly affects the financial stability of all models of the study, supporting the findings (Aslam *et al.*, 2021; Ozkan *et al.*, 2016). This result implies that the large size of banks plays a significant role in stability. Bank leverage has a negative and insignificant impact on FS. All financial stability variables have a positive and significant relationship with market share. These findings corroborate those of Rehman *et al.* (2021) in Asian countries, implying that a larger market share of banks aids to improve bank stability. Foreign ownership positively and significantly affects the financial stability of IBs in all models. These results are contrasting with the findings of Rehman *et al.* (2021), who stated that a large share of the foreign owner has a detrimental effect on financial performance. Besides this, we find that GDP has a positive and significant relationship with IBs' financial stability, whereas inflation has a negative and significant relationship with the FS of Islamic banks. These outcomes are supporting the findings of Aslam and Haron (2021). This finding suggests that a high GDP corresponds to greater national growth, which improves the financial stability of Islamic banks.

5. Conclusion

The impact of ICE and its components on the financial stability of Islamic banks is investigated in this study by using a balanced panel dataset of 94 banks with 1,034 observations from Asian countries over the period 2010–2020. This study assesses the impact of ICE components; a hierarchical 2SYS-GMM estimation technique was used while controlling the size, foreign ownership, and macroeconomic variables. This study is unique in that it used a large dataset of 94 Islamic banks that have been in operation for 11 years, which increases the precision results of this study. The findings support the resource-based theory and suggest that increasing ICE leads to improved bank stability. The study's findings corroborate the resource-based theory, which can be employed to boost intangible investment opportunities to establish a long-term competitive advantage, and ICE has the potential to strengthen a bank's financial performance. The findings also discovered a significant positive association between IC components such as SCE and RCE value-created coefficient for Islamic bank financial stability in Asian countries.

This study's findings benefit regulatory authorities in assessing various banks as it will lead to better governance, economic development, and economic policies that will all lead to financial stability in Asian countries and the whole banking system. Furthermore, in this advanced, risk-based banking system, banks should preserve and use their ICE resources in every legal and possible way to improve efficiency and maintain financial stability. Governments and legislators should increase data transparency and the legal regime in Asian banks by considering the human development system. Additionally, top management of the banking sector should take advantage of the benefits of both SCE and RCE to improve their financial stability. SCE can be improved by implementing various internal control processes in accordance with corporate governance best practices. To reap the benefits of ICE, banks should consider the perspectives of stakeholders. Thus, the needs of not only the shareholders but also the employees, customers, investors, and debtholders should be considered, and increased financial stability will be achieved as a result. Furthermore, because Islamic banks are still in their early stages, they can maintain their growth momentum by making the best use of ICE resources during times of distress.

This research has some limitations. First, consider the fact that the research focused on Islamic banks from Asian Muslim countries and excluded other countries and industries from this study. It has probable legal and regulatory constraints, particularly differences in legal frameworks between developing and developed countries, which impact intellectual capital financial reporting and efficiency. Second, while this study uses the value-added intellectual coefficient (VAIC), there are other ways to assess intellectual capital performance. Admittedly, this study does not include all banks due to a lack of data. These constraints indicate the potential for future research. Thereby, future research should look into this and use a diverse sample of people from developed and developing countries and a dynamic panel estimator.

References

Alhassan, A. L. and Asare, N. (2016). Intellectual capital and bank productivity in emerging markets: Evidence from Ghana. *Management Decision*, *54*(3), 589–609.

Aslam, E. and Haron, R. (2021). Corporate governance and banking performance: The mediating role of intellectual capital among OIC countries. *Corporate Governance: The International Journal of Business in Society*, *21*(1), 111–136.

Aslam, E. and Haron, R. (2020). The influence of corporate governance on intellectual capital efficiency: Evidence from Islamic banks of OIC countries. *Asian Journal of Accounting Research*, *5*(2), 195–208.

Aslam, E., Ur-Rehman, A. and Iqbal, A. (2021). Does corporate governance matter for asset quality of Islamic banks? *Bulletin of Monetary Economics and Banking*, *24*(2), 221–236.

Aslam, E., Ur Rehman, A. and Iqbal, A. (2023). The mediating role of intellectual capital in corporate governance and financial efficiency of Islamic banks. *Corporate Governance*, ahead-of-print. https://doi.org/10.1108/CG-06-2022-0276.

Buallay, A., Hamdan, A. M., Reyad, S., Badawi, S. and Madbouly, A. (2020). The efficiency of GCC banks: The role of intellectual capital. *European Business Review*, *32*(3), 303–404.

Buallay, A. M. (2017). The relationship between intellectual capital and firm performance. *Corporate Governance and Organizational Behavior Review*, *1*(1), 32–41.

Chahal, H. and Bakshi, P. (2015). Examining intellectual capital and competitive advantage relationship: Role of innovation and organizational learning. *International Journal of Bank Marketing*, *33*(3), 376–399.

Dalwai, T., Singh, D. and Singh, A. (2021). Intellectual capital, bank stability and risk-taking: Evidence from Asian emerging markets. *Competitiveness Review: An International Business Journal*, *32*(6), 995–1024.

Edvinsson, L. and Malone, M. S. (1997). *Intellectual Capital: The Proven Way to Establish Your Company's Real Value by Finding Its Hidden Brainpower*. New York: Piatkus, Harper Business.

Elnahass, M., Trinh, V. Q. and Li, T. (2021). Global banking stability in the shadow of COVID-19 outbreak. *Journal of International Financial Markets, Institutions and Money, 72*, 101322.

Festa, G., Rossi, M., Kolte, A. and Marinelli, L. (2021). The contribution of intellectual capital to financial stability in Indian pharmaceutical companies. *Journal of Intellectual Capital, 22*(2), 337–359.

Hameed, A. A. and Anwar, K. (2018). Analyzing the relationship between intellectual capital and organizational performance: A study of selected private banks in Kurdistan. *International Journal of Social Sciences & Educational Studies, 4*(4), 39–52.

Hashim, M. J., Osman, I. and Alhabshi, S. M. (2015). Effect of intellectual capital on organizational performance. *Procedia-Social and Behavioral Sciences, 211*(1), 207–214.

Jetmiko, J. (2018). Analysis on the effect of intellectual capital on growth and financial performance of Islamic banking. *Indonesian Journal of Business and Economics, 1*(1), 92–109.

Kennedy, P. (2008). *A Guide to Econometrics*. Queensland, Australia: John Wiley & Sons.

Lukman, H. and Tanuwijaya, H. (2021). The effect of financial performance and intellectual capital on firm value with CSR as a mediating variable in banking industry. In *Ninth International Conference on Entrepreneurship and Business Management (ICEBM 2020)* (pp. 353–359).

Maji, S. G. and Hussain, F. (2021). Technical efficiency, intellectual capital efficiency and bank performance in emerging markets: The case of India. *Journal of Advances in Management Research, 18*(5), 708–737.

Mention, A.-L. and Bontis, N. (2013). Intellectual capital and performance within the banking sector of Luxembourg and Belgium. *Journal of Intellectual Capital, 14*(2), 286–309.

Nawaz, T. (2019a). Exploring the nexus between human capital, corporate governance and performance: Evidence from Islamic banks. *Journal of Business Ethics, 157*(2), 567–587.

Nawaz, T. (2019b). Intellectual capital profiles and financial performance of Islamic banks in the UK. *International Journal of Learning and Intellectual Capital, 16*(1), 87–97.

Onumah, J. M. and Duho, K. C. T. (2019). Intellectual capital: Its impact on financial performance and financial stability of Ghanaian banks. *Athens Journal of Business and Economics, 5*(3), 243–268.

Ousama, A. A., Hammami, H. and Abdulkarim, M. (2019). The association between intellectual capital and financial performance in the Islamic banking industry. *International Journal of Islamic and Middle Eastern Finance and Management, 13*(1), 75–93.

Ozkan, N., Cakan, S. and Kayacan, M. (2016). Intellectual capital and financial performance: A study of the Turkish banking sector. *Borsa Istanbul Review, 17*(3), 190–198.

Poh, L. T., Kilicman, A. and Ibrahim, S. N. I. (2018). On intellectual capital and financial performances of banks in Malaysia. *Cogent Economics & Finance, 6*(1), 1–15.

Rehman, A. U., Aslam, E. and Iqbal, A. (2021). Intellectual capital efficiency and bank performance: Evidence from Islamic banks. *Borsa Istanbul Review, 22*(1), 113–121.

Shamsuddin, A., Mun, C. Y., Danial, N. A. B. A., Yusn, N. S. B., Adham, N. B. M. and Din, N. A. B. M. (2017). The influence of intellectual capital towards corporate governance practices in top 100 ASEAN companies. *International Journal of Business, Economics and Law, 13*(1), 55–64.

Siswanti, I. and Sukoharsono, E. G. (2019). Intellectual capital and financial performance of Islamic banks in Indonesia. *Institutions and Economies, 5*(1), 31–49.

Ting, I. W. K., Chen, F.-C., Kweh, Q. L., Sui, H. J. and Le, H. T. M. (2021). Intellectual capital and bank branches' efficiency: An integrated study. *Journal of Intellectual Capital, 23*(4), 1–16.

Ullah, A., Pinglu, C., Ullah, S., Qian, N. and Zaman, M. (2021). Impact of intellectual capital efficiency on financial stability in banks: Insights from an emerging economy. *International Journal of Finance & Economics, 26*(2), 1–14.

Ur Rehman, S., Elrehail, H., Alsaad, A. and Bhatti, A. (2021). Intellectual capital and innovative performance: A mediation-moderation perspective. *Journal of Intellectual Capital, 23*(5), 998–1024.

Vo, D. H. (2018). Should bankers be concerned with intellectual capital? A study of the Thai banking sector. *Journal of Intellectual Capital, 19*(5), 897–914.

Xu, J., Haris, M. and Irfan, M. (2022). The impact of intellectual capital on bank profitability during COVID-19: A comparison with China and Pakistan. *Complexity, 22*(1), 1–10.

Xu, J. and Liu, F. (2020). The impact of intellectual capital on firm performance: A modified and extended VAIC model. *Journal of Competitiveness, 12*(1), 161.

Xu, J. and Liu, F. (2021). Nexus between intellectual capital and financial performance: An investigation of Chinese manufacturing industry. *Journal of Business Economics and Management, 22*(1), 217–235.

Xu, J. and Wang, B. (2019). Intellectual capital, financial performance and companies' sustainable growth: Evidence from the Korean manufacturing industry. *Sustainability (Switzerland)*, *10*(12), 1–15.

Zukhri, N., Rahayu, S., Hidayati, H. and Rosalina, E. (2021). Intellectual capital in customer's perception of Sharia banking in Pangkalpinang. *Society*, *9*(1), 72–82.

https://doi.org/10.1142/9781800614321_0005

Chapter 5

The Impact of Regulatory Capital Pressure on Profitability and Risk: Evidence from Tunisian Banks

Rim Zakraoui[*,‡] **and Dorra Mezzez Hmaied**[†,§]

[*] *Institut de Financement du Développement du Maghreb Arabe (IFID), Banque Centrale de Tunisie, Tunisia*

[†] *Laboratoire d'Economie et de Finance Appliquées, Institut des Hautes Etudes Commerciales de Carthage, Université de Carthage, Carthage, Tunisia*

[‡] *zakraoui.reem@outlook.com*

[§] *dorra.hmaied@ihec.ucar.tn*

Abstract

This paper analyses the effect of regulatory pressure on bank behavior, using a sample of Tunisian banks covering the period 2005–2020. First, the paper examines the impact of regulatory capital on bank profitability and risk. Second, it contributes to the literature which has received scant attention from researchers investigating the nonlinear impact of regulatory pressure on bank behavior. Third, we consider different determinants of bank profitability and risk. Finally, we use both static and dynamic models to test for the persistence of bank profitability and risk, as well as to make sure that the results are not biased by endogeneity. The results suggest that regulatory capital pressure improves bank profitability and stability. This effect is, however, conditioned by the existence of a certain threshold, after which stringent capital regulation may have adverse effects. Our results have important policy implications on optimal bank capital regulation.

Keywords: Banking, regulatory capital, bank performance, profitability, risk, political instability

1. Introduction

The debate between bank managers and regulators about regulatory intervention casts doubt on the impact of regulatory capital on bank behavior (Corcoran, 2010; Jakovljevi *et al.*, 2015; Manlagnit, 2015). The questions are still being investigated as to whether capital should be regulated and whether the current regulation is effective in mitigating bank risk (Persaud, 2009; Gopinath, 2010; Hanson *et al.*, 2011) or whether banks should be able to freely set their optimal capital level (Miller, 1995; Calomiris and Berry, 2004; Aiyar *et al.*, 2015).

Regulatory authorities are torn over the costs and benefits of bank capital. On the one hand, stringent capital requirements protect depositors' interest, provide banks with a cushion to absorb unexpected losses, and inspire confidence in the banking sector. On the other hand, capital requirements impose social costs in terms of the availability and the cost of lending which, if not taken seriously, can jeopardize economic growth. Indeed, bank managers are not incentivized to raise capital over debt, mainly due to three reasons eloquently summarized by Aiyar *et al.* (2015): First, if managers act against the interest of shareholders and are able to extract personal gains from keeping a high default risk, they are more likely to opt for leverage, since the probability of default rises when the bank is increasingly leveraged. Second, the social costs of a banking crisis (e.g., tightening of the credit supply and disruption of the payment system) are not internalized by the bank's stakeholders. Hence, bank managers receive no incentives to maintain a prudent management of risk. Third, the presence of safety nets that protect creditors' interests creates incentives for bank managers and shareholders, whose interests are now aligned with those of the managers to "game these safety nets" by keeping a high default risk. This situation is more dangerous when depositors are not able to monitor the risk portfolio of banks, due to the asymmetry of information and high costs of monitoring. This is the reason why some countries have given explicit deposit insurance schemes to protect the interest of depositors, since bank depositors are not protected by the standard covenants of debt contracts.

Banks that choose to raise new equity to comply with regulatory capital may see their profits deplete, due to the costly nature of equity financing compared to leverage (Myers, 1977; Myers and Majluf, 1984). Banks can offset high equity costs by passing this cost on to borrowers by charging higher interest rates (King, 2010). However, higher interest rates affect the ability of borrowers to pay back the amounts borrowed and, in turn, increase borrower defaults and ultimately bank instability (Martynova, 2015). Hence, the effect of capital requirements on bank risk and profitability remains ambiguous. In addition, empirical studies investigating the effect of regulatory capital often focus on developed economies. Scant attention has been paid to developing countries in Africa and Asia. Given these disparities between developing and developed countries, we are uncertain if the impact of regulatory requirements on bank behavior has been the same for both. We chose the Tunisian banking sector because scant attention has been paid to the Tunisian context and because banks remain at the heart of the financial system. In addition, the Tunisian banking industry provides an interesting context to explore, since it has never witnessed a banking crisis and banking is thought to be the most profitable sector in the country.

There are several novel elements in this study. First, unlike most empirical studies, we do use the capital ratio to account for capital requirements. We use the risk-weighted ratio, taking into account the bank's risky portfolio. Moreover, we focus on the linear impact of bank capital regulation but also take into account the possibility that the impact may shift after a certain threshold. This aspect of capital regulation has long been disregarded by earlier works, but we believe it is essential to gauge the real effect of capital regulation. Second, our analysis builds on previous studies on the effects of specific and macroeconomic variables on bank profitability and risk. However, we turn the spotlight on a rather neglected variable that we believe is driving the relationship, and that is political instability. The variable may seem evident in the Tunisian context and in most countries; yet, to our knowledge, we are the first to consider political stability as a driving force of bank profitability and stability. Third, we use both static and dynamic models to test for the persistence of bank profitability and risk, as well as to make sure that the results are not biased by endogeneity. Finally, this analysis allows insightful suggestions for future regulatory policies, while also taking inspiration from different countries' regulatory systems.

The results indicate that regulatory capital pressure improves bank profitability and stability. This effect is, however, conditioned by the existence of a certain threshold after which stringent capital regulation may have adverse effects. Our results have important policy implications on optimal bank capital regulation. The remainder of this paper is structured in the following manner: The following section reviews theoretical and empirical literature. Section 3 describes the methodology, while Section 4 presents the results and findings. Section 5 presents the results of the robustness check, while Section 6 concludes this study.

2. Capital Pressure and Bank Behavior: Theoretical and Empirical Review

Several theoretical and empirical studies have examined the impact of regulatory capital pressure on bank behavior. Theoretically, Kahane (1977), Koehn and Santomero (1980), and Kim and Santomero (1988) have used the mean–variance framework to model bank portfolio selection, in order to understand the dynamics between the introduction of more stringent capital requirements and bank risk-taking incentives. They show that, when banks are faced with more stringent capital requirements, they expect a reduction in their profits. This is commonly referred to as the "*expected income effect*". Under this theory, banks engage in excessive risk-taking, in order to remain profitable. Hence, this theory challenges the ability of capital requirements to curb bank excessive risk-taking (Koehn and Santomero, 1980; Kim and Santomero, 1988; Rochet, 1992). Indeed, when banks are pressured to raise capital, they do so by substituting leverage with risky assets. This means that banks would have incentives to raise their portfolio risk exposure when confronted with involuntary, regulatory-induced increases in capital (Merton, 1972; Kahane, 1977; Koehn and Santomero, 1980; Kim and Santomero, 1988).

Several theories tend to explain the role of capital requirements in bank risk-taking. The option pricing theory posits that banks can maximize shareholder equity value by maximizing the option value of the deposit insurance through greater risky assets and leverage. The problem that arises from this particular type of bank behavior is that banks can increase shareholder value at the expense of their depositors, by exploiting the deposit insurance subsidy induced by the flat rate deposit insurance pricing. This situation is referred to as the "moral hazard" hypothesis. Capital requirements can restrict this bank behavior by forcing shareholders to increase their "skin in the game", thus diminishing the value of the deposit insurance put option. Notwithstanding the contribution of the theory of options valuation applied by Merton (1977) to the conventional wisdom, this framework was criticized for overlooking the presence of market frictions. In particular, information asymmetry was not taken into account in the option pricing theory (Dewatripont and Tirole, 1994).

On the other hand, the theory of bankruptcy cost avoidance, introduced by Orgler and Taggart (1983), sought to explain the reason why the optimal level of capital that banks hold will be in excess of the regulatory minimum. This relationship depends on the trade-off between tax rewards from deposit financing and costs of leverage, in terms of bankruptcy costs, higher reserve requirements, and diseconomies of scale that stem from the production of deposit services. Similar to the aforementioned theory, the buffer theory predicts that a bank, which is holding capital levels just above the regulatory minimum, may reduce its risk exposure or increase its capital level as a protection against the violation of the regulatory minimum capital requirements (Marcus and Shaked, 1984; Milne and Whalley, 2001; Milne, 2004). This allows them to avoid costs arising from a supervisory intervention, in case of a breach of the capital requirements. This theory is challenged, however, by the "*gambling for resurrection*" hypothesis under which banks holding capital levels below the minimum required may increase the risk of their asset portfolio in the hope of garnering higher returns, in order to increase their capital and comply with the regulation in force.

The theory of the disciplinary role of debt offers another view of the nexus. This theory postulates that equity capital does not confer the same control rights as those of creditors. Debt holders are informed about the real outcomes of bank investment, otherwise only known by bank managers (Diamond, 1984; Ramakrishnan and Thakor, 1984; Calomiris and Kahn, 1991). These control rights make it harder for bank managers to serve their own interests in keeping a high default rate, by taking excessive risk, and by creating incentives for them to improve their job performance. Under this theory, capital requirements weaken the disciplinary role of debt, since it decreases the level of leverage.

A large body of theoretical literature also sought to shed light on the relationship between capital regulation and bank profitability. This is explained by the important effect of profitability on the willingness of bank owners and managers to comply with regulations.

The theory of irrelevancy of Modigliani and Miller (1958) was the starting point for research relative to bank capital structure and profitability. Under this theory, capital has a neutral effect on bank cash flows and, in turn, profits. This theory was later challenged by many others over the simplicity of its assumptions. Myers and Majluf (1984) introduced the signaling theory to describe the reaction of the market after a firm announces equity offerings. They document that, when banks or any other firm resorts to external equity, outside investors will not be able to accurately value the bank's future earnings prospects due to information asymmetry. This information asymmetry causes adverse selection. This phenomenon can be witnessed in the stock market after a firm announces equity offerings, which are generally followed by a drop in its share price, forcing them to raise capital at prices well below fair value. Capital requirements impose adverse selection costs, not just when banks are below the minimum requirements but also to include adjustment costs to a new minimum.

The trade-off theory posits that regulatory capital reduces bank profitability due to higher costs of capital, compared to leverage. However, this effect is coupled with a decrease in risks which, in turn, would lower the costs of insolvency demanded by shareholders, to compensate for higher default risk. The trade-off theory argues that, in equilibrium, banks will choose an optimal level of capital which allows them to offset costs and benefits which, in turn, would imply a neutral effect at the margin. However, the aforementioned theory was criticized due to the fact that banks are, generally, pressured to hold a capital level in excess of their optimal level, as required by the 37 binding capital requirements imposed by regulators. This, in turn, would result in additional costs imposed on banks (Miller, 1995; Buser *et al.*, 1981).

Empirically, the relationship between capital and risk has been widely discussed. No consensus has been reached yet on the matter. Hovakimian and Kane (2000) analyzed the effect of an increase in capital requirements on the risk behavior of U.S. commercial banks. They find that regulatory capital ratios do not curb bank risk-taking incentives. On the contrary, they find that capital requirements increase the risk-taking incentives of poorly capitalized banks more than well-capitalized banks. Similarly, Bhattacharya (2013) attempted to compare the change in the risk-taking behavior of U.S. banks before and after the implementation of capital requirements in 1980. The author argues that, contrary to what the regulatory and supervisory authorities would expect, capital requirements increased bank risk-taking. He explains that since binding capital requirements reduced the lending activity of banks by more than half, banks had no other way than to increase their risky asset portfolio to generate income, in order to keep shareholders happy.

Other studies documented the success of capital requirements in limiting bank excessive risk-taking. Rime (2001), using a sample of Swiss banks during the period 1989–1995, found that regulatory pressure has a positive impact on bank capital, due to harsh consequences if banks fail to comply with the Swiss capital requirement, which may lead to bank closure and takeover. Hendrickson and Nichols (2001) argue that we cannot lump financial regulation into one basket. They claim that certain types of regulations (e.g., deposit insurance schemes) increased bank risk-taking, whereas other types of regulations (e.g., capital requirements, lending, and deposit rate regulations) decreased bank risk-taking incentives and improved bank stability. Barth *et al.* (2004) find that the impact of regulation differs across countries, regions, and income groups.

Another strand of literature has shown that capital stringency is less effective when certain aspects of markets are present. Agoraki *et al.* (2011) and Lee and Lu (2015) argue that regulatory capital only reduces bank risk for banks with relatively small market power. For banks with strong market power, the effectiveness of such regulation can be minimal or, in extreme cases, reversed (Agoraki *et al.*, 2011). On a similar note, Behr *et al.* (2010) argue that to be able to achieve the desired effect of regulatory capital, market concentration has to be low. Similarly, Laeven and Levine (2009) reveal that the effectiveness of capital requirements depends on bank ownership concentration. They explain that the more concentrated the ownership, the greater the bank's incentives to take on higher risks to offset utility losses imposed by capital requirements. Camara *et al.* (2013)

argue that the different responses to higher capital requirements are ascribed to the differences in capital levels among banks. Well-capitalized banks, with capital ratios above the minimum required, adjust their risk and capital in the same direction, whereas poorly capitalized banks (below the minimum required) reduce their risky assets portfolio to comply with regulatory capital ratios.

Furthermore, empirical evidence on the effect of regulatory capital on bank profitability is not conclusive on the matter. Several studies show that regulatory compliance seemed to improve bank profits (Coccorese and Girardone 2017; Berger and Bouwman, 2013; Bitar *et al.*, 2016; Kundid and Pavic, 2021; Swamy, 2018), while other studies find that, on the contrary, regulatory capital diminishes bank profitability (Goddard *et al.*, 2010; Chishty, 2011). Other studies find that regulatory pressure has no effective impact on bank profitability (Ngo, 2006).

Berger and Bouwman (2013) analyzed the implications of higher capital on bank performance, using a sample of U.S.-based banks during the financial crises. They document a positive relationship between capital and bank profitability. In Europe, Goddard *et al.* (2004) investigated the determinants of European banks' profitability, using cross-sectional data during the 1990s. The results showed that capital requirements improved bank profitability. Along the same line, Kundid and Pavic (2021) investigated the relationship between our key variables, using a sample of 24 commercial banks from the Croatian banking sector between 2011 and 2016. They document a positive and strong association between regulatory capital and profitability, consistent with the capital buffer theory when using return on assets and net interest margin as bank profitability indicators. However, the relationship does not hold with return on equity as a profitability indicator. In Asia, Swamy (2018), using a sample of Indian commercial banks between 2002 and 2011, examined the effect of new capital regulations under Basel III proposals on Indian banks' profitability. He finds that an increase in the ratio of capital to risk-weighted assets has a positive impact on bank profitability. Similarly, Le and Nguyen (2020) examined the relationship between capital and bank profitability, using a sample of 30 Vietnamese banks between 2007 and 2019, and found a positive association between capital and profitability. Notably, they documented an inverted U-shaped relationship with the bank capital ratio. The relationship is more significant for highly profitable banks than for less profitable ones. In Africa, Madugu *et al.* (2019) argue that capital requirements reduced bank profitability in Ghana. Ajayi *et al.* (2019) find a strong and positive association between capital and the profitability of Deposit Money Banks (DMBs) in Nigeria. They recommend that policymakers should focus on capital adequacy, as well as monitoring and evaluating its implications on the banking industry in Nigeria.

Nevertheless, several other studies have reported that regulatory requirements had no significant impact on bank profitability. Ngo (2006) showed no significant relationship between capital and profitability. Similarly, De Bandt *et al.* (2018) used a sample of 25 French banks for the period 2007–2014 to investigate the effect of higher capital requirements on bank profitability. They report that French banks were unfazed by higher capital restrictions.

Thus, we develop the following three hypotheses:

- **Hypothesis 1:** Regulatory capital has a negative impact on bank profitability.
- **Hypothesis 2:** Regulatory capital follows a "U-shaped" form.
- **Hypothesis 3:** Regulatory capital has a positive impact on bank stability (negative impact on bank risk).

3. Empirical Investigation

3.1. *Sample selection and data sources*

We start with a sample encompassing the 11 banks listed on the Tunisian stock exchange. However, we decided to exclude one bank due to extreme underperformance, which may cause a problem of outliers. We use a final sample of 10 Tunisian banks, relevant to the period 2005–2020. The rationale behind our sample choice is that these 10 banks provide 80% of financing to the economy. Thus, the type of data used for this study is a balanced panel dataset. Our study period covers periods of boom and bust in the Tunisian economy and growth in bank balance sheets. Our data are hand-collected from different but complementary sources from bank annual reports, statistics provided by the Financial Market Council (CMF), and the annual reports of Association Professionnelle Tunisienne des Banques et des Etablissements Financiers (APTBEF). We also used data provided by the CBT and the World Bank to further enhance the quality of our data.

3.2. *Dependent variables*

3.2.1. *Return on average assets (ROAA)*

Following Chen *et al.* (2018), we use the return on average assets to proxy for bank profitability. Hence, we compute ROAA as the ratio of net income to average total assets. This ratio indicates the asset intensity of each bank. A high ROAA signifies that the bank has a higher asset intensity and vice versa.

$$ROAA = \frac{Net\ income}{Average\ total\ assets}$$

3.2.2. *Z-score*

Z-score is a measure of bank stability and an inverse measure of bank risk-taking. The value given after computing our Z-score for each bank can be highly skewed. Therefore, we use the natural logarithm of Z-score. We will refer to the natural logarithm of banking Z-score as a Z-score in the remaining of this thesis. We also compute the standard deviation of ROA using 3-year rolling windows. By using the 3-year rolling window scale, instead of the full sample period, we allow time variation of the standard deviation and give a more accurate estimation of bank risk in each year (Beck *et al.*, 2013). Several papers multiply Z-score by -1 to get an appropriate measure of the bank's risk-taking (Ashraf, 2017; Mourouzidou-Damtsa *et al.*, 2017). We keep the value given by the Z-score measure but provide the inverse interpretation for the relationship between regulatory capital and bank risk. A high level of Z-score indicates that the bank is considered to be a low-risk bank, meaning that it has to go through several drops in its profits to fall into insolvency. Likewise, a low level of Z-score indicates that bank risk is high. Z-score is computed as follows:

$$Z\text{-}score = \frac{ROA + CAR}{\sigma ROA}$$

3.3. *Independent variables*

We use the Basel minimum capital adequacy ratio as a proxy for regulatory requirements. The ratio is calculated by summing Tier 1 and Tier 2 capital and dividing by the risk-weighted assets (RWA). Several empirical studies have also used the ratio of capital to risk-weighted to account for regulatory imposed capital (Adjeitsey, 2015; Afriyie and Akotey, 2013). We follow the methodology of Le and Nguyen (2020), whereby they use the square value of bank regulatory capital to test if the relationship is nonlinear and increases profits up to a threshold, before dropping afterward. This is commonly referred to as a "U-shaped" form. If regulatory capital is, indeed, nonlinear and follows a "U-shaped" form, this reveals serious implications of regulatory decisions on bank behavior. Bank managers claim that capital regulation reduces bank profitability due to social costs.

3.4. *Control variables*

- *Bank-specific characteristics*
  - **Size:** We use the number of operating branches to account for bank size. The rationale for using this proxy for bank size is that by using the natural logarithm of total assets, we fall into multicollinearity problems when two or more explanatory variables are highly correlated and render our estimation spurious. Large banks, at least in the Tunisian context, tend to open more branches.
  - **Net interest margin:** We use the ratio of net interest margin to total loans to measure the interest-based activity of Tunisian banks.
  - **Liquidity risk:** To proxy for bank liquidity risk, we follow Carsemar *et al.* (2021) and use the ratio of Loan to Deposits (LTD). This ratio measures how much loans are being financed by depositors' funds and can predict the potential liquidity risk a bank can face in a situation of a bank run.
  - **Credit risk:** We use the ratio of Loan Loss Reserves (LLR) in Model 1 since loan loss reserves are deducted from bank profits and directly impact bank profitability. We use the ratio of NPLs to total loans (NPL) in Model 2 to account for asset quality

because we believe that NPLs have a stronger impact on the overall risk and stability of a bank.

- **Cost efficiency:** We use the ratio of operating costs, which consists mainly of labor costs to total operating income, to account for bank inefficiency.
- **Lending policy:** Lending policy refers to the bank's strategic choices when it comes to its growth and development. In our models, we use asset growth to proxy for bank lending policy.
- **Diversification:** We use the ratio of non-interest income to total operating income (DIVER) in Model 1. This ratio provides information about the bank's income structure but also showcases the weight of non-traditional income. We use the ratio of net commissions to payroll and benefits expenditure (COMOP) to account for diversification in Model 2. This is because banks are more likely to sustain their normal activity if they are able to meet their short-term financial obligations, including payroll and benefits.

- *Macroeconomic conditions*
  - **Political instability:** We use the score of political stability provided by the World Bank multiplied by (-1) to assess the impact of political instability on bank profitability and stability.
  - **Business cycle:** We use real GDP per capita growth rate to account for the business cycle. Real GDP growth is generally used to measure economic growth and to assess the business cycle.
  - **Inflation:** We use the yearly inflation rate to account for inflation.

Because we believe that the effect of liquidity and credit can take some time to affect bank stability and profitability, we use the one-period lagged of each proxy. Using lagged values of independent variables is also empirically justified because it can reduce the possible impact of reverse causality in our empirical models.

3.5. *Model specification*

We construct two models to investigate the relationship between regulatory capital and ROAA and Z-score, along with other control variables. Since this study uses panel data, we will present two statistical methods: fixed effect OLS and GLS.

We also include the regulatory capital variable squared to test whether the relationship is nonlinear. Therefore, our first model will be written as follows:

$$\begin{aligned}\text{ROAA}_{it} = {} & \alpha + \beta_1\text{CAP}_{it} + \beta_2\text{CAP}^2_{it} + \beta_3\text{CTI}_{it} + \beta_4\text{SIZE}_{it} \\ & + \beta_5\text{AG}_{it} + \beta_6\text{LLR}_{it-1} + \beta_7\text{LTD}_{it-1} + \beta_8\text{RENDC}_{it} \\ & + \beta_9\text{DIVER}_{it} + \beta_{10}\text{POL}_t + \beta_{11}\text{INF}_t + \beta_{12}\text{GDP}_t + \epsilon_{it}\end{aligned} \tag{1}$$

Our second model will be written as follows:

$$\begin{aligned}Z\text{-score}_{it} = {} & \alpha + \beta_1\text{CAP}_{it} + \beta_2\text{GCP}_{it} + \beta_3\text{CTI}_{it} + \beta_4\text{SIZE}_{it} \\ & + \beta_5\text{AG}_{it} + \beta_6\text{NPL}_{it-1} + \beta_7\text{LTD}_{it-1} + \beta_8\text{ROAA}_{it} \\ & + \beta_9\text{COMOP}_{it} + \beta_{10}\text{POL}_t + \beta_{11}\text{INF}_t \\ & + \beta_{12}\text{GDP}_t + \epsilon_{it}\end{aligned} \tag{2}$$

where a $Z\text{-score}_{it}$ is our stability proxy, CAP_{it} is the regulatory capital, GCP_{it} is the growth rate of bank capital, LTD_{it-1} is the lagged value of loan to deposit ratio, NPL_{it-1} is the lagged value of NPLs to total loans, ROAA_{it} is the return on average assets, SIZE_{it} is the number of operating branches, CTI_{it} is the cost to income ratio, AG_{it} is the asset growth rate, COMOP_{it} is the ratio of net commissions over operating income, POL_t is the political instability score, INF_t is the inflation ratio, and GDP_t is the real growth rate.

4. Results and Discussion

First, we test the presence of multicollinearity by following the same method recommended by Wooldridge (2015) in which he considers the existence of multicollinearity if the correlation coefficient between two variables is greater than 0.7. All the correlation coefficients are less than 0.7, suggesting a low chance of multicollinearity bias in our estimations.

4.1. Descriptive statistics

There are 160 observations from 10 Tunisian commercial banks listed on the stock exchange over a 16-year period. Table 1 displays the descriptive statistics of the key variables included in the two models. As noted by several other studies, we witness some variations in the mean and standard deviation of the variables (Ashraf, 2017; Chen *et al.*, 2018).

We note that the mean values presented in Table 1 characterizing banks are generally larger than their median, which indicates that in our sample, smaller and medium-sized banks outnumber large banks.

The financial stability of the Tunisian banking industry, measured by the Z-score, has an average value of 3.51 with a standard deviation of 3.43 and quite a significant gap between the minimum value of −16.12 and the maximum value of 10.08.

Table 1. Descriptive statistics.

Variable	Obs.	Mean	Std. Dev.	Min.	0.25	Median	0.75	Max.
Z-score	160	3.51	3.43	−16.12	3.44	3.93	4.67	10.08
ROAA	160	0.01	0.011	−0.05	0.00	0.01	0.02	0.04
CAP	160	0.11	0.04	−0.06	0.10	0.11	0.13	0.22
GCP	159	0.11	0.17	−0.32	0.01	0.08	0.17	0.99
CTI	160	0.47	0.11	0.25	0.39	0.47	0.53	0.84
SIZE	160	130.5	35.42	39	103.5	125.5	150	207
AG	150	0.08	0.07	−0.08	0.03	0.08	0.13	0.25
LLR	160	0.51	0.17	0.06	0.43	0.53	0.61	0.95
LTD	160	1.10	0.15	0.65	0.97	1.12	1.20	1.45
COMOP	160	0.51	0.15	0.24	0.40	0.49	0.61	0.91
RENDC	160	0.07	0.01	0.05	0.06	0.07	0.08	0.10
NPL	160	0.17	0.11	0.06	0.09	0.13	0.20	0.57
DIVER	160	0.46	0.12	0.22	0.37	0.44	0.51	0.77
INF	160	0.05	0.01	0.01	0.04	.044	0.06	0.08
GDP	160	0.01	0.03	−0.09	0.00	0.02	0.03	0.06
POL	160	0.49	0.48	−0.21	−0.04	0.68	0.89	1.14

Notes: Z-score: bank stability; ROAA: return on average assets; CAP: regulatory capital ratio; GCP: growth rate of capital; CTI: cost to income ratio; SIZE: the number of operating branches banking; AG: asset growth ratio; LLR: loan loss reserves; LTD: loan-to-deposit ratio; COMOP: net commissions to operation costs ratio; RENDC: net interest margin ratio; NPL: non-performing loans ratio; DIVER: non-interest income to total operating income; INF: inflation rate; GDP: real GDP per capita growth rate; POL: political instability.

For our profitability variable, Tunisian bank performance does not stray from the trend witnessed worldwide. Bank ROAA is positive but not very high. The average value of ROA is 1% with a maximum value of 4.4% and a minimum value of −4.5%. This is in line with the average 1% ROA recorded for the banking industry worldwide (Borio *et al.*, 2017). The overall performance of the Tunisian banking industry is attributed to the interest margin charged on loans granted with an average value of 6.83%. Tunisian banks in our sample have an average regulatory capital ratio of 11.32%, much higher than the 10% minimum requirement of the CBT and the 8% minimum requirement of the Basel committee. The median regulatory capital sits at 11.05%. Tunisian banks keep regulatory capital ratios in the range of 10.75–20.70%, except for the years 2013 and 2014, in which a systemically important bank saw its equity drop to negative levels. This implies that Tunisian banks tend to keep a considerable buffer to absorb unexpected losses.

4.2. *The impact of regulatory capital on bank profitability*

Table 2 displays our results for Model 1 in which ROAA is the dependent variable. The fixed effect regressions are presented as a baseline specification from which we depart by examining the Generalized Least Squares (GLS) estimates which control for heteroskedasticity and autocorrelation.

For the first specification, we evidence a positive impact of regulatory capital on bank profitability. This means that regulatory pressure did not curb bank profits. Interestingly, regulatory capital improves Tunisian banks' profitability. Our result confirms the findings of Baker and Wurgler (2013), who interpret these higher realized returns as proxying for higher expected returns *ex ante* and concluded that shareholders in well-capitalized banks require higher returns. This can also be ascribed to the fact that since banks are constrained to increase capital commensurately with their risk-weighted assets, they increase the monitoring and screening of their borrowers in order to select the most solvent borrowers who are able to pay back the principal borrowed with interest (Altunbas *et al.*, 2007). Our

Table 2. Estimation using OLS and GLS for ROAA.

	(1) Fixed Effects ROAA	(2) GLS ROAA	(3) Random Effects ROAA	(4) GLS ROAA
CAP	0.067***	0.066***	0.113***	0.119***
	(0.017)	(0.013)	(0.027)	(0.023)
CAP^2			−0.304**	−0.308***
			(0.128)	(0.111)
CTI	−0.038***	−0.032***	−0.032***	−0.033***
	(0.01)	(0.003)	(0.006)	(0.003)
SIZE	0.032***	0.013***	0.013***	0.012***
	(0.005)	(0.002)	(0.003)	(0.002)
AG	0.019**	0.009***	0.024***	0.008**
	(0.009)	(0.003)	(0.008)	(0.003)
LLLR	0.002	0.013***	0.01***	0.011***
	(0.005)	(0.003)	(0.004)	(0.003)
LLTD	−0.024***	−0.009***	−0.012***	−0.008***
	(0.007)	(0.002)	(0.004)	(0.002)
RENDC	0.252***	0.079**	0.23***	0.085**
	(0.077)	(0.036)	(0.063)	(0.036)
DIVER	−0.058	0.168***	0.143**	0.158***
	(0.165)	(0.042)	(0.072)	(0.042)
POL	−0.001	−0.002**	−0.004***	−0.002**
	(0.002)	(0.001)	(0.002)	(0.001)
INF	0.028	0.029	0.037	0.027
	(0.041)	(0.02)	(0.042)	(0.02)
GDP	0.046***	0.027***	0.022	0.023***
	(0.016)	(0.008)	(0.016)	(0.008)
cons	−0.128***	−0.057***	−0.067***	−0.055***
	(0.026)	(0.011)	(0.016)	(0.011)
Obs	150	150	150	150

Note: Standard errors are in parentheses $^{***}p < 0.01$, $^{**}p < 0.05$, $^{*}p < 0.1$.

result contrasts with the expected income theory, in which capital requirements are thought to reduce bank profitability.

Furthermore, the coefficient of regulatory capital squared (CAP^2) in regression (4) is negative and statistically significant. This finding confirms the view that stringent capital requirements help improve bank profitability, up to a certain threshold. After that, an increase in capital is more likely to reduce bank profitability. This is commonly referred to as a "U-shaped" form relationship. Le and Nguyen (2020) have also documented a U-shaped relationship between bank capital requirements and bank profitability.

Moreover, the coefficient of cost inefficiency is negative and significant. This finding is consistent with the view that efficient management provides banks with the opportunity to improve their profitability. Hence, as conventional wisdom posits, efficient use of labor can only positively affect bank profits (Bourke, 1989; Khediri and Ben-Khedhiri, 2011). We also find that size is positively correlated with profitability. Our findings are in line with the size–profitability hypothesis, whereby larger banks benefit from economies of scale and scope, which in turn lead to higher profits (Le and Nguyen, 2020; Zhang *et al.*, 2008). The positive association between size and bank profitability in the Tunisian context can also be explained by the "stewardship theory", which suggests that managers' interests align with those of the bank owners. Based on this argument, bank profitability will benefit managers as well as bank owners (Donaldson and Davis, 1991; Davis *et al.*, 1997). We use asset growth to proxy for bank growth strategy and lending policy. We document a positive relationship between asset growth and bank profits. This can be explained by the fact that growth in assets translates to higher interest income, which in turn leads to improved profitability.

We find the coefficient of the net interest margin ratio (RENDC) to be positive and significant. This result is expected since Tunisian banks' profitability generally stems from their traditional interest-based activities. In addition, the coefficient for our diversification variable is positive and statistically significant. This means that higher diversification entails higher returns. This finding is in line with the findings of Kohler (2015), Ahamed (2017), and Li (2021), who documented a positive association between diversification and bank profitability.

Interestingly, credit risk has a positive and significant coefficient. This can be explained by the risk–return hypothesis under which bank shareholders expect to be compensated with higher returns for the increases in risk. The coefficient of the liquidity risk variable is negative and significant. This implies that liquidity risk negatively affects bank profitability. This can be explained by the fact that illiquid banks face higher funding costs, which in turn reduce their profitability. Our findings are in line with the findings of Bassey and Moses (2015), who also document a negative impact of liquidity risk on bank profitability.

For macroeconomic conditions, political instability negatively affects economic growth and foreign direct investment, which in turn would lead to less lending and lower profits. Moreover, we observe that the coefficient of real GDP per capita is positive and significant for our first model. This implies that economic growth stimulates bank profitability. We also document a non-significant relationship between inflation and bank profitability. Our findings are in line with that of Jokipii and Monnin (2013), who also found no clear evidence of inflation on profitability.

4.3. *The impact of regulatory capital on bank risk (stability)*

Table 3 displays the results for Model 2, in which Z-score is the dependent variable. The fixed effect regressions are presented as a baseline specification from which we depart by examining the Generalized Least Squares (GLS) estimates which control for heteroskedasticity and autocorrelation.

We find a positive and significant relationship between regulatory capital and bank stability. This implies that regulatory capital boosts Tunisian banks' solvency. This result may be ascribed to the constant effort of Tunisia's regulatory bodies, headed by the CBT, to ensure the resilience of the Tunisian banking industry through recapitalization. Another explanation is that higher regulatory capital increases shareholders' "skin in the game", in turn improving bank efficiency in terms of screening and monitoring of borrowers. Another possible explanation is that managers tend to work harder to offset the negative impact of the social costs of capital financing by generating more profits through the expansion of their income sources and asset growth. The coefficient of the capital growth rate (GCP) is negative and significant. This implies that regulatory capital can also take a "U-shaped" form and increase bank risk-taking and instability. This can also signal that regulatory capital is close

Table 3. Estimation using OLS and GLS for Z-score.

	(1) Fixed Effects Z-score	**(2) GLS Z-score**
CAP	0.546^{***} (0.069)	0.045^{***} (0.001)
GCP	-0.023^{**} (0.01)	-0.001^{***} (0)
CTI	0.039 (0.043)	0.074^{***} (0)
SIZE	-0.117^{***} (0.029)	0.008^{***} (0)
AG	0.087^{***} (0.031)	-0.009^{***} (0)
LNPL	-0.089^{***} (0.027)	-0.071^{***} (0)
LLTD	0.035^{*} (0.02)	0.019^{***} (0)
ROAA	1.545^{***} (0.317)	0.676^{***} (0.002)
COMOP	−0.02 (0.027)	0.05^{***} (0)
POL	0.011 (0.007)	-0.009^{***} (0)
INF	0.074 (0.151)	0.012^{***} (0)
GDP	−0.064 (0.077)	0.057^{***} (0)
cons.	0.701^{***} (0.181)	-0.085^{***} (0.001)
Obs.	160	160

Note: Standard errors are in parentheses $^{***}p < 0.01$, $^{**}p < 0.05$, $^{*}p < 0.1$.

to the threshold which would inverse the relationship between capital requirements and bank risk. We test the nonlinearity hypothesis later in our robustness tests.

Moreover, the results show a positive and significant coefficient of the Cost-to-Income (CTI) ratio. This implies that cost inefficiency has a negative effect on bank risk and a positive effect on bank stability. One possible explanation for this is that Tunisian banks are investing in skilled staff who would potentially improve their stability and decrease their risk exposure through better screening and monitoring of borrowers in the long run. Our finding is in contrast with the result documented by Alber (2017) and Dutta and Saha (2021) whose findings show a positive and significant association between efficiency and stability, as well as with that of Yakubu and Bunyaminu (2021) who do not find any significant association between efficiency and bank stability.

We report a positive effect of size on bank stability, hence a negative effect on bank risk. This can be justified by the fact that larger banks tend to benefit from greater investment opportunities, greater negotiating powers, and economies of scale and scope, which reduce their probability of default. Le Nguyen (2020) explains that large banks tend to be more profitable and have lower bankruptcy costs, which generally foster bank stability and reduce their default risk. Our finding is consistent with those of De Haan and Poghosyan (2012), who also document a positive association between size and bank stability. However, it is in contrast to past literature documenting a negative relationship between size and stability (Altaee *et al.*, 2013; Laeven *et al.*, 2014; Kohler, 2015; Ali and Puah, 2018).

We find that credit risk is negatively associated with bank stability. This finding is in line with economic logic since an accumulation of NPLs can deplete a bank's capital and render a bank insolvent. This finding is in line with Ghenimi *et al.* (2017), who find that credit risk is positively correlated to bank instability because it is associated with higher probabilities of default. Interestingly, the coefficient of our liquidity risk variable is positive and significant. This can be explained by the fact that our ratio also takes account of the lending activity of the bank financed by the cheapest form of liability, which is depositors' funds. This finding is in contrast with that of Ghenimi *et al.* (2017) and Ali and Puah (2019).

We find that profitability is positive and significant. This finding is to be expected because profitability increases bank capital via retained earnings, which boosts bank stability and reduces bank insolvency risk. This result contradicts the one obtained by Srairi (2013) and Imbierowicz and Rauch (2014), who found a negative effect of ROA on banking stability. In addition, we find that diversification is positively associated with bank stability. This implies that diversification has helped Tunisian banks mitigate their risk of insolvency. Our findings are in line with past literature that documented a positive relationship between diversification and bank stability (Litan, 1985; Wall and Eisenbeis, 1984; De Jonghe, 2010), although in contrast to literature that documented the adverse effect of diversification (Lepetit *et al.*, 2008; Abedifar *et al.*, 2013).

Furthermore, we document a negative (positive) relationship between asset growth and stability (risk). This confirms empirical wisdom that associated rapid asset growth with increase in risk. Our findings are in line with those of Abedifar *et al.* (2013), which show that asset growth is associated with higher risks and reduced bank stability.

For macroeconomic conditions, we find that the coefficient of the political instability variable is negative and significant. This implies that political instability increased bank risk of insolvency since it negatively affects the banks' main source of income, which is heavily influenced by market conditions. The coefficient of real GDP per capita is positive and significant in the risk model. This implies that economic growth boosts bank stability. Contrary to Model 1, we document a positive (negative) relationship between inflation and bank stability (risk) for Model 2. This finding is in line with that of Yakubu and Bunyaminu (2021), who also document a positive relationship between inflation and bank stability.

5. Robustness Check

For robustness, we re-estimate Models 1 and 2 using a dynamic approach. Studies have shown that most economic and financial relationships are dynamic. Dynamic models differ from static models in respect of the presence of lagged dependent variables among the other independent variables.

Bank profitability tends to persist due to the influence of long-lasting economic shocks and market conditions (Berger *et al.*, 2000). On these grounds, it is reasonable to expect the relationship to be dynamic and adopt a model in which lagged profitability variables are included. We also test whether bank stability can showcase a persistence effect and if regulatory capital can have a "U-shaped" form relationship with stability (risk taking), like that reported in our profitability model.

The least squares estimation technique produces biased and inconsistent coefficients when lagged dependent variables are present and dynamic relationships need to be modeled using dynamic appropriate techniques, such as the Generalized Method of Moments (GMM) and Two-Stage Least Squares (2SLS) regression analysis. However, Judson and Owen (1999) performed Monte Carlo simulation to test the bias in the coefficient in least squares estimation and found that the bias tends to approach zero when T increases. For the sake of caution, however, we perform our robustness test using the Two-Stage Least Squares (2SLS) regression analysis. We chose this estimation

Table 4. Durbin–Wu–Hausman test for endogeneity.

	ROAA	***Z*-score**
Durbin (score) chi2(1)	1.7818	2.2896
p-value	0.6189	0.5145
Wu–Hausman F(1,114)	1.58421	2.0079
p-value	0.6630	0.5708

Table 5. Over-identifying restrictions test.

	ROAA	***Z*-score**
Sargan (score)	1.7818	2.2896
p-value	0.6189	0.5145
Basmann chi2(3)	1.58421	2.0079
p-value	0.6630	0.5708

technique instead of the GMM estimation, since the latter requires "small T, large N" panels, meaning few time periods and many individuals (Arellano and Bond, 1991; Arellano and Bover 1995; Blundell and Bond 1998).

Tables 6 and 7 display the regression results after testing for endogeneity[1] and over-identifying[2] restrictions. Table 6 displays regression results for the 2SLS estimation, in which ROAA is the dependent variable.

The coefficient of the one-period lagged value of ROAA is positive and significant. This implies that Tunisian banks' profitability showcases a persistence effect, meaning that banks that performed well in the past year tend to perform well the following year.

Even though the magnitude of coefficients generated by the 2SLS regression varies from the GLS to some extent, the impact of our

[1]We performed the Hausman endogeniety test to determine whether our regulatory capital ratio variable is endogenous. We use the second and third lags of regulatory capital (CAP) and NPLs' ratio as instruments. We fail to reject the null hypothesis (Table 4), meaning that our regulatory capital variable is exogeneous.

[2]Table 5 reports our over-identifying restrictions test result. We fail to reject the null hypothesis for both of our models. Hence, we can confirm that our instruments are valid.

Table 6. Robustness check using instrumental variable regression using ROAA.

ROAA	Coef.	St. Err.	*t*-value	*p*-value	(95% Conf.	Interval)	Sig.
LROAA	0.205	0.066	3.11	0.002	0.076	0.335	***
CAP	0.086	0.026	3.28	0.001	0.034	0.137	***
CAP^2	−0.239	0.121	−1.98	0.048	−0.475	−0.002	**
CTI	−0.026	0.006	−4.28	0	−0.038	−0.014	***
SIZE	0.01	0.003	3.86	0	0.005	0.016	***
AG	0.029	0.007	4.01	0	0.015	0.043	***
LLLR	0.01	0.004	2.82	0.005	0.003	0.017	***
LLTD	−0.012	0.003	−3.42	0.001	−0.018	−0.005	***
RENDC	0.19	0.06	3.18	0.001	0.073	0.307	***
DIVER	0.116	0.067	1.72	0.085	−0.016	0.248	*
POL	−0.004	0.001	−2.67	0.008	−0.007	−0.001	***
INF	0.041	0.039	1.04	0.298	−0.036	0.117	
GDP	0.03	0.015	2.07	0.038	0.002	0.059	**
Constant	−0.054	0.016	−3.43	0.001	−0.084	−0.023	***
Mean dependent var		0.011	SD dependent var			0.011	
R-squared		0.800	Number of obs			150	
Chi-square		599.776	Prob > chi2			0.000	

Note: $^{***}p < 0.01$, $^{**}p < 0.05$, $^{*}p < 0.1$.

independent variables is basically consistent. All our independent variables have economically reasonable signs. Regulatory capital remains positive and significant. However, the coefficient of the ratio squared is negative. This further confirms the nonlinearity of the capital–profitability hypothesis and is in line with the "U-shaped" nature of the relationship documented in the GLS regression. Table 7 displays regression results of the 2SLS estimation, in which Z-score is the dependent variable. The coefficient of the one-period lagged value of Z-score is not significant. This implies that bank stability or risk-taking does not tend to persist. We find that the coefficient of the regulatory capital ratio is positively correlated with bank stability (negatively correlated with bank risk), which confirms the results of the static model. However, the coefficient of CAP^2 is negative and significant, which further showcases the nonlinearity of the capital–risk hypothesis and is in line with the "U-shaped" nature of the relationship documented in the GLS regression.

Table 7. Robustness check using instrumental variable regression using Z-score.

Z-score	Coef.	St. Err.	t-value	p-value	(95% Conf.	Interval)	Sig.
LZ-score	−0.029	0.044	−0.66	0.508	−0.116	0.057	
CAP	1.409	0.083	16.92	0.000	1.246	1.572	***
CAP^2	−4.824	0.368	−13.11	0.000	−5.545	−4.103	***
GCP	−0.029	0.007	−3.94	0.000	−0.044	−0.015	***
CTI	−0.027	0.021	−1.28	0.200	−0.068	0.014	
SIZE	0.002	0.009	0.24	0.807	−0.016	0.021	
AG	0.04	0.021	1.94	0.052	0	0.08	*
LNPL	−0.042	0.015	−2.76	0.006	−0.072	−0.012	***
LLTD	0.005	0.01	0.50	0.616	−0.014	0.023	
ROAA	0.317	0.193	1.64	0.101	−0.061	0.696	
COMOP	−0.022	0.012	−1.86	0.063	−0.045	0.001	*
POL	−0.002	0.004	−0.51	0.609	−0.01	0.006	
INF	−0.041	0.097	−0.42	0.671	−0.232	0.15	
GDP	0.097	0.043	2.27	0.023	0.013	0.181	**
Constant	−0.047	0.073	−0.64	0.523	−0.191	0.097	
Mean dependent var		0.034	SD dependent var			0.035	
R-squared		0.831	Number of obs			150	
Chi-square		736.145	Prob > chi2			0.000	

Note: $^{***}p < 0.01$, $^{**}p < 0.05$, $^{*}p < 0.1$.

6. Conclusion

Bank capital is considered to be the center of microprudential and macroprudential regulations in banking all over the world. The Basel Accords view capital as the most important target to ensure the resilience and the stability of the financial system. Capital regulation can be considered as the effective medicine to prevent future illness within the financial system. Yet, it is legitimate to ask if the medicine can kill the patient.

Our empirical investigation reveals very interesting findings. First, we find that regulatory capital ratios at first improve bank profitability and reduce bank risk. However, when regulatory pressure reaches a certain threshold, the positive effect of regulatory capital is diminished and regulatory capital may reduce bank profitability and increase risk-taking incentives. This means that the profitability and risk-taking behavior of Tunisian banks is not linear and follows a "U-shaped" form. This implies that bank managers retain some truth in their claims about the social costs of regulatory capital. In addition, we also find that Tunisian banks' performance tends to persist over time. This may insinuate that banks increase their capital by means of retained earnings. However, we do not find evidence of the persistence of bank risk. In addition, we find that diversification has helped mitigate bank risk and that political instability reduced bank profits and increased bank fragility.

Regulators should be able to re-design capital standards in line with the optimal social capital, whereby bank profitability is not compromised and regulators are ensured of the soundness and solvency of banks. However, the optimal social capital is very difficult to determine, due to the complexity of the banking activity and the divergence of interests between regulators and banks. We propose that regulatory authorities include the leverage ratio — equity to total assets ratio — proposed by Basel III and set at 3% as a complement to the regulatory risk-weighted requirements, in order to improve the resilience of the Tunisian banking sector and to curb banks' incentives to engage in regulatory arbitrage. Indeed, since risk-weighted capital ratios are prone to errors and since regulators cannot have full information about the risk portfolio, banks can meet capital requirements without having to raise equity capital considered to have the best loss-absorbing capacity. This behavior has been documented by Jackson (1999), whose findings show that banks, in response to capital requirements, increase their average risk-weighted asset ratio, whereas the leverage ratio kept declining. The U.S., for instance, has kept the minimum leverage ratio — which existed prior to the implementation of the Basel Framework — at 3% for "strong" banks and 4% for other banks. Regulators in the U.S. claim that the leverage ratio is the more binding constraint on bank activities.

We also propose the introduction of contingent capital, otherwise known as "CoCos". Contingent capital is a form of hybrid debt, which converts automatically into equity capital when a trigger event is met. The advantage brought by CoCos is that bank capital increases automatically in situations of distress, providing banks with additional loss-absorbing capacities. Contingent capital provides banks with additional capital in times of need, while also preserving the disciplinary role of debt, since subscribers to CoCos will closely monitor bank compliance. Another advantage of contingent capital is that the

Central Bank of Tunisia can set the trigger conditions of contingent capital, for example, when the leverage ratio reaches a pre-specified limit or when Tier 1 capital requirements are no longer met.

A few limitations in this study can be identified. First, more evidence is needed on the impact of regulatory capital on bank profitability and risk before any generalization of our results can be made. Second, due to data availability, our empirical investigation was only conducted on the 10 major listed Tunisian banks covering the period 1999–2005; hence, the results of this study cannot be assumed to extend beyond this group of banks or to different study periods. The use of only quantitative data — accounting data to be exact — in itself can also be seen as a limitation to some extent, since bank risk and profitability may also depend on other qualitative variables that we did not take into account, which may affect the richness of our research data. Moreover, this study focuses on the banking sector and not the overall financial system, which can be considered both a delimitation and limitation. Another limitation of our study is that we do not consider insurance deposit schemes when determining the relationship between bank risk and regulatory capital. However, the Tunisian Bank Deposit Guarantee Fund started operating in 2018, which is considered too recent to influence bank behavior. We propose, for future research, investigating the impact of an alternative "regulatory capital" Z-score as an indicator for the likelihood that a bank's regulatory capital drops below a given threshold.

References

Abedifar, P., Molyneux, P. and Tarazi, A. (2013). Risk in Islamic banking. *Review of Finance, 17*, 2035–2096.

Adjeitsey, G. (2015). Effect of credit risk exposure on the profitability of rural banks in Ghana, a case of Atwima Kwanwoma rural bank limited. Unpublished MBA thesis, Kwame Nkrumah University of Science and Technology.

Afriyie, H. O. and Akotey, J. O. (2013). Credit risk management and profitability of rural banks in the Brong Ahafo of Ghana. *European Journal of Business and Management, 5*, 24–35.

Agoraki, M., Delis, M. and F. Pasiouras, F. (2011). Regulations, competition and bank risk-taking in transition countries. *Journal of Financial Stability, 7*, 38–48.

Ahamed, M. (2017). Asset quality, non-interest income, and bank profitability: Evidence from Indian banks. *Economic Modeling*, *63*, 1–14.

Aiyar, S., Calomiris, C. W. and Wieladek, T. (2015). How to strengthen the regulation of bank capital: Theory, evidence, and a proposal. *Journal of Applied Corporate Finance*, *27*, 27–36.

Ajayi, S., Ajayi, H. F., Enimola, D. J. and Orugun, F. I. (2019). Effect of capital adequacy ratio (CAR) on profitability of deposit money banks (DMB's): A study of DMB's with international operating license in Nigeria. *Research Journal of Finance and Accounting*, *10*, 84–91.

Alber, N. (2017). Banking efficiency and financial stability: Which causes which? A panel analysis. In Tsounis, N., and Vlachvei, A. (eds.) *Advances in Applied Economic Research*. Springer Proceedings in Business and Economics. Cham: Springer.

Ali, M. and Puah, C. H. (2018). Does bank size and funding risk effect banks' stability? A lesson from Pakistan. *Global Business Review*, *19*, 1166–1186.

Altaee, H. H. A., Talo, I. M. A. and Adam, M. H. M. (2013). Testing the financial stability of banks in GCC countries: Pre and post financial crisis. *International Journal of Business and Social Research*, *3*, 93–105.

Altunbas, Y., Carbo, S., Gardner, E. and Molyneux, P. (2007). Examining the relationship between capital, risk and efficiency in European banking. *European Financial Management*, *13*, 49–70.

Arellano, M. and Bond, S. (1991). Some tests of specification for panel data: Monte Carlo evidence and an application to employment equations. *The Review of Economic Studies*, *58*, 259–277.

Arellano, M. and Bover, O. (1995). Another look at the instrumental variable estimation of error-components' models. *Journal of Econometrics*, *68*, 29–51.

Ashraf, B. (2017). Political institutions and bank risk-taking behavior. *Journal of Financial Stability*, *29*, 13–35.

Baker, M. and Wurgler, J. (2013). Do strict capital requirements raise the cost of capital? Banking regulation and the low-risk anomaly. *National Bureau of Economic Research, Working Paper 19018*.

Barth, J. R., Caprio, G. and Levine, R. (2004). Bank regulation and supervision: What works best? *Journal of Financial Intermediation*, *13*, 205–248.

Bassey, G. E. and Moses, C. E. (2015). Bank profitability and liquidity management: A case study of selected Nigerian deposit money banks. *International Journal of Economics, Commerce and Management*, *3*, 1–24.

Beck, T. and Cull, R. (2013). Banking in Africa. *World Bank Policy Research Working Paper No. 6684.*

Behr, P., Schmidt, R. H. and Xie, R. (2010). Market structure, capital regulation and bank risk- taking. *Journal of Financial Services Research, 37*, 131–158.

Berger, A. N. and Bouwman, C. H. S. (2013). How does capital affect bank performance during financial crises? *Journal of Financial Economics, 109*, 146–76.

Berger, A. N., DeYoung, R., Genay, H. and Gregory F. U. (2000). Globalisation of financial institutions: Evidence from cross-border banking performance. *Brookings-Wharton Papers on Financial Services*, January, 23–120.

Bhagat, S., Bolton, B. and Lu, J. (2015) Size, leverage, and risk-taking of financial institutions. *Journal of Banking and Finance, 59*, 520–537.

Bhattacharya, H. (2013). Capital regulation and rising risk of banking industry: A financial accounting perspective. *Academy of Banking Studies Journal, 12*, 31–59.

Bitar, M., Saad, W. and Benlemlih, M. (2016). Bank risk and performance in the MENA region: The importance of capital requirements. *Economic Systems, 40*, 398–421.

Blundell, R. and Bond, S. (1998). Initial conditions and moment restrictions in dynamic panel data models. *Journal of Econometrics, 87*, 115–143.

Borio, C., Gambacorta, L. and Hofmann, B. (2017) The influence of monetary policy on bank profitability. *International Finance, 20*, 48–63.

Bourke, P. (1989). Concentration and other determinants of bank profitability in Europe, North America and Australia. *Journal of Banking and Finance, 13*, 65–79.

Buser, S., Chen, A. and Kane, E. (1981). Federal deposit insurance, regulatory policy, and optimal bank capital. *Journal of Finance, 36*, 51–60.

Calomiris, C. W. and Berry, W. (2004). Bank capital and portfolio management: The 1930s "capital crunch" and the scramble to shed risk. *The Journal of Business, 77*, 421–455.

Calomiris, C. W. and Kahn, C. M. (1991). The role of demandable debt in structuring optimal banking arrangements. *American Economic Review, 81*, 497–513.

Camara, B., Lepetit, L. and Tarazi, A. (2013). Ex ante capital position, changes in the different components of regulatory capital and bank risk. *Applied Economics*, 45, 4831–4856.

Carsemar, E., Abbam, A. and Queku, Y. N. (2021). Bank capital, liquidity and risk in Ghana. *Journal of Financial Regulation and Compliance, 30*, 149–166.

Chen, Y.-K., Shen, C.-H., Kao, L. and Yeh, C.-Y. (2018). Bank liquidity risk and performance. *Review of Pacific Basin Financial Markets and Policies*, *21*, 1850007.

Chishty, K. A. (2011). The impact of capital adequacy requirements on profitability of private banks in India. *International Journal of Research in Commerce and Management*, *2*, 122–129.

Coccorese, P. and Girardone, C. (2017). Bank capital and profitability: Evidence from a global sample. *Essex Finance Centre Working Papers, No. 19480.*

Corcoran, C. (2010). A reassessment of regulated bank capital on profitability and risk. *The International Business and Economics Research Journal*, *9*, 97–100.

Dautovic, E. (2019). Has regulatory capital made banks safer? Skin in the game vs moral hazard. *ESRB Working Paper No. 91.*

Davis, E. P. (2001). *Banking Soundness — Financial Stability Nexus.* Organiser Financial Stability e-group.

De Bandt, O., Camara, B., Pessarossi, P. and Rose, M. (2014). Est-ce que la structure du capital affecte la profitabilité des banques? Quelques résultats avant et après la crise financière pour les banques significatives en France.

De Haan, J. and Poghosyan, T., (2012). Bank size, market size, market concentration and bank earnings volatility in the U.S. *Journal of International Financial Markets and Institutions and Money*, *22*, 35–54.

De Jonghe, O. (2010). Back to the basics in banking? A micro-analysis of banking system stability. *Journal of Financial Intermediation*, *19*, 387–417.

Devereux, M., Johannesen, N. and Vella, J. (2015). Can taxes tame the banks? Evidence from European bank levies. *Said Business School Working Paper*, *5*, 520–537.

Dewatripont, M. and Tirole, J. (1994). *The Prudential Regulation of Banks.* Cambridge, Massachusetts: MIT Press.

Diamond, D. W. (1984). Financial intermediation and delegated monitoring. *The Review of Economic Studies*, *51*, 393–414.

Donaldson, L. and Davis, J. H. (1991). Stewardship theory or agency theory: CEO governance and shareholder returns. *Australian Journal of Management*, *16*, 49–64.

Dutta, K. D. and Saha, M. (2021). Do competition and efficiency lead to bank stability? Evidence from Bangladesh. *Future Business Journal*, *7*, 1–12.

Elnahass, M., Trinh, V. Q. and Li, T. (2021). Global banking stability in the shadow of Covid-19 outbreak. *Journal of International Financial Markets, Institutions and Money*, *72*, 101322.

Elnahass, M., Marie, M. and Elgammal, M. (2022). Terrorist attacks and bank financial stability: Evidence from MENA economies. *Review of Quantitative Finance and Accounting*, *59*, 383–427.

Ghenimi, A., Chaibi, H. and Omri, M. A. B. (2017). The effects of liquidity risk and credit risk on bank stability: Evidence from the MENA region. *Borsa Istanbul Review*, *17*, 238–248.

Goddard, J., Liu, H., Molyneux, P. and Wilson, J. O. S. (2010). Do bank profits converge? *European Financial Management*, *31*, 35–46.

Goddard, J., Molyneux, P. and Wilson, J. O. S. (2004). The profitability of European banks: A cross-sectional and dynamic panel analysis. *The Manchester School*, *72*, 363–381.

Gopinath, S. (2010). *Macro-prudential Approach to Regulation — Scope and Issues*. St. Louis: Federal Reserve Bank of St Louis.

Hanson, S. G., Kashyap, A. K. and Stein, J. C. (2011). A macroprudential approach to financial regulation. *Journal of Economic Perspectives*, *25*, 3–28.

Hendrickson, J. M. and Nichols, M. W. (2001). How does regulation affect the risk-taking of banks? A US and Canadian perspective. *Journal of Comparative Policy Analysis*, *3*, 59–83.

Hovakimian, A. and Kane, E. J. (2000). Effectiveness of capital regulation at U.S. commercial banks, 1985 to 1994. *The Journal of Finance*, *55*, 451–468.

Imbierowicz, B. and Rauch, C. (2014). The relationship between liquidity risk and credit risk in banks. *Journal of Banking and Finance*, *40*, 242–256.

Jackson, P., Furfine, C., Groeneveld, H., Hancock, D., Jones, D., Perraudin, W., Radecki, L. and Yoneyama, M. (1999). *Capital Requirements and Bank Behaviour: The Impact of the Basel Accord*, No. 1. Basel: Bank for International Settlements.

Jakovljevi, S., Degryse, H. and Ongena, S. (2015). A review of empirical research on the design and impact of regulation in the banking sector. *Annual Review of Financial Economics*, *7*, 423–443.

Jokipii, T. and Milne, A. (2011). Bank capital buffer and risk adjustment decisions. *Journal of Financial Stability*, *7*, 165–178.

Judson, R. A. and Owen, A. L. (1999). Estimating dynamic panel data models: A guide for macroeconomics. *Economics Letters*, *65*, 9–15.

Kahane, Y. (1977). Capital adequacy and the regulation of financial intermediaries. *Journal of Banking and Finance*, *1*, 207–218.

Khediri, K. B. and Ben-Khedhiri, H. (2011). Determinants of bank net interest margin in Tunisia: A panel data model. *Applied Economics Letters*, *18*, 1267–1271.

Kim, D. and Santomero, A. M. (1988). Risk in banking and capital regulation. *Journal of Finance, 43*, 1219–1233.

King, M. R. (2010). Mapping capital and liquidity requirements to bank lending spreads. *BIS Working Paper No. 324.*

Koehn, M. and Santomero, A. M. (1980). Regulation of bank capital and portfolio risk. *Journal of Finance, 35*, 1235–1250.

Kohler, M. (2015). Which banks are more risky? The impact of business models on bank stability. *Journal of Financial Stability, 16*, 195–212.

Kundid N. A. and Pavić, A. (2021). Croatian banks' profitability under capital requirements pressure. *Management, 26* (Special Issue), 17–43.

Laeven, L. and Levine, R., (2009). Bank governance, regulation, and risk-taking. *Journal of Financial Economics, 93*, 259–275.

Laeven, L., Ratnovski, L. and Tong, H. (2014). Bank Size and Systemic Risk. IMF Staff Discussion Note 14/04.

Le, T-D-Q. and Nguyen, D-T. (2020). Capital structure and bank profitability in Vietnam: A quantile regression approach. *Journal of Risk and Financial Management, 13*, 168–181.

Lee, K. and Lu, W. (2015). Do bank regulation and supervision matter? International evidence from the recent financial crisis. *Journal of Financial Economic Policy, 7*, 275–288.

Lepetit, L., Nys, E., Rous, P. and Tarazi, A. (2008). Bank income structure and risk: An empirical analysis of European banks. *Journal of Banking and Finance, 32*, 1452–1467.

Li, X., Feng, H., Zhao, S. and Carter, D. A. (2021). The effect of revenue diversification on bank profitability and risk during the COVID-19 pandemic. *Finance Research Letters, 43*, November 2021, 101957.

Litan, R. E. (1985). Evaluating and controlling the risks of financial product deregulation. *Yale Journal on Regulation, 3*, 1–52.

Madugu, A. H., Ibrahim, M. and Amoah, J. O. (2019). Differential effects of credit risk and capital adequacy ratio on profitability of the domestic banking sector in Ghana. *Transnational Corporations Review, 12*(1), 37–52.

Manlagnit, M. C. V. (2015). Basel regulations and banks' efficiency: The case of the Philippines. *Journal of Asian Economics, 39*, 72–85.

Marcus, A. J. and Shaked, I. (1984). The valuation of FDIC deposit insurance using option pricing estimates. *Journal of Money, Credit, and Banking, 16*, 446–460.

Martynova, N. (2015). Effect of bank capital requirements on economic growth: A survey. De Nederlandsche Bank Working Paper No. 467.

Merton, R. C. (1972). An analytic derivation of the efficient frontier. *Journal of Financial and Quantitative Analysis, 7*, 1851–1872.

Merton, R. C. (1977). An analytic derivation of the cost of deposit insurance and loan guarantees. *Journal of Banking and Finance, 1*, 3–11.

Miller, M. H. (1995). Do the M&M propositions apply to banks? *Journal of Banking and Finance, 19*, 483–489.

Milne, Alistair K. L. (2004). The inventory perspective on bank capital. *Cass Business School Research Paper*, Available at SSRN: https://ssrn.com/abstract=576062 or http://dx.doi.org/10.2139/ssrn.576062.

Milne, A. and Whalley, A. E. (2001). Bank capital regulation and incentives for risk-taking. *Cass Business School Research Paper.*

Modigliani, F. and Miller. M. H. (1958). The cost of capital, corporation finance, and the theory of investment. *The American Economic Review, 48*, 261–297.

Mourouzidou-Damtsa, S., Milidonis, A. and Stathopoulos, K. (2017). National culture and bank risk-taking. *Journal of Financial Stability, 40*, 132–143.

Myers, S. C. (1977). Determinants of corporate borrowing. *Journal of Financial Economics, 5*, 147–175.

Myers, S. C. and Majluf, N. S. (1984). Corporate financing and investment decisions when firms have information that investors do not have. *Journal of Financial Economics, 13*, 187–221.

Naceur, S. and Kandil, M. (2009). The impact of capital requirements on banks' cost of intermediation and performance: The case of Egypt. *Journal of Economics and Business, 61*, 70–89.

Ngo, P. T. H. (2006). A theory of precautionary regulatory capital in banking. *International Review of Finance, 6*, 99–128.

Orgler, Y. E. and Taggart, R. A. Jr. (1983). Implications of corporate capital structure theory for banking institutions. *Journal of Money, Credit, and Banking, 15*, 212–221.

Persaud, A. (2009). A different approach to financial regulation. *Economic and Political Weekly, 44*, 34–37.

Ramakrishnan, R. T. S. and Thakor, A. V. (1984). Information reliability and a theory of financial intermediation. *The Review of Economic Studies, 51*, 415–432.

Rime, B. (2001). Capital requirements and bank behaviour: Empirical evidence from Switzerland. *Journal of Banking and Finance, 25*, 789–805.

Rochet, J.-C. (1992). Capital requirements and the behaviour of commercial banks. *European Economic Review, 36*, 1137–1170.

Samet, A., Boubakri, N. and Boubaker, S. (2018). Does public–private status affect bank risk taking? Worldwide evidence. *Journal of International Financial Markets, Institutions and Money, 53*, 287–306.

Srairi, S. (2013). Ownership structure and risk-taking behaviour in conventional and Islamic banks: Evidence for MENA countries. *Borsa Istanbul Review*, *13*, 115–127.

Swamy, V. (2018). Basel III capital regulations and bank profitability. *Review of Financial Economics*, *36*, 307–320.

Wall, L. D. and Eisenbeis, R. A. (1984). Risk considerations in deregulating bank activities. *Economic Review (Federal Reserve Bank of Atlanta)*, *69*, 6–19.

Wooldridge, J. (2015). *Introductory Econometrics: A Modern Approach*, 6th edn. USA: Cengage Learning.

Yakubu, I. N. and Bunyaminu, A. (2021). Regulatory capital requirement and bank stability in Sub-Saharan Africa. *Journal of Sustainable Finance and Investment*, *9*, 1–13.

Zhang, Z., Jun, W. and Qiong-fang, L. (2008). Impacts of capital adequacy regulation on risk-taking behaviours of banking. *Systems Engineering-Theory and Practice*, *28*, 183–189.

PART II

Systematic Risk and Risk Management

https://doi.org/10.1142/9781800614321_0006

Chapter 6

Banking Stability: The Impact of Financial Sector Heterogeneity on Systemic Risk in Financial Crises and Economic Recessions

Carlos León[*,†,‡], **Zihao Liu**[*,§], **and Luc Renneboog**[*,¶]

[*] *Tilburg University, Tilburg, The Netherlands*
[†] *Financial Network Analytics*
[‡] *carlos@fna.fi*
[§] *liuzihao.connor@gmail.com*
[¶] *luc.renneboog@tilburguniversity.edu*

Abstract

Financial institutions' heterogeneity, a high degree of dissimilarity across multiple dimensions, including business focuses, correlated asset holdings, capital structures, and funding sources, reduces systemic risk. We empirically test this hypothesis using a bank holding company (BHC) level heterogeneity index based on granular balance sheet, income statements, cash flow statements, and off-balance-sheet information for U.S. bank holding companies over a sample period spanning the second quarter of 2000 to the fourth quarter of 2021. We find that the BHC-level heterogeneity negatively correlates with BHC-level systemic risk, SRISK, measured both at the global and local levels. We also construct a sector-heterogeneity index and demonstrate that a reduction of heterogeneity occurred in the U.S. financial sector prior to both the Great Recession (2007–2009) and the COVID-19 Recession, especially for the largest

[§]Corresponding author.

BHCs. As such, a declining level of financial sector heterogeneity may exacerbate the consequences of systemic shocks.

Keywords: Financial institutions, bank holding companies, COVID-19, great recession, FDIC, financial markets, financial crises, economic recessions, heterogeneity, systemic risk, Dodd–Frank

1. Introduction

About a decade and a half after the collapse of Lehman Brothers (September 2008), systemic risk — the risk that many market participants in the financial sector are simultaneously struck by significant losses, which then spread through the economic system — is still not well understood (Benoit *et al.*, 2017; Elliott and Golub, 2022). The complexity of financial networks and the intricacies of interconnectedness brought about by implicit and explicit contracts and financial infrastructure (including payment, securities settlement, remittance, credit reporting, and central counterparty systems) obscure our understanding of systemic risk. The global financial crisis, often called the Great Recession, that commenced in 2007 has set off new explorations into correlated asset holdings in financial institutions and the negative externalities that a build-up in the systemic risk (through contagion effects) can have not only on the financial system but also on the real economy. In the extreme, if there are only homogeneous banks in the financial sector and all banks are exposed to the same tail risk simultaneously due to similar or correlated business focuses, capital structures, asset holdings, lending portfolios, and funding sources, the financial system as a whole can be easily undercapitalized. A systemic crisis in the financial sector may then spill over to non-financial sectors due to, for example, a fall in credit supply from the financial industry.

This chapter focuses on cross-sectional heterogeneity at the bank holding company (BHC) level as a novel resilience factor to systemic risk. We also study the U.S. financial sector's aggregate heterogeneity index and systemic risk. In a systemic crisis, healthy financial institutions can be swept along and fail together with distressed banks unless the government intervenes, possibly at very high costs to the real economy. It goes without saying how important it is to correctly understand the channels that enhance systemic risk. We can then minimize the probability of a downfall of the financial system.

We study the degree of heterogeneity of financial institutions by examining BHCs in the U.S. and find that BHC-level heterogeneity negatively correlates with systemic risk. The BHCs are the top-tier financial holding corporations that directly control one or more depository institutions, such as commercial banks. A BHC often owns other financial institutions, such as hedge funds and insurance companies. Moreover, the public FR Y-9 filings to the Federal Reserve Bank (FRB) of Chicago offer an interesting laboratory to study the multidimensional heterogeneity of financial institutions. The FR Y-9 filings offer granular financial information on BHCs (and include a balance sheet, an income statement, a cash flow statement, and detailed supporting schedules, including a schedule of off-balance-sheet items for each BHC). In particular, there are two steps to construct our BHC-level heterogeneity index. First, we use book information's pairwise Euclidean distance (PED) to calculate the dissimilarity between two BHCs. Second, we use all PEDs of each BHC to the rest of the BHCs in our sample as an input measure for the heterogeneity index at the BHC level. Our heterogeneity index is based on BHCs' granular financial information (365 features) for each quarter from 2000Q2 to 2021Q4 (87 quarters). We use equal weights for each standardized accounting feature as our benchmark case. BHC-level distance is then calculated using the size-weighted average of the PEDs of a BHC to the rest of the BHCs in the U.S.

In the empirical tests, we relate our heterogeneity measure to the widely used systemic risk measure at a BHC level, i.e., the so-called SRISK measure (Acharya *et al.*, 2017; Brownlees and Engle, 2017). The measure can estimate the severity of capital losses of a financial institution in a prolonged recession, such as the Great Recession. The firm-level SRISK measure considers a firm's market information and book information. More specifically, the SRISK incorporates the asset prices and funding liquidity risk by using publicly available information, such as stock prices and quasi-leverage of a firm. The approach is consistent with the stress tests that the banking regulators have performed in the U.S. and Europe on systemically important financial institutions (SIFIs) since 2008.

An increase in our BHC-level heterogeneity measure decreases the BHC-level SRISK. In our baseline case, a 1% (or one standard deviation) increase in the value-weighted BHC-level heterogeneity decreases the systemic risk of the average BHC by approximately 0.2936%[1] (or US$59.3 million)[2] after controlling for BHC characteristics and year-quarter fixed effects. In order to address the right-skewness in the distribution in the systemic risk measures and thus reduce biases of our estimations, we apply an inverse hyperbolic transformation (Bellemare and Wichman, 2020; Norton, 2022). Bank heterogeneity can mitigate systemic risk because correlated asset holdings can expose financial institutions to a similar degree of tail risk and induce contemporaneous failure (an aggregate expected capital shortfall) in the financial sector (Albuquerque *et al.*, 2019; Allen *et al.*, 2012; Duarte and Eisenbach, 2021). In this chapter, we show that the gradual decrease in financial institutions' heterogeneity is an essential factor that should be considered by the supervisory authorities responsible for financial stability. Our measure of BHC-level heterogeneity is economically meaningful and easy to implement.

We capture the heterogeneity in the financial sector by a quarterly index composed by aggregating our BHC-level heterogeneity measures. We document that our size-weighted heterogeneity index shows a higher level of heterogeneity for the financial sector than the equally weighted index, consistent with the literature on bank interconnectedness (Chen, 2022) and herding behavior (Jin Cai, 2022). This signifies that there are a few large banks that are interconnected with many small banks, which tend to mimic peers' investment, funding, and lending portfolios and exploit implicit and explicit government guarantees. In case of financial distress, the government may stimulate large banks to acquire a number of interconnected failing small banks or bail out many small (similar) banks directly.

This chapter contributes to the literature on systemic risk and, more specifically, to the strand of literature proposing systemic risk measurement based on balance sheet information. While over the past decade, the literature has focused on contagion as a consequence of direct interconnectedness among financial institutions, the

[1]The elasticity coefficient is reported in column (5) of Table 3.

[2]In Table 2, one standard deviation of heterogeneity (value-weighted Euclidean distance or VWD — see the following for a definition) equals 3.35, and the mean of the VWD is 20.39. Thus, one standard deviation increase in VWD translates to an increase of 4.82% (3.35/20.39×29.36%) in the average SRISK (of US$1.23 billion), which equals US$59.3 million (4.82% × US$1.23 billion).

research on heterogeneity or homogeneity in the financial sector is only a recent phenomenon (Abduraimova and Nahai-Williamson, 2021; Chu *et al.*, 2020; Duarte and Eisenbach, 2021; Fricke, 2016; Fricke and Roukny, 2020). In line with Duarte and Eisenbach (2021), we find that the effect of heterogeneity on systemic risk can be significant and varies over time. We further contribute to the literature by measuring the effect of heterogeneity on systemic risk by relaxing the assumption that banks are homogeneous (and are similar in terms of asset size, which is one of the most systemic-important factors). Moreover, our heterogeneity measure is based on a granular balance sheet and off-balance-sheet information.

We focus on a "going concern externality", the negative spillover caused by an aggregate expected shortfall or systemic shock in the financial sector which can occur with or without bank runs, and hence do not assume the failure of an individual bank (Hufeld *et al.*, 2017). Acharya *et al.* (2017) and Brownlees and Engle (2017) calculate the systemic expected shortfall of a firm in terms of its likelihood to be undercapitalized conditional on a globally distressed financial system and call the respective systemic expected shortfall "SRISK". Specifically, we focus on how BHC-level heterogeneity can decrease the government's *ex post*-required capital injection ("SRISK") to sustain a well-functioning financial system after a systemic shock. Our results have implications for how macroprudential regulation can be improved by incorporating BHC-level heterogeneity into an *ex ante* systemic risk tax, a CEO incentives' cap, stress tests, or recapitalization of financial firms during systemic crises. We also contribute to the literature that studies financial institutions' indirect connections that are created by the investment, funding, and lending portfolios and by a wide range of other market-based business activities such as proprietary trading, broker-dealer services, and securitization, and — more broadly — a supply of various financial market services, from advisory to hedging. Finally, this chapter also contributes to new insights into the systemic risk during the latest COVID-19 recession (Duan *et al.*, 2021; Elnahass *et al.*, 2021; Trinh *et al.*, 2022).

This chapter also helps explain the amplification mechanisms of systemic risk (Benoit *et al.*, 2017), i.e., how a small shock can lead to significant impacts. A higher heterogeneity at a BHC level can increase the sector resilience and decrease a BHC's contribution to systemic risk. A typical example would be a downside shock to real estate values (Reinhart and Rogoff, 2009a, 2009b; Sufi and Taylor, 2021); financial institutions could be distressed at the same point in time when the downside risks of their homogeneous investment holdings, e.g., mortgage-backed securities (MBS), manifest themselves simultaneously. When financial institutions cannot obtain more liquidity by selling MBS, their financial intermediation is paralyzed, and the aggregate capital supply in the financial markets falls significantly. The negative externalities extend to the real economy (Bongaerts *et al.*, 2021; Mian *et al.*, 2015; Shleifer and Vishny, 1992).

This research may be helpful for macroprudential policymakers, financial institutions, and retail investors as it considers systemic risk from a novel channel (homogeneity) that amplifies the systemic risk during economic downturns. This chapter proceeds as follows: Section 2 defines heterogeneity and systemic risk. Section 3 documents our datasets and empirical measurements (systemic risk, heterogeneity measures, and control variables). In Section 3, we discuss the relation between heterogeneity and systemic risk. We conclude in Section 4 with some policy implications and develop a plan for further research in Section 5.

2. Heterogeneity and Systemic Risk

At the basis of the decreasing heterogeneity of the financial institutions (and the potential increase in systemic risk) lie three reasons: (i) the pursuit of optimal diversification, (ii) rational herding behavior motivated by government guarantees, and (iii) relative performance evaluation (RPE) of bank managers. The first reason for the financial system to become more homogeneous is optimal diversification of financial institutions' investment and funding portfolios without consideration for negative externalities to the whole system, which makes a joint failure of the financial system more likely (Chu *et al.*, 2020; Girardi *et al.*, 2021; Haldane and May, 2011; Wagner, 2010, 2011). A second reason why homogeneity leads to higher systemic risk is rational herding behavior by financial institutions: mimicking their peers' investment or funding decisions leads to holding highly correlated assets or similar risks. Consequently, banks take advantage of expected government bailouts and "too-many-to-fail" guarantees (Altinoglu and Stiglitz, 2022; Farhi and Tirole, 2012; Grieser *et al.*, 2022; Silva, 2019). Even though rational herding behavior may be beneficial in risk-sharing among financial institutions, the likelihood of joint failure increases. This can induce negative externalities to the real economy.

Meanwhile, there is recent literature on a novel source of systemic risk regarding incentive pay for bank managers. This incentive loop could lead to a more homogenous financial sector and increase systemic risk. A financial institution with a relative performance evaluation (RPE) contract for the top managers may invest more in rival firms' correlated asset holdings. Since their variable compensation is benchmarked to the performance of rival firms, the firm manager can lower her pay volatility (Albuquerque *et al.*, 2019; Arifa *et al.*, 2021; Armstrong *et al.*, 2021; Cziraki, 2018; Koudijs *et al.*, 2021).

A few empirical papers on financial institutions' homogeneity and contribution to systemic risk need to be highlighted. Gandhi and Purnanandam (2022) find that U.S. commercial banks become more homogeneous in terms of risk exposures after the implementation of the first stress test under the Dodd–Frank Act in 2013. Their theoretical model and empirical findings raise consistent concerns about the increasing homogeneity in the banking system. They do not find such an increase for non-bank financial firms or non-financial firms. However, the empirical findings focus on bank stock returns without further investigation of systemic risk measures. We contribute to this literature by offering a novel heterogeneity measure and further research on empirical systemic risk measures. We will empirically show that the heterogeneity decreases in the banking sector and answer the question as to whether heterogeneity mitigates systemic risk. Duarte and Eisenbach (2021) briefly discuss the effect of heterogeneity on their systemic risk measure — aggregate vulnerability (AV) — within a theoretical framework. Still, they do not measure heterogeneity directly or separate the effect from the bank size.

Jian Cai *et al.* (2018) studied indirect interconnectedness using syndicated loan portfolios and confirmed that bank-level risk diversification does not consider the whole financial system's negative externalities. In addition, without referring to systemic risk empirically, León (2020) found cross-sectional homogeneity in the Colombia banking sector based on granular balance sheet information without a time series dimension or investigating the negative externalities. In contrast to the above papers testing the systemic risk empirically, our heterogeneity measurement is based on much more granular and refined data with a time dimension. We contribute to the empirical literature by offering a better BHC-level heterogeneity measure based on granular balance sheet and off-balance-sheet accounts (rather than syndicated loan portfolios). We show that the U.S. financial sector has become less heterogeneous over the past decade. Our BHC-level heterogeneity measure negatively associates with BHC-level systemic risk.

3. Data and Measurements

3.1. *Bank holding companies (BHCs)*

We focus on BHCs because they are the most comprehensive type of financial institution and the most significant contributors to the total assets of the financial sector. The BHCs are the top-tier holding corporations directly controlling one or more banks. In addition to commercial banks, BHCs often control other financial subsidiaries, such as insurance companies, securities broker-dealers, and investment banks. A significant parent BHC in the U.S. is usually a universal financial institution with several domestic bank subsidiaries and non-banking and foreign subsidiaries. The BHC can eventually engage in a broad range of financial services, including lending, deposit-taking, insurance, securities dealing and underwriting, real estate, private equity, leasing and trust services, and asset management. Therefore, studies on BHCs also offer insights into the broader shadow banking system (Gelman *et al.*, 2022; Irani *et al.*, 2021). Finally, BHCs are the focus of government supervision. BHCs are required to file FR Y-9C reports, which we obtain from the Bank Regulatory database on the Wharton Research Data Services platform. These public reports contain detailed public financial information, e.g., capital structure, deposit collection, derivative contracts, and employee benefits. Large banks with total assets over US$1 billion starting in the 2015Q1 (with total assets over US$500 million between 2006Q1 and 2014Q4 and over US$150 million before 2006Q1) are obliged to supply FR Y-9C forms.

The financial sector in this chapter is represented by 74 prominent U.S. BHCs that include systemically important financial institutions (SIFIs), such as JPMorgan Chase & Co, Bank of America, and Citigroup. This sample is not only representative but also quite comprehensive. In 2020, the total assets of BHCs (US$19 trillion) stand for about 15.4% of the total assets of U.S. financial institutions (US$123.1 trillion[3]) (that include banks, insurance, capital markets, consumer finance, diversified financial services, mortgage REITs, and thrift and mortgage finance). Meanwhile, this sample of BHCs stands for around 92.7% of the consolidated total assets of all commercial banks (US$20.5 trillion) in 2020.[4]

Since 1986, a total of 3,057 individual items of balance sheet and off-balance-sheet information have been available quarterly for each BHC. However, not all these items are numerical as they also consist of textual notes. Some items are not always available across the whole sample period (e.g., the item BHCAP859 — common equity tier 1 capital is only available since 2014Q1), which is why we drop these variables for calculating our heterogeneity measurements. In order to avoid double accounting for the granular features, we also exclude summary accounts such as total assets and total liabilities from our measures. Instead, we only include the individual accounts without the summarizing accounts. The data cover three recessions (2001, 2008, and the COVID-19 recession in 2020) and three financial crises (the bursting of the dot-com bubble in 2000, the large financial crisis of 2007/8 leading to the Great Recession, and the crisis of 2011). Eventually, we constructed a database with 365 items, available quarterly from 2000Q2 to 2021Q4. The variables, comprising total assets, combined thrift assets, mortgage servicing assets and goodwill, income statement variables such as the sale of common stock, salaries and employee benefits, and other interest expenses, are harvested from the FR-Y9 reports. The report also includes off-balance-sheet items, such as foreign exchange swaps, foreign exchange futures contracts, and equity derivative futures contracts. A more detailed description of the FR-Y9 reports

---

[3]Data source: https://www.statista.com/statistics/421697/financial-institutions-assets-usa/.

[4]Data source: https://www.federalreserve.gov/releases/h8/20220128/.

of BHCs is presented in Appendix 1, and a detailed list of balance sheet and off-balance-sheet items can be found in the Online Appendix.[5]

3.2. *Measurements of systemic risk*

In terms of managing systemic risk, regulators such as the Financial Stability Oversight Council (FSOC)[6] should ensure that potential distress in the financial sector does not stop financial institutions from performing their intermediation functions needed by the real economy. This is not an easy task since systemic risk measurement is still an interdisciplinary challenge that combines insights from banking, microeconomics, macroeconomics, econometrics, and network theory. We denote the "system" as the U.S. financial sector and define "systemic risk" as the risk of undercapitalization of the entire U.S. financial sector, most likely triggered by the bankruptcy of one or more large and interconnected institutions (Berger *et al.*, 2022; Montagna *et al.*, 2020). A financial firm is systemically risky if the firm's distress could lead to a negative externality (high social costs) to the real economy (Benoit *et al.*, 2017; Elliott and Golub, 2022).

As mentioned in the introduction, two strands of literature mainly study systemic risk. The first strand focuses on contagion without a presumption of an aggregate expected shortfall or a systemic shock in financial networks. The central economic insight is that the distress of a BHC at a critical node within the financial network, possibly due to maturity mismatching, could make the whole system collapse (Allen *et al.*, 2012; Allen and Gale, 2000; Chen, 1999; Gorton and Metrick, 2012). This strand of literature is the so-called "runs externality" literature since it does not assume an aggregate expected shortfall or systemic shock but focuses on bank runs triggered by an individual

[5]For a detailed list of items, please refer to our Online Appendix: https://www.dropbox.com/sh/ldu00q0mqewnogz/AACV4jXqDcmBbzR-RZgFMsUka?dl=0.

[6]FSOC was created in the U.S. following the Dodd–Frank Wall Street Reform after the 2007–2009 financial crisis. FOSC has the responsibilities to monitor and address the overall risks to financial stability.

bank failure (Diamond and Dybvig, 1983; Diamond and Rajan, 2001, 2005, 2011; Farboodi, 2021).[7]

The second strand of literature focuses on the "going concern externality". It emphasizes an aggregate expected shortfall or systemic shock, which can occur with or without bank runs in the financial sector. This literature mainly attempts to measure the firm-level contribution to systemic risk conditional on a systemic event based on market prices or macroeconomic indicators. De Jonghe (2010) measures a bank's systemic importance through its tail beta, i.e., the probability of a sharp decline of its stock price conditional on a crash in a banking index. More recently, Tobias and Brunnermeier (2016) used a standard regulatory measure of Value-at-Risk (VaR) to calculate the CoVaR, i.e., the change in the VaR of the overall financial system induced by a single bank being under distress. Acharya *et al.* (2017) and Brownlees and Engle (2017) calculate the systemic expected shortfall of a firm in terms of its likelihood to be undercapitalized conditional on a distressed financial system. They call the respective systemic expected shortfall "SRISK". This measure focuses on cross-sectional characteristics of financial institutions and has been widely used in the literature. For a more detailed literature review on systemic risk measures, please refer to Bisias *et al.* (2012) and Giglio *et al.* (2016).

This chapter is most related to the systemic risk measures based on detailed balance sheet information. Duarte and Eisenbach (2021) construct an index of aggregate vulnerability (AV) to fire sales based on the BHCs' balance sheet information and the "vulnerable bank" framework of Greenwood *et al.* (2015). Compared to the market-based systemic risk measures, balance-sheet-based measures signal increased systemic risk ahead of a crisis (e.g., at least five years ahead for AV). This chapter empirically measures the effect of heterogeneity

[7]The "runs externality" focuses on the externality based on the liability structure of a firm which contributes to the propensity of runs and forced fire sales without a presumption of an aggregate expected shortfall or a systemic shock. It is well-understood that the maturity mismatching can lead to a financial crisis, i.e., financial firms rely extensively on short-term financing such as deposits which induces the risk that the financing of these firms cannot be rolled over when the economy experiences a shock.

on systemic risk with more granular features, and we found opposite results compared to Duarte and Eisenbach (2021). Finally, a new strand of literature applies machine learning methodologies to systemic risk measures (Liu and Pun, 2022).

We use the $\mathrm{SRISK}_{i,t}$ measure (of BHC i at time t) of Acharya *et al.* (2017) and Brownlees and Engle (2017), which is a comprehensive systemic risk measure that merges both market and balance sheet information. $\mathrm{SRISK}_{i,t}$ is defined as the expected capital shortfall of a financial institution conditional on a prolonged and distressing market decline. We mainly use the global model for $\mathrm{SRISK}_{i,t}$ that applies the stress test using the MSCI All-Country World Index decline by around 40% (equivalent to US$100 billion).[8] We also show results based on a domestic version of $\mathrm{SRISK}_{i,t}$ based on a decline of 40% of the S&P 500 Index. $\mathrm{SRISK}_{i,t}$ is one of the most used reduced-form analytical measurements that captures the systemic importance of a financial institution in terms of its contribution to the undercapitalization of the financial system at times of distress. In contrast to a firm's own risk measurement, e.g., expected shortfall ($ES_{i,t}$), which treats institutions' risk in isolation, $\mathrm{SRISK}_{i,t}$ helps the regulator to supervise excessive risk-taking at an institutional level along the systemic risk dimension. For instance, a firm with the highest value of $\mathrm{SRISK}_{i,t}$ contributes most to the undercapitalization of the financial sector during a crisis. This measure hinges on market-based measurements (i.e., equity volatility and correlation of the firm and market returns) as well as balance sheet information (i.e., the size and the degree of leverage of a financial firm). It should be noted that $\mathrm{SRISK}_{i,t}$ captures the tail dependency in a non-causal sense: the calculation is based on the expected value of one endogenous variable conditioned on the value of another endogenous variable. This means that if the financial sector is distressed and cannot function anymore when a substantial economic recession arises, the sector can by itself further worsen the economic downturn.

We gratefully acknowledge that we are allowed to use the NYU Volatility Laboratory (V-Lab)'s Systemic Risk database, which covers 1,218 publicly traded global financial institutions from 72 countries of which 156 are from the U.S. since March 2000. By

[8]There can be different variations of SRISK by applying, e.g., different time horizons, market indexes, and threshold of financial distress.

merging the BHC database and the SRISK datasets, we ended up with an unbalanced quarterly time series of 74 U.S. BHCs from 2000Q2 to 2021Q4.[9]

The $\text{SRISK}_{i,t}$ is a function of a firm's size, leverage, and risk, and it is formally defined as follows:

$$\text{SRISK}_{i,t} = E_t(\text{Capital Shortfall}_{i,t+h} | \text{Crisis Return}_{m,t+1:t+h}) \tag{1}$$

$$\text{SRISK}_{i,t} \approx [k(1 - L_{i,t}) - (1 - k)(1 - \text{LRMES}_{i,t})L_{i,t}]A_{i,t} \tag{2}$$

where m stands for the market index that we use (MSCI All-Country World Index for the global model and S&P 500 Index for the domestic model), k is the prudential level of equity relative to assets (for the U.S., this is an 8% prudential capital ratio), h is the time horizon for the market decline (which we set at 6 months), $L_{i,t}$ is the ratio of the market value of equity to the quasi-market value of assets (defined as $A_{i,t}$) of BHC i at time t (i.e., the book value of total assets plus the market value of equity minus the book value of equity), and LRMES is the Long-Run Marginal Expected Shortfall (i.e., the decline in expected equity value if another financial crisis were to arise). The $\text{LRMES}_{i,t}$ is calculated as follows: $\text{LRMES}_{i,t} = -E_t(R_{i,t+1:t+h} | R_{m,t+1:t+h} < d)$, where $R_{i,t+1:t+h}$ is a multiperiod arithmetic equity return of BHC i between period $t + 1$ and $t + h$, $R_{m,t+1:t+h}$ is a multiperiod arithmetic equity return of the market m between period $t + 1$ and $t + h$, and d is the six-month crisis threshold for the global market with a default value of 40%. The above equations show that SRISK is a function of the size of the BHC, its leverage, and its expected capital shortfall conditional on a systemic event. SRISK is higher for a BHC with a larger size, higher leverage ratio, and higher sensitivity to a systemic event.

Meanwhile, we can use the aggregate bank-level systemic risk to construct a system-wide measure of financial distress (Brownlees and Engle, 2017):

$$\text{SRISK}_t = \sum_i^N (\text{SRISK}_{i,t})_+ \tag{3}$$

[9]Please note that the bankrupt Lehman Brothers Holdings Inc. is not in our sample as it is not included in the Bank Regulatory database.

where $(x)_+$ denotes $\max(x, 0)$ and i and t are the same as introduced above. The aggregate SRISK can be interpreted as the total amount of capital that the government would need to inject into the financial system in order to bailout the distressed financial institutions after a systemic event. This aggregate amount excludes the capital surpluses of BHCs (i.e., negative $\text{SRISK}_{i,t}$), which is a fair approach considering that capital surpluses cannot easily be transferred from interbank loans or following mergers and acquisitions when the market turns very illiquid.

We can observe in Figure 1 that the aggregate SRISK is relatively low after the dot-com bubble because this crisis was mainly in the telecommunications, media, and technology (TMT) sectors. Our sample represents financial institutions that BHCs control. Therefore, our aggregate SRISK measure does not always capture all the systemic events outside the financial sector. The measure focuses on financial firms which are more sensitive to leverage. SRISK reached its highest peak after the Lehman Brothers bankruptcy of September 2008. It stayed high with peaks when the European sovereign debt crisis significantly worsened (June 2010 and October 2011). So, using a sub-sample of the financial institutions, the aggregate systemic

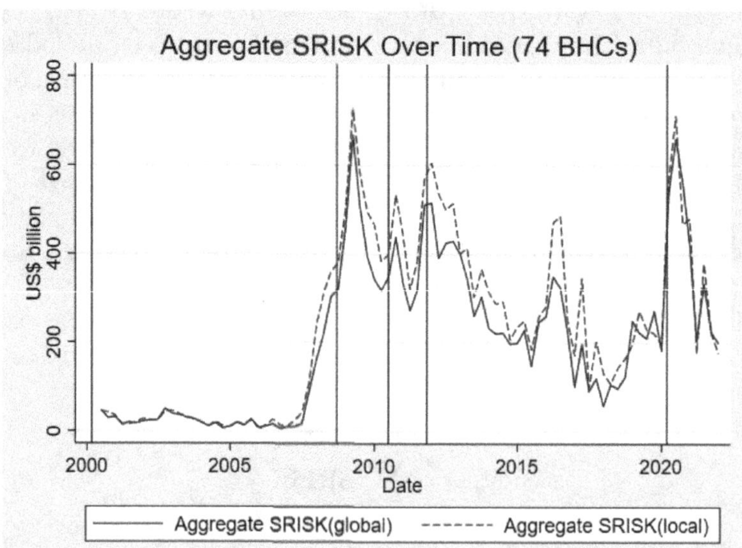

Figure 1. Aggregate SRISK.

risk results capture the significant patterns in the broader sample (95 large financial institutions) of Brownlees and Engle (2017). This indicates that our sample of the 74 largest BHCs (which stand for 15.4% of the total assets of the U.S. financial sector) proxies for the whole financial sector reasonably well and hence also relates to its systemic risk.

During the COVID-19 recession, the aggregate systemic risk reached about the same level as in the Great Recession. Therefore, the COVID-19 pandemic is a systemic-important event worth further attention. Our results are consistent with the latest empirical findings that the pandemic induced an increased systemic risk in the global financial sectors (Duan *et al.*, 2021; Trinh *et al.*, 2022).

Finally, we can see that the overall patterns of the global SRISK and domestic SRISK are almost identical. So, for the rest of this chapter, we will focus the results on the global SRISK for reasons of parsimoniousness. Besides, the level of the domestic SRISK is almost always above the level of the global SRISK. We can interpret that the American BHCs are more sensitive to a decline in the domestic capital market. Nevertheless, we leave a more detailed investigation of the divergence of the two measures for further research.

Figure 1 shows the quarterly time series of aggregate SRISK_t from June 2000 to December 2021, which amounts to 87 quarters. The five vertical lines indicate (i) the peak of dot-com bubble in January 2000, (ii) the bankruptcy of the Lehman brothers in September 2008, (iii) the European sovereign debt crises in June 2010, and (iv) October 2011, and (v) the WHO declaring COVID-19 as a pandemic, respectively.

Finally, we can also interpret the SRISK in terms of a systemic risk share:

$$\text{SRISK}\%_{i,t} = \frac{\text{SRISK}_{i,t}}{\text{SRISK}_t} \text{ if } \text{SRISK}_{i,t} > 0 \tag{4}$$

In Table 1, we show that the $\text{SRISK}\%_{i,t}$ rank is consistent with the systemic importance of financial institutions. For example, Citigroup Inc., JPMorgan Chase & Co, Bank of America Corporation, and Wells Fargo & Company have been the most systemically important BHCs since the demise of Lehman Brothers in the fourth quarter of 2008 (see also Brownlees and Engle, 2017). While at the end of 2016, Wells Fargo & Company and JPMorgan Chase & Co are no longer

Table 1. The SRISK% rankings of the top 10 bank holding companies.

Rank	BHC Name	SRISK (US$ Billion)	SRISK%
2008Q4			
1	Citigroup Inc.	134.67	29.45
2	JPMorgan Chase & Co.	117.25	25.64
3	Bank Of America Corporation	100.84	22.06
4	Wells Fargo & Company	38.58	8.44
5	Pnc Financial Services Group, Inc.	11.21	2.45
6	Suntrust Banks, Inc.	7.63	1.67
7	Regions Financial Corporation	7.22	1.58
8	Capital One Financial Corporation	5.81	1.27
9	Fifth Third Bancorp	5.73	1.25
10	KeyCorp	5.57	1.22
2012Q4			
1	Bank Of America Corporation	99.15	24.78
2	Citigroup Inc.	91.03	22.75
3	JPMorgan Chase & Co.	85.35	21.33
4	Goldman Sachs Group, Inc.	41.35	10.34
5	Morgan Stanley	39.67	9.92
6	Bank Of New York Mellon Corporation	8.59	2.15
7	Suntrust Banks, Inc.	4.96	1.24
8	Capital One Financial Corporation	4.43	1.11
9	Pnc Financial Services Group, Inc.	3.83	0.96
10	Regions Financial Corporation	3.56	0.89
2016Q4			
1	Citigroup Inc.	32.95	32.65
2	Bank Of America Corporation	30.09	29.82
3	Morgan Stanley	16.39	16.24
4	Goldman Sachs Group, Inc.	10.60	10.51
5	Ally Financial Inc	7.37	7.31
6	State Street Corporation	2.83	2.81
7	Capital One Financial Corporation	0.68	0.67
8	Associated Banc-Corp	−0.17	0.00
9	BankUnited, Inc.	−0.37	0.00
10	Valley National Bancorp	−0.37	0.00

Table 1. (*Continued*)

Rank	BHC Name	SRISK (US$ Billion)	SRISK%
2020Q4			
1	Citigroup Inc.	107.77	25.80
2	Wells Fargo & Company	80.47	19.27
3	Bank Of America Corporation	63.41	15.18
4	Goldman Sachs Group, Inc.	37.82	9.06
5	JPMorgan Chase & Co.	37.75	9.04
6	Morgan Stanley	14.00	3.35
7	Bank Of New York Mellon Corporation	11.19	2.68
8	Capital One Financial Corporation	7.39	1.77
9	State Street Corporation	7.26	1.74
10	Ally Financial Inc.	6.80	1.63

as systemically risky as in 2008, the other two BHCs have retained their systemic importance. Meanwhile, Goldman Sachs Group and Morgan Stanley increased their systemic riskiness over our sample period.

Table 1 reports the ranking, the BHC-level systemic risk, and the systemic risk share for each of the top 10 bank holding companies (BHCs) that contributed the most to the aggregate systemic risk in the last quarter of 2008, 2012, 2016, and 2020, respectively. The sample period is from 2000Q2 to 2021Q4. The systemic share $\text{SRISK\%}_{i,t}$ is calculated as follows:

$$\text{SRISK\%}_{i,t} = \frac{\text{SRISK}_{i,t}}{\text{SRISK}_t} \text{ if } \text{SRISK}_{i,t} > 0$$

where $\text{SRISK}_{i,t}$ stands for the daily time series BHC-level systemic risk (based on global model) for each BHC i at the last trading day at the end of quarter t, and the aggregate systemic risk is calculated as $\text{SRISK}_t = \sum_i^N (\text{SRISK}_{i,t})_+$. There are 87 cross-sectional tables whose results are similar to Table 1 and can be found in the Online Appendix.

3.3. *Measurements of heterogeneity*

Various heterogeneity measures quantify the dissimilarity of any pair of BHCs based on their granular balance sheet and off-balance-sheet information. The basic idea is that if two BHCs have different investment, funding, and lending strategies and pursue similar other business activities, such as broker-dealer services, these activities are visible on the granular balance sheet and off-balance-sheet accounts. There is not a single heterogeneity measure that has been singled out in the literature as a superior measure, and Fricke (2016) shows that the Euclidean distance (Jian Cai *et al.*, 2018), generalized Jaccard similarity (Pool *et al.*, 2015), connectedness (Anton and Polk, 2014), and cosine similarity (Falato *et al.*, 2018) measures are highly correlated (at 88% or higher). We therefore start with the Euclidean distance to capture the degree of heterogeneity of any pair of BHCs. The larger the Euclidean distance, the more dissimilar the two BHCs are. While we calculate the Euclidean distance as a measure of heterogeneity, Jian Cai *et al.* (2018) use the banks' syndicated loan portfolios as the basis for the Euclidean distance to calculate their interconnectedness. That choice significantly biases the proximity measurement because syndicated loans are merely a small fraction of a BHC's balance sheet and may not even be the most important systemic factor. In contrast, we include all BHC's activities, on and off the balance sheet. As we cannot cap the Euclidean distance to a range of 0–1 (as do Jian Cai *et al.* (2018) since they use portfolio weights adding up to 1), we use a Z-score measurement (by subtracting the mean of the specific account[10] across BHCs and dividing by its standard deviation) to capture the financial information on the regulatory reports (FR Y-9) of the BHCs and avoid data issues regarding scale or dispersion. This transformation improves the identification of the effects of our heterogeneity measure.

The BHC-level heterogeneity measure, i.e., pairwise Euclidean distance (PED) between BHC i and BHC $j (i \neq j)$, in the following

[10]Balance sheet, income statement, cash flow statement, and supplementing information in the FR Y-9 reports — see Appendix 1.

F-dimension space is

$$\text{PED}_{i,j,t} = \sqrt{\sum_{f=1}^{F}(x_{i,f,t} - x_{j,f,t})^2} \tag{5}$$

where $x_{i,f,t}$ is the standardized feature f in the financial statements at quarter t for BHC i. The distance between the two BHCs is determined by the total value of the squared distance for each item in the financial statements. So, if all the features of the two BHCs are exactly the same, $\text{PED}_{i,j,t} = 0$ (complete feature matching).

The benchmark heterogeneity measure of one BHC to the rest of the BHCs is measured using value-weighted Euclidean distance (VWD). VWD is based on the BHC's total assets and above pairwise Euclidean distance:

$$\text{VWD}_{i,t} = \sum_{j \neq i} x_{i,j,t} \cdot \text{PED}_{i,j,t} \tag{6}$$

where $x_{i,j,t}$ is the weight given to BHC j in the computation of BHC i's dissimilarity. The value weights in the above formula, $x^{VW}_{i,j,t}$, are the value weights between any BHC i and j and n_t is the total number of BHCs at time t such that

$$x^{vw}_{i,j,t} = \frac{a_{j,t}}{\sum_i a_{i,t}} \tag{7}$$

where $a_{i,t}$ is the total asset of BHC i in quarter t. As a robustness check, we will also use equal-weighted Euclidean distance (EWD) where $x^{EW}_{i,j,t}$ are the equal weights such that

$$x^{EW}_{i,j,t} = \frac{1}{(n_t - 1)} \tag{8}$$

and n_t is the number of BHCs in our sample at quarter t. This EWD is a useful benchmark as it enables us to understand whether or not value weighing is important (Duarte and Eisenbach 2021, for instance, do not allow for heterogeneous bank sizes when measuring homogeneity).

3.4. *Control variables*

In principle, we do not need to include the traditional control variables from the BHCs' balance sheets in our empirical analysis to avoid "bad controls" (Ahern and Dittmar, 2012; Cinelli *et al.*, 2021); indeed, our heterogeneity measure already incorporates the detailed book information of the BHCs. Still, as the illiquidity of a systemically important financial institution may matter, several aggregate and cross-sectional factors could explain a firm's "systemicness" (Tobias and Brunnermeier, 2016). It is well known that the bank size and leverage at both the aggregate and the cross-sectional levels are essential to systemic risk (Duarte and Eisenbach, 2021). We therefore include BHCs' total assets to capture that larger firms contribute more to systemic risk and may associate with the "too-big-to-fail" concept (Berndt *et al.*, 2022). We use the equity to total assets ratio as our leverage measure, loans to total assets (including leases) as liquidity measure (Ari *et al.*, 2021), and return on equity (ROE) as profitability. We also include the ratio of deposits to total assets as a proxy for solvency, as in Laeven *et al.* (2016). All control variables are obtained from the Bank Regulatory Database.

4. Empirical Results

4.1. *Summary statistics*

The summary statistics of the systemic risk measures (described in Section 3.2), the proximity measurement (the value-weighted pairwise Euclidean distance ($\text{VWD}_{i,t}$) described in Section 3.3), and the control variables (see Section 3.4) are presented in Table 2 and are based on 5,898 bank-quarter observations for the SRISK series and 5,294 bank-quarter observations for the distance measures ($\text{VWD}_{i,t}$ and $\text{EWD}_{i,t}$ series) over the period 2000Q2–2021Q4. The two samples differ because some public financial institutions are not categorized as BHCs over the entire sample period. For example, the Bank Regulatory database only included Goldman Sachs Group from 2008. The average global $\text{SRISK}_{i,t}$ is around US$1.23 billion which is much lower than the corresponding value, namely, US$25.33 billion, reported by Jian Cai *et al.* (2018) on an international sample. We attribute the differences to the fact that we also consider the most recent decade (2011–2021), during which sufficient capital buffers were accumulated subsequent to the Great Recession. Furthermore, Jian Cai *et al.* (2018) focus on lead arrangers (commercial banks)

Table 2. Summary statistics.

Variable	Obs.	Mean	St. Dev.	Min.	25th perc.	Median	75th perc.	Max.
Systemic risk measures								
Global $SRISK_{i,t}$ (US$ billion)	5,898	1.23	16.37	−131.62	−4.89	−0.45	4.40	153.85
Global asinh ($SRISK_{i,t}$)	5,898	−0.278	1.835	−5.573	−2.29	−0.432	2.187	5.729
Domestic $SRISK_{i,t}$ (US$ billion)	5,995	2.25	17.15	−135.68	−3.77	−0.20	5.85	160.73
Domestic asinh ($SRISK_{i,t}$)	5,995	−0.036	1.825	−5.603	−2.038	−0.196	2.467	5.773
BHC characteristics								
$VWD_{i,t}$	5,294	20.39	3.35	8.42	15.25	21.31	23.55	26.45
$EWD_{i,t}$	5,294	15.18	3.89	10.03	11.88	13.66	22.75	26.13
Total Assets (US$ billion)	5,294	187.22	463.46	0.19	4.87	30.43	391.28	3757.58
Book Equity (US$ billion)	5,294	18.31	44.37	0.02	0.48	3.30	44.48	294.13
Return on Equity (ROE)	5,294	0.06	0.08	−1.99	0.02	0.06	0.13	0.62
Book Equity/Total Assets	5,294	0.11	0.05	0.03	0.07	0.10	0.14	0.92
Loans/Total Assets	5,280	0.59	0.19	0.00	0.32	0.66	0.77	0.96
Deposits/Total Assets	4,993	0.53	0.14	0.00	0.37	0.54	0.69	0.85

of syndicated loans, whereas our sample only includes U.S. BHCs. BHCs have been under increasing regulatory pressure to reduce systemic risk. For instance, the Dodd–Frank Wall Street Reform and Consumer Protection Act was passed in 2010, and the Volcker Rule was enacted on July 21, 2015. Table 2 shows high variation in our $\text{VWD}_{i,t}$ measure; the standard deviation amounts to 3.35. The changes of our heterogeneity index are related to the systemic risk measures. It should be noted, however, that the absolute threshold of an optimal heterogeneity level is not yet well understood (and is only discussed in Engle and Ruan 2018). Therefore, we focus on the relative changes in our heterogeneity index and offer preliminary evidence on the threshold.

Finally, the median of the main dependent variable ($\text{SRISK}_{i,t}$) is negative and right-skewed, whereas our key variable of interest ($\text{VWD}_{i,t}$) only has positive values. Therefore, adjusting the dependent variable by using inverse hyperbolic sine transformation (or arcsinh) is suggested in econometrics literature (Bellemare and Wichman, 2020; Norton, 2022). The arcsinh approximates the traditional natural logarithm but allows retaining zero and negative economic observations. However, the interpretation of the coefficients is not straightforward; in Section 4.2, we follow Bellemare and Wichman (2020) with regard to the interpretations of elasticities.

Table 2 shows the summary statistics of the systemic risk measures. Both global $\text{SRISK}_{i,t}$ based on a 40% decline in the MSCI World Index and the domestic $\text{SRISK}_{i,t}$ based on a 40% decline in the S&P 500 Index are reported as the corresponding normalized systemic risk measures based on inverse hyperbolic transformation following Bellemare and Wichman (2020). We also show the heterogeneity measurements (the value-weighted pairwise Euclidean distance, $\text{VWD}_{i,t}$, and the equally weighted pairwise Euclidean distance, $\text{EWD}_{i,t}$), total assets values, book equity, return on equity, equity ratio, loans to total assets, and deposits ratio. These summary statistics are mainly based on two databases: the Bank Regulatory Database for BHC features and the NYU Volatility Laboratory (V-Lab)'s Systemic Risk database. We create a merged panel dataset of 74 BHCs based on the above datasets and report $\text{SRISK}_{i,t}$ which stands for the systemic capital shortfall for each BHC i at the last trading day at the end of quarter t. The time series consists of 87 bank-quarter observations for 74 unique BHCs (see Appendix 2).

4.2. *Aggregate heterogeneity and systemic risk*

The aggregate heterogeneity indices of the financial sector, both equally and asset-weighted, and the quarterly averages of BHC-level systemic risk ($\text{SRISK}_{i,t}$) are summarized in Figure 2. We see that the overall patterns of the two aggregate indices are similar and that they diverge the most during the 2009 financial crisis. This can be interpreted as bank size being a crucial factor in heterogeneity measures. In the subsequent analyses, we will use the weighted average version of our sector-heterogeneity index for our benchmark analyses. The heterogeneity of the financial sector was low on average prior to the 2009 financial crisis. The weighted VWD index dropped to the lowest level in the first half of our sample period before the bankruptcy of Lehman Brothers and the peak of aggregate systemic risk in 2008. Immediately after the bankruptcy of Lehman Brothers, the heterogeneity index increased significantly and reached its highest level in 2011. Subsequently, there is a decline in the sector-heterogeneity index spanning the past decade. Similar to the decline of our heterogeneity index prior to the Great Recession that commenced in 2008, the index declined to a relatively low level before

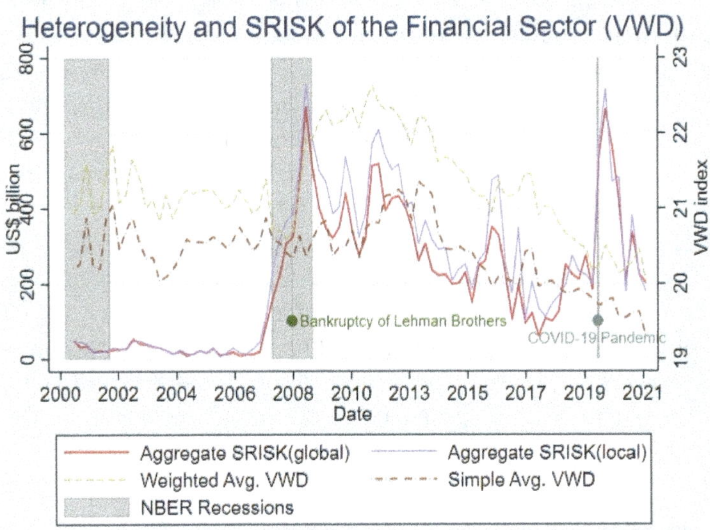

Figure 2. Decreasing heterogeneity of the financial sector.

the COVID-19 recession, which correlates with a peak in aggregate systemic risk in 2020.

From these observations, we can derive two preliminary conclusions. First, the changes in the heterogeneity index are associated with changes in systemic risk. Second, the level of heterogeneity has implications for systemic risk and could be used to identify future crises. The relatively low level of sector heterogeneity prior to the two most recent economic recessions shows some preliminary evidence of a threshold of sector heterogeneity that can trigger economic recessions. The drop in heterogeneity of the financial sector shortly before the bankruptcy of Lehman Brothers can be potentially explained by fire sales and devaluation of common asset holdings, such as mortgage-backed securities (MBS), collateral debt obligations (CDO), and credit default swaps (CDS). Finally, we can see a gradual decrease in the heterogeneity in the financial sector over the past decade, consistent with Gandhi and Purnanandam (2022). Figure 2 implies that a uniform prudential policy without consideration of sector heterogeneity could eventually lead to a homogeneous financial sector and increase systemic risk.

Figure 2 shows the decreasing heterogeneity of the financial sector. The heterogeneity (VWD) is measured by the weighted average of bank-level pairwise Euclidean distance (PED) across bank holding companies (BHCs) based on asset size (yellow dashed line) and equally weighted bank-level PED across BHCs (brown dot-dashed line). The y-axis on the left shows the value of the systemic risk, the y-axis on the right shows the level of the sector-heterogeneity index, and the x-axis shows the time (in years). The gray areas from left to right are the recessions defined by the National Bureau of Economic Research, including the peak of the dot-com bubble in January 2000, the bankruptcy of Lehman Brothers in September 2008, and the COVID-19 recession, respectively. The solid lines capture the level of aggregate systemic risk. The red solid line represents the SRISK based on the assumption of a global recession and the purple solid line is the SRISK based on a domestic recession in the U.S. (Acharya *et al.*, 2017; Brown and Engle, 2017).

4.3. *BHC-level heterogeneity and systemic risk*

This section describes the cross-sectional relationship between the BHC-level heterogeneity measures and systemic risk. We also test which characteristics of BHCs (size, profitability, leverage, solvency, and liquidity) are associated with higher systemic risk by means of a panel regression where we control for the year-quarter and bank fixed effects:

$$\text{arcsinh}(\text{SRISK}_{i,t}) = \alpha + \beta_0 \cdot \text{VWD}_{i,t} + \gamma \cdot \text{Control}_{i,t} + \lambda_t + \omega_i + \epsilon_{i,t} \quad (9)$$

where the dependent variable $\text{arcsinh}(\text{SRISK}_{i,t})$ is the inverse hyperbolic sine transformation of the daily time series of systemic capital shortfall matched with the BHC accounting information at the last trading day in each quarter. The variable of interest $\text{VWD}_{i,t}$ is the quarterly time series of value-weighted pairwise Euclidean distances based on-balance- and off-balance-sheet accounts. In Table 3, we report, in addition to the transformed systemic risk measure, the original values of $\text{SRISK}_{i,t}$ for robustness checks. We also include year-quarter (λ_t) and individual BHC fixed effects (ω_i) and apply robust standard errors by using the Eicker–Huber–White estimator. We conduct a Hausman test to decide between fixed-effect or random-effect models. The Hausman test rejects the null hypothesis that the relationship between the dependent and independent variables is affected by random effects, which is why we opt for fixed-effects models.

Table 3 shows that the control variables do not change much of the model's explanatory power as they could be "bad controls" (Section 4.1); we will mainly discuss the results from the models of columns (1) and (5). Our primary variable of interest, namely, our BHC-level heterogeneity measure $\text{VWD}_{i,t}$, is negatively related to systemic risk (at the 95% level of statistical significance) in column (1), as hypothesized. An increase in VWD by one standard deviation decreases the systemic risk by, on average, around US$0.236[11] billion for the average BHC (or almost 19.2%[12] of the average value of $\text{SRISK}_{i,t}$). The $\text{VWD}_{i,t}$ mean is 20.39 with a standard deviation of about 3.35 in Table 2. This finding is economically significant since, as we can observe in Table 1, an increase of US$0.236 billion raises a BHC's rank of the SRISK% ranking in 2008Q4 (during the Great Recession). For example, Fifth Third Bancorp's SRISK% ranking can

---

[11] $-0.0705 \times 3.35 = -0.236$.

[12] $0.236/1.23 = 19.2\%$.

Table 3. Bank-level heterogeneity and systemic risk.

(US$ billion)	**(1)**	**(2)**	**(3)**	**(4)**	**(5)**	**(6)**	**(7)**	**(8)**
	SRISK$_{i,t}$				**arcsinh(SRISK$_{i,t}$)**			
Key variables								
VWD$_{i,t}$	−0.0705**		−0.0653**		−0.0123***		−0.0103**	
	[0.0304]		[0.0321]		[0.00450]		[0.00472]	
EWD$_{i,t}$		−0.134***		−0.142***		−0.00565		−0.00324
		[0.0361]		[0.0390]		[0.00438]		[0.00461]
Control variables								
Total Assets (TA)	0.0290***	0.0289***	0.0296***	0.0295***	0.00190***	0.00189***	0.00185***	0.00184***
	[0.00306]	[0.00305]	[0.00312]	[0.00311]	[0.000260]	[0.000260]	[0.000262]	[0.000262]
Profitability (ROE)			−7.604**	−7.636**			−1.797***	−1.817***
			[3.542]	[3.575]			[0.631]	[0.632]
Leverage (Equity/TA)			−35.10***	−35.04***			−4.564***	−4.534***
			[7.630]	[7.616]			[0.968]	[0.965]
Liquidity (Loans/TA)			−0.508	−0.273			−0.452	−0.438
			[2.758]	[2.754]			[0.307]	[0.306]
Solvency (Deposits/TA)			−6.132***	−6.602***			0.847***	0.839***
			[1.612]	[1.653]			[0.204]	[0.207]

Calculated (semi-) elasticities								
$\xi(\text{SRISK}_{i,t}, \text{VWD}_{i,t})$	-1.169^{**}		-1.082^{**}		-0.2936^{***}		-0.2475^{**}	
					[0.1077]		[0.1130]	
$\xi(\text{SRISK}_{i,t}, \text{EWD}_{i,t})$		-1.654^{***}		-1.752^{***}		-0.1015		-0.0582
						[0.0787]		[0.0827]
Fixed effects								
Year-quarter	Yes	Yes	Yes	Yes	Yes	Yes	Yes	Yes
Bank-level	Yes	Yes	Yes	Yes	Yes	Yes	Yes	Yes
Constant	-2.863^{***}	-2.233^{***}	4.575^{*}	5.546^{**}	-0.362^{***}	-0.524^{***}	0.0330	-0.134
	[0.820]	[0.804]	[2.720]	[2.689]	[0.104]	[0.0856]	[0.303]	[0.299]
Obs.	4693	4693	4404	4404	4693	4693	4404	4404
Adj. R-squared	0.541	0.541	0.543	0.544	0.616	0.616	0.623	0.622

be replaced by KeyCorp with an increase of US$0.236 billion regarding SRISK. Recall that the SRISK measures the expected capital shortfall at the firm-level conditional on a market crisis.

This panel regression includes both the negative (capital surplus) and positive (capital shortfall) observations of $\text{SRISK}_{i,t}$ for BHCs i at time t. As discussed in Section 4.1, we apply inverse hyperbolic sine transformation for our dependent variable in columns (5)–(8) and follow Bellemare and Wichman (2020) to retransform the coefficients into elasticity interpretations. For comparison, we also calculated semi-elasticities in the models of columns (1)–(4) using the sample means of the dependent variable. According to semi-elasticity[13] in column (1), a 1% increase in bank-level heterogeneity decreases the systemic risk by approximately 1.17% on average. After controlling for the skewness of the dependent variable, we observe from column (5) that a 1% increase in bank-level heterogeneity decreases systemic risk by around 0.2936% on average. The significant changes (at the 99% level) in economic magnitudes and statistical significance of the coefficients in the models of columns (5)–(8) emphasize the importance of controlling for the skewness of our dependent variable.

The baseline regression is as follows:

$$\begin{aligned}\text{arcsinh}(\text{SRISK}_{i,t}) = \alpha + \beta_0 \cdot \text{VWD}_{i,t} \\ + \gamma \cdot \text{Control}_{i,t} + \omega_t + \sigma_i + \epsilon_{i,t}\end{aligned}$$

where the dependent variable $\text{arcsinh}(\text{SRISK}_{i,t})$ is the inverse hyperbolic sine transformation of daily time series of systemic capital shortfall matched to the last trading day in each quarter. $\text{VWD}_{i,t}$ is a quarterly time series of value-weighted pairwise Euclidean distance based on balance sheet and off-balance-sheet accounts provided in the Bank Regulatory Database. We also report the results for the original values of $\text{SRISK}_{i,t}$ and equally weighted pairwise Euclidean distance ($\text{EWD}_{i,t}$). The control variables include total assets, the equity ratio (leverage), return on equity (ROE), loans to total assets (liquidity), and deposits ratio to solvency. Semi-elasticities are calculated

[13] We construct the semi-elasticity using the regression coefficients of the original dependent variables $\text{SRISK}_{i,t}$ divided by the sample mean.

based on sample means, while retransformed elasticities for inverse hyperbolic sine transformation are calculated based on Bellemare and Wichman (2020). We also include year-quarter (λ_t) and individual fixed effects (σ_i) for the regression and estimate robust standard errors using the Eicker–Huber–White estimator. A Hausman test rejects the null hypothesis that the relation between the dependent and independent variables is influenced by random effects, which suggests the use of fixed-effects models. Robust standard errors are in parentheses ($^{***}p < 0.01$, $^{**}p < 0.05$, $^{*}p < 0.1$).

4.4. *Heterogeneity and systemic risk during recessions*

In this section, we focus on the cross-sectional relationship between the BHC-level heterogeneity and the systemic risk during the recessions measured by the NBER (the dot-com bubble, the bankruptcy of Lehman Brothers in September 2008, and the COVID-19 recession). In addition to the independent variables included in the models discussed in Section 4.3, we add an interaction term between an NBER recession indicator and our BHC-level heterogeneity measure and estimate the following equation:

$$\begin{aligned}\mathrm{SRISK}_{i,t} &= \alpha + \beta_1 \cdot \mathrm{Recession}_t \cdot \mathrm{VWD}_{i,t} + \beta_2 \cdot \mathrm{VWD}_{i,t} \\ &\quad + \gamma \cdot \mathrm{Control}_{i,t} + \phi \cdot \mathrm{Cluster}_{i,t} + \lambda_t + \omega_i + \epsilon_{i,t} \qquad (10)\end{aligned}$$

where $\mathrm{Recession}_t$ is a dummy variable equal to one during NBER recessions and 0 otherwise; $\mathrm{Recession}_t \cdot \mathrm{VWD}_{i,t}$ is the interaction term between the recession dummy and the BHC-level heterogeneity measure. The other independent and dependent variables are the same as the ones defined in Section 4.3. Our BHC-level heterogeneity measure $\mathrm{VWD}_{i,t}$ is still negatively related to bank-level systemic risk but with higher statistical significance (at the 99% statistical significance level) and economic magnitudes in Table 4 compared to the levels in Table 3. In addition, the coefficient of the interaction term $\mathrm{Recession}_t \cdot \mathrm{VWD}_{i,t}$ is also positively related to systemic risk (at the 95% statistical significance level in column (1) and 99% level in column (3)). Therefore, our BHC-level heterogeneity measure contributes more to the systemic risk during recession periods. A one

Table 4. The impact of recessions.

(US$ billion)	(1)	(2)	(3)	(4)	(5)	(6)	(7)	(8)
	$\mathbf{SRISK}_{i,t}$				$\mathbf{arcsinh(SRISK}_{i,t})$			
Key variables								
$\mathrm{VWD}_{i,t}$	−0.106***		−0.105***		−0.0125***		−0.0108**	
	[0.0323]		[0.0345]		[0.00464]		[0.00492]	
$\mathrm{VWD}_{i,t} \times Rec.$	0.263**		0.279***		0.00163		0.00310	
	[0.104]		[0.104]		[0.0148]		[0.0148]	
$\mathrm{EWD}_{i,t}$		−0.128***		−0.141***		−0.00733		−0.00539
		[0.0373]		[0.0409]		[0.00456]		[0.00487]
$\mathrm{EWD}_{i,t} \times Rec.$		−0.0345		−0.00498		0.0103		0.0123
		[0.123]		[0.124]		[0.0132]		[0.0131]
Control variables	No	No	Yes	Yes	No	No	Yes	Yes
Calculated (semi-) elasticities								
$\xi(\mathrm{SRISK}_{i,t}, \mathrm{VWD}_{i,t})$	−1.757***		−1.741***		−0.2989***		−0.2581**	
					[0.1111]		[0.1176]	
$\xi(\mathrm{SRISK}_{i,t}, \mathrm{EWD}_{i,t})$		−1.580***		−1.740***		−0.1316		−0.0968
						[0.0819]		[0.0874]
Fixed effects								
Year-quarter	Yes	Yes	Yes	Yes	Yes	Yes	Yes	Yes
Bank-level	Yes	Yes	Yes	Yes	Yes	Yes	Yes	Yes
Constant	−2.900***	−2.248***	4.575*	5.540**	−0.362***	−0.519***	0.0330	−0.121
	[0.819]	[0.794]	[2.721]	[2.666]	[0.105]	[0.0847]	[0.303]	[0.299]
Obs.	4,693	4,693	4,404	4,404	4,693	4,693	4,404	4,404
Adj. R-squared	0.541	0.541	0.543	0.544	0.616	0.616	0.622	0.622

standard deviation increase in $\mathrm{VWD}_{i,t}$ can increase the systemic risk by around US$1.08 billion for the average BHC. We can attribute the positive correlation to rational herding behavior that could be induced by government guarantees. If a BHC is very different from its peers, it may be less likely to be saved by the government during a recession. Nevertheless, after we control for the skewness of the dependent variable in columns (5)–(8), the interaction terms' coefficients are no longer statistically significant. Thus, the net effects of heterogeneity during recessions are yet inconclusive.

The regression is constructed as follows:

$$\begin{aligned}\operatorname{arcsinh}(\mathrm{SRISK}_{i,t}) = \alpha + \beta_1 \cdot \mathrm{Recession}_t \cdot \mathrm{VWD}_{i,t} + \beta_2 \cdot \mathrm{VWD}_{i,t} \\ + \gamma \cdot \mathrm{Control}_{i,t} + \lambda_t + \omega_i + \epsilon_{i,t}\end{aligned}$$

where the dependent variable $\operatorname{arcsinh}(\mathrm{SRISK}_{i,t})$ is the inverse hyperbolic sine transformation of daily time series of systemic capital shortfall matched to the last trading day in each quarter. $\mathrm{VWD}_{i,t}$ is a quarterly time series of value-weighted pairwise Euclidean distance ($\mathrm{VWD}_{i,t}$) based on balance sheet and off-balance-sheet accounts provided in the Bank Regulatory Database. We report the results for the original values of $\mathrm{SRISK}_{i,t}$ and equally weighted pairwise Euclidean distance ($\mathrm{EWD}_{i,t}$). $\mathrm{Recession}_t$ is the NBER-based recession indicator that covers the dot-com bubble (April 2000–November 2000), the 2008 financial crisis (Jan 2009–June 2009), and the COVID-19 pandemic (March 2020–April 2020). The control variables include total assets, equity ratio (leverage), loans to the total assets (liquidity), and deposits ratio (solvency). Semi-elasticities are calculated based on sample means, while retransformed elasticities for inverse hyperbolic sine transformation are calculated based on Bellemare and Wichman (2020). We also control for year-quarter (λ_t) and individual fixed effects (σ_i) and estimate robust standard errors by using the Eicker–Huber–White estimator. A Hausman test rejects the null hypothesis that the relation between the dependent and independent variables is influenced by random effects, which suggests the use of fixed-effects models. Robust standard errors are in parentheses ($^{***}p < 0.01$, $^{**}p < 0.05$, $^{*}p < 0.1$).

5. Conclusions

A decrease in the heterogeneity of bank holding companies can amplify the aggregate expected capital shortfalls and is therefore correlated with systemic risk. While individual banks may diversify by holding different loan, lending, and investment books, this diversification choice may make them more similar, augmenting systemic risk. Hence, by holding similar (optimal) portfolios, bank managers (possibly inadvertently) herd by investing in correlated asset holdings and adopting a similar capital structure to exploit implicit or explicit government guarantees. Furthermore, by maximizing the private benefits from reward-based compensation schemes, bank managers may induce negative externalities to the real economy through augmenting systemic risk.

We observed a drop in heterogeneity in the financial sector prior to the financial crisis related to the Great Recession and the COVID-19 recession. We also noted a continued decrease in heterogeneity during the past decade and that BHC-level heterogeneity negatively correlates with bank-level systemic risk. Therefore, this chapter suggests that cross-sectional heterogeneity at BHC and at aggregate levels is relevant to the microprudential and macroprudential policies. It is crucial to consider heterogeneity to better monitor, intervene, or regulate and eventually reduce the magnitude of a future possible joint failure of financial institutions and hence the whole financial system.

6. Further Research

As the heterogeneity at the BHC level and the aggregate level for the financial sector contributes to systemic risk, a natural next step would be to delve deeper into the economic mechanisms. First, regarding the issue of diversification, one could collect data on detailed investment, funding, and lending portfolios of each of the BHCs. Furthermore, following Chu *et al.* (2020), incorporating geographic diversification of BCHs in the systemic risk analysis is an interesting path forward. Moreover, a more in-depth time series analysis with higher frequency (e.g., with daily and weekly data) could be pursued.

Second, in relation to the rational herding behavior mechanism, we can test the hypothesis that BHCs that implement a relative performance evaluation (RPE) for the top managers' compensation have investment portfolios that are more correlated with those of their peers (Albuquerque *et al.*, 2019). This would give insight into how incentive pay contributes to systemic risk, which has hardly been discussed in the extant literature. Moreover, a further extension of the framework of Duarte and Eisenbach (2021) with a focus on the heterogeneity effects is warranted.

Finally, one could also expand the focus toward the incorporation of other financial institutions, such as insurance companies and pension funds. For example, the interconnectedness of the financial section with the insurance sector could be an important contributor to systemic risk (Billio *et al.*, 2012). As Hufeld *et al.* (2017) state, insurance companies and pension funds invest in illiquid assets and cannot tolerate considerable downside risk; an increase in their aggregate risk can contaminate other financial institutions during a recession and bring the whole financial system down.

Appendices

Appendix 1: The FR Y-9 Report

Description: This report collects basic financial data from domestic bank holding companies (BHC), savings and loans holding companies (SLHC), intermediate holding companies (IHCs), and security holding companies (SHC) on a parent-only basis in the form of balance sheet data, income statements, and the supporting schedules relating to investments, cash flows, and memoranda items.

Purpose: The information is used to assess and monitor the financial condition of parent holding companies.

Background: The report was initiated as the FR Y-9 in 1978. In 1985, the report was revised to parallel the Report of Condition and Income (Call Report) for commercial banks, and in June 1986, it was extensively revised and split into FR Y 9LP (parent-company-only statements) and FR Y 9C (consolidated statements). In September 1990, a cash flow statement was added to the FR Y-9LP. In keeping with the revisions to the filing criteria for the FR Y-9C, the asset-size threshold for filing the FR Y-9LP was increased from US$150 million to US$500 million, from US$500 million to US$1 billion, and from US$1 billion to US$3 billion effective from the March 2006, March 2015, and September 2018 report dates respectively. Consistent with the Call Report, the content and structure of this report are frequently revised in consideration of developments in the banking industry and changes in supervisory, regulatory, and analytical needs. This report is required under Regulation Y and the Bank Holding Company Act of 1956, as amended. The Dodd–Frank Wall Street Reform and Consumer Protection Act (the Dodd–Frank Act) was enacted on July 21, 2010. Title III of the Dodd–Frank Act abolished the Office of Thrift Supervision (OTS) and transferred all former OTS authorities (including rulemaking) related to SLHCs to the Federal Reserve, effective as of July 21, 2011. The Federal Reserve also became responsible for the consolidated supervision of SLHCs beginning July 21, 2011. During 2011, the Board finalized its proposal exempting a limited number of SLHCs from regulatory reporting using the Board's existing regulatory reports and providing a two-year phase-in approach for regulatory reporting for all other SLHCs, starting from March 31, 2012. Section 165 of the Dodd–Frank Act directs the Federal Reserve to establish enhanced prudential standards for bank holding companies (BHCs) and foreign banking organizations (FBOs) with total consolidated assets of US$50 billion or more. On June 1, 2016, the Federal Reserve approved the proposal to require FBOs with total consolidated assets of US$50 billion or more to establish U.S. intermediate holding companies (IHCs) over all their U.S. subsidiaries. The IHCs are subject to U.S. Basel III, capital planning, Dodd–Frank stress testing, liquidity, risk management requirements, and other U.S. regulations. Effective July 1, 2016, U.S. Intermediate Holding companies were required to file certain reports under the Federal Reserve's Regulation YY.

Respondent Panel: This report is filed by the parent company of large BHCs, SLHCs, IHCs, and SHCs and is required for large BHCs, SLHCs, and IHCs with total consolidated assets of US$3 billion or more. In addition, BHCs, SLHCs, IHCs, and SHCs meeting certain criteria may be required to file this report regardless of size. When such BHCs, SLHCs, IHCs, or SHCs are tiered holding companies, each of the subsidiary holding companies' files separate reports.

Frequency: Quarterly, from the last calendar day of the quarter onwards.

Public Release: Data are published in the Federal Reserve Bulletin and the Federal Reserve's Uniform Bank Holding Company Performance Report (BHCPR). With a few exceptions, microdata are considered public information and are available through the Board's Freedom of Information Office.

Appendix 2: The Sample of Bank Holding Companies

Ticker	Legal Name	Ticker	Legal Name
AIG	American International Group, Inc	MI	Marshall & Ilsley
ALLY	Ally Financial, Inc	MS	Morgan Stanley
AMP	Ameriprise Financial, Inc	MTB	M&T Bank Corp
ASB	Associated Banc-Corp	NCC	National City Corporation
BAC	Bank of America Corp	NTRS	Northern Trust Corp
BK	Bank of New York Mellon Corp/The	NYCB	New York Community Bancorp, Inc
BKU	BankUnited, Inc	OZK	Bank OZK
BOH	Bank of Hawaii Corp	PACW	PacWest Bancorp
BOKF	BOK Financial Corp	PB	Prosperity Bancshares, Inc
C	Citigroup, Inc	PBCT	People's United Financial, Inc
CBSH	Commerce Bancshares, Inc/MO	PNC	PNC Financial Services Group Inc/The
CFFN	Capitol Federal Financial, Inc	PNFP	Pinnacle Financial Partners, Inc
CFG	Citizens Financial Group, Inc	RF	Regions Financial Corp
CFR	Cullen/Frost Bankers, Inc	RJF	Raymond James Financial, Inc
CIT	CIT Group, Inc	SCHW	Charles Schwab Corp/The
CMA	Comerica, Inc	SEIC	SEI Investments Co
COF	Capital One Financial Corp	SF	Stifel Financial Corp
CYN	City National Corp/CA	SIVB	SVB Financial Group
DFS	Discover Financial Services	SNV	Synovus Financial Corp
ETFC	E*TRADE Financial Corp	STI	SunTrust Banks, Inc
EWBC	East West Bancorp, Inc	STL	Sterling Bancorp/DE

(Continued)

(*Continued*)

Ticker	Legal Name	Ticker	Legal Name
FAF	First American Financial Corp	STT	State Street Corp
FCNCA	First Citizens BancShares, Inc/NC	TCBI	Texas Capital Bancshares, Inc
FHB	First Hawaiian, Inc	TCF	TCF Financial Corp
FHN	First Horizon National Corp	TFC	Truist Financial Corp
FITB	Fifth Third Bancorp	TROW	T Rowe Price Group, Inc
FNB	FNB Corp/PA	UBSI	United Bankshares, Inc/WV
FNFG	First Niagara Financial Group Inc	UMBF	UMB Financial Corp
FULT	Fulton Financial Corp	UMPQ	Umpqua Holdings Corp
GS	Goldman Sachs Group, Inc/The	USB	US Bancorp
HBAN	Huntington Bancshares, Inc/OH	VLY	Valley National Bancorp
HCBK	Hudson City Bancorp, Inc	WAFD	Washington Federal, Inc
HWC	Hancock Whitney Corp	WAL	Western Alliance Bancorp
IBKC	IBERIABANK Corp	WBS	Webster Financial Corp
ISBC	Investors Bancorp, Inc	WFC	Wells Fargo & Co
JPM	JPMorgan Chase & Co	WTFC	Wintrust Financial Corp
KEY	KeyCorp	ZION	Zions Bancorporation

Appendix 3: Online Appendix

Online appendix link (a shared Dropbox folder):

https://www.dropbox.com/sh/ldu00q0mqewnogz/AACV4jXqDcmBbzR-RZgFMsUka?dl=0.

References

Abduraimova, K. and Nahai-Williamson, P. (2021). Solvency distress contagion risk: network structure, bank heterogeneity and systemic resilience. *Bank of England Working Paper No. 909.* Retrieved from https://ssrn.com/abstract=3796283.

Acharya, V. V., Pedersen, L. H., Philippon, T. and Richardson, M. (2017). Measuring systemic risk. *The Review of Financial Studies*, *30*(1), 2–47.

Ahern, K. R. and Dittmar, A. K. (2012). The changing of the boards: The impact on firm valuation of mandated female board representation. *The Quarterly Journal of Economics*, *127*(1), 137–197.

Albuquerque, R., Cabral, L. and Guedes, J. (2019). Incentive pay and systemic risk. *The Review of Financial Studies*, *32*(11), 4304–4342.

Allen, F., Babus, A. and Carletti, E. (2012). Asset commonality, debt maturity and systemic risk. *Journal of financial economics*, *104*(3), 519–534.

Allen, F. and Gale, D. (2000). Financial contagion. *Journal of Political Economy*, *108*(1), 1–33.

Altinoglu, L. and Stiglitz, J. E. (2022). Collective moral hazard and the interbank market. *NBER Working Paper No. 29807.*

Anton, M. and Polk, C. (2014). Connected stocks. *The Journal of Finance*, *69*(3), 1099–1127.

Ari, A., Chen, S. and Ratnovski, L. (2021). The dynamics of non-performing loans during banking crises: A new database with post-COVID-19 implications. *Journal of Banking & Finance*, *133*, 106140.

Arifa, S., Donovanb, J., Gopalanc, Y. and Morrise, A. (2021). Pay for Prudence.

Armstrong, C., Nicoletti, A. and Zhou, F. S. (2022). Executive stock options and systemic risk. *Journal of Financial Economics*, 146(1), 256–276.

Bellemare, M. F. and Wichman, C. J. (2020). Elasticities and the inverse hyperbolic sine transformation. *Oxford Bulletin of Economics and Statistics*, *82*(1), 50–61.

Benoit, S., Colliard, J.-E., Hurlin, C. and Pérignon, C. (2017). Where the risks lie: A survey on systemic risk. *Review of Finance*, *21*(1), 109–152.

Berger, A. N., Curti, F., Mihov, A. and Sedunov, J. (2022). Operational risk is more systemic than you think: Evidence from US bank holding companies. *Journal of Banking & Finance*, *143*, 106619.

Berndt, A., Duffie, D. and Zhu, Y. (2022). The decline of too big to fail. Available at SSRN 3497897. Retrieved from https://ssrn.com/abstract=3497897.

Billio, M., Getmansky, M., Lo, A. W. and Pelizzon, L. (2012). Econometric measures of connectedness and systemic risk in the finance and insurance sectors. *Journal of Financial Economics*, *104*(3), 535–559.

Bisias, D., Flood, M., Lo, A. W. and Valavanis, S. (2012). A survey of systemic risk analytics. *Annual Review of Financial Economics*, *4*(1), 255–296.

Bongaerts, D., Mazzola, F. and Wagner, W. (2021). Fire sale risk and credit. Available at SSRN 3783199. Retrieved from https://ssrn.com/abstract=3783199.

Brownlees, C. and Engle, R. F. (2017). SRISK: A conditional capital shortfall measure of systemic risk. *The Review of Financial Studies, 30*(1), 48–79.

Cai, J. (2022). Bank herding and systemic risk. *Economic Systems, 46*(4), 101042.

Cai, J., Eidam, F., Saunders, A. and Steffen, S. (2018). Syndication, interconnectedness, and systemic risk. *Journal of Financial Stability, 34*, 105–120.

Chen, Y. (1999). Banking panics: The role of the first-come, first-served rule and information externalities. *Journal of Political Economy, 107*(5), 946–968.

Chen, Y. (2022). Bank interconnectedness and financial stability: The role of bank capital. *Journal of Financial Stability, 61*, 101019.

Chu, Y., Deng, S. and Xia, C. (2020). Bank geographic diversification and systemic risk. *The Review of Financial Studies, 33*(10), 4811–4838.

Cinelli, C., Forney, A. and Pearl, J. (2020). A crash course in good and bad controls. *Sociological Methods & Research*, 00491241221099552.

Cziraki, P. (2018). Trading by bank insiders before and during the 2007–2008 financial crisis. *Journal of Financial Intermediation, 33*, 58–82.

De Jonghe, O. (2010). Back to the basics in banking? A micro-analysis of banking system stability. *Journal of Financial Intermediation, 19*(3), 387–417.

Diamond, D. W. and Dybvig, P. H. (1983). Bank runs, deposit insurance, and liquidity. *Journal of Political Economy, 91*(3), 401–419.

Diamond, D. W. and Rajan, R. G. (2001). Liquidity risk, liquidity creation, and financial fragility: A theory of banking. *Journal of Political Economy, 109*(2), 287–327.

Diamond, D. W. and Rajan, R. G. (2005). Liquidity shortages and banking crises. *The Journal of Finance, 60*(2), 615–647.

Diamond, D. W. and Rajan, R. G. (2011). Fear of fire sales, illiquidity seeking, and credit freezes. *The Quarterly Journal of Economics, 126*(2), 557–591.

Duan, Y., El Ghoul, S., Guedhami, O., Li, H. and Li, X. (2021). Bank systemic risk around COVID-19: A cross-country analysis. *Journal of Banking & Finance, 133*, 106299.

Duarte, F. and Eisenbach, T. M. (2021). Fire-sale spillovers and systemic risk. *The Journal of Finance, 76*(3), 1251–1294.

Elliott, M. and Golub, B. (2022). Networks and economic fragility. *Annual Review of Economics, 14*, 665–696.

Elnahass, M., Trinh, V. Q. and Li, T. (2021). Global banking stability in the shadow of Covid-19 outbreak. *Journal of International Financial Markets, Institutions and Money, 72*, 101322.

Engle, R. F. and Ruan, T. (2018). How much SRISK is too much? Available at SSRN 3108269.

Falato, A., Favara, G. and Scharfstein, D. (2018). Bank risk-taking and the real economy: Evidence from the housing boom and its aftermath.

Farboodi, M. (2021). Intermediation and voluntary exposure to counterparty risk. *NBER Working Paper No. 29467.*

Farhi, E. and Tirole, J. (2012). Collective moral hazard, maturity mismatch, and systemic bailouts. *American Economic Review*, *102*(1), 60–93.

Fricke, D. (2016). Has the banking system become more homogeneous? Evidence from banks' loan portfolios. *Economics Letters*, *142*, 45–48.

Fricke, D. and Roukny, T. (2020). Generalists and specialists in the credit market. *Journal of Banking & Finance*, *112*, 105335.

Gandhi, P. and Purnanandam, A. (2022). United they fall: Bank risk after the financial crisis. Available at SSRN 4091626. Retrieved from https://ssrn.com/abstract=4091626.

Gelman, M., Goldstein, I. and MacKinlay, A. (2022). Bank diversification and lending resiliency. Available at SSRN 4147790. Retrieved from https://ssrn.com/abstract=4147790.

Giglio, S., Kelly, B. and Pruitt, S. (2016). Systemic risk and the macroeconomy: An empirical evaluation. *Journal of Financial Economics*, *119*(3), 457–471.

Girardi, G., Hanley, K. W., Nikolova, S., Pelizzon, L. and Sherman, M. G. (2021). Portfolio similarity and asset liquidation in the insurance industry. *Journal of Financial Economics*, *142*(1), 69–96.

Gorton, G. and Metrick, A. (2012). Securitized banking and the run on repo. *Journal of Financial Economics*, *104*(3), 425–451.

Greenwood, R., Landier, A. and Thesmar, D. (2015). Vulnerable banks. *Journal of Financial Economics*, *115*(3), 471–485.

Grieser, W., Hadlock, C., LeSage, J. and Zekhnini, M. (2022). Network effects in corporate financial policies. *Journal of Financial Economics*, *144*(1), 247–272.

Haldane, A. G. and May, R. M. (2011). Systemic risk in banking ecosystems. *Nature*, *469*(7330), 351–355.

Hufeld, F., Koijen, R. S. and Thimann, C. (2017). *The Economics, Regulation, and Systemic Risk of Insurance Markets*. UK: Oxford University Press.

Irani, R. M., Iyer, R., Meisenzahl, R. R. and Peydro, J.-L. (2021). The rise of shadow banking: Evidence from capital regulation. *The Review of Financial Studies*, *34*(5), 2181–2235.

Koudijs, P., Salisbury, L. and Sran, G. (2021). For richer, for poorer: Bankers' liability and bank risk in New England, 1867 to 1880. *The Journal of Finance*, *76*(3), 1541–1599.

Laeven, L., Ratnovski, L. and Tong, H. (2016). Bank size, capital, and systemic risk: Some international evidence. *Journal of Banking & Finance, 69*, S25–S34.

León, C. (2020). Banks in Colombia: How homogeneous are they? *Revista de economía del Rosario, 23*(2), 4.

Liu, R. and Pun, C. S. (2022). Machine-Learning-enhanced systemic risk measure: A Two-Step supervised learning approach. *Journal of Banking & Finance, 136*, 106416.

Mian, A., Sufi, A. and Trebbi, F. (2015). Foreclosures, house prices, and the real economy. *The Journal of Finance, 70*(6), 2587–2634.

Montagna, M., Torri, G. and Covi, G. (2020). On the origin of systemic risk. Available at SSRN 3699369. Retrieved from https://ssrn.com/abstract=3699369.

Norton, E. C. (2022). The Inverse Hyperbolic Sine Transformation and Retransformed Marginal Effects. *NBER Working Paper No. 29998.*

Pool, V. K., Stoffman, N. and Yonker, S. E. (2015). The people in your neighborhood: Social interactions and mutual fund portfolios. *The Journal of Finance, 70*(6), 2679–2732.

Reinhart, C. M. and Rogoff, K. S. (2009a). The aftermath of financial crises. *American Economic Review, 99*(2), 466–472.

Reinhart, C. M. and Rogoff, K. S. (2009b). *This Time Is Different.* USA: Princeton University Press.

Shleifer, A. and Vishny, R. W. (1992). Liquidation values and debt capacity: A market equilibrium approach. *The Journal of Finance, 47*(4), 1343–1366.

Silva, A. F. (2019). Strategic liquidity mismatch and financial sector stability. *The Review of Financial Studies, 32*(12), 4696–4733.

Sufi, A. and Taylor, A. M. (2021). Financial crises: A survey. *NBER Working Paper No. 29155.*

Tobias, A. and Brunnermeier, M. K. (2016). CoVaR. *The American Economic Review, 106*(7), 1705.

Trinh, V. Q., Cao, N. D. and Elnahass, M. (2023). Financial stability: A 'vaccine' for tail risk of the global banking sector in the shadow of the pandemic. *The European Journal of Finance, 29*(7), 726–753.

Wagner, W. (2010). Diversification at financial institutions and systemic crises. *Journal of Financial Intermediation, 19*(3), 373–386.

Wagner, W. (2011). Systemic liquidation risk and the diversity–diversification trade-off. *The Journal of Finance, 66*(4), 1141–1175.

https://doi.org/10.1142/9781800614321_0007

Chapter 7

Analysis of the Systemic Risk in the Turkish Banking Sector[a]

Mert Malkoç*,‡ and İlkay Şendeniz-Yüncü†,§

**Middle East Technical University, The Institute of Applied Mathematics, Ankara, Turkey*

†Middle East Technical University, Department of Business Administration, Ankara, Turkey

‡malkoc.mert@metu.edu.tr

§sendeniz@metu.edu.tr

Abstract

In this chapter, we aim to see the effects of the foreign exchange (FX) debt level of Turkish banks on the riskiness of the banking sector between January 2008 and December 2021. We use two explanatory variables: the ratio of foreign loans to total assets and the ratio of Turkish Lira denominated deposits to total credits. Our results show that an increase in the ratio of foreign loans to total assets triggers an increase in the riskiness of the banking sector. However, the ratio of Turkish Lira-denominated deposits to total credits does not have a significant effect on the volatility measure.

Keywords: Foreign exchange, systemic risk, Turkish banking sector

[a]This chapter is a part of Mert Malkoç's MSc studies under the supervision of İlkay Şendeniz-Yüncü at Middle East Technical University.

1. Introduction

In this chapter, we study the effects of the macroeconomic environment on the structure of banking sector risk in Turkey. Amid the rapid dollarization and the high inflation rate, Turkish banks are exposed to exchange rate risk. The roots of these risks need to be analyzed through a historical perspective beginning from the 2008 Mortgage crisis aftermath, which resulted in a serious amount of liquidity injection by monetary authorities when foreign borrowing had become attractive and cheap for Turkish banks.

Since it is an option for the banks to access foreign debt, this method was applied to extend the credit pool of the banks. The risks related to the Turkish economy were lower, and the exchange rates were relatively stable at the beginning of the 2010s. Combined with the positive real interest rates, this formed an access opportunity for Turkish banks to foreign funds in foreign currencies. However, after it was seen that the adverse effects of the crisis started to disappear and an increase in the interest rates was necessary, which resulted in pressure on the Turkish Lira, a risky environment for the Turkish banking sector occurred. Turkish banks deal with the increased exchange rate risk with very high levels of leverage compared to the beginning of the 2010s. The rapid depreciation of the Turkish Lira combined with the high level of external debt creates a difficult environment for Turkish banks. This study, however, does not focus on the microlevel of the individual banks in Turkey but instead follows a more general path to explain the overall risks in the sector.

This chapter contributes to the literature by analyzing the risks in the Turkish banking sector via balance sheet items. We analyze both the riskiness of the sector and the consequent moves made by the sector rather than focusing solely on the policy implications. Instead of focusing on microlevel risks of the Turkish banking sector, this chapter studies the industry-level foreign exchange risk. We have two explanatory variables: the ratio of borrowings from abroad (hereinafter "foreign loans") to total assets and the ratio of total deposits to total credits.

Results of this study indicate that the short-term needs of the sector increased. Although it may be expected that an increase in the ratio of total deposits to total credits would have an impact on reducing the volatility, namely, exchange rate change in this study, it is not the case in this model. The variable is statistically insignificant in explaining the changes in the exchange rate. The ratio of foreign loans to total assets is entered into the regression with a positive sign and it is statistically significant. An increase in the ratio will cause an increase in the volatility measure as well.

According to the results of this study, some macroprudential policies can be advised to reduce foreign exchange risk of the sector. Since the increase in foreign loans triggers an increase in the foreign exchange rate, policies related with the foreign borrowings of the sector can be implemented to prevent the rise of the FX risk.

We focus on assessing the FX risk for the Turkish banking sector by establishing a volatility model which includes foreign loans, total assets, total deposits, and total credits. The model is created upon two independent variables (the ratio of foreign loans to total assets and the ratio of total deposits to total credits) and one dependent variable (USD/TRY exchange rate change). The analyses are held for the January 2008 and December 2021 period via monthly data. As well as assessing the FX risk of the sector, this chapter also focuses on the policy shifts made by the sector in the same period. Money market statistics and borrowing activities of the banks are assessed to see the policy shifts in the sector. The results show that the model established in this study is statistically significant in explaining the foreign exchange rate changes. The level of foreign loans has a significant impact on the volatility measure. An increase in the foreign borrowing will trigger the same response in the foreign exchange rate. Although it may be expected that an increase in the total deposits to total credits ratio would reduce the volatility, the findings suggest no significant effect.

2. Literature Review

Huang *et al.* (2019) study the systemic risk in the Chinese banking system for 16 banks by estimating the marginal expected shortfall

(MES), the systemic impact index (SII), the vulnerability index (VI), and the conditional value at risk (CoVaR) for the 2007–2014 period to capture different aspects of the systemic risk. Their findings indicate that systemic risk in the Chinese banking system declined following the global financial crisis; however, it began to rise in 2014. A similar study analyzes the Korean banking sector. Yun and Moon (2014) use MES and CoVaR to examine the systemic risk in the Korean banking sector. Their analyses show that, first, although these two systemic risk measures are different in defining the contributions to systemic risk, both are qualitatively similar in explaining the cross-sectional differences in systemic risk contributions across banks. Second, it was found that certain bank characteristic variables such as size and leverage ratio are essential to explain systemic risk contributions. Elnahass *et al.* (2022) investigate the effect of systematic risk for 14 countries in the Middle East and North Africa (MENA) region between 2010 and 2018 by using CoVaR analyses and state that high systemic risks for the banks escalate the instability of financial markets. Sengul and Yilmaz (2019) study the systemic risk in the Turkish banking sector using MES and Δ CoVaR values for six Turkish banks. Their findings indicate that although the measures contribute separate rankings for the systemic risks, they are qualitatively similar in explaining the cross-sectional differences in systemic risk contributions. The study shows that the VaR of an individual bank affects the bank's systemic risk contribution in terms of cross-sectional and time-series dimensions. In addition, the authors did not find a close link between leverage ratios and systemic risk contributions although an increase in leverage ratios causes an increase in systemic risk contribution in the long term. Lastly, it is found that the size of a bank is weakly related to systemic risk contribution. Another study done by Fan *et al.* (2021) investigates the systemic risk of the Turkish banking sector using a systemic risk measurement framework of the fractional Brownian motion method. The study focuses on the period between 2014 and 2019. The results suggest that the systemic risk peaked in 2017, and between 2016 and 2018, the banking sector was unstable. However, after the government stimulation, the overall risks were reduced.

Wang *et al.* (2015) use the Merton model to estimate the systemic risk of China's banking industries. They choose the data of Chinese listed banks on a 5-year basis (2007–2011). The model focuses on the change in bank asset price and view of the risk of infection. The authors conclude that the probability of a crisis in the Chinese banking system is low in terms of asset value analysis. However, it is also advised to prevent risk by improving the single bank risk resisting ability, improving the asset pricing mechanism, blocking risk transmission channels, and strengthening external supervision.

De Nicolo *et al.* (2005) study the effect of deposit dollarization on the financial deepening of the onshore financial system, the causes of deposit dollarization, and banking risk for 100 countries between 1990 and 2001. Their findings suggest that dollarization helps the economy to have more monetary depth than otherwise in inflationary environments. Ozsoz (2008) investigates the effects of the financial dollarization on commercial bank performance between 1991 and 2004. The study is conducted with bank-level data in 11 developing countries, and it shows that dollarization is not directly related to bank profitability. The analysis of loan loss provisions indicates the significant effect of FX deposits on the changes in the banks' bad loans to their overall loan portfolio ratios.

Karasoy (1995) studies the Turkish banking sector's exchange rate risk management with a portfolio model. Both the foreign exchange and domestic currency-denominated items are included to analyze how changes in interest rates in foreign and domestic currencies and the volatility affect the portfolio structure of a Turkish bank. It is indicated that state and private Turkish banks are more sensitive to the changes in interest rates than the changes in the volatility of exchange rates. In contrast, the exchange rate risk and the interest rate changes are highly effective in explaining foreign banks' foreign exchange rate behavior. Demir (2021) analyzes the financial performance of the Turkish banking sector between 2009 and 2019 by using "Multi-Criteria Decision Making" methods. For the evaluation, 14 financial criteria are used in the proposed model. After determining the model's weights by Rank Order Centroid (ROC) and Indifference Threshold-based Attribute Ratio Analysis (ITARA) methods, the weights are combined based on the Bayesian approach to find the final weight coefficients. After observing the most critical performance criteria, lastly, the Combinative Distance-based Assessment (CODAS) method is used to analyze the performance of the Turkish banking sector. The analyses indicate a significant instability in the Turkish banking sector.

Caglayan *et al.* (2021) examine dollarization in the Turkish banking sector between 2002 and 2018 with quarterly data. The authors state a significant currency mismatch problem in banks' balance sheets. It is argued that less than 30% of the foreign-denominated deposits turn into foreign-denominated credit. Moreover, for banks, a greater currency imbalance signals that they are more likely to extend their domestic currency loans. Deposit dollarization helps the banks profit more from their domestic currency-denominated loans, but this method also increases the exposure to the exchange rate risk.

Schularick and Taylor (2012) study credit growth with money, credit, and macroeconomic indicators. They analyze these indicators for 14 countries between 1870 and 2008. Their findings suggest that credit growth is a powerful indicator when predicting financial crises. Another finding of the study is that large financial systems are inclined to have more crises. According to the article, the authors argue that endogenous credit growth can generate economic instability although detailed research is suggested. However, it should be noted that not every credit growth is a signal of crisis. In periods of financial development and innovation, credit growth can boost economic activity.

3. Data and Methodology

To see the effects of the FX debt level of Turkish banks on the riskiness of the banking sector, monthly data are used between January 2008 and December 2021. The large dataset helps us to see the change in the riskiness of the sector. The data source is the Central Bank of the Republic of Turkey (CBRT) Electronic Data Delivery System (EDDS) database. Variable names and descriptions are presented in Table 1.

We have two explanatory variables: the ratio of foreign loans to total assets and the ratio of total deposits to total credits. It may be

Table 1. Variable names and descriptions.

Variable Name	Description
V	USD/TRY exchange rate change
FL	Foreign loans (borrowings from abroad)
TA	Total bank assets
TD	Total deposits in the banking system
TC	Total credits extended by the banking system

expected that an increase in the ratio of foreign loans to total assets will trigger an increase in the riskiness of the sector by causing a depreciation in the Turkish Lira. On the contrary, an increase in the ratio of total deposits to total credits may have an appreciation effect on the Turkish Lira by decreasing the demand for foreign currency, reducing the overall risk in the Turkish banking system. Our model is as follows:

$$V = \alpha + ß_1 FL/TA + ß2TD/TC + \varepsilon \quad (1)$$

First, we need to outline the currency risk for Turkish banks. In our analysis, after liquidity options became available for Turkish banks, they used foreign borrowing heavily to increase resources. When the US Dollar/Turkish Lira exchange was relatively stable, this might have been a profitable method for the Turkish banks to follow; however, after the Turkish economy became more fragile and the Turkish Lira started to lose value, the above-mentioned method created problems for the Turkish banks. The ratio of foreign debt to total credits was about 90% for a long time between January 2008 and May 2013. Although the ratio started to decline over time, still a very huge portion of the debt was foreign currency denominated.

Second, the gradual increase in the CBRT funding of the Turkish banks can also be observed in our data. The CBRT debt to total debts ratio starts as low as 0.001%. However, it started to surge and reached a level as high as 17% as of December 2021. Moreover, the increasing needs of the sector can be observed from the level of short-term financing. Since open market operations are important to keep the financial markets stable, this side of the balance sheet signals an important need for the banking sector. The movements in these data can give us a clue regarding the increased short-term needs of the Turkish banking sector (see Figure 1).

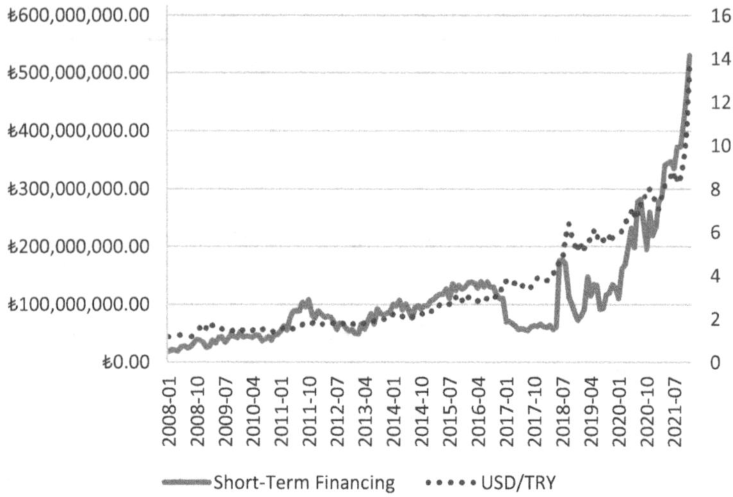

Figure 1. Short-term financing and FX rate.

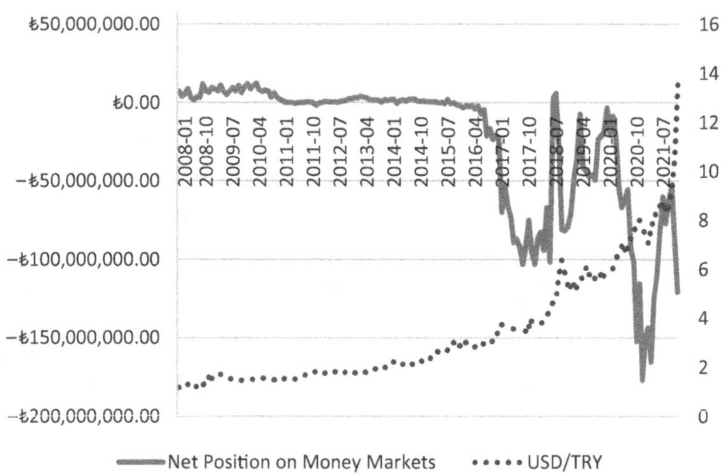

Figure 2. Net position on money markets and FX rate.

Another proof of the increasing needs of Turkish banks can be seen in the net position in the money markets. Although the series shows stability until mid-2016, after that, there are huge fluctuations as can be seen in Figure 2. With some exceptions, the sector was lending to the market until September 2015; however, after that, it started to borrow from the market. There is an increase in the amount borrowed over time especially after mid-2016 whereas the amount lent remained stable. After mid-2016, the debt from the money market increased by more than 300%, from 7 billion TRY to 23.4 billion TRY. Banks changed their positions in money markets. The increasing needs of the sector pushed the lending from the money markets. The amount lent to the market stayed around 2–4 billion TRY whereas, with some outliers, the amount borrowed was 73 billion TRY on average.

Although the ratio of the sources of borrowing is analyzed, it is also important to note that the amount is getting bigger. In Figure 3, this increase can be seen. Total foreign debt, which includes the loans from foreign banks and foreign funds, was 45 billion Turkish Liras in January 2008. This amount increased over the 13-year period and reached 756 trillion Turkish Liras. Adding the depreciation of the Turkish Lira against the US Dollar over the past years, there is a significant level of exchange rate risk for Turkish banks.

Figure 3 shows that the exchange rate follows the pattern of the level of foreign debt. Banks have a very high level of foreign debt, which requires high demand for foreign currencies since these debts require regular payments. In our case, the US Dollar/Turkish Lira

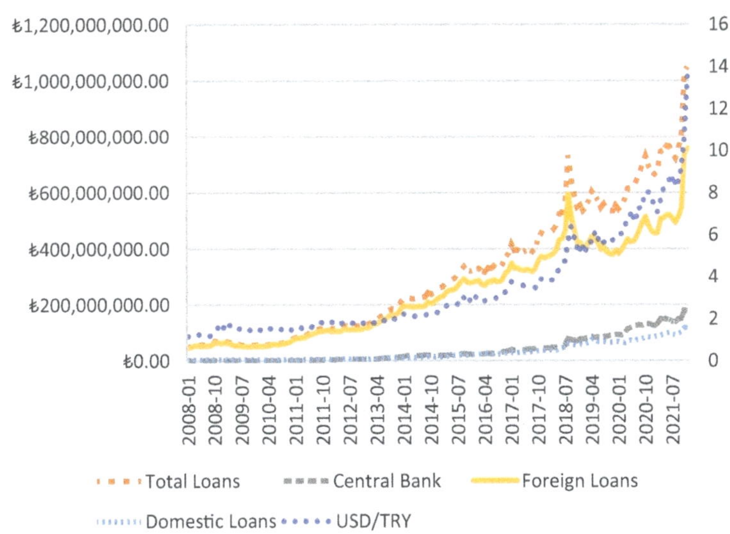

Figure 3. Distribution of total loans (TL) and FX rate.

exchange rate follows the pattern of the foreign-denominated debts of the banking sector with a small lag. This indicates that banks form their expectations accordingly.

As the exchange rate increases, it is expected that due to the increased levels of currency mismatch risk, the Turkish banks will try to close their foreign loans to reduce their risk. However, in Figure 4, in the last 3 months of 2021, there is an increase in the FL/TA ratio due to the increase in the exchange rate. Between November and December 2021, the US Dollar/TRY exchange rate increased by 29%. There is a 20% decrease in both the foreign loans and total assets that are expressed in terms of US dollars, whereas an increase is observed in both items in terms of Turkish Liras. Since all of the foreign loans are denominated in foreign currency unlike the total assets, a rapid increase in the exchange rate causes the FL/TA ratio to increase. In total assets, there are TRY-denominated items, and an increase in those items compensates for the exchange rate effect although not fully. Therefore, this unexpected movement in the ratio can be explained as the exchange rate effect on the FL/TA ratio.

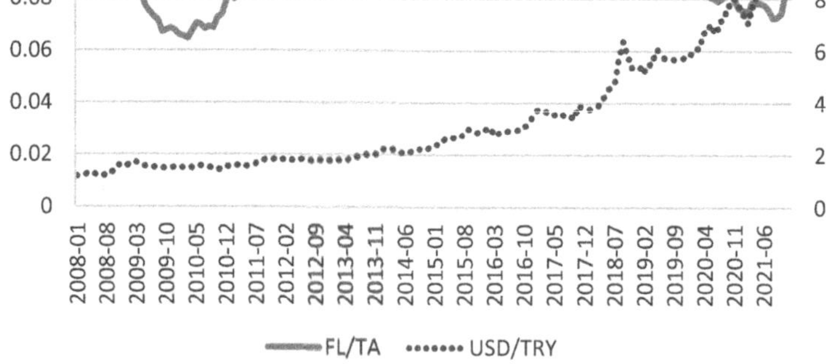

Figure 4. FL/TA and FX rate.

Moreover, the Turkish banking sector's domestic debt levels have risen between January 2008 and December 2021. Therefore, it can be said that banks are trying to reduce their foreign debts and turn those liabilities to TRY-denominated debt. Although the level of domestic debt (excluding the CBRT) is relatively low compared to foreign debt, it has risen from 3.5 billion TRY to 115 billion TRY over 13 years.

Figures 5 and 6 show that although an increase in the foreign loans in terms of Turkish Lira is evident in the data, when we turn this debt into US Dollars terms, there is a decrease in the foreign loans. This implies that the depreciation of TRY surpasses the decrease in foreign loans. In these two figures, the exchange rate risk becomes obvious. This reduction in the number of foreign loans points out a switch in Turkish banks' policies. There are three sources of liabilities for banks to support their credit channels: foreign loans, loans from the central bank, and deposits. Since the foreign loans are reduced in terms of US Dollars, it can be said that the banks increase the proportion of the funds taken from the CBRT and deposits to give credit.

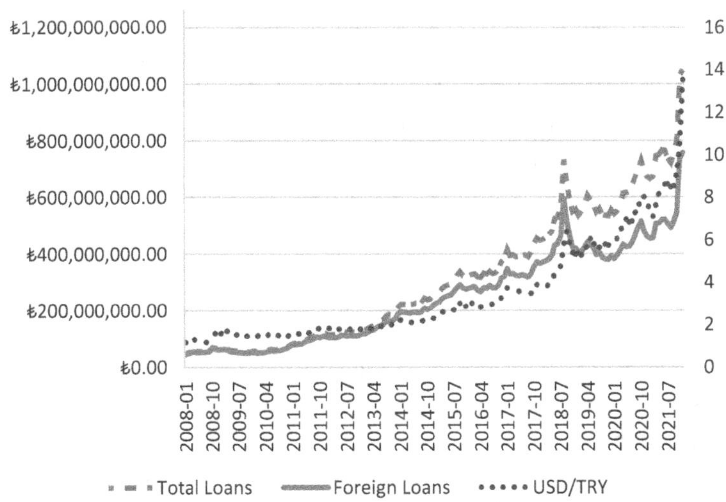

Figure 5. Foreign and total loans (TL) and FX rate.

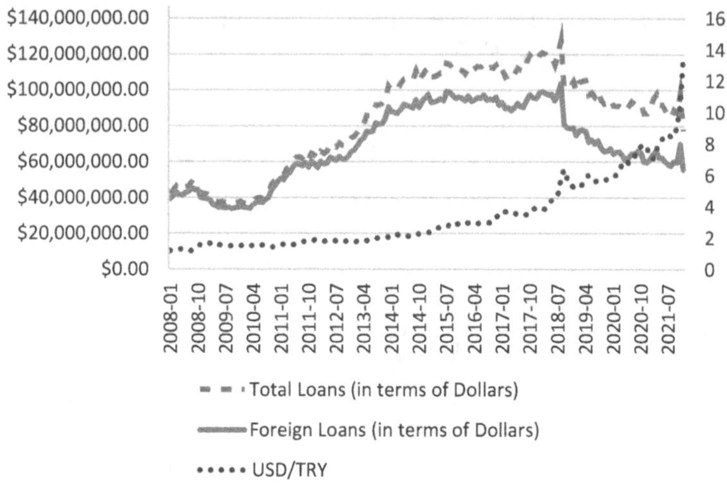

Figure 6. Foreign and total loans ($) and FX rate.

It is also important to make interpretations from the comparison of the credit and deposit pool of the Turkish banking sector. The main tool for this part of the data analysis is the ratio of total deposits to total credits. This ratio will show how the Turkish banks are mobilizing their main source of operation. A very low ratio would indicate that banks are not making full use of their resources. A very high ratio would signal a proxy for risk. The time series on this ratio will show the responses of the banking system as well. Therefore, it is expected that the ratio will be useful to gauge the Turkish banking system's health by showing the sector's ability to cover its loans with its deposits. Although the maturity of the said instruments should be considered to provide a more detailed analysis, it is not within the scope of this study.

In Figure 7, it is seen that in January 2008, Turkish banks had a ratio that is bigger than 1. This indicates that the level of total deposits is bigger than total credits. The ratio reached its peak in March 2009 at a level of 1.49, then it started to decline. It continued to fall until January 2018, declining to 0.84. After January 2018, there was an increasing trend in the ratio. The ratio exceeded 1 in December 2019 and continued to increase with small ups and

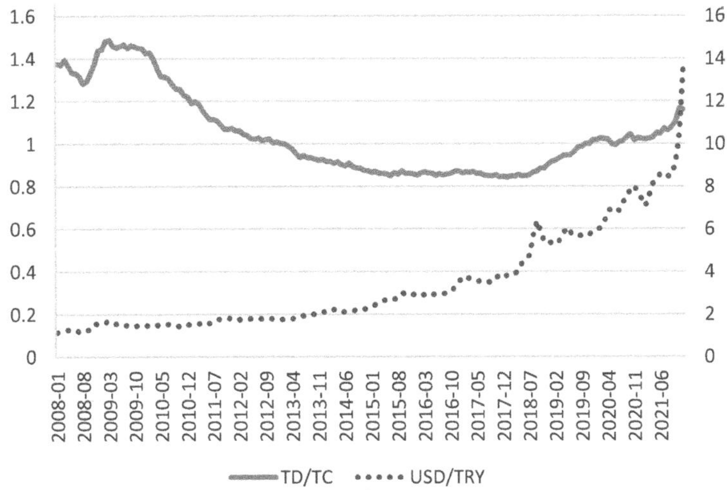

Figure 7. TD/TC and FX rate.

downs. Moreover, there was a shift in banks' policies in January 2018. Until January 2018, the ratio continued to decline. After that, banks started to increase their deposits faster than they did before. Although the level of credit continued to increase, the level of deposits increased faster after January 2018 and the ratio of total deposits to total credits started rising.

To see the policy shift clearly, the time series of total deposits to total credits ratio is divided into two separate categories. The first part covers the period between January 2008 and January 2018, as shown in Figure 8. The lowest value of TD/TC ratio is the separating point for the two periods. The second part starts in February 2018 and ends in December 2021, as shown in Figure 9.

Before conducting the regression analysis, it is necessary that the time series which will enter the equation should be statistically stationary.

After conducting the HEGY test for stationarity, the results of which are shown in Tables 2, 3, and 4, it is found that all three series have unit root problem. After taking the first difference of all three series, the regression analysis is conducted (see Table 5).

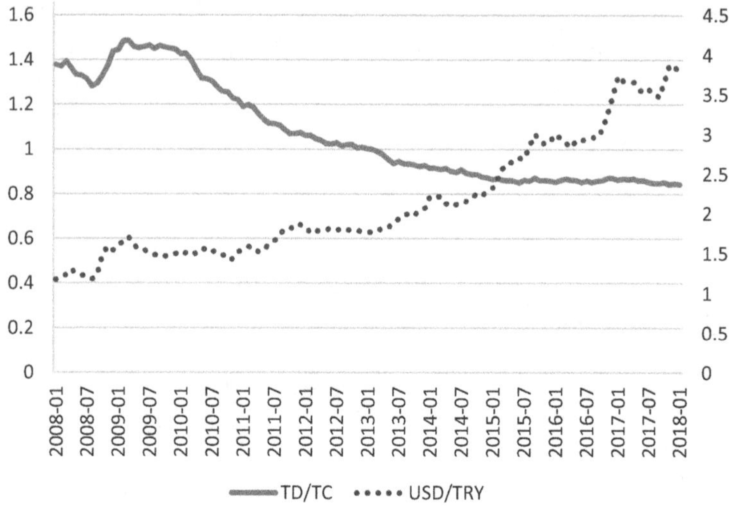

Figure 8. Before minimum of TD/TC.

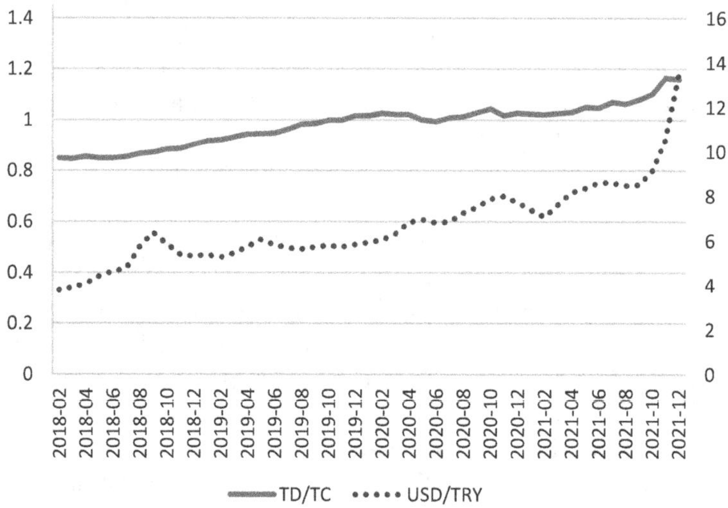

Figure 9. After minimum of TD/TC.

Table 2. HEGY test results for series V.

	Statistic	***p*-value**
tpi_1	−2.049	0.10
tpi_2	−4.545	0.01
Fpi_3:4	7.991	0.01
Fpi_5:6	11.004	0.01
Fpi_7:8	13.125	0.01
Fpi_9:10	13.309	0.01
Fpi_11:12	14.945	0.01
Fpi_2:12	22.586	NA
Fpi_1:12	21.401	NA

Table 3. HEGY test results for series FL/TA.

	Statistic	***p*-value**
tpi_1	−2.081	0.10
tpi_2	−2.992	0.01
Fpi_3:4	13.204	0.01
Fpi_5:6	11.070	0.01
Fpi_7:8	11.160	0.01
Fpi_9:10	11.104	0.01
Fpi_11:12	15.968	0.01
Fpi_2:12	127.352	NA
Fpi_1:12	135.287	NA

Table 4. HEGY test results for series TD/TC.

	Statistic	***p*-value**
tpi_1	−1.895	0.10
tpi_2	−2.731	0.01
Fpi_3:4	6.993	0.01
Fpi_5:6	16.006	0.01
Fpi_7:8	13.735	0.01
Fpi_9:10	6.574	0.01
Fpi_11:12	19.012	0.01
Fpi_2:12	112.362	NA
Fpi_1:12	159.840	NA

Table 5. Regression analyses.

Coefficients	Estimate	Standard Error	t-value	p-value
Intercept	0.002	0.003	0.722	0.471
FL/TA	7.80	0.993	7.855	5.1e−13
TD/TC	0.278	0.198	1.408	0.161
Multiple R		0.279		
Adjusted R Square		0.270		
Residual Standard Error		0.039		
Degrees of Freedom		163		
Significance F		2.6e−12		
F-statistic		31.56		

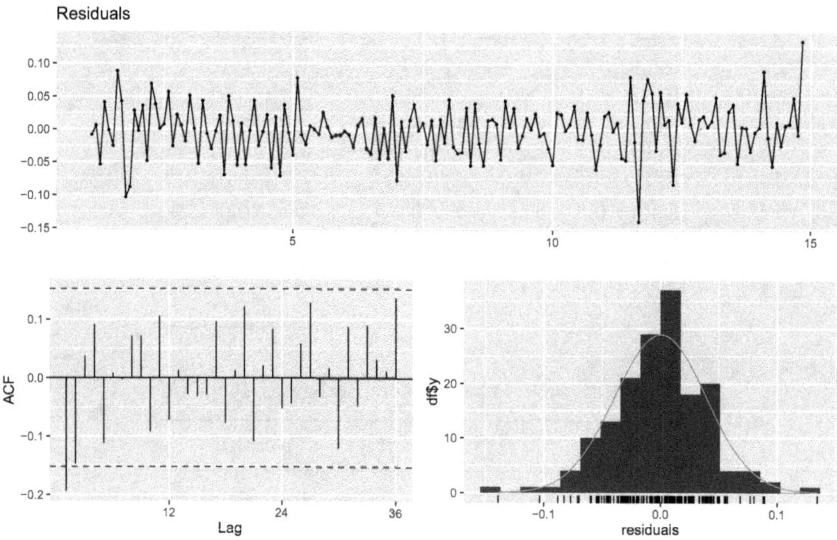

Figure 10. Residuals.

As Figure 10 indicates, the residuals in our model have a normal distribution and do not have an autocorrelation problem.

As p-value indicates in Table 6, there is no autocorrelation problem for the error terms in the model.

As is seen in Table 7, the error terms have normal distribution in our model.

Table 6. Breusch–Godfrey test results.

Breusch–Godfrey Test	
LM Test	28.906
Df	24
p-value	0.224

Table 7. Shapiro–Wilk normality test results.

Shapiro–Wilk Normality Test	
W	0.989
p-value	0.251

4. Conclusion

The model we constructed aimed to explain the change in the US dollar/TRY exchange rate, namely, volatility, between January 2008 and December 2021. We aimed to do so with two different ratios, which are the ratio of foreign loans to total assets (FL/TA) and the ratio of total deposits to total credits (TD/TC). It may be expected that an increase in FL/TA will trigger an increase in the volatility measure by causing a depreciation in the Turkish Lira. On the other hand, an increase in TD/TC may have an appreciation effect on the Turkish Lira by decreasing the volatility measure and reducing the overall risk in the Turkish banking system.

After testing for stationarity in the time series of the data, it is found that all three series (FL/TA, TD/TC, and V) have unit root problem. Therefore, differenced series are used for the above-mentioned series. Then the regression analysis is conducted and it is seen that the regression model has normally distributed residuals and the model's error terms do not have an autocorrelation problem. The independent variable FL/TA enters the equation significantly with a positive sign. An increase in FL/TA will trigger an increase in the the exchange rate change. However, the results indicate that TD/TC is statistically insignificant. The p-value for the whole model indicates that the model is statistically significant.

Over the 13-year period, it is seen that banks are changing their positions. As the exchange rate increases, the weight and amount of foreign loans in the Turkish banking sector decrease. Short-term needs increased as money market statistics indicate. The ratio of total deposits to total credits first decreases and then increases. As banks are reducing their foreign loan financing, this is an expected outcome. The funding from the CBRT increased as well.

Although it is expected that TD/TC ratio would have an effect on the volatility variable, it is not the case in this model. Contrary to the initial hypothesis, an increase in the ratio of TD/TC has no effect on volatility. However, FL/TA ratio is statistically significant and enters the equation with the expected sign. An increase in this ratio will trigger an increase in our volatility measure, which is the change in the US dollar/Turkish lira exchange rate.

As a further study, an analysis can be conducted to see whether such high levels of debt may cause cyclical foreign borrowing. Due to the increased risks of the Turkish economy, this means borrowing with higher interest rates. Even if we assume that the amount borrowed would be used to pay back a portion of the foreign debt, the interest payments will have an impact on the liabilities of the Turkish banks. Additionally, future research can investigate whether Turkish banks use these short-term funds to pay their foreign loans. If this is true, maturity mismatch risk arises. Although it is evident that the short-term needs of banks increased, a detailed analysis is needed to show if these funds are used for paying foreign loans back. Further analysis can be conducted to see if Turkish banks used the foreign loans to give credit in terms of Turkish liras, how these foreign funds are utilized, and if the Turkish banking sector managed the currency mismatch risks by adjusting its positions. There is an increased demand for TRY-denominated funds from the Turkish banking sector. This increased demand may be inflationary.

Although the model in this chapter focuses on deposits and foreign loans, there are other factors influencing the exchange rate changes. Those factors such as political and macroeconomic risks are not within the scope of this study. A limitation is that the individual bank performances are not included and the level of dollarization is not studied. It would be interesting to conduct an analysis to see which banks are contributing most to the FX risk.

There are some policy implications for the banking sector. According to the results of this study, some macroprudential policies can be advised to reduce the foreign exchange risk of the sector.

References

Caglayan, M., Pham, T. and Talavera, O. (2021). Dollarization, pass-through, and domestic lending: Evidence from Turkish banking. *Emerging Markets Finance and Trade*, *57*, 3190–3201.

Demir, G. (2021). Analysis of the financial performance of the Turkish banking system by using ROC-ITARA-CODAS methods. *Gümüşhane University Journal of Social Sciences Institute*, *12*, 831–847.

De Nicolo, G., Honohan, P. and Ize, A. (2005). Dollarization of bank deposits: Causes and consequences. *Journal of Banking & Finance*, *29*, 1697–1727.

Elnahass, M., Marie, M. and Elgammal, M. (2022). Terrorist attacks and bank financial stability: Evidence from MENA economies. *Review of Quantitative Finance and Accounting*, *59*, 383–427.

Fan, H., Feng, L. and Zhou, R. (2021). Research on systemic risk of the Turkish banking industry based on a systemic risk measurement framework of the fractional Brownian motion. *Discrete Dynamics in Nature and Society*, 2021, 1–13.

Huang, Q., De Haan, J. and Scholtens, B. (2019). Analysing systemic risk in the Chinese banking system. *Pacific Economic Review*, *24*, 348–372.

Karasoy, A. T. (1995). Management of exchange rate risk in Turkish banking sector: A model and tests. *Discussion Papers, Research Department, Central Bank of Turkey.*

Ozsoz, E. (2008). Bank performance in dollarized economies. PhD Dissertation, Fordham University.

Schularick, M. and Taylor, A. (2012). Credit booms gone bust: Monetary policy, leverage cycles, and financial crises, 1870-2008. *American Economic Review*, *102*, 1029–1061.

Sengul, S. and Yilmaz, E. (2019). Measuring systemic risks in the Turkish banking sector. *Business and Economic Research Journal*, *10*, 1071–1084.

Wang, Y., Shan, X. and Geng, J. (2015). Estimating the systemic risk of China's banking industries based on Merton model. *Applied Mathematics & Information Sciences*, *9*, 957–964.

Yun, J. and Moon, H. (2014). Measuring systemic risk in the Korean banking sector via dynamic conditional correlation models. *Pacific-Basin Finance Journal*, *27*, 94–114.

https://doi.org/10.1142/9781800614321_0008

Chapter 8

Building Bank Resilience Through Risk Management Competency Development

Eric H. Y. Koh
Faculty of Business and Economics, Universiti Malaya, Kuala Lumpur, Malaysia
erickoh@um.edu.my

Abstract

This chapter studies the use of a proposed integrated competency development approach to address the challenges which a bank's risk management function faced during the COVID-19 pandemic. It studies the challenges and regulatory reforms after the 2008 Global Financial Crisis. It argues that these reforms were not sufficient to address the challenges in the longer term. It revisits the key features of the proposed integrated approach to risk management competency development. Next, it studies and identifies four major challenges together with the corresponding risk management competency development requirements. It finds that these requirements can be inferred from the proposed integrated approach. It proposes that this integrated approach is, and will likely remain, relevant to helping banks build resilience as they confront future pandemics and challenges.

Keywords: Financial crisis, risk management, competency development, banks, integrated, resilience, uncertainty, pandemic, risk, actionable

1. Introduction

Even as banks were grappling with the aftermath of the 2008 Global Financial Crisis (GFC), another crisis struck in 2020: the COVID-19 pandemic.[1] Initially brushed off as merely a local phenomenon in Wuhan, China, it subsequently spread and shook the world in unprecedented ways, speed, and scale across all aspects of people's lives. Businesswise, this pandemic has negatively impacted sales, cash flow, liquidity, margins, and growth. In fact, some businesses have collapsed.

Consequently, banks have been caught up in yet another big distraction and disruption since 2020. They have to grapple with many fluid situations and uncertainties for which guidance from the past was almost non-existent. As banks dealt with the urgent tasks, they may by now be familiar with some new norms such as social distancing, which has in turn accelerated digitalization. Cashless and contactless payments have substantially replaced traditional forms of financial services. However, amid these distractions and disruptions, banks should still reflect on whether their post-GFC reformation journey is still on track. In short, banks should consider whether they are still heading toward building enduring resilience which can withstand other potential future shocks. Resilience may be defined as "the ability to deal with adversity, withstand shocks, and continuously adapt and accelerate as disruptions and crises arise over time" (World Economic Forum and McKinsey & Company, 2022, p. 5). In other words, resilience is not about surviving one crisis but, rather, about enduring the test of time as we face one crisis after another.

Some ten years after the CFG, several leading global banks continued to shock the world with huge blunders. Examples include institutions which were fined or charged for mishandling mortgages, manipulating interbank rates reporting, engaging in money laundering financing, engaging in securities fraud, and at least one suffered a huge trading loss on derivatives (Hurtado, 2013; Wright, 2017). This sense of frustration and hopelessness is well reflected in former

[1] In fact, at the time of writing, we are confronted by the Russia–Ukraine crisis and the monkeypox outbreak.

British premier Gordon Brown's lamentation that banks have failed to learn from the GFC (Arnold, 2017).

Similar to what we saw in the aftermath of the GFC, we now see a flurry of activities toward tackling the immediate challenges posed by the COVID-19 pandemic. Likewise, just as in post-GFC period, we see many discussions on specific areas. For instance, banking publications tend to discuss technical risk or regulatory areas (Hartmann, 2010; Van Greuning and Bratanovic, 2009) but not human development areas. Meanwhile, learning-related publications tend to cover notional human engagement or development concepts but not how they may apply to a bank. Similarly, in the aftermath of the COVID-19 pandemic, we see banking publications largely discussing the pandemic's generally adverse impact on areas such as the 116 banking sectors' financial performance and stability (Elnahass *et al.*, 2021), the U.S. banks' systemic risk or betas (Walker *et al.*, 2020), and the 45 countries' bank stock prices (Demirguc-Kunt *et al.*, 2020).

These publications provide some useful gauges and indicative public policy responses. But they are area specific and do not provide sufficiently granular and comprehensive guidance for banks to build enduring resilience. The post-GFC regulatory measures and reforms may have aided in strengthening the overall banking sector. This helped mitigate the COVID-19 pandemic's unprecedented effects on banks (Financial Stability Board, 2021). But regulatory measures and reforms are by themselves inadequate. Likewise, other quick fixes, such as engaging the best consultants, recruiting the top bankers, and implementing the most advanced systems, may show some short-term results but these may not be effective and sustainable in the longer term.

Instead, each bank needs to properly plan and run its own journey toward developing its risk management competency in an integrated manner to better weather the many storms ahead. Competency refers to three items as represented by the human hands, head, and heart. It refers not only to the requisite technical skills (hands) but also to the pertinent knowledge (head) and the bank staff members' attitudinal traits (heart) to effectively manage its risk management function. Toward this end, this chapter builds on Koh's (2019b) proposed integrated approach to risk management competency development.

Specifically, it has three objectives, namely, (1) to revisit the key outputs of the proposed competency development approach, (2) to identify the requirements arising from the COVID-19 pandemic, and (3) to assess the adequacy of this approach in light of the COVID-19 pandemic.

2. Revisiting a Proposed Integrated Approach to Competency Development

Koh's (2019b) proposed an integrated approach that serves to help a bank to continuously facilitate its risk management function's competency development endeavor. There are two main outputs. The first is a list of 23 actionable items which will be discussed in Section 2.2. This list effectively serves as a working checklist of the items required to continuously develop the bank's risk management competency. The second output is a five-theme model that substantially summarizes these actionable items through a factor analysis exercise. This five-theme model will be discussed in Section 2.3. It provides a more summarized way of reviewing and updating competency development matters. These five themes encompass 18 of the 23 actionable items. The remaining five actionable items do not clearly form any factor and are deemed standalones in nature. The following three sub-sections discuss why the proposed approach is integrated, the formulation of the 23 actionable items, and the five-theme model, respectively.

2.1. *An integrated approach*

This proposed competency development approach is integrated in that it brings together three interconnected and established strategy concepts, namely, core competencies, dynamic competencies, and learning organization. These concepts are still widely discussed; they were popularized largely by Hamel and Prahalad (1994), Teece (2007), and Senge (2006), respectively.

Each concept focuses on one key area, namely, the continuous stretching of competencies, adapting to external changes, and nurturing an internal environment which encourages and enables continuous learning. Most studies examine each concept separately. Despite their individual strengths, Koh (2019b) argues that these concepts are interconnected because there are some subtle similarities and concomitantly subtle differences pertaining to their goals and focus areas. Besides, each concept contributes uniquely to competency development in a way that is not as obvious, clear, or explicit as the other two concepts. Hence, these concepts complement one another. When these three concepts are merged, they provide a more comprehensive and integrated approach to competency development.

2.2. *The 23 actionable items*

The concepts' key variables were inferred through literature reviews of those three concepts on competency development. These variables were then translated into 23 actionable items that apply to a bank's risk management function. The translation process was done through a review of pertinent banking and risk management context literature. The actionable items were further rechecked through interviews with leading Chief Risk Officers.

Furthermore, these 23 actionable items were studied through a questionnaire survey of bank risk management professionals. They do not merely allude to some broad or abstract notions but also provide a list of actionable items. Nonetheless, the questionnaire does not pretend to be an exhaustive list. It should be used together with the three concepts in mind and should be reviewed regularly for updates and relevance.

2.3. *The five-theme model*

A factor analysis was performed on the survey responses. The outcome suggests that these actionable items could be meaningfully summarized through five themes which grouped together 18 of the 23 actionable items. That is, the grouping of like actionable items into each of the pertinent themes makes both statistical and conceptual sense. Table 1 briefly describes these five themes and the remaining five standalone actionable items.

Table 1. An integrated approach to risk management competency development.

Themes/Actionable Items	Brief Explanation
Themes	
T1. Active learning	Learning meaningfully, willingly, continuously, and purposively in an environment which fosters such behavior. Examples of pertinent actionable items include having a culture which respects risk considerations, having enriching prior experience in other functions, and regularly relooking into the relevance of pertinent competency profiles.
T2. In the bank's interest	Staff members seriously reflect, discuss, and act in the bank's interest rather than for selfish motives. Examples of pertinent actionable items include professional and sincere discussions to reflect on probable future events, aligning staff members' goals to those of the bank, and constructive discussions among staff members from various other functions.
T3. Proactive	Self-driven in keeping updated and equipped for continuous development. Examples of pertinent actionable items include being aware of new techniques in risk management, keeping updated on regulatory matters, and being proactive to pursue professional development.
T4. Stretch	Stretch one's thinking rather than being limited to typical sources of competencies. Examples of pertinent actionable items include engaging or applying quantitative expertise from other disciplines to complex derivatives and engaging other external parties to gain insights into emerging or probable trends and hence, the pertinent implications for competency development.
T5. Broader perspective	View things from a broader perspective, taking into account interconnections of events and risk implications. Examples of pertinent actionable items include adopting a "comprehensive view" and "enterprise-wide risk management".
The five standalone actionable items	
A1. Aware of new products	Proactive in being aware of new banking products.
A2. Learn from past lessons	Discuss and reflect on lessons learned from past events.

Table 1. (*Continued*)

Themes/Actionable Items	Brief Explanation
A3. Codify and institutionalize knowledge	Record and retain as explicit knowledge instead of merely being tacit knowledge that resides in few staff members.
A4. Exercise judgment	Exercise judgment instead of overly relying on quantitative risk models.
A5. Keep abreast of international developments	Regularly track and be updated with global industry events.

3. The COVID-19 Pandemic

There are many issues arising from the COVID-19 pandemic. The list will probably never be complete as we are still adapting and learning daily. Nonetheless, the following sub-sections highlight the four key themes arising from a literature review on how the pandemic affects the risk management of banks.

3.1. *Increased uncertainty and volatility*

The COVID-19 pandemic struck unexpectedly and swiftly created chaos worldwide. Just as in the case of other industries, banks had to quickly adjust to new norms of working which were triggered by social distancing, movement restrictions, and lockdowns, both locally and internationally. The pandemic was unprecedented as most people did not see it coming and did not expect it to have such wide-reaching and huge ramifications. For banks, the lack of reliable data in the midst of huge uncertainty, volatility, dynamic, and fluid conditions made it extremely difficult to assess credit quality and portfolio risk (Basel Committee on Banking Supervision, 2022a; Deloitte Malaysia, 2020; KPMG, 2022).

The challenges were compounded by the public policymakers' expectations that banks would provide financing in a counter-cyclical manner at a time when a global economic downturn was imminent (Demirguc-Kunt *et al.*, 2020; Elnahass *et al.*, 2021). Not only did banks have to address their internal operational matters but they also had to assess more credit requests in the midst of public policy support which may couch the borrowers' true risk conditions. In other words, banks were attacked on two fronts: increased volumes and complexity in the midst of physical restrictions and in a highly uncertain environment.

One possible way to address these challenges is to mobilize a crisis-era "war room". This "war room" comprises a core group of highly experienced risk professionals (and supported by staff from the business, finance, legal, and compliance functions) to coordinate the bank's response during a crisis (Gwynne *et al.*, 2020). Broadly speaking, this calls for making a delicate trade-off judgment between providing what the bank's customers and society need versus protecting the bank's financials. More specifically, it also involves making quick but well-reasoned adjustments to the credit underwriting criteria against the backdrop of limited data and great uncertainty.

Likewise, banks had to exercise greater judgment by considering the possible limitations, non-reliability, and interdependencies of their risk models (Laurent *et al.*, 2020). This contrasts with the largely risk model-driven decision-making approach in more normal circumstances. During the COVID-19 pandemic, risk professionals had to be more vigilant as many underlying assumptions, parameters, and data of their models became inaccurate, incomplete, or irrelevant very quickly.

In sum, the highly uncertain and volatile scenarios call for greater exercise of judgment to make pertinent adjustments and to consider the possible limitations inherent in the quantitative risk models. This corresponds with the standalone actionable item A4 "exercise judgment" in Table 1.

3.2. *A global crisis and more to come?*

Initially, the COVID-19 outbreak was seen as a faraway domestic issue in Wuhan, China. Many blamed the alleged poor hygiene standards and practices. When the Chinese authorities imposed strict lockdowns to contain the outbreak, many criticized them for human rights violations. However, to the surprise of many, COVID-19 quickly spread across the world to become a global pandemic.

Governments worldwide had no choice but to impose some forms of lockdowns to contain the COVID-19 pandemic.

This points to the importance of keeping abreast with key international developments. What happens in one country can quickly transmit to another country and, in fact, to many countries globally. In actuality, travel restrictions and border closures had accelerated digitalization and triggered supply chain disruptions. Accelerated digitalization happened due to the increased demand for technology solutions to facilitate contactless transactions, remote work interface, and video conferencing. While digitalization facilitated transactional efficiencies and mitigated the limitations in face-to-face contact, it also raised concerns in terms of technology and cybersecurity risks. These risks increase because of potential security weaknesses in "work from home" settings and greater reliance on outsourced service providers. This led to increased incidences of phishing, malware, and ransomware attacks (Financial Stability Board, 2021).

While the world is still grappling with the COVID-19 pandemic, the Russia–Ukraine crisis has unleashed another wave of global repercussions. This crisis has exacerbated cybersecurity threats and supply chain disruptions (White *et al.*, 2022). These cyberattacks may affect others who are not the original targets, i.e., those related to the Russian and Ukrainian governments.

The COVID-19 pandemic had already disrupted global supply chains because of border closures, travel restrictions, and factory schedule disruptions. This was exacerbated by the Russia–Ukraine crisis because they are the major suppliers of gas, wheat, and fertilizer ingredients, all of which are basic necessities. The supply chain disruptions have also seen price increases which affect business margins and cash flows. Besides, there is a decline in globalization or offshoring activities and an increase in nearshoring instead (White *et al.*, 2022).

In sum, the risk management function needs to be even more aware of international developments and their potential impact on the bank's business. Events that seem so far away can quickly become a reality in one's backyard. This corresponds to the standalone actionable item labeled A5 "keep abreast of international developments" in Table 1.

3.3. *A bigger picture in the midst of the pandemic*

Reflecting on the unprecedented COVID-19 pandemic, Lim and Heng (2022) propose a broader perspective by studying some historical, social, economic, and political contexts and developments. They argue that excessive human economic greed had led to the over-encroachment of nature and environment. This in turn led to several zoonotic pandemics, from the 1918 Spanish flu to the 1997 Avian flu, 2009 Swine flu, and 2003 SARS, all of which were relatively small compared with the COVID-19 pandemic that triggered unprecedented consequences.

Lim and Heng (2022) point out some flaws and fractures in society as shown by increasing economic inequalities, environmental degradation and climate crisis, the inability of health systems to cope with calamities, and domestic populist political stance that led to the weak handling of the pandemic. We also see economic growth being driven more by debt, speculation, and asset bubbles rather than being led by productivity and income gains. This results in an unstable financial system which sees one financial crisis morphing into another. In short, the issues of climate change, potential future pandemics, and financial system instability are among the biggest global risks now. We tend to study these issues in isolation when, in fact, they are closely intertwined.

A period of uncertainty also requires us to move away from the typical, largely quantitative approach to analyzing portfolio risk sources. Typically, banks would identify the likely winners and losers in each sector. However, having a broader, integrated qualitative-quantitative approach may mean studying the narrative connections between how COVID-19 evolved and future business outlook rather than waiting to input financial statement data into credit risk models (Wee *et al.*, 2021). Likewise, it is not enough to merely study and manage model limitations. Instead, one also needs to adopt a broader perspective of considering the interdependencies among the models used (Laurent *et al.*, 2020).

In sum, in the midst of the uncertainties during the pandemic, one needs to also adopt a broader perspective or a more comprehensive view to make sense of what is going on in order to better manage risks. This corresponds to Theme T5 "broader perspective" in Table 1.

3.4. *Broader-based competencies*

As the COVID-19 pandemic further complicates the fragile financial system, the risk management function needs to have a broader-based range of competencies. It cannot work in its own silo but has to properly engage other functions and integrate pertinent broad-based competencies (Koh, 2019a).

In terms of engaging other functions, the risk management function should be a strategic value partner rather than being perceived as a passive control function. For instance, the risk management function may facilitate a more proactive and dynamic approach to managing model risks and clarify how the models link to the bank's risk appetite (Laurent *et al.*, 2020). Additionally, Wee *et al.* (2021) suggest that some risk management functions are already coordinating calls for action and helping the business functions navigate the turmoil by using scenario analytics and modeling enhancements.

Integrating broad-based competencies includes a better appreciation of data analytics and even non-financial risks, especially environmental, social, and governance (ESG) matters. This may be exemplified in terms of how COVID-19-related data should be best incorporated into credit risk models (Basel Committee on Banking Supervision, 2022a). Moreover, as banks aspire to better leverage data, risk management functions should recruit data analytics talent so as to build more sophisticated data-related competencies (Bellens and Watson, 2020).

Meanwhile, non-financial risks, such as ESG and particularly on climate change, have been intensifying since 2019 when the European Union first incorporated climate-related risks as a key driver. There is grave concern that climate-related risks may trigger systemic risks in the banking sector. Hence, there is a need to better understand climate-related risks to encourage environment-friendly activities or investments and to dissuade the non-environment-friendly ones. As of June 2022, the Basel Committee on Banking Supervision (2022b) had issued 18 high-level principles for managing and supervising climate-related financial risks.

In sum, as the pandemic increases the complexities of risk challenges confronting banks, the risk management function needs to actively interact with other functions as a valued business partner.

Table 2. COVID-19: competency development requirements.

Key Challenges from COVID-19 Pandemic	Themes/Actionable Items (from Table 1)
3.1 Increased uncertainty and volatility	A4. Exercise judgment
3.2 A global crisis and more to come?	A5. Keep abreast of international developments
3.3 A bigger picture	T5. Broader perspective
3.4 Broader-based competencies	T1. Active learning

Further, increasing complexity calls for building a broader-based range of competencies. This corresponds to Theme T1 "active learning" in Table 1.

Sections 3.1–3.4 discuss some new developments arising from the COVID-19 pandemic. Each new development presents challenges and calls for competency development requirements that correspond to two standalone actionable items and two themes. The two standalone actionable items are "exercise judgment" and "keep abreast with international developments". Meanwhile, the two themes are "broader perspective" and "active learning".

Table 2 summarizes the discussions in this section. It shows the four key challenges arising from the COVID-19 pandemic. It also depicts the corresponding themes or actionable items of the proposed integrated competency development approach.

4. Conclusion

This chapter discussed the challenges that banks faced in the aftermath of the GFC and the apparent indications that they may have not really learned from the crisis. Meanwhile, the COVID-19 pandemic caught many by surprise and added complexities to the challenges. Regulatory reforms are necessary but not sufficient. Thus, this chapter proposed that banks adopt an integrated approach to develop their risk management competency.

This chapter revisited the key outputs of Koh's (2019b) proposed integrated approach to competency development. It brought together three interrelated competency development concepts and mapped them to the risk management competency development requirements as inferred from literature, interviews, and a survey. The main outputs are in the form of 23 actionable items and five themes of like actionable items.

Next, this chapter studied the key challenges and the pertinent risk management competency development requirements arising from the COVID-19 pandemic. The analysis suggests that these requirements can be found in the proposed competency development approach through two actionable items and two themes. This suggests that the proposed approach could have helped the banks' risk management functions address the COVID-19 pandemic issues and will probably be applicable for future pandemics and challenges.

Acknowledgment

Financial support from the Tun Ismail Ali Chair Research Grant (Grant Number GA013-2021) is gratefully acknowledged.

References

Arnold, M. (2017). Banks have not learnt lessons of 2008 crisis, says Gordon Brown. *Financial Times*. 31 October.

Basel Committee on Banking Supervision (2022a). Newsletter on Covid-19 related credit risk issues. 2 March.

Basel Committee on Banking Supervision (2022b). Principles for the effective management and supervision of climate-related financial risks. Bank for International Settlements.

Bellens, J. and Watson, M. (2020). How resiliency in risk management is the new top priority for banks. Ernst & Young Global Limited, UK.

Deloitte Malaysia (2020). Covid-19: Impact on financial institutions, and how to respond. April 2020.

Demirguc-Kunt, A., Pedraza, A. and Ruiz-Ortega, C. (2020). Banking sector performance during the Covid-19 crisis. *Policy Research Working Paper, Issue 9363*. The World Bank, Washington, D.C.

Elnahass, M., Trinth, V. Q. and Li, T. (2021). Global banking stability in the shadow of Covid-19 outbreak. *Journal of International Financial Markets, Institutions & Money*, *72*, 101322.

Financial Stability Board (2021). Lessons learnt from the Covid-19 pandemic from a financial stability perspective: Interim report.

Gwynne, S., O'Kelly, R., Sommer, M. and Dedeaga, C. (2020). Five actions for corporate banks in response to Covid-19. Oliver Wyman.

Hamel, G. and Prahalad, C. K. (1994). *Competing for the Future*. Boston, MA: Harvard Business School Press.

Hartmann, P. (2010). Interaction of market and credit risk. *Journal of Banking & Finance, 34*(4), 697–702.

Hurtado, P. (2013). Ex-JPMorgan employees indicted over $6.2 billion loss. Bloomberg. 17 September. http://www.bloomberg.com/news/print/2013-09-16/ex-jpm-trader-and-supervisor-indicted-by-u-s-grand-jury.jury.html.

Koh, E. H. Y. (2019a). Practitioner insight on risk management practices. In R. Zainudin, S.-G. Chan and A. R. Shahrin (eds.) *The Malaysian Banking Industry: Policies and Practices After the Asian Financial Crisis*. Milton Park, Abingdon: Routledge, pp. 125–153.

Koh, E. H. Y. (2019b). *Risk Management Competency Development in Banks an Integrated Approach*. Singapore: Palgrave Macmillan.

KPMG. (2022). A new risk management playbook for banks.

Laurent, M.-P., Weyenbergh, F. V., Plantefeve, O. and Tejada, M. (2020). Banking models after Covid-19: Taking model-risk management to the next level. McKinsey & Company.

Lim, M. H. and Heng, M. S. H. (2022). *Covid-19 and the Structural Crises of Our Time*. Singapore: ISEAS Publishing.

Senge, P. M. (2006). *The Fifth Discipline — The Art and Practice of the Learning Organisation*. London: Random House Business Books.

Teece, D. J. (2007). Explicating dynamic capabilities: The nature and microfoundations of (sustainable) enterprise performance. *Strategic Management Journal, 28*(13), 1319–1350.

Van Greuning, H. and Bratanovic, S. B. (2009). *Analysing Banking Risk — A Framework for Assessing Corporate Governance and Risk Management*, 3rd edn. Washington: The International Bank for Reconstruction and Development/The World Bank.

Walker, J., Geyfman, V. and Tekatli, N. (2020). An examination of the stability of bank betas during extreme market volatility: The case of the financial crisis and the pandemic. *Banking & Finance Review, 12*, 15–31.

Wee, K., Karsov, K., Lai, C. and Mogul, Z. (2021). Non-financial risks reshape banks' credit portfolios. Boston Consulting Group — International Association of Credit Portfolio Management.

White, O., Buehler, K., Smit, S., Greenberg, E., Mysore, M., Jain, R., Hirt, M., Govindarajan, A. and Chewning, E. (2022). War in Ukraine: Twelve disruptions changing the world. McKinsey & Company.

World Economic Forum and McKinsey & Company (2022). Resilience for sustainable, inclusive growth.

Wright, W. (2017). Have we learned our lessons from the financial crisis? Don't bank on it. *The Telegraph*. 8 October.

https://doi.org/10.1142/9781800614321_0009

Chapter 9

Resilience in the EU Banking Sector and Beyond

Lucia Alessi*, Francesca E. Di Girolamo†, and Marco Petracco-Giudici‡

European Commission — Joint Research Centre, Ispra, Italy
**lucia.alessi@ec.europa.eu*
†francesca.di-girolamo@ec.europa.eu
‡marco.petracco@ec.europa.eu

Abstract

This chapter reviews scientific work conducted in support of the policy-making processes of the European Commission in reforming the financial sector. It first discusses how the introduction of new prudential requirements, resolution, and supervision tools in the aftermath of the Global Financial Crisis has allowed for a considerable reduction in the risk of systemic crises. This chapter also discusses how further benefits could come from further harmonization of resolution and insolvency frameworks, as well as from the completion of the Banking Union, including the introduction of a European Deposit Insurance Scheme, and of a European Safe Asset. Finally, this chapter briefly overviews more recent research underpinning policy efforts to enhance financial resilience toward the risks linked to climate change and the green transition, as well as to the impacts of the digital transformation.

Keywords: Financial stability, systemic risk, climate risk, digital finance

1. Introduction

In the decade following the global financial crisis, the EU put forward a number of policy measures to improve the regulatory framework for the financial sector and enhance deposit protection. The initiatives introduced a set of harmonized rules within the European Union with the ultimate objective of creating a safer and more transparent financial sector for the EU single market, notably by shielding public finances from the effect of bank failures and improving the robustness of financial institutions. A single rulebook was proposed in 2009 to lay down capital requirements for banks, ensure better protection for depositors, and regulate the prevention and management of bank failures. On the grounds of this, the Banking Union was created later on with the rationale of breaking the circle between banks and sovereigns and further aligning responsibility for banking supervision, resolution, and funding of banks in the Eurozone by transferring bank supervision of significant institutions and resolution to the European level.

The COVID-19 pandemic and the recent geopolitical events highlighted the importance of having a healthy financial sector to absorb unexpected shocks. These circumstances have also revealed the power of a joint European response to handle a crisis. An effective and interconnected financial framework has in fact proved essential to avoid financial fragmentation and to safeguard financial stability.

Evidence of the benefit of these financial reforms also emerges from the literature. Against this background, the chapter reviews the scientific work produced in support of the policymaking process of the European Commission leading to the main measures proposed and adopted by regulators to limit the effect of bank losses and failures on the whole financial sector. The set of these financial instruments is generally referred to as the "financial safety net", as the final objective is strengthening the banking sector and ensuring that bank failures are resolved with minimal costs to taxpayers, in the case of future crises, which can never be ruled out.

Despite the progress, much more needs to be done to ensure that the financial sector remains resilient to new risks that might emerge in relation to the challenges posed by climate change and the digital transition. This chapter also provides an overview of the main outstanding issues with respect to banking regulation and presents work assembling scientific evidence on the effectiveness of different safety net tools proposed by the Commission over the past years. Moreover, this chapter elaborates on evidence supporting the need to move forward on the missing elements of the overall framework, such as a European Deposit Insurance Scheme. Finally, this chapter discusses ongoing scientific work on the new challenges ahead as the structural changes that come with the twin transitions, green and digital, exposing banks to a number of emerging risks.

2. Risk and Crisis Management Framework

During the global financial crisis, the national government injected large amounts of capital and provided liquidity support to bail out their stressed national banks to avoid domino effects that could systemically affect the banking sector and damage the real economy. The expectation of a potential public intervention encouraged risk-taking by banks thus amplifying moral hazard behaviors. For example, Cariboni *et al.* (2014) shed light on the fact that large banks were likely to benefit relatively more from government support, and the empirical work estimates that the implicit public subsidies enjoyed by the largest European banks in past years amount to 0.5–0.8% of EU 27 GDP.

Immediately following the crisis, regulators at global level highlighted the urgency of improving risk management frameworks, reducing the moral hazards, and preventing contagion effects in the banking system to avoid the fact that the default of one individual institution could produce negative effects toward the rest of the system or extend far beyond the banking sector itself. Consequently, the EU took decisive action to create a safer and sounder financial sector for the EU single market by revising and expanding the crisis prevention and management framework for banks. This involved enhancing the uniformity of existing common rules and the introduction of new rules where needed. The initiatives triggered comprehensive changes to European financial legislation and to the financial supervisory architecture. A recent study by Carmassi *et al.* (2019) shows that the ability of the euro area banking system to absorb losses while minimizing costs to taxpayers has significantly increased over the last ten years. This is seen as a consequence of the reduction in the average probability of default of banks from 2007 to 2017 and an increase in banks' loss-absorbing capacity, due to the introduction of the new resolution framework.

This section provides an overview of the actions taken by policy-makers and regulators to enhance the safety/soundness of the banking sector and at the same time increase the protection of taxpayers after the financial crisis of 2008.

2.1. *Depositors' protection*

Deposit insurance was introduced a long time ago by virtue of Directive 94/10/EC with the specific aim to protect depositors' savings. The legislative text laid down the foundation for the establishment of Deposits Guarantee Schemes (DGSs) in all EU Member States. Their ultimate responsibility is to provide a guarantee to a certain amount of customer's deposits in the event of insolvency of their credit institution. The underlying objective is to maintain financial stability by strengthening depositor confidence and discouraging bank runs. In this regard, the DGSs, directive ensured that, regardless of where the deposits were located in the Union, depositors would always be afforded a minimum standard of protection. Several of the details of the implementation of DGSs were however left at the national level.

When the global turmoil broke out, this lack of standardization led to significant differences in protection across different DGSs, as the scope or level of coverage, financing of the schemes, maximum payout delays, and rules for cooperation across borders were not fully harmonized (Cariboni *et al.*, 2008). This fragmented system turned out to be detrimental for financial stability and some of the schemes proved to be under-effective during the financial stress of 2008.

Based on then ongoing analytical work by JRC on reform of the 1994 DGS Directive, the Commission fixed wide differences in scope and level of coverage with an "emergency" Directive in March 2009: 2009/14/EC "amending Directive 94/19/EC on deposit-guarantee schemes as regards the coverage level and the payout delay".

A revised DGS framework was finally adopted in 2014 with Directive 2014/69/EU. The revised framework imposed harmonized rules to prevent unavailability of funds that might jeopardize financial stability; it harmonized the level of protection to 100 000 EUR per depositor per bank and stipulated that all DGSs should reach an *ex ante* target level of financing equal to 0.8% of the amount of covered deposits of its members by July 2024. Recently, several authors discussed the role of DGSs in the new regulatory framework. While Bodellini (2021) supports the view that these national schemes are pivotal in preserving financial stability, Boccuzzi (2022) discusses how uncertainties and inconsistencies in the legal framework could undermine the effectiveness of a DGS intervention.

In the context of analytical work on the revision of DGS directive, the JRC, together with researchers from academia and representatives from the European Commission's Directorate-General for Financial Stability, Financial Services, and Capital Markets Union,[1] developed a model for estimating the funding needs of DGSs under a range of crisis scenarios.

The model was proposed for the first time by De Lisa *et al.* (2011) to quantify an optimal target level for the Italian Deposit Guarantee Scheme fund. Campolongo *et al.* (2010) applied the model for the first time in 2010 to estimate the size of losses that are not covered by banks' capital requirements in a time of crisis and are therefore passed on to other components of the financial safety net.

The model was eventually adopted as a reference model of JRC as the Systemic Model of Banking Originated Losses (SYMBOL). The model has then been extensively used in analytical work in support of the EU regulatory reform in the banking sector (see Benczur *et al.* 2016 for a description of the model and Hordijk *et al.* 2018 for a review of the model and further references).

2.2. *Prudential requirements*

The Basel Committee on Banking Supervision approved in summer 2010 an update of the "Basel Framework" for prudential capital known as Basel III[2] with the final goal of promoting a more resilient banking sector, reducing the probability of individual bank failures, and reducing the creation and transmission of systemic risk. Among others, the package consists of capital adequacy requirements to be

[1]On 1 November 2014, the DG Internal Market and Services was dissolved and its components integrated into other DGs. A large section of the DG was integrated into the new DG for Financial Services.

[2]See https://www.bis.org/bcbs/basel3.htm?m=2572.

applied to all internationally active banks to ensure that each financial institution sets aside an appropriate level of capital relative to its riskiness. Few years later, the European Commission adopted a Regulation (575/2013) and a Directive (Capital Requirements Directive IV 2013/36/EU) to transpose the minimum standards on bank capital adequacy proposed by the Basel Committee into EU law. The EU legislative texts aim to enhance the quality and quantity of capital held by banks in their balance sheet. The new rules introduced a new definition of capital, revised the framework for credit risk, and imposed that all banks hold a capital conservation buffer of 2.5% on top of the regulatory minimum of 8% of risk-weighted assets. To reduce pro-cyclicality, counter-cyclical buffers that could be run down in a period of stress were introduced.

To address the issue of systemic riskiness of large banks, a tighter treatment was reserved for the list of banks identified by the Financial Stability Board (FSB) as Global Systemic Important Banks (GSIBs). These are mandated to set aside extra capital buffers due to their size and systemic importance.

Quantitative work by Marchesi *et al.* (2013) supported the European Commission in the implementation of such proposals, by investigating the macroeconomic benefit and costs entailed by the implementation of Basel III. Building on the already existing SYMBOL model and a simplified macroeconomic framework, the authors estimate the reduction in the probability of occurrence of a systemic banking crisis under higher levels of capitalization and the different definition of capital contained in the new regulatory framework. The model then derives the distribution of excess losses affecting the banking system due to banks' defaults. The macroeconomic benefits arise from the avoidance of the expected fall in GDP that follows a systemic banking crisis, thanks to the reduction in the probability of having a crisis. Costs derive instead from the increase in lending rates introduced by banks as a reaction to the tighter Basel III capital requirements that in turn induce a decrease in non-financial firms' investments and a drag in GDP growth. Results show that Basel III reduces the probability of a systemic banking crisis, and the reduction depends on the initial level of banks' capital and on the subsequent level of recapitalization. Regarding the macroeconomic impact of Basel III, findings reveal that the net benefits of implementing Basel III are always positive, and their aggregate value is maximal in the scenario where the capital conservation buffer is introduced on top of an 8% base requirement. As illustrated by Zedda and Cannas (2020), higher capitalization not only has the effect of enhancing the resilience of banks against future crises but it also has the potential of reducing contagion risk and therefore reducing systemic risk.

A set of amendments to the Basel framework was tabled over the next few years, proposing the revision of leverage and liquidity requirements and of the framework for market risk prudential requirements.

In line with these revised Basel standards, the European Commission implements the liquidity standards by imposing stricter liquidity requirements for banks in the CRDIV, so as to enhance the short-term (Liquidity Coverage Ratio, LCR) and long-term (Net Stable Funding Ratio, NSFR) resilience to liquidity disruptions. The LCR was fully implemented by the end of 2018, and the NSFR came into effect in 2021.

In a revised Capital Requirement Regulation published in 2016, the European Commission includes additional capital rules for activities in the trading book exposed to market risk and addresses the need of limiting institutions' exposure to the risk of excessive leverage. The revised package proposes a change in the capital requirements of credit institutions to reflect the appropriate riskiness of the trading book and imposes a binding 3% leverage ratio.

In support of the discussion on these issues, Alessi *et al.* (2016) performed an *ex ante* quantitative evaluation to estimate the effects of changes to market risk capital and leverage requirements. First, the authors identify assets' categories associated with retail and trading activities. Second, a panel analysis is used to estimate the level of trading RWAs under a common set of risk weights. Third, the estimated riskiness of trading activities is translated into an increase in capital requirements. Finally, the estimated new capital level is used to feed the SYMBOL model and generate losses in the event of a banking crisis. Results of the simulation before and after the introduction of the legislative changes are compared to arrive at an estimation of the impacts. Benefits are measured as reduction in banks' losses that need to be absorbed by different levels of the financial safety net. The main findings show that when higher capital requirements are imposed on the trading book, public finance contingent liabilities from the banking sector, in case of a systemic crisis, would be reduced by up to 15% compared to a situation where banks only hold base capital requirements. However, owing to the fact that capitalization of credit institution is higher than the minimum required, the new legislative proposal does not imply an additional capital burden on most banks and does not reduce potential contingent liabilities. When focusing on the leverage ratio, authors find that the 3% requirement is binding for many institutions, thus imposing substantially higher capitalization needs, which could also reduce potential contingent liabilities up to 48% compared to the minimum capital baseline.

2.3. *Bank recovery and resolution framework*

As already emphasized, the ability of authorities to manage failing banks has been severely tested over the course of the financial crisis. The high degree of integration in the EU financial services market and the lack of tools and preparedness to wind down banks in an orderly manner hampered the capacity of regulators to deal with the crisis, forcing them in many cases to intervene by bailing out institutions instead.

While the increase in capital requirement aims to reduce the probability of failure, the resolution framework is a tool for reducing the impact of failure on the economy and ensuring that the costs are not borne by taxpayers.

The package was designed to ensure resolvability, to guarantee a more intensive/effective supervision, to manage failure of credit institutions of any size, and to ensure smooth market exits whenever needed. While some banks are still harder to resolve due to being heavily interconnected and systemically important, or having a complex structure, by facilitating their resolution, the new Directive addresses the too-big-to-fail problem, thus mitigating the distortionary effect of the implicit subsidy.

The Bank Recovery and Resolution Directive, adopted in spring 2014, grants national authority powers to ensure an orderly resolution of failing banks and provides for a set of instruments that can be applied whenever a bank is in distress. Before a bank is declared failing or likely to fail (FOLF), supervisors can intervene in a timely manner in the operation of banks to stop the escalation of the problem and to prevent failures. When a bank is considered

FOLF and there is a public interest in resolving it, the resolution authorities will intervene in the absence of a private solution. Tools include the possibility to sell the bank or parts of it, to transfer critical functions to a bridge institution, or to transfer non-performing assets to an asset management vehicle. Moreover, it includes the power to bail-in creditors by writing down their claims or converting them into capital, to provide the bank with loss-absorbing or recapitalization resources.[3] Fiordalisi *et al.* (2020) show that investors perceive the new bail-in regime as a credible tool to decrease government interventions, reduce the too-big-to-fail problem, and increase market discipline in the European banking industry. Crespi *et al.* (2019) provide evidence of improved market discipline in the Italian primary bond market.

Furthermore, the BRRD grants national resolution authorities the possibility to complement the resolution intervention with alternative financing arrangements funded *ex ante* by the industry. This refers to the setup of a National Resolution Fund to be used in case of a bank failure to ensure an orderly resolution and an effective application of the resolution tools. All financial institutions have to contribute to the funding of their national funds by paying an annual fee according to their size and risk profile. The European Commission (2012) expands on the approach presented in Marchesi *et al.* (2013)[4] and makes use of the SYMBOL model together with a simplified macroeconomic framework to quantify the appropriate size of National Resolution Funds, and to analyze different combinations of funding from resolution schemes and the loss-absorbing capacity (TLAC)[5] of a bank. That is to say funding needs are obtained from the distribution of losses in excess of capital plus recapitalization needs of defaulted banks, and the size mainly depends on the severity

[3]The rationale behind this is to reduce contagions across banks. By allocating the cost of resolving a bank to the shareholders and creditors of the bank itself (with the bail-in), the framework reduces moral hazard and negates the possibility that banks will automatically be rescued by the government, as occurred in the global financial crisis.

[4]The reverse timing on the references is due to an embargo on the publication of the scientific report while the Impact Assessment of the proposals was being drafted.

[5]Total regulatory capital plus long-term bail-in able liabilities.

of the crisis that such tools would be asked to withstand. Model calculations identify optimal parameters for TLAC and the size of the resolution fund. These model-based optimal values provide support to the choices of values of 8% of Total Liability and Own Funds (TLOF) to be held by banks and of 1% of total covered deposits for the national resolution funds target, which were selected by the co-legislators.

Having established Resolution Funds, one of the main challenges of the European Commission was the development of a methodology to design the banks' contributions. Specifically, Article 94 of the BRRD establishes that the banks are required to pay an annual contribution based on two components: first, a flat contribution based on a size component and second, a risk adjustment. The former is proportional to the amount of total liability excluding own funds and covered deposits. The risk adjustment takes into account the risk profile of each bank and is defined on a number of risk indicators, some of which depend upon balance sheet information. In 2014, the Commission published a delegated act to spell out the technical details of the methodology to calculate banks' contribution to the resolution funds. The analyses reported in Cannas *et al.* (2014) contributed by assessing alternative designs of the composite risk indicator measuring the risk adjustment and addressing the distributional impacts of several alternative technical options for the calculation methodology.

2.4. *Proposal on structural reforms*

Besides the regulatory reforms described in previous sections, the European Commission also reflected on a potential structural reform of the banking sector to address the too-big-to-fail concern. This initiative was adopted following an assessment carried out by the High-Level Expert Group presided by Erkki Liikanen, governor of Finland's central bank. Back in 2011, Commission Barnier set up this group with the mandate to assess the need for structural separation of banks' activities. The conclusions argued that additional reforms seemed to be necessary in order to correct incentives for excessive risk raking, complexity, and interconnectedness in the banking sector. The group thus recommended a separation of the trading book from the rest of the assets. To tackle this issue, the European

Commission proposed a regulation to stop the largest financial institutions from engaging in risky trading activities using money invested by customers.

The JRC (European Commission 2014a) contributed to the proposal with several analyses. Pagano *et al.* (2014) assess the impact of different designs on the rules for selecting banks that would be candidates for structural separation based on different definitions of trading activities and calculate optimal cut-off points for selection based on cluster analysis.

Cariboni *et al.* (2014), already mentioned above, estimate the implicit subsidy for large and complex institutions that are "too big to fail" by looking at the difference between ratings with and without government support.

Petracco *et al.* (2014) conduct a panel analysis of average risk weights for different asset classes that can be reconducted to trading and commercial banking activities, and find evidence for incentives toward trading activities implied by the then current structure of capital requirements for market risk.

Cannas *et al.* (2014) estimate some benefits and costs of the proposed separation by making use of a version of the SYMBOL model on "counterfactual" credit institutions separated into commercial and trading entities and a set of behavioral scenarios for banks' and markets' reactions and adaptations.

Results of the analysis suggest that owing to the separation, a higher part of the losses in case of crisis would be absorbed by their shareholders with respect to other creditors. Model results also estimate a reduction in total losses, though this would not necessarily translate in further reductions of contingent liabilities once all other financial reforms on capital requirements and resolvability of banks are factored in.

In a separate piece of work expanding the framework developed for the assessment of potential candidates (Pagano *et al.*, 2014), Campolongo *et al.* (2015) conduct a cluster analysis of balance sheet data to identify banks with different business models and compare their results with the proposed rules for determining potential candidates.

The Commission eventually decided to withdraw the proposal in July 2018, as it was recognized that its purpose had in the meantime largely been addressed by other regulatory measures. For example,

Ayadi *et al.* (2020) show that banks have reconsidered their strategies after the regulatory reforms of the European banking sector. That is to say the authors find that larger, less profitable, and riskier banks are more likely to change their business model to effectively improve their performance.

2.5. *Comprehensive assessment of the safety net in the EU*

Since the approval of the prudential reforms, a number of quantitative studies have been developed to discuss the impact of the new safety net tools and of the package as a whole.

Concerning the bail-in, the work by Galliani and Zedda (2014) shows that, while limited crises tend to be absorbed by the system, serious crises amplify at each turn until it becomes impossible to stop them without external intervention. However, results when including bail-in show that a bail-in of 8% of total bank balance sheet can be effective in making the system more robust to absorb losses and in breaking the vicious circle thus preventing contagion between banks and public finances. Making use of data on government bonds' holdings from the Transparency Exercise of the European Central Bank and a version of the SYMBOL model including a macro module for sovereign default risk, Fontana and Langedijk (2019) look at the impact of reducing home bias, bail-in, resolution tools, and bank recapitalization support on the bank–sovereign loop. They show that reducing home bias has limited impacts, while bail-in and the new tools can be effective in breaking the loop, which otherwise could more than double the effect of an initial shock on bank losses and the sovereign risk premium. Finally, Beck *et al.* (2021) show that a bail-in coupled with management changes can mitigate the potentially negative impact of bank failures on credit supply and thus provide supporting evidence for this resolution tool.

The literature on the overall assessment of the whole new banking package attempts to look at the combined impact of the new capital definitions and requirements, and the tools for bank recovery and resolution, including bail-in. These quantitative studies mainly focus on the reduction in public finance costs. The European Commission (2014b) performed a comprehensive assessment of the financial reforms adopted by the EU with the Economic Review of the

Financial Regulation Agenda report. Results (based on the SYMBOL model) show that the overall benefits of higher capital requirement combined with the bail-in and national resolution funds are expected to outweigh the cost. That is to say macroeconomic benefit, measured in terms of avoided GDP loss, amounts to 0.6–1.1% of EU GDP per year. On the contrary, the macroeconomic costs have been quantified to be about 0.3% of EU GDP per year. In more detail, increased capital requirement results in a 22% reduction in the potential public finance costs associated with a banking crisis. Considering the bail-in and the resolution funds, the reduction reaches more than 90% assuming that the new regulatory framework is fully effective in stopping contagion in the system. A few years later, empirical works by Benczur *et al.* (2016) and Cariboni *et al.* (2016) also discussed the distribution of losses across equity holders, bondholders, safety net tools, and public sector when using the SYMBOL model. The first paper extends the results of the European Commission along different lines. First, the authors model the single resolution fund for countries in the Banking Union (see the following). Second, the analysis assesses the impact analyzing different data vintages. Third, the paper allows for a more sophisticated correlation structure among banks. Despite these differences, results do not change. In particular, the authors estimate the joint distribution of bank losses in excess of capital, under the new level of capital and safety net tools, such as bail-in and resolution funds. Aggregating data over the entire banking system, the model allows one to assess the overall reduction in potential public finance costs deriving from the adopted policies. Results show that final contingent losses decrease from 3.7% of EU GDP to 0.5%. In particular, increased capitalization decreases financing needs by about 30% and the bail-in tool seems to play a larger role in reducing financing needs by 60%. In the second paper, the authors also discuss where bank losses go when the bail-in is applied, as different classes of investors may be concerned. Findings reveal that most of the bank bonds are held by domestic financial institutions, despite some heterogeneity across countries. The paper concludes that more research is needed to improve the understanding of the composition of bank creditors. Finally, Bellia *et al.* (2020a), the FSB (2020), and Bellia *et al.* (2020b, 2021a) also develop a set of event studies based on CDS data and equity returns, aimed at assessing market perception of the reforms in solving the too-big-to-fail problem. Results from these studies point to a reduced perception of public subsidies. Moreover, some of the results point to a change over time of this perception, with the event of being included in the GSIB's list generating less reactions over time, thus pointing to a lower expectation on the government support.

2.6. *The establishment of the banking union*

The global financial crisis and the subsequent sovereign debt crisis of 2010–2012 made clear how interconnected the European banking market was, especially in the euro area where the single currency played a pivotal role in accelerating the integration of the financial system. At that time, the doom loop (so-called bank-sovereign nexus) was at the heart of the eurozone debt crisis. Despite being engaged in cross-border activities, banks remained closely linked to their Member State of origin by the presence of local supervision. Moreover, "home bias" in government bond purchases led them to hold large amounts of their own government debt. An initial shock originating either in the banking or sovereign sector could thus be amplified by the feedback relation. Therefore, the idea of strengthening the banking sector, breaking the sovereign–bank nexus, and enhancing the level playing field of banks in the Eurozone gained momentum.

The European Commission investigated additional measures to harmonize and centralize at the EU level the responsibility for supervision, resolution, and funding in the Eurozone. This idea led to the establishment of the Banking Union, a fundamental milestone designed to preserve financial stability and avoid exacerbating the bank–sovereign vicious loop. The Banking Union coupled with the single rulebook is made of three main pillars: the Single Supervisory Mechanism (SSM), the Single Resolution Mechanism (SRM), and the European deposit guarantee scheme (EDIS).

The SSM is a system for supervision of financial institutions in the EU, exercised by the European Central Bank (ECB) and the National Supervisory Authorities of the participating Member States. In preparation for its new supervisory role, the ECB announced a Comprehensive Assessment of all banks which were likely to become subject to its direct supervision. Calò *et al.* (2021) show that the CA and institution of the SSM succeeded in making the financial system of the Eurozone more resilient. That is to say banks under the SSM remit proved to have a persistently higher Tier 1 capital ratio. Over the medium term, this seems to have been achieved by increasing their capitalization level without shrinking their assets, and the impact appears to be concentrated in jurisdictions that are ranked in the bottom half of the ranking of institutional and supervisory quality before the introduction of the reform. The importance of increased capitalization and micro supervision in improving the resilience of banks is also supported by the findings of Alessi *et al.* (2021a), who look at the determinants of the coverage ratio of Non-Performing Loans (NPLs) and its components.

The SRM aims to resolve effectively and efficiently non-viable banks. It is made up of national resolution authorities and a central resolution authority, namely, the Single Resolution Board (SRB). An essential part of the SRM is the Single Resolution Fund (SRF), a supranational fund administered by the SRB, which replaced the National Resolution Fund of all Member States participating in the Banking Union in 2016.

EDIS refers to the establishment of a common depositor protection mechanism, which is still under discussion. The EDIS proposal builds on the system of national DGSs regulated by Directive 2014/49/EU which ensures that all deposits up to €100,000 are protected through national schemes. The EDIS would mark an important step toward reinforcing financial stability, reducing the vulnerability of national deposit guarantee schemes to large local shocks, ensuring that the level of depositor confidence in a bank would not depend on the bank's location, and further weakening the link between banks and their national sovereigns. An effects analysis of this proposal is presented in European Commission (2016). The report includes a section based on the SYMBOL model looking at the impact of alternative design options on the capacity of EDIS to absorb shocks of different dimensions, vis-a-vis the current nationally based system. So far, few studies have investigated the potential impact and rationale of introducing EDIS in the Banking Union. Among others, Jokivuolle and Pennacchi (2019) suggest alternative design features that could significantly reduce subsidies and mitigate moral hazard distortions. Panetti (2020) reviews the rationale for EDIS and the merit of alternative designs in preventing bank runs and ensuing sovereign crises. Fernandez-Aguado *et al.* (2022) show that the scheme may be an appropriate incentive to reduce moral hazard in the Banking Union.

2.7. *The 2023 Commission proposal for a revised crisis management and deposit insurance framework*

The challenges posed by the COVID-19 health crisis have been a severe test after the entry into force of the new insolvency and resolution framework. Elnahass *et al.* (2021) show that the pandemic has had detrimental effects on several indicators of financial performance and financial stability of banks in several regions in 2019 and 2020. In a related study, Trinh *et al.* (2022) examine tail risk developments for banks during the COVID-19 pandemic. Results show that different components of bank tail risk have increased during the health crisis but less so for stronger banks. The authors thus argue that banks with higher profitability and market value, and lower volatility, were indeed better placed to tackle the crisis effectively and hence less likely to suffer extreme equity devaluations. Deniz *et al.* (2022) document the resilience of banks during the pandemic, with findings pointing at macroprudential policy as a driver of such resilience, with credit growth limits, reserve requirements, and dynamic provisioning decreasing bank riskiness. Kasinger *et al.* (2021) highlight the need for early and realistic assessment of loan losses. Similarly, Apergis (2022) points out the importance of developing a realistic loan value assessment to incentivize banks to acknowledge their NPL situation early on. Özlem Dursun-de Neef and Schandlbauer (2021) also suggest that the crisis impacted the quality of lenders with evidence of an increase in worse-capitalized banks' loans, while better-capitalized peers tended to decrease lending. In this context, Bellia *et al.* (2023b) and European Commission (2022) support the general view that, while COVID-19 has been impacting banks, the implementation of the financial regulatory agenda and the establishment of the Banking Union helped banks to remain resilient during the pandemic. Nonetheless, the authors argue that by depending on banks' individual exposure to affected economic sectors, a surge in defaulted loans could materially erode banks' capital base. Both papers put forward an attempt to model the consequences on banks' balance sheet of the extraordinary policy measures taken in response to the pandemic, namely, the moratoria on loans' repayments to offer temporary relief to borrowers, and guarantees for loans to the private sector granted by the governments. Results show that, while the situation has generally strongly improved since the start of the reform process and the system is resilient even to large shocks, in case of a severe deterioration of the macrofinancial situation, some countries would remain vulnerable to contingent liabilities' risk stemming from the banking sector. Uncovered excess losses and recapitalization needs could exceed 1% of GDP in multiple countries and more than 2% of GDP in a few cases.

Experience with the application of the current crisis management for the banking sector seemed to indicate that the predictability of the current framework could be impacted by various elements. Parisi *et al.* (2020) measure and estimate possible liquidity gaps in resolution and show that, under adverse circumstances, the instruments currently available to provide liquidity support to financial institutions in the euro area would be insufficient. In particular, small and medium institutions have more limited loss-absorbing capacity. Bank for International Settlements (2020) discusses the limitations of the current EU bank failure management framework: (i) pointing at shortcomings of the national component of the resolution/insolvency frameworks in some countries, (ii) pointing at issues with the bail-in of creditors as a condition for the use of resolution funding, and (iii) commenting on the stringency of caps imposed for the use of deposit guarantee funds to support resolution actions. In addition, elements of fragmentation also still prevail, such as the fact that depositors benefit from different levels and types of guarantees across countries.

To address these issues and enable the framework to fully achieve its objective, the European Commission in 2023 has put forward a legislative proposal for a reformed bank crisis management and deposit insurance (CMDI) framework. The proposal, adopted by the Council in April 2023, improves the rules for handling bank failures while preserving financial stability, protecting depositors, and further limiting the use of public financial resources. The JRC has contributed to the impact assessment (European Commission, 2023a) of the proposed revision of the CMDI with a broad assessment of policy options for managing bank crises in an orderly and economically efficient manner by protecting financial stability and depositors while reducing recourse to taxpayers' money. The first is the harmonization of protection of deposits arising from Temporary High Deposits Balances (THBs) in excess of the coverage limit — resulting from important life events, such as real estate transactions — whose level of protection diverges across countries. EBA (2019) proposed to the Commission a number of recommendations, who then had to choose a policy option striking a balance between the additional costs borne by banks or DGSs and the need to protect depositors. Bellia *et al.* (2023d) developed an analysis to assess the financial impact of harmonizing the coverage of THBs on households and DGSs. Findings reveal that an EU-wide harmonization of the level of protection up to 500,000 might be successful in improving the protection of household wealth in the majority of countries, with respect to the actual situation. This level of protection is estimated to have a limited impact on DGSs, translating into an increase of 0–3% in covered deposits. As part of this initiative, the European Commission issued a request for advice to the European Banking Authority (EBA) to provide quantitative evidence on the difficulties faced by the financial sector in accessing resolution funds under the current framework and the role that the DGS could play in resolution. The European Banking Authority (EBA) together with the JRC provides estimates of the potential loss-absorption capacity of banks under different funding options and creditor hierarchies in resolution and insolvency. The models identify policy solutions that can facilitate the use of deposit guarantee schemes in crises outside of payout events. EBA (2021) tackles these issues by relying on analytical frameworks developed with the JRC, and results of the SYMBOL model, to assess benefits and advantages brought about by potential changes in the legislative framework. With respect to the recovery and resolution framework, results show that some small- and medium-sized banks may face difficulties in issuing certain financial instruments for the purpose of meeting requirements for total loss-absorbing capacity. Another issue relates to insolvency laws. As the hierarchy of creditor claims is not harmonized in the EU, the existence of these differences cannot ensure an overall consistent approach across Member States. This might have consequences for the role that DGS plays in resolution (under certain conditions, with the aim of reducing losses to depositors) and even for banks that are resolved. In fact, before resolving a bank, resolution authorities must ensure that the application of resolution tools would not make creditors worse off than they would have been in ordinary insolvency. The SYMBOL model has therefore been used by the EBA to assess the allocation of simulated losses to various categories of instruments in the institution's balance sheet, with respect to the hierarchy of claims, to show which class of instruments would be impacted and ultimately to provide an overview of the institution's internal loss-absorbing capacities. Following the write-down and bail-in of instruments, Resolution Funds could make a contribution. The analysis further considers to what extent the DGS could contribute to meeting the minimum loss absorption threshold of 8% TLOF under appropriate conditions and the effects of alternative depositor preference options.

Despite the progress in promoting a stable and integrated financial system in the European Union, further adjustments to the regulatory framework are still warranted to avoid financial fragmentation, to safeguard financial stability, and to guarantee a financial sector that fulfills its role in society. Owing to the global concerns affecting the EU, including climate change and the recent increase in commodity prices, banks and other financial intermediaries will possibly be subject to balance sheet pressures and significant deterioration in their asset quality. An effective and interconnected financial framework is therefore essential to avoid financial fragmentation and to safeguard financial stability. It does not come as a surprise that there is a need to further enhance and increase the resilience of the European financial sector toward systemic events, by substantially facilitating private risk-sharing across borders, while at the same time reducing the need for public risk-sharing.

2.8. *Policy options still under discussion*

This section looks at areas where work on further improvements is ongoing, and policy options are being discussed for implementation.

The first area for further adjustment is depositors' protection. Deposit guarantee schemes are in fact still national, and as such, depositors could enjoy different levels and types of guarantees depending on their location. EDIS remains one of the missing pieces which would underpin stability in the banking sector by sharing the risks deriving from the minimum coverage of bank deposits and by further weakening the link between banks and their national sovereigns.

In the European Commission (2023), the JRC has expanded work presented in the European Commission (2016) looking at the outcomes of possible alternative designs of EDIS. Recent research investigates the role of EDIS when providing liquidity support in terms of effectiveness, defined as the ability to reimburse depositors, and in terms of efficiency, defined as the ability to reimburse depositors at lower cost.

The modeling framework is based on the SYMBOL model, which simulates bank failures and the corresponding multiple pay-outs hitting the Deposits Guarantee Schemes (DGSs) and the common resolution fund. The simulation is developed at the individual bank level and results are then aggregated at the country/banking union level. The assessment focuses on the amount of covered deposits that are not protected in the event of a banking crisis given that banks' funds are insufficient. JRC results provide the Commission with scientific evidence that joint financial means such as the European Deposit Insurance Scheme would provide a higher level of protection than a scheme based solely on national Deposit Guarantee Schemes. The more resources are mutualized, the more effective and efficient the system is. Pooling of resources in fact (i) increases the probability of full protection of the covered deposits without liquidity shortfall and (ii) delivers a higher efficiency for various EDIS designs creating room for lowering the target level and consequently the cost for the baking sector.

Last, the JRC also contributed to the discussion on European safe assets. Notably, Bellia *et al.* (2019) developed a modeling framework which proved that the emission of safe assets would very strongly limit the sovereign bank doom loop in case a financial crisis strikes the EU financial sector after the emission of debt for shock absorption and recover. Contingent fiscal liabilities would be reduced by around 75%, capping potential losses to less than 1% of GDP for the euro area as a whole and for the vast majority of countries individually. The work has been expanded in Bellia *et al.* (2021b) to estimate the impacts of the emission of common issuance bonds, grants, and ECB support programs in the context of a hypothetical financial crisis that could have been induced by the COVID-19 downturn.

The paper finds a combination of grants and loans to be optimal for attenuating the sovereign banks' loop.

3. Climate Risk

Climate change, together with probably being the most prominent threat facing humanity, represents a new source of financial systemic risk since its impact could spread across the entire financial sector. Financial risks stemming from climate change can be grouped into two macro categories.[6]

The first one is physical risk, which arises from climate-related catastrophic events becoming more frequent and more severe owing to climate change. We are already witnessing extreme floods, heatwaves, and droughts in Europe and beyond, as well as increasingly destructive hurricanes and other hazards in other parts of the world, together with chronic hazards, such as rising sea levels. These physical risks can affect the financial system. The first climate-related bankruptcy happened already in California in 2018, as a local insurance company could not meet its obligations toward policyholders hit by devastating wildfires. The next in line could be a bank, whose borrowers may find themselves unable to repay their debts. For instance, they might be hit by a flood, causing losses and damages to their real estate properties, plants, and facilities. As another example, firms in a particular region could face difficulties owing to heatwaves and droughts, e.g., if they are active in the agriculture sector, which may result in an increase of unlikely-to-pay and non-performing loans.

The second type of financial risk related to climate change is the so-called transition risk, which arises from the changes in strategies, policies, or investments that come with the low-carbon transition. Essentially, transition risk stems from the financing of economic activities that will need to be abandoned in the low-carbon transition. These activities are related to fossil fuels or particularly

[6]The seminal speech delivered by Mark Carney in 2015, when he was the Governor of the Bank of England, "Breaking the Tragedy of the Horizon — climate change and financial stability", also identified liability risks together with physical and transition risks.

energy-inefficient production processes and buildings. The risk is that relevant physical assets, for example, a coal mine, will become stranded and the associated investment will result in a financial loss. Financing a new plant today based on an obsolete, energy-inefficient or polluting technology is like investing in videotapes the day the first CD came out. Notably, transition risk also encompasses regulatory risk, i.e., the risk that more polluting firms may be in trouble owing to stricter environmental regulation. We need reliable data and methodologies to assess financial institutions' exposures to these particular economic activities and related risks.

In the face of climate-related financial risks, it is of paramount importance to ensure that banks and financial institutions at large are well equipped to withstand potential impacts, which may become systemic. The financial industry as a whole needs to identify, measure, and monitor these risks. Moreover, relevant policy measures might need to be implemented to ensure financial stability. In particular, while individual banks are exposed to various degrees of climate-related risks, which justifies a microsupervisory approach, the global dimension of climate-related financial risks makes a macroprudential framework also suitable to address the impact of climate change on the financial system.

Against this background, this section overviews selected scientific works assessing climate risks for the system and developing climate stress tests, with a focus on providing quantitative evidence on the magnitude of climate risk for the European financial sector. It concludes by making proposals on how to increase the resilience of the banking sector to climate transition risks.

3.1. *Assessing financial exposures to climate risk*

3.1.1. *Transition risk*

Accurate metrics are the logical starting point for a broader assessment of climate risks. Looking at transition risk, the most obvious metric to measure the impact of an activity on climate change is the associated greenhouse gas (GHG) or CO_2 emissions, which can be normalized by revenues. However, emissions data are not exempt from issues (Papadopoulos, 2022). First, emissions data are scarce. The most populated databases only have Scope 1 (i.e., direct) emission data or estimates for around a thousand firms for the EU as a whole (against 25 million EU firms in total). Even focusing only on listed companies, direct emissions are available for only around 25% of them, while data on indirect emissions are only available for a handful of companies.[7] Second, there exist large discrepancies across different data providers, in particular for indirect emissions.

An alternative approach to the use of GHG emissions is the methodology proposed in Battiston *et al.* (2017), the so-called Climate Policy Relevant Sectors (CPRS). The success of this approach is due to the use of information that is actually widely available, i.e., the economic sector where the investee of the borrower firm is active. The approach consists in mapping NACE sectors[8] to CPRS, which include in particular the fossil fuel sector, the transport sector, buildings, as well as energy-intensive activities. CPRS re-group NACE sub-sectors in a meaningful way for sustainability analysis, as, for example, NACE subsectors related to the extraction, manufacturing, and sale of fossil fuels belong to different NACE macrosections. Based on CPRS, one can calculate the share of a financial portfolio that will be impacted, one way or another, by the transition. However, CPRS are not able to tell whether a particular financial asset will most likely outperform (for example, a mortgage extended to buy a zero-emission building) or underperform (for example, a loan extended to buy old and inefficient real estate) in the transition.

Alessi and Battiston (2022) overcome this limitation of the CPRS approach by providing a methodology to estimate the exposure of a financial portfolio to transition risk, still only using the NACE sector of the counterpart as input. To do so, they develop transition-risk exposure coefficients (TEC) associated with all relevant NACE sectors, which can be used to estimate the exposure of individual assets in the portfolio to transition risk. For example, while all NACE sectors in the fossil fuel CPRS are associated with a TEC of 100%,

[7] This is particularly concerning, as for several sectors what really matters is Scope 2 and in particular Scope 3 emissions. For example, fossil fuel extraction is associated with relatively low direct emissions but responsible for huge amounts of Scope 3 emissions.

[8] The NACE classification is the standard classification of economic activities in use in the European Union. It should be noted, however, that the classification of firms into NACE sectors also varies to some extent across data providers.

the NACE sector "real estate activities" are associated with a TEC of 70%, corresponding to the share of energy inefficient buildings in the EU.[9] By using their proposed TEC on confidential security-by-security data on European investors' bond and equity portfolios, Alessi and Battiston (2022) estimate an overall exposure to transition risk of 5.5%. In particular, the exposure of investment funds, banks, and insurers is estimated at 6.1%, 1.7%, and 5.0%, respectively. Remarkably, these estimates are considerably higher when considering equity exposures only, e.g., reaching 15% for banks.

3.1.2. *Physical risk*

The measurement of financial exposures to physical risk is, if possible, even more complicated. The main issue is that in this case, a crucial input is the geolocation of physical assets underlying relevant financial assets. For example, the exposure of a firm loan to physical risk depends on the location of the plants of the counterpart, based on which one can assess the risk that these facilities could be hit by, e.g., a flood. The same applies to mortgages, where the underlying property is also often the collateral against which the mortgage is extended. Hence, in case of a natural hazard, not only could the borrower become unable to repay the loan but the collateral could also massively depreciate. Some of these geo-locational data banks may have, although possibly in a format that makes it hard to retrieve and use. For example, the information could be available only in a printed format for older mortgages, or not adequately digitally stored, as it is only meant to become relevant if the loan would become non-performing and the bank would need to repossess collateral. Some of these data are therefore hardly accessible, if at all, to banks, supervisors, and researchers, in particular regarding the location of the plants.[10]

These data on the location of collateral and plants need to be combined with maps that give information on the risk of various natural disasters for a particular territory. The market is developing various

[9]This estimate is in turn based on relevant definitions in the regulation establishing the EU Taxonomy for Sustainable Activities.

[10]Some databases report information on the location of firms' facilities, but the number of firms for which the location of their plants is available is comparatively very small.

solutions for "firm-level physical risk assessments". However, there is no transparency on how these assessments are derived, which makes it impossible to evaluate their accuracy. In particular, one would need to know exactly what climate change scenarios are considered and how missing observations — the vast majority — are imputed. Against this background, we support the use of official, open source, and science-based data on climate-risk-related natural hazards. In particular, the JRC manages the Risk Data Hub,[11] which is the designated platform in the new EU Strategy on Adaptation to Climate Change for the collection of data on climate-related losses and physical climate risk from the public and private sectors. Relevant risk maps for various hazards are available with granularity up to Local Administrative Units, while underlying maps have a precision of up to 100 meters for floods. The JRC also runs the PESETA project,[12] which provides climate scenarios for EU Member States.

3.2. *Climate stress testing*

Having measured the exposure of financial institutions to climate transition and physical risks, the next step is to understand the consequences that the materialization of these risks could have at the individual and systemic levels.

3.2.1. *Transition risk*

Climate transition stress testing is inherently different from traditional stress testing. The latter aims to test the resilience of the financial system, or parts of it, to an economic shock, such as a large-scale recession. It then derives consequences for the financial system, e.g., in terms of non-performing loans and general losses. Climate-transition stress testing, on the contrary, aims — or should aim — to test the resilience of the financial system to risks related to the transition, which can materialize also in the absence of a generalized economic contraction. Actually, the concept of and a strategy for "Green Growth" have already existed for the past dozen years (OECD, 2011). While a "disorderly transition" caused by the implementation of strict climate policies (NGFS, 2019) could happen if

[11] Available at https://drmkc.jrc.ec.europa.eu/risk-data-hub#/.

[12] https://joint-research-centre.ec.europa.eu/peseta-projects/jrc-peseta-iv_en.

the process struggles to gain traction, the baseline scenario so far remains that of an "orderly transition". However, given that investors are forward-looking, financial shocks can originate within the financial system itself and get amplified by financial dynamics that can rapidly get out of control and impact the real economy, creating negative feedback loops, as has happened already with the Global Financial Crisis.

Alessi *et al.* (2022a) developed such a stress test for the banking system, where stress does not originate from the real economy but due to a sudden repricing of assets financing polluting activities. In particular, they modelled a fire sale on "high-carbon" assets, starting with an extremely small depreciation of such assets, which would however trigger the default of particularly vulnerable banks. These defaults would in turn lead to further depreciations, which would cause further bankruptcies. The authors found that the process could lead to around 400 billion in losses for the EU banking system, corresponding to 1% of total assets or 3% of GDP and just below the amount of losses due to the Global Financial Crisis.

Whether a repricing of "polluting" assets is plausible is a question we can answer based on a growing scientific literature. Several papers have looked into the reaction of investors to particular events, such as the Paris Agreement, and have investigated the existence of a "green taste" among investors, in bonds and equity markets. For example, Monasterolo and de Angelis (2020) found that investors did start to consider low-carbon stocks as a good investment opportunity after the Paris Agreement but did not penalize carbon-intensive stocks yet. The Paris Agreement was also studied by Alessi *et al.* (2023a), who found that it caused a reduction in European investor's exposure to carbon-intensive assets. Looking at the first global Climate Strike in 2019, Ramelli *et al.* (2021a) found evidence of a subsequent decrease in the stock price of high-carbon firms, in the form of significantly negative abnormal returns. Ramelli *et al.* (2021b) looked at the election of Trump and Biden, finding that firms' climate-related performance and expected future performance affected their stock market valuations around those events. Looking at the overall stock market dynamics, as opposed to particular events, Alessi *et al.* (2021d) coined the term greenium referring to the risk premium attached by investors to greener and more transparent stocks, showing that they have been on average willing to ask for lower returns, ceteris paribus, to hold greener and more transparent stocks.

Alessi *et al.* (2021c) showed that this greenium actually decreases, i.e., green investments are perceived as less risky, when the transition becomes more credible, e.g., after the Paris Agreement. In a value-at-risk framework, Alessi *et al.* (2023b) found that fossil fuel companies are riskier than their industrial peers, at the global level, and have become incrementally riskier after the Paris Agreement as well as during the COVID-19 pandemic. They have also become increasingly systemic, according to Caporin *et al.* (2022). Finally, Alessi *et al.* (2022b) showed that uncertainty around the "fundamental" value of the stock price of high-carbon firms has increased in the recent period.

3.2.2. *Physical risk*

When assessing the financial impacts of climate-related physical risks, insurers are obviously in the spotlight. Notably, whenever the insurance sector is unable to cover related economic losses, climate-related hazards also affect public finances. Particularly in the face of extreme catastrophes, there is a need for public intervention. On this, Bellia *et al.* (2023a) estimate that the value of assets exposed to floods each year in the EU could be higher than 30 billion, with only 38% of potential losses covered by insurance. The authors calculate that if the insurance coverage is raised to 75% of total exposures in each country, uncovered losses would reduce by more than 50% on average. However, total premiums written would need to double to reach this objective.

Looking at banks, a key ingredient of stress tests on physical risks is the impact of firm loans. Evidence on this particular channel is provided, among others, by Fatica *et al.* (2021) by analyzing how European manufacturing firms have fared after the floods occurred in the 2007–2018 period. They find significant and persistent negative effects on firms' assets, which decrease by around 3% and up to 7%, with no clear signs of full recovery even after 8 years. Sales, employment, wages, and productivity are also mostly negatively impacted after a firm is hit by a flood. Highly indebted firms are particularly vulnerable, probably because of the destruction or depreciation of the physical capital pledged as collateral.[13]

[13]These results are in line with Faiella and Natoli (2018), who find that lending to non-financial firms is negatively correlated with their flood risk exposure.

With respect to other acute physical risks, i.e., natural disasters, beyond floods, Morana and Sbrana (2019) show that global warming risk is significantly undervalued in the catastrophe bonds market, where about 50% of the outstanding risk capital is exposed to (Atlantic) hurricanes. With respect to chronic physical risks — those linked to steady changes — Goldsmith-Pinkham *et al.* (2021) show that the risk of rising sea level started to be priced in municipal bonds in 2013, with a larger effect for longer maturities. As for temperatures, evidence at firm or asset level is scarce. By focusing on a variety of aggregate economic variables, some works show a negative effect of higher mean temperatures and extreme temperatures (Gallup *et al.* 1999, Dell *et al.* 2009 and 2012, Hsiang 2010), while Addoum *et al.* (2020) find only a mild relation between temperature and growth based on US data.

Finally, Ojea-Ferreiro *et al.* (2022) use the NGFS scenarios (NGFS, 2019) to quantify the financial market impact of the materialization of transition risk versus physical risk. Indeed, in the case of a transition, the former risk would be preponderant, while in the absence of it, climate change would lead to catastrophic consequences. They find that banks would experience more negative consequences in the case of a disorderly transition than in the case of no transition. On the contrary, real estate firms would suffer more in a "hot house world" scenario because of the impacts of natural hazards on their immovable assets.

To conclude, it is worth discussing what financial regulators and the financial industry can do to increase the resilience of the system to climate risks. In general, increased capital buffers to account for increased risks are an option. Looking at transition risks and banks in particular, Alessi *et al.* (2022a) calculate that an additional buffer corresponding to 0.5% of Risk-Weighted Assets (RWA) on average would be sufficient to protect the system from a fire sale of high-carbon assets. However, as shown in Alessi *et al.* (2023a), transition risk tends to shift to less regulated financial institutions and jurisdictions where climate action is less incisive; hence, policy action should be coordinated at the global level.

As for financial institutions themselves, they can of course become safer by selling polluting assets and cutting credit lines to high-carbon clients. It should be emphasized, however, that this is not the only way banks have to protect their balance sheet from climate transition risk — and it is in fact a risky path, owing to its potentially systemic consequences. A much better way to make their balance sheets greener is to actually engage with firms to promote their own green transition. Analogously, with respect to physical risk exposures, financial institutions should promote the adoption of climate adaptation measures by their counterparts.

4. Digital Finance

Digital finance is a broad term used to describe the application of technology to financial intermediation and accessory services. While finance has a comparatively long history of digitalization, the term in particular tends to refer to the set of technologies which are driving the latest wave of the "digital revolution", such as mobile applications, Artificial Intelligence (AI) and machine learning, biometrics, big data analytics, cryptography and distributed ledgers, and cloud computing.

These are technologies that, not unlike in other sectors, seem to have the potential to allow the creation of new services or the establishment of new business models.

The introduction of these tools, either by incumbents or new entrants, has the potential for lowering the barrier to accessing financial services, lowering prices to consumers, and allowing easier and more reliable access to credit.

At the same time, from a financial stability point of view, even positive disruption in the financial sector could present some risks if not managed correctly.

Also, new products and services, eventually provided by unregulated operators, while allowing greater access to financial services, could leave open the possibility of fraud and misuse, exposing consumers to risks.

Following the surge in the value of Bitcoin over 2015 and 2016, all financial regulators became alerted not only to the importance of new digital technologies for finance but also to the fact that change could be happening very rapidly. The European Commission in particular was very quick in recognizing the potential of digital finance and the necessity of early involvement of regulators. This would allow establishing supervisory convergence, in order for the European financial sector to better embrace the opportunities brought by the digital revolution. With the aim of developing a framework that could allow rapid rollout and scaling of solutions in the single market, while preserving financial stability and high standards of consumer protection, the Commission therefore launched a "FinTech action plan" in 2018.

This was followed in 2020 by a "Digital Finance Package" including a digital finance strategy, a legislative proposal on crypto assets and on digital operational resilience, and a revised retail payments strategy.

The goal of these initiatives is to increase the competitiveness and global reach of the EU financial sector while not decreasing the standards of consumer protection and stability achieved with the reforms that followed the financial crisis.

Moving in parallel to these developments, Central Banks have been discussing the opportunity of adopting digital equivalents of their official currencies. The European Central Banks published a report on "Digital Euro" in 2020, looking at potential advantages and disadvantages, concluding that a digital euro could become essential under a number of scenarios and could support progress toward other strategic initiatives of the Eurosystem. At the same time, further analysis and consideration of alternative design options were advised, in order to maximize benefits and avoid undesirable consequences. Following the publication of the report, in 2021, the Eurosystem launched the "Digital Euro project". The project envisages an investigation phase of 24 months, following a preliminary experimentation phase conducted by the European Central Bank and selected national central banks. In parallel, in 2023, the European Commission has adopted a legislative proposal for a framework regulating essential aspects of a possible digital euro as a form of Central Bank money. Contributing to these exercises and to the Impact Assessment of the new regulation (European Commission, 2023b), Petracco-Giudici and Di Girolamo (2023) and Bellia and Cales (2023c) explore the potential impacts of different levels of substitution of CBDC for bank deposits on bank balance sheets and profitability. Results show that, for preferred scenarios for the initial introduction of a CBDC, impacts should not present issues for the financial stability and profitability of banks.

In this context, it is important to keep monitoring developments in digital and cryptofinance, with the purpose of horizon scanning and knowledge building, as well as supporting the work of the Commission in this very important area.

As digital finance is a technology-driven phenomenon, as the first approach, it is necessary to look at high-level aspects of technologies involved in the digital transformation of finance, including distributed ledger technology (DLT) and blockchain as well as cybersecurity.

Muftic (2016) provides an overview of the mechanics and characteristics of virtual currencies based on DLTs, and early trends and initiatives in the application of DLTs to other domains.

Flore (2018) provides an early assessment of the potential of digital currencies to disrupt the global market for remittances, constituting a very important channel of foreign currency for several nations.

Anderberg *et al.* (2019) in their report on blockchain look at several issues tied to blockchain and transformations in digital finance, noting how it has potential for transformation in several areas, from payment systems to the distribution of liabilities. However, the authors note how the technology, and legislative and standards frameworks, is for the time being, limiting its diffusion.

Cagnin *et al.* (2020) use a foresight process approach to analyze a set of issues tied to open strategic autonomy and identify the development of a European Central Bank digital currency as an important step to "future-proof" the euro.

Hassan *et al.* (2021) scan applications of distributed ledger technologies for the pursuit of social and public good, including their potential uses for alternative organizational models in finance.

Baldini *et al.* (2020) provide an overview of research on cybersecurity at JRC. While not looking directly at potential financial stability impacts, they offer insights on the evolution of cybersecurity risks and countermeasures, which are particularly important in a more and more digitized and digitally dependent financial sector.

On a more granular level, the dynamics of cryptocurrencies are investigated, analyzing determinants of the price formation process, in particular, trying to disentangle speculative demand in order to assess the usability and suitability of Bitcoin as a potential substitute for traditional currencies.

Ciaian *et al.* (2016a) conduct an analysis of Bitcoin price dynamics using the Barro model and price data up to 2015, concluding that investor interest and attractiveness seem to be the main determinants of Bitcoin prices, rather than macroeconomic developments. In a related paper (Ciaian *et al.*, 2016), the same authors suggest that, while Bitcoin prices will remain mainly driven by speculative investments, Bitcoin will not be able to compete with standard currencies. In a later piece of work, Ciaian *et al.* (2020) again look at price determinants using high-frequency data and a GARCH approach. They estimate transaction and speculative demand models and this time find that both factors seem to impact Bitcoin price formation.

Research is continuing in this field; by way of example, Alessi *et al.* (2021b) look into price determinants of Bitcoin using a panel approach applied to high-frequency data and a large collection of annotated news items. In particular, the authors look at how sentiment news in different languages affect quotes on exchanges in different parts of the world.

Price dynamics of cryptocurrencies also have implications for risk management, and their suitability as investments rather than as pure currency substitutes.

From the Operational Risk point of view, Ciaian *et al.* (2021) employ an ARDL model to study how the security of the Bitcoin digital ledger depends on prices and mining rewards, concluding that the relationship seems geographically differentiated but tends to quickly revert to an equilibrium level after price shocks.

Concentrating on portfolio allocation strategies and risk management, Van der Auwera *et al.* (2020) provide an overview of risk issues and risk management for cryptocurrencies, and include chapters applying risk management techniques to cryptocurrencies, as well as an assessment of potential impact in portfolio management under some alternative scenarios and measures.

Issues tied to the potential for digital currencies continue to remain central, with recent developments in Bitcoin and "stablecoins" prices bringing these instruments to the center of attention in the first half of 2022.

The Commission is currently engaged in continuing legislative work in accordance with the digital finance strategy, which has a four-year horizon.

Research continues in this critical area, supporting the work on digital euro and conducting research on societal impacts of digitalization, including digitalization of finance, and cybersecurity.

5. Conclusions

This chapter has reviewed the work conducted in support of the policymaking processes of the European Commission in reforming the financial sector following the Great Financial Crisis, including the more recent efforts to enhance financial resilience toward the risks linked to climate change and the green transition, as well as to the impacts of the digital transformation.

In regard to the first objective, the findings of the works illustrated here provide evidence supporting the main choices behind the creation of the financial safety net following the Great Financial Crisis and its follow-up sovereign crisis.

In particular, quantitative work shows how the introduction of new prudential requirements, resolution, and supervision tools has allowed for a considerable reduction in the risk of systemic crises and the subsequent contingent liabilities stemming from the financial sector while at the same time not imposing an excess burden on its financing capacity. Follow-up studies support the idea that markets have been incorporating a reduced expectation of "too-big-to-fail" problems. Despite the recent Commission proposal for a revised resolution and insolvency framework, research presented here points to the possibility of capturing further benefits from the completion of the Banking Union, including the introduction of a European Deposit Insurance Scheme, and the introduction of a European Safe Asset.

While in general the research presented here supports the idea that the European financial system is now much more resilient and better able to withstand large sudden shocks, it also highlights the possibility that new sources of risk might need further attention due to the appearance of challenges tied to climate change and the green transition and to the transformation of the financial sector due to the digital transition. Research on the vulnerability of financial assets to physical and transition risks is starting to overcome data limitations to produce estimates of the exposure of various assets and players to these risks, also due to the elaboration of more detailed scenarios and climate-related hazards. Research on the one hand illustrates how investors are becoming aware of risks tied to carbon-intensive assets and are starting to incorporate these into pricing of both carbon-intensive and "green" assets. On the other side, research is supporting the idea that these risks could be relevant also for credit institutions, as they could be material and also have the potential for triggering disorderly transitions, supporting the necessity of climate stress testing and eventually the explicit consideration of these risks in prudential requirements. Finally, the digital transition is seen to have the potential to affect the financial sector, by generating opportunities for the creation of new products, services, and eventually new business models. This seems especially true in the realm of currencies, where digital currencies are rapidly moving from fringe assets to Central Bank money. Continued research in this area will allow policymakers to keep building knowledge of these phenomena with the aim of producing regulations that will allow market and institutional players to develop solutions while maintaining high standards of market integrity and consumer protection.

References

Addoum, J. M., Ng, D. T. and Ortiz-Bobea, A. (2020). Temperature shocks and establishment sales. *The Review of Financial Studies, 33*(3), 1331–1366.

Alessi, L., Cannas, G., Di Girolamo, F., Ossola, E., Papanagiotou, E., Petracco-Giudici, M. and Rossi, E. (2016). Estimation of potential benefits of the implementation of the fundamental review of the trading book and leverage ratio. JRC Science for Policy Brief Report. EUR 28269 EN. Luxembourg (Luxembourg): Publications Office of the European Union. JRC103768.

Alessi, L., Cannas, G., Maccaferri, S. and Petracco-Giudici, M. (2017). The European deposit insurance scheme: Assessing risk absorption via SYMBOL. *JRC Working Papers in Economics and Finance, 2017/12*. Publications Office of the European Union, Luxembourg. JRC109381.

Alessi, L., Bruno, B., Carletti, E., Neugebauer, K. and Wolfskeil, I. (2021a). Cover your assets: Non-performing loans and coverage ratios in Europe. *Economic Policy, 36*(108), 685–733.

Alessi, L., Ghysels, E., Petracco-Giudici, M. and Zhe, W. (2021b). Bitcoin and news around the world in twenty-six languages. Conference Paper, Crypto Assets Lab 2021.

Alessi, L., Ossola, E. and Panzica, R. (2021c). When do investors go green? Evidence from a time-varying asset-pricing model. *European Commission – Joint Research Centre, Working Papers in Economics and Finance 2021/13.*

Alessi, L., Ossola, E. and Panzica, R. (2021d). What greenium matters in the stock market? The role of greenhouse gas emissions and environmental disclosures. *Journal of Financial Stability, 54*, 100869.

Alessi, L. and Battiston, S. (2022). Two sides of the same coin: Green taxonomy alignment versus transition risk in financial portfolios. *International Review of Financial Analysis, 84*, 102319.

Alessi, L., Di Girolamo, F., Petracco-Giudici, M. and Pagano, A. (2022a). Accounting for climate transition risk in banks' capital requirements. *European Commission – Joint Research Centre, Working Papers in Economics and Finance, 2022/08.*

Alessi, L., Hirschbuehl, D. and Rossi, A. (2022b). A sustainability transition on the move? Evidence based on the disconnect from market fundamentals. *European Commission – Joint Research Centre, Working Papers in Economics and Finance*, 2022/10.

Alessi, L., Battiston, S. and Kvedaras, V. (2023a). Over with carbon? Investors' reaction to the Paris Agreement and the US withdrawal. *Journal of Financial Stability* (forthcoming).

Alessi, L., Cojoianu, T. F. and Hoepner, A. G. F. (2023b). Fossil fuels: Are they worth the (downside) risk? *European Commission — Joint Research Centre, Working Papers in Economics and Finance 2022-10.*

Anderberg, A., Andonova, E., Bellia, M., Calès, L., Inamorato Dos Santos, A., Kounelis, I., Nai Fovino, I., Petracco-Giudici, M., Papanagiotou, E., Sobolewski, M., Rossetti, F. and Spirito, L. (2019). Blockchain now and tomorrow. In S. Figueiredo Do Nascimento and A. Roque Mendes Polvora (eds.). EUR 29813 EN, Publications Office of the European Union, Luxembourg. JRC117255.

Apergis, N. (2022). Convergence in non-performing loans across EU banks: The role of COVID-19. *Cogent Economics & Finance, 10*(1), 2024952–202.

Ayadi, R., Bongini, P., Casu, B. and Cucinelli, D. (2021). Bank business model migrations in Europe: Determinants and effects. *British Journal of Management, 32*(4), 1007–1026.

Baldini, G., Barrero, J., Chaudron, S., Coisel, I., Draper Gil, G., Duch Brown, N., Eulaerts, O., Geneiatakis, D., Hernandez Ramos, J., Joanny, G., Junklewitz, H., Kampourakis, G., Kerckhof, S., Kounelis, I., Lewis, A., Martin, T., Nai Fovino, I., Nativi, S., Neisse, R., Nordvik, J., Papameletiou, D., Reina, V., Ruzzante, G., Sanchez Martin, J., Sportiello, L., Steri, G. and Tirendi, S. (2020). Cybersecurity, our digital anchor. In I. Nai Fovino, G. Barry, S. Chaudron, I. Coisel, M. Dewar, H. Junklewitz, G. Kampourakis, I. Kounelis, B. Mortara, J. Nordvik and J. Sanchez Martin (eds.). EUR 30276 EN.

Battiston, S., Mandel, A. and Monasterolo, I. (2017). A climate stress-test of the financial system. *Nature Climate Change*, *7*, 283–288.

Beck, T., Da-Rocha-Lopes, S. and Silva, A. F. (2021). Sharing the pain? Credit supply and real effects of bank bail-ins. *The Review of Financial Studies*, *34*(4), 1747–1788. April 2021.

Bellia, M., Calès, L., Frattarolo, L., Maerean, A., Monteiro, D., Petracco-Giudici, M. and Vogel, L. (2019). The sovereign-bank nexus in the Euro area: Financial and real channels, (122), 5–28.

Bellia, M., Heynderickx, W., Maccaferri, S. and Schich, S. (2020a). Do CDS markets care about the G-SIB status? *JRC Working Papers in Economics and Finance, 2020/02.*

Bellia, M. and Maccaferri, S. (2020b). Banks' bail-in and the new banking regulation: An EU event study. *JRC Working Papers in Economics and Finance, issue no. 2020/07.*

Bellia, M., Maccaferri, S. and Schich, S. (2021a). Limiting too-big-to-fail: Market reactions to policy announcements and actions. *Journal of Banking Regulation.*

Bellia, M., Calès, L., Frattarolo, L., Monteiro, D. and Petracco-Giudici, M. (2021b). COVID-19: The stabilising impact of EU bond issuance on sovereigns and banks. *Quarterly Report on the Euro Area (QREA)*, *20*(3), 17–28.

Bellia, M., Di Girolamo, F., Pagano, A. and Petracco-Giuidici, M. (2023a). Climate protection gap: Evidences for public finances and insurance premiums. *European Commission - Joint Research Centre, Working Papers in Economics and Finance* (Forthcoming).

Bellia, M., Di Girolamo, F. E., Pagano, A., Orlandi, F., Pamies, S. and Petracco-Giudici, M. (2023b). Impact of banks losses on public finances. *ECFIN Working Papers* (Forthcoming).

Bellia, M., Calès, L. (2023c). Bank profitability and central bank digital currency. *JRC Working Papers in Economics and Finance, 2023/6.*

Bellia, M., Calès, L., Di Girolamo, F., Joossens, E. and Petracco-Giudici, M. (2023d). Quantitative analysis on selected deposits insurance issues for purposes of impact assessment, Publications Office of the European Union, Luxembourg, 2023, 76.

Benczúr, P., Cannas, G., Cariboni, J., Di Girolamo, F., Maccaferri, S. and Petracco, M. (2016). Evaluating the effectiveness of the new EU bank regulatory framework: A farewell to bail-out? *Journal of Financial Stability, 33.*

Bank for International Settlements (2020). Bank failure management in the European banking union: What's wrong and how to fix it. Occasional Paper No 15, July 2020.

Bodellini, M. (2012). The optional measures of deposit guarantee schemes: Towards a new bank crisis management paradigm? *European Journal of Legal Studies, 13*(1) (Spring 2021), 341–376.

Boccuzzi, G. (2022). Deposit guarantee schemes: Role and functioning in banking crises. In *Banking Crises in Italy.* Palgrave Studies in Financial Instability and Banking Crisis Regulation. Cham: Palgrave Macmillan.

Cagnin, C., Muench, S., Scapolo, F., Stoermer, E. and Vesnic Alujevic, L. (2021). Shaping and securing the EU's Open Strategic Autonomy by 2040 and beyond, EUR 30802 EN.

Calo', S., Gregori, W. Petracco, M. and Rancan, M. (2021). Has the comprehensive assessment made the European financial system more resilient? *Working Papers 2021-08, Joint Research Centre, European Commission.*

Campolongo, F., De Lisa, R, Zedda, S., Vallascas, F. and Marchesi, M. (2010). Deposit insurance schemes: Target fund and risk-based contributions in line with Basel II regulation. JRC Scientific and Technical Report. EUR 24281 EN.

Campolongo, F., Cariboni, J., Ndacyayisenga, N. and Pagano, A. (2015). Banks under X-rays: Business model choices and trading. *Journal of Financial Economic Policy, 7*(4), 377–400.

Cannas, G., Cariboni, J., Foryś, M., Joensson, H., Langedijk, S., Marchesi, M., Ndacyayisenga, N., Pagano, A. and Petracco-Giudici, M. (2014a). Annex A10 quantitative estimation of a part of the costs and benefits of bank structural separation requirements in European Commission.

Cannas, G., Maccaferri, S., Cariboni, J. and Petracco-Giudici, M. (2014b). JRC technical work supporting commission second level legislation on risk based contributions to the (single) resolution fund. JRC Science for Policy Report.

Caporin, M., Fontini, F. and Panzica, R. (2022). The systemic risk of US oil and natural gas companies. *European Commission – Joint Research Centre, Working Papers in Economics and Finance, 2022/11.*

Cariboni, J., Vanden Branden, K., Campolongo, F. and De Cesare, M. (2008). Deposit protection in the EU: State of play and future prospects. *Journal of Banking Regulation, 9*(2), 82–101. JRC38190.

Cariboni, J., Joensson, H., Kazemi Veisari, L., Magos, D., Papanagiotou, E. and Planas, C. (2014). Annex A4.2: Size and determinants of implicit state guarantees to EU banks in European Commission.

Cariboni, J., Fontana, A., Langedijk, S., Maccaferri, S., Pagano, A., Petracco-Giudici, M., Rancan, M. and Schich, S. (2016). Reducing and sharing the burden of bank failures. *OECD Journal: Financial Market Trends, 2015*(2), 29–61.

Carmassi, J., Corrias, R. and Parisi, L. (2019). Is taxpayers' money better protected now? An assessment of banking regulatory reforms ten years after the global financial crisis. *Macroprudential Bulletin, 7*.

Ciaian, P., Rajcaniova, M. and Kancs, D. (2016). The economics of BitCoin price formation. *Applied Economics, 48*(19), 1799–1815.

Ciaian, P., Kancs, D. and Rajcaniova, M. (2020). The price of BitCoin: GARCH evidence from high frequency data. *Journal of Investment Strategies, 9*(4), 1–18.

Ciaian, P., Kancs, D. and Rajcaniova, M. (2021). The economic dependency of bitcoin security. *Applied Economics, 53*(49), 5738–5755.

Crespi, F., Giacomini, E. and Mascia, D. (2019). Bail-in rules and the pricing of Italian bank bonds. *European Financial Management* (European Financial Management Association), *25*(5), 1321–1347.

De Lisa, R., Zedda, S., Vallascas, F., Campolongo, F. and Marchesi, M. (2011). Modelling deposit insurance scheme losses in a Basel II framework. *Journal of Financial Services Research, 40*(3), 123–141.

Dell, M., Jones, B. F. and Olken, B. (2009). Temperature and income: Reconciling new cross-sectional and panel estimates. *American Economic Review, 99*, 198–204.

Dell, M., Jones, B. F. and Olken, B. (2012). Temperature shocks and economic growth: Evidence from the last half century. *American Economic Journal: Macroeconomics, 4*, 66–95.

Deniz, I., Ali, M. and Tomoe, M. (2023). Does macroprudential policy alleviate the adverse impact of COVID-19 on the resilience of banks? *Journal of Banking & Finance, 147*(C), 106419.

Elnahass, M., Trinh, V. Q. and Li, T. (2021). Global banking stability in the shadow of Covid-19 outbreak. *Journal of International Financial Markets, Institutions and Money, 72*.

European Banking Authority (2019). Opinion of the European Banking Authority on deposit guarantee scheme payouts. EBA-Op-2019-14. European Commission (2012). SWD(2012)166. Commission Staff Working Document Impact Assessment. Accompanying the document PROPOSAL FOR A DIRECTIVE OF THE EUROPEAN PARLIAMENT AND OF THE COUNCIL establishing a framework for the recovery and resolution of credit institutions and investment firms and amending Council Directives 77/91/EEC and 82/891/EC, Directives 2001/24/EC, 2002/47/EC, 2004/25/EC, 2005/56/EC, 2007/36/EC and 2011/35/EC and Regulation (EU) No 1093/2010.

European Commission (2014a). Commission Staff Working Document Impact Assessment, Accompanying the document Proposal for a

Regulation of the European Parliament and of the Council on structural measures improving the resilience of EU Credit Institutions and the Proposal for a Regulation of the European Parliament and of the Council on reporting and transparency of securities financing transactions, 2014. SWD/2014/030/final.

European Commission (2014b). COMMISSION STAFF WORKING DOCUMENT Economic Review of the Financial Regulation Agenda Bibliography and Annexes Accompanying the document COMMUNICATION FROM THE COMMISSION TO THE EUROPEAN PARLIAMENT, THE COUNCIL, THE EUROPEAN ECONOMIC AND SOCIAL COMMITTEE AND THE COMMITTEE OF THE REGIONS A reformed financial sector for Europe. ANNEX 4: QUANTITATIVE MODELLING OF BENEFIT.

European Commission (2016). Effects analysis on the European deposit insurance scheme (EDIS).

European Commission (2022). Fiscal Sustainability Report 2021. European Economy. Institutional Paper 171.

European Commission (2023a). COMMISSION STAFF WORKING DOCUMENT IMPACT ASSESSMENT REPORT Accompanying the Proposals for a DIRECTIVE OF THE EUROPEAN PARLIAMENT AND COUNCIL amending Directive 2014/59/EU as regards early intervention measures, conditions for resolution and financing of resolution action, REGULATION OF THE EUROPEAN PARLIAMENT AND COUNCIL amending Regulation (EU) 806/2014 as regards early intervention measures, conditions for resolution and financing of resolution action, DIRECTIVE OF THE EUROPEAN PARLIAMENT AND COUNCIL amending Directive 2014/49/EU as regards the scope of deposit protection, use of deposit guarantee schemes funds, cross-border cooperation, and transparency.

European Commission (2023b). COMMISSION STAFF WORKING DOCUMENT IMPACT ASSESSMENT REPORT Accompanying the documents Proposal for a Regulation of the European Parliament and of the Council on the establishment of the digital euro and Proposal for a Regulation of the European Parliament and of the Council on the provision of digital euro services by payment services providers incorporated in Member States whose currency is not the euro and amending Regulation (EU) 2021/1230 of the European Parliament and the Council and Proposal for a Regulation of the European Parliament and of the Council on the legal tender of euro banknotes and coins.

Faiella, I. and Natoli, F. (2018). Natural catastrophes and bank lending: The case of flood risk in Italy. Questioni di Economia e Finanza

(Occasional Papers) 457, Bank of Italy, Economic Research and International Relations Area.

Fatica, S., Katay, G. and Rancan, M. (2022). Floods and firms: Vulnerabilities and resilience to natural disasters in Europe. *European Commission – Joint Research Centre, Working papers in Economics and Finance* (Forthcoming).

Fernández-Aguado, P., Martínez, E., Ruíz, R. and Ureña, A. (2022). Evaluation of European deposit insurance scheme funding based on risk analysis. *International Review of Economics & Finance* (Elsevier), *78*(C), 234–247.

Financial Stability Board. (2020). Evaluation of the effects of too-big-to-fail reforms, a consultation report. Technical Appendix.

Fiordalisi, F., Minnucci, F., Previati, D. A. and Ricci, O. (2020). Bail-in regulation and stock market reaction. *Economics Letters, 186*, 108801. January 2020.

Flore, M. (2018). How blockchain-based technology is disrupting migrants' remittances: A preliminary assessment, EUR 29492 EN.

Fontana, A. and Langedijk, S. (2019). The bank-sovereign loop and financial stability in the Euro area. *JRC Working Papers in Economics and Finance, 2019/10.*

Goldsmith-Pinkham, P. S., Gustafson, M., Lewis, R. and Schwert, M. (2021). Sea level rise exposure and municipal bond yields. Jacobs Levy Equity Management Center for Quantitative Financial Research Paper.

Gallup, J. L., Sachs, J. D. and Mellinger, A. D. (1999). Geography and economic development. *International Regional Science Review, 22*, 179–232.

Hassan, S., Brekke, J. K., Atzori, M., Bodó, B., Meiklejohn, S., De Filippi, P., Beecroft, K., Rozas, D., Orgaz Alonso, C., Martínez Vicente, E., Lopéz Morales, G. and Figueras Aguilar, A., (2020). Scanning the European ecosystem of distributed ledger technologies for social and public good. In A. Roque Mendes Polvora, A. Hakami and E. Bol (eds.). EUR 30364 EN.

Hordijk, L. and Kancs, D., Kok, C., Ongena, S., Pelizzon, L., Cariboni, J., Heynderickx, W., Maccaferri, S., Pagano, A. and Petracco-Giudici, M. (2018). Review of the SYMBOL model, EUR 29233 EN.

Hsiang, S. M. (2010). Temperatures and cyclones strongly associated with economic production in the Caribbean and Central America. *Proceedings of the National Academy of Sciences, 107*, 15367–72.

Jokivuolle, E. and Pennacchi, G. (2019). How to design the European deposit insurance scheme. VoxEu. 31 May 2019.

Kasinger, J., Krahnen, J. P., Ongena, S., Pelizzon, L., Schmeling, M. and Wahrenburg, M. (2021). Non-performing loans-new risks and policies? SAFE White Paper, No. 84. Commissioned by the European Parliament upon request of the Economic and Monetary Committee. Economic Governance Support Unit (EGOV) Directorate-General for Internal Policies.

Marchesi, M., Petracco-Giudici, M., Cariboni, J., Zedda, S. and Campolongo, F. (2013). Macroeconomic cost-benefit analysis of Basel III minimum capital requirements and of introducing Deposit Guarantee Schemes and Resolution Funds. JRC Scientific and Policy. Report EUR 24603 EN.

Monasterolo, I. and de Angelis, L. (2020). Blind to carbon risk? An analysis of stock market reaction to the Paris Agreement. *Ecological Economics, 170*, 106571.

Morana, C. and Sbrana, G. (2019). Climate change implications for the catastrophe bonds market: An empirical analysis. *Economic Modelling, 81*(C), 274–294.

Muftic, S. (2016). Overview and analysis of the concept and applications of virtual currencies. EUR 28386 EN.

NGFS (2019). A call for action: Climate change as a source of financial risk. First Comprehensive Report, Network for Greening the Financial System, Paris, France.

OECD (2011). *Towards Green Growth, OECD Green Growth Studies.* OECD Publishing, Paris.

Özlem Dursun-de Neef, H. and Schandlbauer, A. (2021). COVID-19 and lending responses of European banks. *Journal of Banking & Finance, 133*, 106236.

Papadopoulos, G. (2022). Discrepancies in corporate GHG emissions data and their impact on firm performance assessment. European Commission – *Joint Research Centre, Working Papers in Economics and Finance, 2022/12.*

Pagano, A., Cariboni, J., Marchesi, M. and Ndacyayisenga, N. (2014). Annex A8: Trading activities and bank structural separation: Possible definitions and calibration of screening in European Commission.

Panetti, E. (2020). The European deposit insurance scheme: Economic rationale, issues and policy solutions. SUERF Policy Note, Issue No 146, April 2020.

Parisi, L., Chalamandaris, D., Amamou, R., Torstensson, P. and Baumann, A. (2020). Liquidity in resolution: Estimating possible liquidity gaps for specific banks in resolution and in a systemic crisis. Occasional Paper Series No 250/November 2020.

Petracco-Giudici, M., Marchesi, M., Rossi, A., Ndacyayisenga, N. and Cariboni, J. (2014). Annex A5: Analysis of possible incentives towards trading activities implied by the structure of banks's minimum capital requirements in European Commission.

Petracco, M. and Di Girolamo, E. (2023). Central bank digital currency and European banks' balance sheets. Publications Office of the European Union, Luxembourg, JRC132239.

Ramelli, S., Ossola, E. and Rancan, M. (2021a). Stock price effects of climate activism: Evidence from the first global climate strike. *Journal of Corporate Finance*, *69*, 102018.

Ramelli, S., Wagner, A. F., Zeckhauser, R. J. and Ziegler, A. (2021b). Investor rewards to climate responsibility: Stock-price responses to the opposite shocks of the 2016 and 2020 U.S. elections. *The Review of Corporate Finance Studies*, *10*(4), 748–787.

Trinh, V. Q., Cao, N. D. and Elnahass, M. (2022). Financial stability: A 'vaccine' for tail risk of the global banking sector in the shadow of the pandemic. *The European Journal of Finance*, 1–28.

Van der Auwera, E., Schoutens, W., Petracco-Giudici, M. and Alessi, L. (2020). Financial risk management for cryptocurrencies.

Zedda, S. and Cannas, G. (2020). Analysis of banks' systemic risk contribution and contagion determinants through the leave-one-out approach. *Journal of Banking and Finance*, *112*, 2020.

Zedda, S. and Galliani, C. (2014). Will the bail-in break the vicious circle between banks and their sovereign? *Computational Economics*, *45*(4), 597–614.

PART III

Implications from Macroeconomic Factors

https://doi.org/10.1142/9781800614321_0010

Chapter 10

Market Illiquidity and the Bank Lending Channel

Sergio Sanfilippo-Azofra*, **María Cantero-Saiz**†, **and Begoña Torre-Olmo**‡

The University of Cantabria — Santander Financial Institute (SANFI), Santander, Spain

**sergio.sanfilippo@unican.es*

†*maria.cantero@unican.es*

‡*maria.torre@unican.es*

Abstract

This study analyses how stock and bond market illiquidity affect the bank lending channel. Our empirical analysis comprises a sample of 862 listed banks from 21 OECD countries between 2002 and 2015. We find that the bank lending channel plays an important role in the transmission mechanism of the monetary policy when financial markets are very liquid. However, as market liquidity decreases, the bank lending channel becomes less relevant and ends up being ineffective.

Keywords: Market illiquidity, monetary policy, bank lending channel, banks, shocks, loan supply, OECD countries, financial crisis, interest rates, transmission mechanism

1. Introduction

In the last two decades, the role played by banks in the transmission mechanism of monetary policy has been a recurrent topic of research. In this regard, the bank lending channel of monetary policy has received a lot of attention because changes in banks' loan supply have enormous consequences for an economy. The traditional view of the bank lending channel considers that monetary policy restrictions lead to a reduction in banks' access to deposits, which gives rise to a decline in their loan supply (Bernanke and Blinder, 1988). This loan supply reduction depends on different bank characteristics, such as size, liquidity, and capitalization, which have been widely analyzed in the context of the traditional view of the bank lending channel (Kashyap and Stein, 1995, 2000; Kishan and Opiela, 2006; Cantero-Saiz *et al.*, 2022).

However, the traditional view of the bank lending channel has been reformulated by other authors because the dependence of banks on financial market-based funds has increased rapidly in the last decades and banks no longer depend only on deposits for funding (Bernanke, 2007; Disyatat, 2011). According to this reformulation of the bank lending channel, monetary policy restrictions increase the cost of market funding for banks, which results in a decline in banks' loan supply. Therefore, apart from bank characteristics, financial market variables could affect the effectiveness of the bank lending channel. In this regard, illiquidity is a key element in the financial market that could alter the financing conditions of the banking industry and thus impact the bank lending channel. Market liquidity shocks increase the cost and reduce the availability of funds in financial markets (Gatev and Strahan, 2006), which could really affect the bank lending channel because banks are especially sensitive to these situations (Diamond and Rajan, 2001b). Moreover, during global market liquidity shocks, investors' funds flow toward safe investments, which can alter banks' loanable funds and, as a result, the way the bank lending channel works (Gatev and Strahan, 2006; Acharya and Mora, 2015).

We directly analyze the effect that market illiquidity has on the potency of the bank lending channel. This aspect, which has not been studied previously, represents a new application of the bank lending channel and thus provides a new contribution to the literature. We analyze how the marginal effect of monetary policy on loan supply varies with the level of both stock and bond market illiquidity including interactions between continuous variables. This approach exploits all the information included in the variables and provides a precise understanding of the relationship between illiquidity and monetary policy.

Our empirical analysis comprises a sample of 862 listed banks from 21 OECD countries between 2002 and 2015. Our analysis is carried out using the System GMM methodology for panel data, which controls for both unobservable heterogeneity and the problems of endogeneity. Our results show that the bank lending channel plays an important role in the transmission mechanism of the monetary policy when financial markets are very liquid. However, the intensity of the bank lending channel decreases as the stock and bond market liquidity declines. Furthermore, when both markets start to become less liquid, the banks' loan supply ceases to be affected by monetary policy shocks, which means that the bank lending channel becomes ineffective. These results are very interesting for the way monetary policy is conducted because they suggest that market liquidity is a key factor that affects the transmission of monetary policy through the bank lending channel.

The remainder of this chapter is structured as follows: The following section reviews the previous literature. Section 3 focuses on the empirical analysis and the discussion of the results. We conclude in Section 4.

2. Literature Review

Monetary policy can affect the economy through different channels, such as the interest rate channel, the exchange rate channel, the asset price and wealth channel, the expectations channel, the risk-taking channel, and the credit channel (Mishkin, 1995; Gambacorta, 2009; Disyatat, 2011; Auer *et al.*, 2019).

The interest rate channel posits that increases in interest rates lead to a reduction in consumption and investment by both families and companies. This leads to a reduction in demand in the economy that puts downward pressure on prices.

The exchange rate channel, which works mainly in open economies, proposes that increases in interest rate give rise to the appreciation of the local currency. This appreciation mainly generates two effects. First, it reduces the local currency prices of imported goods and inputs, which reduces inflationary pressure. Second, it discourages exports and encourages imports. As a result, the demand for domestic goods is reduced and prices are pushed down.

The asset price and wealth channel indicate that interest rate increases tend to reduce the prices of financial assets due to a rise in the discount rate that is applied to cash flows from financial assets. This reduction in the financial wealth of families and companies leads to a decrease in consumption and investment, which in turn puts downward pressure on prices.

The expectation channel focuses on how monetary policy decisions affect agents' expectations about the future evolution of the economy and prices. Thus, a rise in interest rates signals a reduction in economic activity in the future and a reduction in inflationary pressures. For this channel to work properly, it is essential that the central bank has a high level of credibility.

The risk-taking channel proposes that banks take on greater risks when interest rates decrease. This is, on the one hand, because asset managers are trying to get the same nominal returns as when interest rates were higher. On the other hand, when interest rates decrease, banks' perception of risk is lower because this decrease boosts the asset and collateral values and reduces asset volatility (Gambacorta, 2009; Alzuabi, *et al.*, 2021).

The credit channel focuses on the effects that changes in interest rates have on the credit issued by banks to firms and consumers. This channel can be divided into two sub-channels: the balance sheet channel and the bank lending channel. The balance sheet channel operates through the net worth of firms. Restrictive monetary policies damage the balance sheets of indebted firms because they increase their debt services and decrease the value of their assets. As a result, lenders tend to demand greater interest rates which reduces the financing access of firms. The bank lending channel, which is the main topic of this chapter, poses that monetary policy shocks decrease banks' loan supply because they reduce banks' access to loanable funds, such as deposits (Bernanke and Blinder, 1988; Ivashina *et al.*, 2022).

This chapter focuses on the bank lending channel, which has gained a lot of relevance in recent decades. According to this channel, a tightening of monetary policy reduces the supply of bank loans due to a decrease in loanable funds, mainly deposits, available to banks (Bernanke and Blinder, 1988). The decrease in bank deposits after a tightening of monetary policy conditions is mainly due to two effects. First, the increase in the obligatory reserves that commercial banks must hold in central banks reduces the funds available to banks to issue credits (Kashyap and Stein, 1995). Second, monetary policy changes alter the relationship between the return on deposits and that of other assets, which changes the amount of deposits that banks can collect (Ehrmann *et al.*, 2003).

The bank lending channel has been criticized because banks are now more dependent on market-based funds (Romer and Romer, 1990). However, Bernanke (2007) and Disyatat (2011) reformulated the bank lending channel, reiterating the importance of the cost and availability of market-based funds as one of the main elements through which monetary policy changes affect banks' loan supply. This reformulation has given rise to a renewed interest in this channel on which many research papers have recently been published (Albertazzi *et al.*, 2021; Papadamou *et al.*, 2021; Ivashina *et al.*, 2022; Cantero-Saiz *et al.*, 2022). Most previous studies have analyzed the effect of different bank-specific characteristics on the intensity of the bank lending channel. These studies usually find that the loan supply of small and less financially healthy banks (poorly capitalized, less liquid, or riskier) is more affected after monetary policy changes.[1] A few studies have analyzed the relationship between the bank lending channel and certain bank market characteristics, such as market concentration (Olivero *et al.*, 2011; Adams and Amel, 2011), banking competition (Amidu and Wolfe, 2013), sovereign risk (Cantero-Saiz *et al.*, 2014), and financial development (Sanfilippo-Azofra *et al.*, 2018).

Market liquidity is an important factor in the financing of banks because global financial markets are easily accessible now to most banks, which are increasingly becoming more dependent on market-based funds (Gambacorta and Marques-Ibanez; 2011; Almazan *et al.*, 2015; Samarasinghe and Uylangco, 2022). Regarding the reformulation of the bank lending channel, this means that market liquidity might well be a key element in its effectiveness. However, to our knowledge, this is the first empirical study that analyzes market illiquidity as one of the determinants of the bank lending channel.

Market illiquidity could affect the effectiveness of the bank lending channel due to different opposing effects. First, market liquidity

---

[1]See, among others, Kashyap and Stein (1995), Jimborean (2009), and Cantero *et al.* (2018).

shocks increase the cost and reduce the availability of funds in financial markets (Gatev and Strahan, 2006). Banks are particularly sensitive to market liquidity shocks because their loans are relatively illiquid assets and they have to provide liquidity to depositors on demand (Diamond and Rajan, 2001a; Diamond and Rajan, 2001b). When banks need liquidity, they could securitize their loans or use them as collateral to issue loan-backed bonds (Bhattacharya and Thakor, 1993). However, getting liquidity from these activities becomes more difficult and costly when market liquidity is scarce (Cornet *et al.*, 2011). Banks might even reduce their loan supply if they foresee liquidity needs (Diamond and Rajan, 2001b). Consequently, we expect that in illiquid financial markets, monetary policy restrictions, which exacerbate the cost and reduce the availability of funds in financial markets, give rise to a greater reduction in banks' loan supply.

Second, the shortage of market liquidity not only gives rise to an increase in the cost of market financing and a reduction in the availability of funds in financial markets but it also leads to a flow of funds from the financial markets to banks (Saidenberg and Strahan, 1999; Gatev and Strahan, 2006; Gatev *et al.*, 2007). During market liquidity shocks, investors' appetite for risky (and more profitable) assets, such as commercial paper, shares, or corporate bonds, decreases considerably. As a result, they became more willing to hold very safe and liquid assets, such as bank deposits. This effect is called "flight to safety". Bank deposits are considered safer because, first, they are protected by deposit insurance systems, second, banks can get emergency liquidity assistance from central banks, and, third, governments usually bail out banks in financial distress that are too big to fail (Gatev *et al.*, 2007). In this regard, Gatev and Strahan (2006) show a significant increase in bank deposits during the liquidity crisis after the bankruptcy of Penn Central Transportation Company in 1970 and Enron in 2002 or the Russian default in 1998.

Moreover, the inflow of funds that banks experience during liquidity shocks might lower the interest rate of deposits, reducing the financing cost of banks (Gatev and Strahan, 2006). Although banks tend to increase the proportion of liquid assets that they hold because depositors can withdraw their funds on demand, the inflow of funds and the reduction of financing cost that banks experience can boost the loan supply. Thus, the inflow of bank deposits increases the loanable funds available for banks, which together with the decrease in financing cost of banks could hinder the effectiveness of the bank lending channel.

Finally, we need to take into account a third effect. During severe liquidity shocks that even affect the banking industry, investors might well be more willing to move their funds from the financial markets to non-banking safe assets. This effect will neutralize the expected inflow of deposits after shortages of market liquidity, leading to fierce competition for deposits and an increase in their interest rates. According to Acharya and Mora (2015), this is exactly what happened in the United States during the beginning of the financial crisis. From August 2007 to October 2008, liquidity problems in the financial markets gave rise not to an increase in bank deposits in the USA but to an increase in the funding inflow into assets with government guarantees or Treasury securities. The lack of market liquidity forced many banks, especially those with greater liquidity problems or exposed to undrawn commitments, to raise their rates for deposits (Cornett *et al.*, 2011; Acharya and Mora, 2015). This situation did not extend beyond September 2008, when Lehman Brothers failed, due to several government actions that reverted the previous trend in fund flows, leading to a large increase in deposits.[2]

In general, banks tend to increase their holdings of liquid assets during the shocks of liquidity that both seriously affect them and are not followed by an increase in deposits. First, during these episodes, banks' fragility arises because depositors could withdraw large amounts of cash from their back accounts on demand (Diamond and Rajan, 2001a). Second, banks' loans become more illiquid because loans are more difficult to securitize or use as collateral (Bhattacharya and Thakor, 1993). Third, borrowers tend to draw down their pre-existing bank credit lines as raising funds is becoming increasingly difficult (Saidenberg and Strahan, 1999; Gatev *et al.*, 2007). Fourth, banks tend to hold more liquid assets as precautionary liquidity due to the rollover risk (Freixas *et al.*, 1999; Acharya *et al.*, 2011; Unsal and Caceres, 2011; Cantero-Saiz *et al.*, 2014).

[2]See Acharya and Mora (2015) for a more detailed explanation.

During these periods of severe liquidity shocks and lack of inflow of deposits, banks' liquidity hoarding might well lead to a drastic reduction in banks' loan supply. Actually, if market liquidity is so low that banks are seriously affected, banks could be forced to restrict their loan supply in such an abrupt way that they could be unresponsive to monetary policy changes (or even reduce their loans after monetary policy expansions). This seems to have happened during the first years after the onset of the financial crisis when the monetary policy expansion of central banks did not manage to increase banks' loan supply. Banks were reluctant to grant new loans, but they invested their funds in government bonds or increased their cash reserves in their accounts at central banks, which gave rise to the so-called "liquidity trap" (Pollin, 2012).

To sum up, market liquidity could affect the effectiveness of the bank lending channel due to different opposing consequences:

(1) Market-based financing difficulties give rise to an increase in the cost of financing and a reduction in the availability of funds in financial markets. As a result, the effectiveness of the bank lending channel increases.
(2) Flight to safety leads to an increase in deposits and a reduction in their interest rates. As a result, the effectiveness of the bank lending channel decreases.
(3) Liquidity trap leads to a drastic reduction in banks' loan supply. As a result, the bank lending channel stops working properly.

To shed some light on the effect that market illiquidity has on the bank lending channel, in the following section, we conduct an empirical analysis.

3. Empirical Analysis

3.1. *Selection of the sample*

Our sample consists of the listed banks from OECD countries in the Datastream database between 2002 and 2015. We restrict the sample period to end in 2015 because since 2016, the interest rates of some central banks have been zero, or close to zero, and with minor changes. Furthermore, the short-term money market rate was even negative in some countries. Negative interest rates harm bank profitability[3] and thus force banks to inhibit loan supply (Borio and Gambacorta, 2017). This fact completely distorts the bank lending channel, which could give rise to a bias in our results.

According to Olivero *et al.* (2011) and Cantero *et al.* (2018), we remove those listed banks in the following cases:

(1) Banks with negative values of assets, loans, deposits, interest income, and expenses.
(2) Banks with growth rates of loans and/or deposits greater than 300%. Banks with a high loan-to-deposits ratio usually have liquidity problems and highly impaired financial intermediation. This situation generates a funding gap, which biases their loan supply behavior (Van der End, 2016).
(3) Banks with loans 100 times greater than deposits might be evidence of mergers or acquisitions.

We remove the banks with data available for less than six consecutive years between 2002 and 2015 (as we use lagged growth variables) and the banks from countries without the necessary macroeconomic data. The former condition is vital to test for second-order serial correlation and ensure the robustness of the estimates made by System GMM (Arellano and Bond, 1991).

The final sample consists of an unbalanced panel of 862 listed banks from 21 OECD countries between 2002 and 2015. Table 1 shows the number of banks and total observations per country and the year of distribution of our sample. The required data come from the Datastream, IMF databases, the World Development Indicators database, J.P. Morgan, and the central banks of several of the countries analyzed.

3.2. *Econometric model and data*

To analyze the relationship between market liquidity and the bank lending channel, we propose the following model based on the

[3]Banks hardly reduce deposit rates below zero, even when money market interest rates are negative. Therefore, as deposit rates are zero or close to zero, any additional decrease in the interest rates would affect the return on loans without any reduction in the cost of deposits.

Table 1. Sample.

	Number of Observations	Number of Banks
AUSTRALIA	96	7
AUSTRIA	95	7
BELGIUM	36	3
CANADA	128	10
CHILE	96	7
DENMARK	284	23
FRANCE	246	19
GERMANY	127	11
GREECE	76	8
ITALY	228	17
JAPAN	1,163	88
KOREA, REPUBLIC OF	97	8
MEXICO	44	4
POLAND	149	12
PORTUGAL	58	5
SLOVAKIA	41	4
SPAIN	70	5
SWEDEN	56	4
SWITZERLAND	291	25
UNITED KINGDOM	90	7
UNITED STATES	6,525	588
Total	9,996	862

Years	2002	2003	2004	2005	2006	2007	2008	2009	2010	2011	2012	2013	2014	2015	Total
No. of banks	597	644	676	707	718	740	754	742	747	762	764	741	717	687	9,996

approach of Kashyap and Stein (1995):

$$\begin{aligned}
\Delta \ln(\text{loans})_{i,t} = {} & \beta_0 + \beta_1 \Delta \ln(\text{loans})_{i,t-1} + \beta_2 \Delta i_{m,t} + \beta_3 \Delta \ln(\text{GDP})_{m,t} \\
& + \beta_4 \text{SIZE}_{i,t-1} + \beta_5 \text{LIQ}_{i,t-1} + \beta_6 \text{CAP}_{i,t-1} \\
& + \beta_7 \text{SM_ILLIQ}_t + \beta_8 \text{BM_ILLIQ}_t \\
& + \beta_9 (\Delta i_{m,t} * \text{SIZE}_{i,t-1}) + \beta_{10} (\Delta i_{m,t} * \text{LIQ}_{i,t-1}) \\
& + \beta_{11} (\Delta i_{m,t} * \text{CAP}_{i,t-1}) + \beta_{12} (\Delta i_{m,t} * \text{SM_ILLIQ}_t) \\
& + \beta_{13} (\Delta i_{m,t} * \text{BM_ILLIQ}_t) + \sum_{t=1}^{12} \pi_t \text{Year}_t \\
& + \sum_{m=1}^{21} \vartheta_m \text{Country}_m + \varepsilon_{i,t} \qquad (1)
\end{aligned}$$

The dependent variable, $\Delta\ln(\text{loans})_{i,t}$, captures the growth rate in loan supply from bank i in year t relative to year *t-1.* This variable has been widely used in the bank lending channel literature (Altunbas, 2010; Gambacorta and Marques-Ibanez, 2011; Cantero-Saiz, 2014). Moreover, as in many other studies, we introduce this variable lagged one year as an independent variable to control for the persistence effect of the dependent variable.

Δi is the change in the short-term money market rate and represents monetary policy changes. This is the most used variable in the literature to test the existence of the bank lending channel with bank-level data (Olivero, *et al.*, 2011; Alaeddin *et al.*, 2019; Cantero-Saiz *et al.*, 2022). According to this channel, higher interest rates reduce the growth of bank loans.

$\Delta\ln(\text{GDP})$ is the real GDP growth rate. This variable controls for the business cycle, so we expect that higher economic growth rates give rise to an increase in the supply of loans (Olivero *et al.*, 2011).

SIZE is the logarithm of total assets. Large banks usually experience higher loan growth rates (Kashyap and Stein, 2000).

LIQ is the ratio of securities, cash, and funds due from banks to total assets. Liquid banks tend to grant more loans (Kashyap and Stein, 2000; Olivero *et al.*, 2011; Cantero-Saiz *et al.*, 2014).

CAP is the ratio of total equity to total assets. Higher-capitalized banks usually grant more loans (Altunbas *et al.*, 2002; Kishan and Opiela, 2006).

As with many previous studies, we lag the bank variables (SIZE, LIQ, and CAP) for one year to avoid an endogeneity bias (Altunbas *et al.*, 2010; Cantero *et al.*, 2018; Sanfilippo-Azofra *et al.*, 2018).

The main objective of this study is to evaluate the effect that market illiquidity has on the bank lending channel. Thus, we need to capture market illiquidity in the stock market and in the bond market because banks resort to both of them to finance their loan supply. We use Amihud's (2002) illiquidity as a proxy for the stock market illiquidity and the market efficiency coefficient (MEC) as a proxy for the bond market illiquidity. These proxies, which have been widely used in the previous literature (Bernstein, 1987; Acharya and Pedersen, 2005; Karolyi *et al.*, 2012; Broto and Lamas, 2016), are easily aggregated to form global values per year, which is necessary for this study. Moreover, our sample period requires data for a long time series, which, unlike other illiquidity proxies, the ones used in this study comply with.

In this regard, SM_ILLIQ, which is the proxy of the stock market illiquidity, is the market value-averaged Amihud's (2002) illiquidity proxy

$$\text{SM\_ILLIQ}_y = \left(\sum_{i=1}^{n} \text{AMIHUD}_{iy} \cdot \text{AvMV}_{iy}\right) \Big/ \left(\sum_{i=1}^{n} \text{AvMV}_{iy}\right) \tag{2}$$

where AvMV is the average market value of stock i for year y and AMIHUD is the average of the daily ratio of absolute stock return to trading volume.

$$\text{AMIHUD}_{iy} = (1/D_{iy}) \sum_{d=1}^{D_{iy}} (|R_{idy}|/V_{idy}) \tag{3}$$

where D is the number of valid observation days in year y for stock i, R is the return on day d in year y for stock i, and V is the dollar volume (in thousand US dollars) on day d in year y for stock i. Stock i is admitted to the calculation in year y if it has return and volume data for more than 200 days during year y (Amihud, 2002). Moreover, to eliminate outliers, stocks whose estimated value of the variable AMIHUD is at the highest or lowest 1% tails of the distribution are removed (Amihud, 2002).

Regarding bond market, BM_ILLIQ, which is the proxy of the bond market illiquidity, is based on the market efficiency coefficient (MEC).[4]

$$\text{MEC} = \text{Var}(R_t)/(T \cdot \text{Var}(r_t)) \tag{4}$$

where $\text{Var}(R_t)$ is the variance of the logarithm of long-period returns, $\text{Var}(r_t)$ is the variance of the logarithm of short-period returns, and T is the number of short periods in each longer period.

MEC is built on the idea that price movements are more continuous in liquid markets (Sarr and Lybek, 2002). Thus, in these markets, long-term volatility and short-term volatility are inclined to be similar (new orders flow rapidly to correct order imbalances), so MEC tends to be close but below one. However, in less liquid markets, short-term volatility tends to be higher due to price factors like inaccurate price discovery. Thus, in these markets, MEC tends to be considerably below one. Moreover, certain market conditions could reduce short-term volatility, leading to MEC above one (Sarr and Lybek, 2002). To consider this possibility, several authors propose the absolute deviation of MEC from unity (Ekaputra and Asikin, 2012; Broto and Lamas, 2016). Thus, the higher this new measure, the higher the market illiquidity. Thus, the absolute deviation of MEC from unity is defined as follows:

$$\text{AD\_MEC} = |\text{MEC} - 1| \tag{5}$$

One of the advantages of MEC or AD_MEC is that it can be used with indexes, which is very convenient for this study because it allows us to calculate a proxy of the bond market illiquidity without the traditional problems of aggregation. In this regard, we calculate MEC[5] using the J.P. Morgan Global Aggregate Bond Index.[6]

[4]MEC was introduced by Hasbrouck and Schwartz (1988).

[5]For every year, we use the variance of the logarithm of five-day return and one-day return (De Nicolò and Wiegand, 2007).

[6]The J.P. Morgan Global Aggregate Bond Index offers a representation of the global fixed income security market. It includes more than 5,500 investment-grade instruments issued in more than 60 countries and in more than 25 currencies. De Nicolò and Wiegand (2007) use the J.P. Morgan Global Bond Index to calculate the market-efficient coefficient (MEC) in order to estimate liquidity in bond markets.

Then, we calculate the absolute deviation from unity as our bond market illiquidity measure (BM_ILLIQ).

Returning to the variables in Equation (1), we include interactions between the monetary policy variable (Δi) and the bank variables (SIZE, LIQ, and CAP) and the market illiquidity variables (SM_ILLIQ and BM_ILLIQ) to capture the effect of these variables on monetary policy changes. Finally, country and year dummies are introduced in Equation (1) to control for country- and year-specific effects.

To correctly interpret the effect of the changes in monetary policy (Δi) on the growth of loans, we need to bear in mind that we are interacting the variable Δi with other continuous variables (SIZE, LIQ, CAP, SM_ILLIQ, and BM_ILLIQ). Therefore, we have to take the derivative of Equation (1) with respect to Δi to capture the marginal effect of Δi on the growth of loans:

$$(\partial\Delta \ln(\text{loans})_{i,t}/\partial\Delta i_{m,t}) = \beta_2 + \beta_9\text{SIZE}_{i,t-1} + \beta_{10}\text{LIQ}_{i,t-1} + \beta_{11}\text{CAP}_{i,t-1} + \beta_{12}\text{SM\_ILLIQ}_t + \beta_{13}\text{BM\_ILLIQ}_t \tag{6}$$

We normalize the variables (SIZE, LIQ, and CAP) with respect to their mean across all banks in the sample to facilitate the interpretation of our results (Gambacorta, 2005; Altunbas *et al.*, 2010; Cantero-Saiz *et al.*, 2014).

$$\text{SIZE}_{\text{it}} = \text{logA}_{\text{it}} - \left(\sum_{\text{i}=1}^{\text{N}} \text{logA}_{\text{it}}/\text{N}_{\text{t}}\right) \tag{7}$$

$$\text{LIQ}_{it} = (L_{it}/A_{it}) - \left(\left(\sum_{t=1}^{T}\left(\sum_{i=1}^{N}(L_{it}/A_{it})/N_t\right)\right)/T\right) \tag{8}$$

$$\text{CAP}_{it} = (E_{it}/A_{it}) - \left(\left(\sum_{t=1}^{T}\left(\sum_{i=1}^{N}(E_{it}/A_{it})/N_t\right)\right)/T\right) \tag{9}$$

A_{it} is the total assets, L_{it} is the securities, cash, and due from banks, E_{it} is the total equity, and N_t is the number of banks.

The mean of a normalized variable is zero. Thus, the marginal effect of Δi on the growth of loans for an average bank is as follows:

$$(\partial\Delta\ln(\text{loans})_{\text{i,t}}/\partial\Delta \text{i}_{\text{m,t}}) = \beta_2 + \beta_{12}\text{SM\_ILLIQ}_{\text{t}} + \beta_{13}\text{BM\_ILLIQ}_{\text{t}} \tag{10}$$

The marginal effect of the changes in monetary policy (Δi) on the growth of loans, shown in Equation (10), depends on the level of global stock market illiquidity (SM_ILLIQ) and global bond market illiquidity (BM_ILLIQ). Thus, the effectiveness of the bank lending channel will vary for different values of those variables. β_2 captures the marginal effect when the variables SM_ILLIQ and BM_ILLIQ are zero, while β_{12} and β_{13} capture the effect of stock and bond market illiquidity, respectively. In order to interpret the results properly, we will have to calculate the marginal effect and evaluate its significance for different values of SM_ILLIQ and BM_ILLIQ. We will use plots to facilitate the interpretations of the results.

Table 2 shows the descriptive statistics of the variables used in the analysis, and Table 3 presents the correlations between them.

3.3. *Results*

Equation (1) is estimated using a two-step System GMM with robust errors (Arellano and Bond, 1991). Regarding the instruments used in our estimation, following Sanfilippo-Azofra *et al.* (2018), we consider the monetary policy indicator and the macroeconomic variables to be exogenous. Moreover, we consider the bank characteristics and

Table 2. Sample statistics.

	Mean	Std. Dev.	Min.	Max.
Δln(loans)	0.0857	0.1626	−5.2658	1.3741
Δi	−0.0024	0.0119	−0.0766	0.0327
Δln(GDP)	0.0362	0.0590	−0.2075	0.2867
SIZE	15.8248	3.3360	9.9386	26.7037
LIQ	0.2789	0.1333	0.0046	0.9919
CAP	0.0923	0.0422	0.0059	0.7425
SM_ILLIQ	1.6694	0.4725	0.9825	2.2689
BM_ILLIQ	0.1164	0.0744	0.0189	0.2215

Table 3. Correlations.

	Δi	Δln (GDP)	SIZE	LIQ	CAP	SM_ ILLIQ	BM_ ILLIQ
Δi	1						
Δln(GDP)	0.2699	1					
SIZE	0.0436	−0.0803	1				
LIQ	0.0633	−0.0238	0.1385	1			
CAP	−0.0221	0.0444	−0.4287	−0.0259	1		
SM_ILLIQ	−0.5178	−0.3537	0.0000	−0.0263	0.0482	1	
BM_ILLIQ	−0.2051	−0.2972	0.0000	−0.0268	0.0059	0.2750	1

their interactions to be endogenous. Based on the Hansen test of the over-identifying restrictions for the endogenous variables, third lags have been used as instruments.[7] Moreover, we collapsed and factorized the instruments used in our estimation to reduce the overfitting risk but retain almost all information (Mehrhoff, 2009).

Table 4, Model (a) shows the results of the estimation of Equation (1). The coefficient associated with the first lag of the dependent variable is significant and positive, which indicates the persistence effect of the loan supply. $\Delta\ln(\text{GDP})$ has a significant positive coefficient, too. Thus, economic growth stimulates loan supply. Finally, SIZE has a significant and negative coefficient, which means that the size of banks is negatively related to loan supply.

With regard to the presence of the bank lending channel, Model (a) in Table 4 shows that the coefficient associated with the monetary policy indicator Δi is not significant. However, as we are interacting continuous variables, to correctly interpret the effect of the changes in monetary policy (Δi) on the growth of loans, we need to bear in mind that we are interacting the variable Δi with other continuous variables (SIZE, LIQ, CAP, SM_ILLIQ, and BM_ILLIQ). As we mentioned previously, to capture the marginal effect of Δi on the growth of loans, we have to take the derivative of Equation (1) with respect to Δi. As the variables SIZE, LIQ, and CAP are normalized with respect to their mean and the mean of a normalized variable is zero, we use Equation (10) to calculate the marginal effect for an average bank.

[7] The exogenous variables are instrumented by themselves.

Table 4. Results.

	(a)	(b)	(c)
Δln(loans)t-1	0.5386***	0.5142***	0.5062***
	(5.44)	(4.68)	(4.63)
Δln(GDP)t	0.1618***	0.1430**	0.1462**
	(2.67)	(2.26)	(2.27)
Δit	−4.58	−4.1362	−4.1847
	(−1.53)	(−1.51)	(−1.53)
SIZEt-1	−0.0118*	−0.0089	−0.0091
	(−1.64)	(−1.13)	(−1.13)
LIQt-1	0.0029	0.0075	0.0085
	(0.05)	(0.12)	(0.14)
CAPt-1	0.2879	0.5931	0.6173
	(0.33)	(0.65)	(0.67)
SM_ILLIQt	−0.0092	−0.0097	−0.0105
	(−0.37)	(−0.45)	(−0.49)
BM_ILLIQt	−0.04	−0.0521	−0.0539
	(−0.3)	(−0.42)	(−0.44)
Δit*SIZEt-1	−0.5918	−0.4011	−0.4261
	(−0.8)	(−0.56)	(−0.6)
Δit*LIQt-1	6.2281	3.7125	4.1116
	(0.5)	(0.3)	(0.33)
Δit*CAPt-1	31.4696	27.7332	28.0354
	(0.41)	(0.39)	(0.4)
Δit*SM_ILLIQt	1.178	1.0725	1.1240
	(0.9)	(0.87)	(0.9)
Δit*BM_ILLIQt	27.7346**	24.1097*	24.0653*
	(2.12)	(1.95)	(1.95)
Crisis$t$		−0.0051	−0.0065
		(−0.54)	(−0.68)
CBASS_GDPt			0.0494
			(0.94)
Cons.	0.0899***	0.0848***	0.0829***
	(3.36)	(3.02)	(2.92)
Country dummies	Yes	Yes	Yes
Year dummies	Yes	Yes	Yes

(*Continued*)

Table 4. (*Continued*)

	(a)	(b)	(c)
ar(2)	0.222	0.181	0.196
Hansen	0.213	0.232	0.233

Notes: Results of the estimation of Equation (1). $\Delta\ln(\text{loans})_{i,t}$ is the dependent variable and captures the growth rate in loan supply from bank i in year t relative to year *t-1*. Δi is the change in the short-term money market rate and represents monetary policy changes. $\Delta\ln(\text{GDP})$ is the real GDP growth rate. SIZE is the logarithm of total assets. LIQ is the ratio of securities, cash, and funds due from banks to total assets. CAP is the ratio of total equity to total assets. SM_ILLIQ, which is the proxy of the stock market illiquidity, is the market value-averaged Amihud's (2002) illiquidity proxy. BM_ILLIQ, which is the proxy of the bond market illiquidity, is based on the market efficiency coefficient. Coefficients and T-student are associated with each variable. *** indicates a level of significance of 0.01, ** indicates a level of significance of 0.05, * indicates a level of significance of 0.1; ar(2) is the *p*-value of the second-order serial correlation statistic. Hansen is the *p*-value of the over-identifying restriction test.

The marginal effect of the changes in monetary policy (Δi) on the growth of loans, as shown in Equation (10), depends on the level of stock market illiquidity (SM_ILLIQ) and bond market illiquidity (BM_ILLIQ). Thus, in order to interpret the results properly, we will have to calculate the marginal effect for different values of SM_ILLIQ and BM_ILLIQ. To facilitate the interpretations of the results, we use plots that show the marginal effect when the variable SM_ILLIQ changes, but in each of them, we set a specific value for the variable BM_ILLIQ (minimum, 25th percentile, 50th percentile, 75th percentile, and maximum).

Figure 1(a) reports the marginal effect of monetary policy on the growth of loans in relation to the stock market illiquidity (SM_ILLIQ) when the bond market illiquidity (BM_ILLIQ) is set at its minimum (the bond market is very liquid). The figure shows the presence of the bank lending channel when the stock market is very liquid (low values of SM_ILLIQ), so increases in the short-term money market rate negatively and significantly affect banks' loan supply. This negative effect is less intense as stock market liquidity declines and becomes non-significant when the stock market becomes highly illiquid. This result is consistent with the flight-to-safety effect, which considers that the reduction of liquidity gives rise to an inflow of funds to banks, which lessens the effectiveness of the bank lending channel.

Figure 1(b)–(e) shows the marginal effect of monetary policy changes on bank lending when bond market illiquidity increases. In general, the effect of the short-term money market rate (Δi) on bank lending becomes non-significant for most values of SM_ILLIQ when the bond market illiquidity is set at its 25th percentile (Figure 1(b)) and becomes completely non-significant when the bond market illiquidity is set at its 50th percentile (Figure 1(c)). Moreover, when the bond market is very illiquid (75th percentile and maximum), the marginal effect of the short-term money market rate becomes positive and significant, which is the opposite effect of the one proposed by the bank lending channel (Figure 1(d) and (e)). This opposite effect could be related to the financial crisis. Back then, severe financing and liquidity problems forced banks in many countries to reduce their loan supply even when central banks cut their official or target interest rates (Acharya and Mora, 2015). Moreover, during a banking crisis, investors might well be more willing to move their funds from the financial markets to non-banking safe assets, which will neutralize the expected inflow of deposits.

In order to control for the effect of the crisis, we carry out a new analysis by including in Equation (1) the variable CRISIS. This variable takes a value of 1 for a bank during the years that the country in which the bank operates suffered a banking or sovereign debt crisis, and 0 otherwise. To determine when a country experienced a crisis, we follow the tables shown in Laeven and Valencia (2020). Table 4, Model (b) and Figure 2 show the results of this estimation. In general, the results are similar when bond market illiquidity is set at its minimum and at its 25th and 50th percentiles. The bank lending channel is only effective when the stock market and the bond market are very liquid. Thus, increases in the short-term money market rate negatively and significantly affect banks' loan supply when banks have easy access to market financing. This negative effect is less intense, and ends up becoming non-significant, as stock market and bond market liquidity decrease.

Figure 2(d) and (e) shows that when the bond market is very illiquid (75th percentile and maximum), the marginal effect

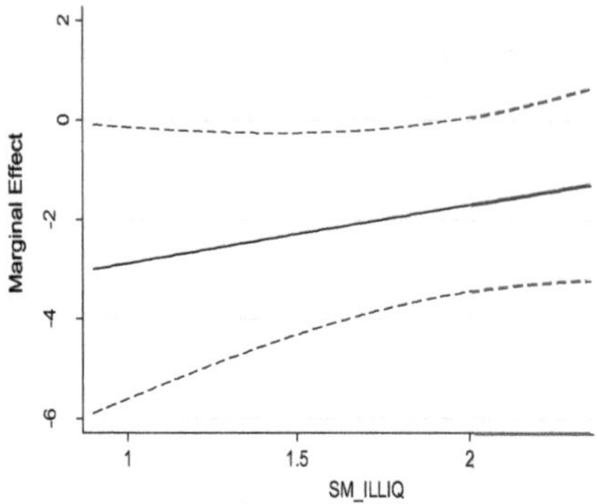

(a) BM_ILLIQ-MIN

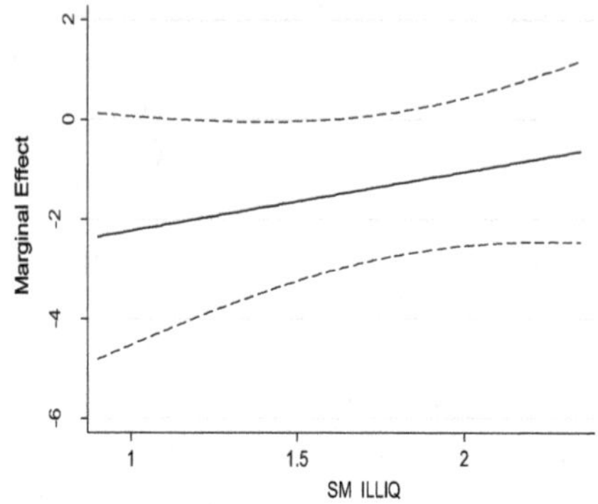

(b) BM_ILLIQ-25th PCTL

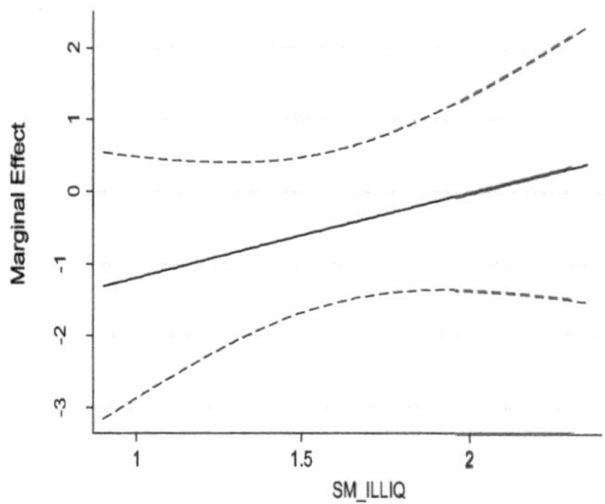

(c) BM_ILLIQ-50th PCTL

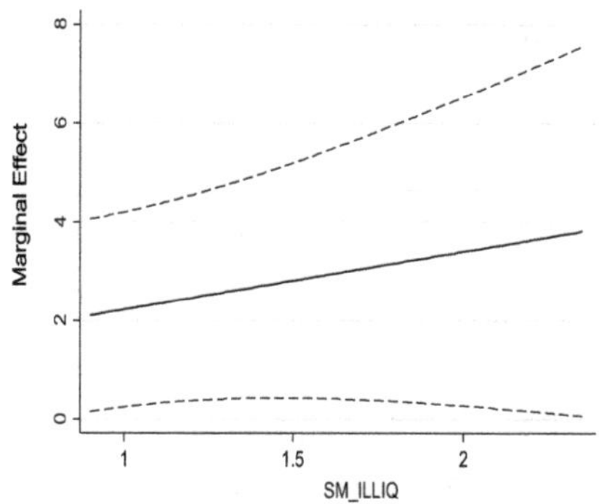

(d) BM_ILLIQ-75th PCTL

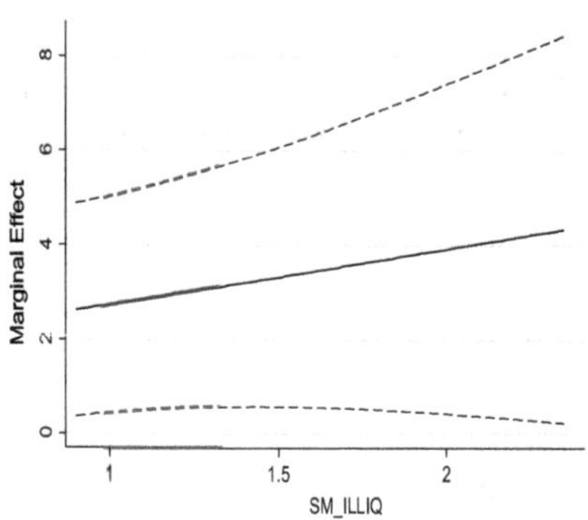

(e) BM_ILLIQ-MAX

Figure 1. Marginal effect of Table 4, Model (a). Marginal effect (—) and upper and lower 90% confidence limit (– – –) of Δi on $\Delta \ln$(loans) in relation to SM_ILLIQ for different values of BM_ILLIQ.

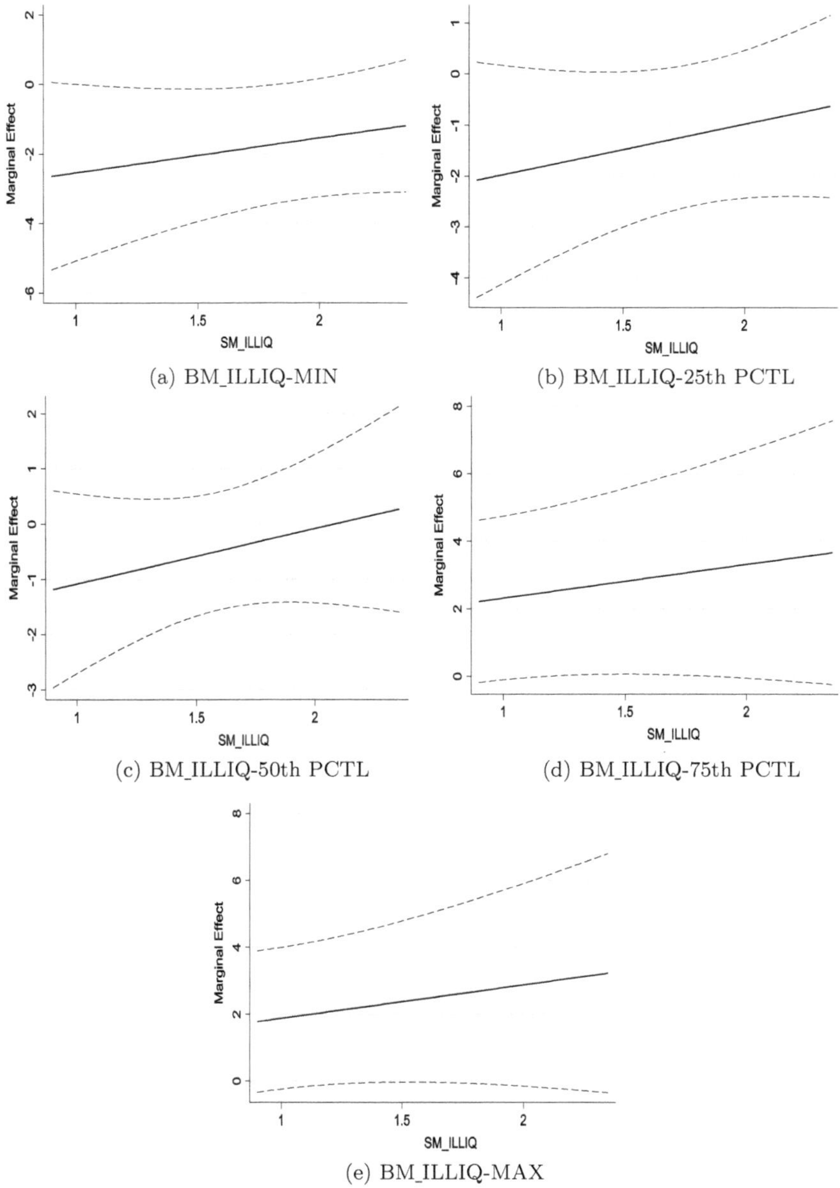

Figure 2. Marginal effect of Table 4, Model (b). Marginal effect (—) and upper and lower 90% confidence limit (– – –) of Δi on Δln(loans) in relation to SM_ILLIQ for different values of BM_ILLIQ.

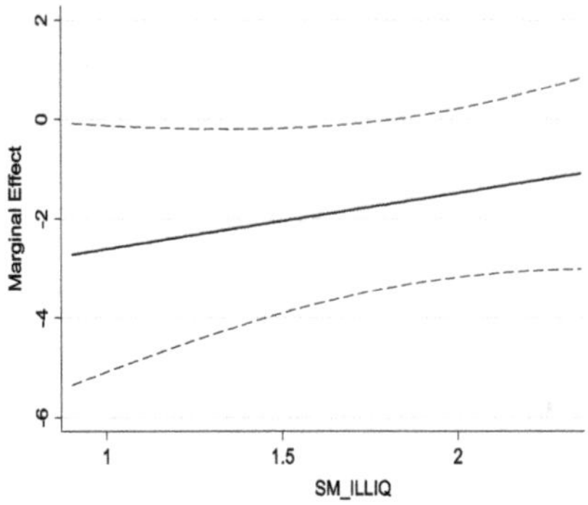

(a) BM_ILLIQ-MIN

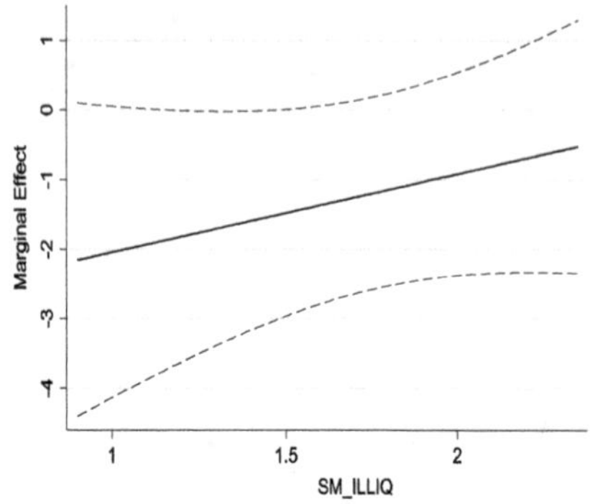

(b) BM_ILLIQ-25th PCTL

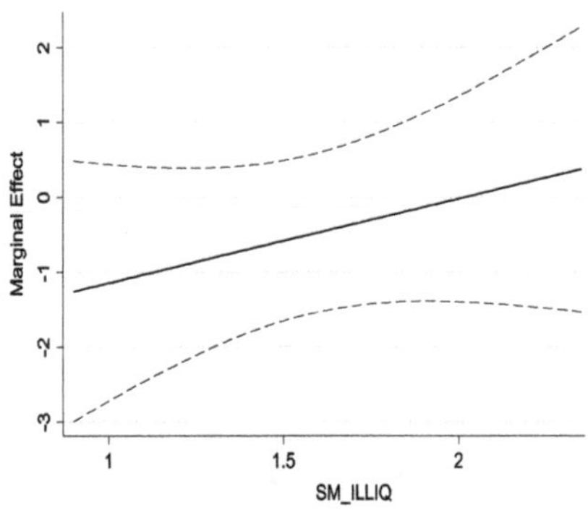

(c) BM_ILLIQ-50th PCTL

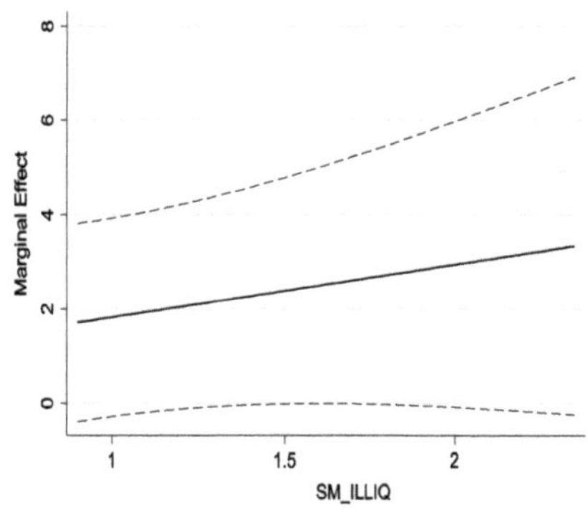

(d) BM_ILLIQ-75th PCTL

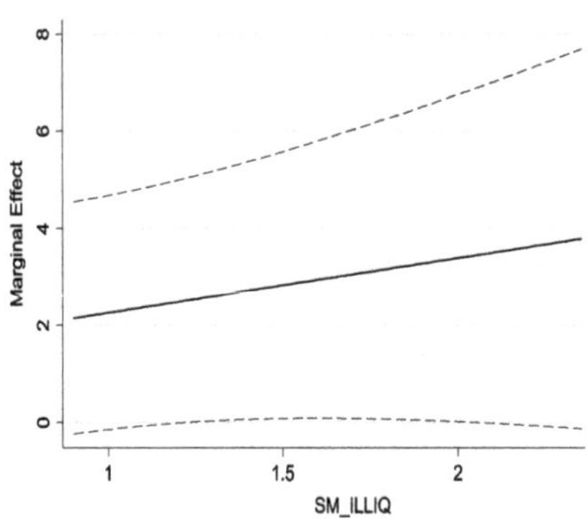

(e) BM_ILLIQ-MAX

Figure 3. Marginal effect of Table 4, Model (c). Marginal effect (—) and upper and lower 90% confidence limit (– – –) of Δi on $\Delta\ln(\text{loans})$ in relation to SM_ILLIQ for different values of BM_ILLIQ.

of the short-term money market rate, instead of being positive and significant as the previous model shows, becomes practically non-significant.

Finally, since in the aftermath of the financial crisis, some central banks carried out quantitative easing programs that expanded their balance sheet, we carry out a new analysis including the variable CBASS_GDP to control for these programs. This variable is the ratio between the total assets of the central bank of the country in which a bank operates and GDP[8] (Fungáčová *et al.*, 2014). The results, which are shown in Model (c) in Table 4 and Figure 3, are quite similar to the ones obtained in Model (b) when the effects of the crisis were controlled. Thus, increases in the short-term money market rate only negatively and significantly affect banks' loan supply when stock markets and bond markets are very liquid.

4. Conclusions

In this paper, we analyze the effect that market illiquidity has on the success of the bank lending channel using a sample from OECD countries. We find that when both stock and bond markets are very liquid, the bank lending channel plays an important role in the transmission mechanism of the monetary policy. However, the intensity of the bank lending channel decreases as the stock and bond market liquidity declines, which is consistent with the flight-to-safety effect. Furthermore, when both markets start to become less liquid, the banks' loan supply ceases to be affected by monetary policy shocks, which means that the bank lending channel becomes ineffective.

These results are very interesting for the way monetary policy is conducted because they suggest that market liquidity is a key factor that affects the transmission of monetary policy through the bank lending channel. When financial markets are illiquid, changes in interest rates do not seem to affect bank lending, so central banks should resort to other monetary policies to stimulate or restrict loan supply. Further analysis is required to understand fully the effects of market liquidity on the transmission mechanism of the monetary policy.

[8]In the case of the banks that operate in a country of the Eurozone, we use the total assets of the European Central Bank and the GDP of the Eurozone.

In fact, the high inflation in 2022 and the war in Ukraine may affect market liquidity conditions and the relationship between market liquidity and the transmission of monetary policy.

References

Acharya, V. V. and Mora, N. (2015). A crisis of banks as liquidity providers. *The Journal of Finance*, *70*(1), 1–43.

Acharya, V. V. and Pedersen, L. H. (2005). Asset pricing with liquidity risk. *Journal of Financial Economics*, *77*(2), 375–410.

Acharya, V. V. and Skeie, D. (2011). A model of liquidity hoarding and term premia in inter-bank markets. *Journal of Monetary Economics*, *58*(5), 436–447.

Adams, R. M. and Amel, D. F. (2011). Market structure and the pass-through of the federal funds rate. *Journal of Banking & Finance*, *35*(5), 1087–1096.

Alaeddin, O., Abojeib, M., Azmi, W., Alchaar, M. O. and Salim, K. (2019). The effectiveness of the bank lending channel: The role of banks' market power and business model. *Contemporary Economics*, *13*(3), 253–269.

Albertazzi, U., Nobili, A. and Signoretti, F. M. (2021). The bank lending channel of conventional and unconventional monetary policy. *Money, Credit and Banking*, *53*(2–3), 261–299.

Almazan, A., Martín-Oliver, A. and Saurina, J. (2015). Securitization and banks' capital structure. *The Review of Corporate Finance Studies*, *4*(2), 206–238.

Altunbas, Y., Fazylov, O. and Molyneux, P. (2002). Evidence on the bank lending channel in Europe. *Journal of Banking & Finance*, *26*(11), 2093–2110.

Altunbas, Y., Gambacorta, L. and Marques-Ibanez, D. (2010). Bank risk and monetary policy. *Journal of Financial Stability*, *6*(3), 121–129.

Alzuabi, R., Caglayan, M. and Mouratidis, K. (2021). The risk-taking channel in the United States: A GVAR approach. *International Journal of Finance and Economics*, *26*(4), 5826–5849.

Amihud, Y. (2002). Illiquidity and stock returns: Cross-section and time-series effects. *Journal of Financial Markets*, *5*(1), 31–56.

Amidu, M. and Wolfe, S. (2013). The effect of banking market structure on the lending channel: Evidence from emerging markets. *Review of Financial Economics*, *22*(4), 146–157.

Arellano, M. and Bond, S. (1991). Some tests of specification for panel data: Monte Carlo evidence and an application to employment equations. *The Review of Economic Studies*, *58*(2), 277–297.

Auer, S., Friedrich, C., Ganarin, M., Paligorova, T. and Towbin, P. (2019). International monetary policy transmission through banks in small open economies. *Journal of International Money and Finance, 90*, 34–53.

Bernanke, B. S. (2007). The financial accelerator and the credit channel speech at the Credit Channel of Monetary Policy in the Twenty-first Century Conference. *Federal Reserve Bank of Atlanta* (Atlanta, Georgia), *15*, 52–66.

Bernanke, B. S. and Blinder, A. S. (1988). Credit, money and aggregate demand. *The American Economic Review, 78*(2), 435–439.

Bernstein, P. L. (1987). Liquidity, stock markets, and market makers. *Financial Management, 16*(2), 54–62.

Bhattacharya, S. and Thakor, A. V. (1993). Contemporary banking theory. *Journal of Financial Intermediation, 3*(1), 2–50.

Borio, C. and Gambacorta, L. (2017). Monetary policy and bank lending in a low interest rate environment: Diminishing effectiveness? *Journal of Macroeconomics, 54*, 217–231.

Broto, C. and Lamas, M. (2016). Measuring market liquidity in US fixed income markets: A new synthetic indicator. *The Spanish Review of Financial Economics, 14*(1), 15–22.

Cantero-Saiz, M., Sanfilippo-Azofra, S., Torre-Olmo, B. and Lopez-Gutierrez, C. (2014). Sovereign risk and the bank lending channel in Europe. *Journal of International Money and Finance, 47*, 1–20.

Cantero, M, Sanfilippo, S., Torre, B. and López, C. (2018). A new approach to the analysis of monetary policy transmission through bank capital. *Finance Research Letters, 24*, 95–104.

Cantero-Saiz, M., Sanfilippo-Azofra, S. and Torre-Olmo, B. (2022). Sovereign risk and the bank lending channel: Differences across countries and the effects of the financial crisis. *Journal of Money, Credit and Banking, 54*(1), 285–312.

Cornett, M. M., McNutt, J. J., Strahan, P. E. and Tehranian, H. (2011). Liquidity risk management and credit supply in the financial crisis. *Journal of Financial Economics, 101*(2), 297–312.

De Nicolo, G. and Wiegand, J. (2007). What is global liquidity? In *IMF World Economic Outlook, International Monetary Fund.*

Diamond, D. W. and Rajan, R. G. (2001a). Banks and liquidity. *American Economic Review, 91*(2), 422–425.

Diamond, D. W. and Rajan, R. G. (2001b). Liquidity risk, liquidity creation, and financial fragility: A theory of banking. *Journal of Political Economy, 109*(2), 287–327.

Disyatat, P. (2011). The bank lending channel revisited. *Journal of money, Credit and Banking, 43*(4), 711–734.

Ekaputra, I. A. and Asikin, E. S. (2012). Impact of tick size reduction on small caps price efficiency and execution cost on the Indonesia stock exchange. *Asian Academy of Management Journal of Accounting and Finance*, *8*(1), 1–12.

Ehrmann, M., Gambacorta, L., Martínez-Pagés, J., Sevestre, P. and Worms, A. (2003). Financial systems and the role of banks in monetary policy transmission in the Euro Area. In I. Angeloni, A. Kashyap and B. Mojon (eds.) *Monetary Policy Transmission in the Euro Area*, pp. 235–269. Cambridge: Cambridge University Press.

Freixas, X., Giannini, G., Hoggarth, G. and Soussa, F. (1999). Lender of the last resort: A review of the literature. *Financial Stability Review*, *7*, 151–167.

Fungáčová, Z., Solanko, L. and Weill, L. (2014). Does competition influence the bank lending channel in the euro area? *Journal of banking & Finance*, *49*, 356–366.

Gambacorta, L. (2005). Inside the bank lending channel. *European Economic Review*, *49*(7), 1737–1759.

Gambacorta, L. (2009). Monetary policy and the risk-taking channel. *BIS Quarterly Review*, December, 43–53.

Gambacorta, L. and Marques-Ibanez, D. (2011). The bank lending channel: Lessons from the crisis. *Economic Policy*, *26*(66), 135–182.

Gatev, E., Schuermann, T. and Strahan, P. E. (2007). Managing bank liquidity risk: How deposit-loan synergies vary with market conditions. *The Review of Financial Studies*, *22*(3), 995–1020.

Gatev, E. and Strahan, P. E. (2006). Banks' advantage in hedging liquidity risk: Theory and evidence from the commercial paper market. *The Journal of Finance*, *61*(2), 867–892.

Hasbrouck, J. and Schwartz, R. A. (1988). Liquidity and execution costs in equity markets. *Journal of Portfolio Management*, *14*(3), 10–16.

Ivashina, V., Laeven, L. and Moral-Benito, E. (2022). Loan types and the bank lending channel. *Journal of Monetary Economics*, *126*, 171–187.

Jimborean, R. (2009). The role of banks in the monetary policy transmission in the new EU member states. *Economic Systems*, *33*(4), 360–375.

Karolyi, G. A., Lee, K. H. and Van Dijk, M. A. (2012). Understanding commonality in liquidity around the world. *Journal of Financial Economics*, *105*(1), 82–112.

Kashyap, A. K. and Stein, J. C. (1995). The impact of monetary policy on bank balance sheets. *Carnegie-Rochester Conference Series on Public Policy*, 42, 151–195.

Kashyap, A. K. and Stein, J. C. (2000). What do a million observations on banks say about the transmission of monetary policy? *American Economic Review*, *90*(3), 407–428.

Kishan, R. P. and Opiela, T. P. (2006). Bank capital and loan asymmetry in the transmission of monetary policy. *Journal of Banking & Finance, 30*(1), 259–285.

Laeven, L. and Valencia, F. (2020). Systemic banking crises database II. *IMF Economic Review, 68*, 307–361.

Mehrhoff, J. (2009). A solution to the problem of too many instruments in dynamic panel data GMM. *Discussion Paper Series 1: Economic Studies 2009, 31.*

Mishkin, F. S. (1995). Symposium on the monetary transmission mechanism. *Journal of Economic Perspectives, 9*(4), 3–10.

Olivero, M. P., Li, Y. and Jeon, B. N. (2011). Competition in banking and the lending channel: Evidence from bank-level data in Asia and Latin America. *Journal of Banking & Finance, 35*(3), 560–571.

Papadamou, S., Sogiakas, D., Sogiakas, V. and Syriopoulos, K. (2021). The role of net stable funding ratio on the bank lending channel: Evidence from European Union. *Journal of Banking Regulation, 22*(4), 287–307.

Pollin, R. (2012). The great US liquidity Trap of 2009–11: Are we stuck pushing on strings? Political Economy Research Institute. *University of Massachusetts Working Papers.*

Romer, C. D. and Romer, D. H. (1990). New evidence on the monetary transmission mechanism. *Brookings Papers on Economic Activity, 1990*(1), 149–213.

Saidenberg, M. R. and Strahan, P. E. (1999). Are banks still important for financing large businesses? *Current Issues in Economics and Finance, 5*(12), 1–6.

Samarasinghe, A. and Uylangco, K. (2022). Stock market liquidity and traditional sources of bank business. *Accounting and Finance, 62*(3), 3107–3145.

Sanfilippo-Azofra, S., Torre-Olmo, B., Cantero-Saiz, M. and López-Gutiérrez, C. (2018). Financial development and the bank lending channel in developing countries. *Journal of Macroeconomics, 55*, 215–234.

Sarr, A. and Lybek. T. (2002). Measuring liquidity in financial markets. *International Monetary Fund, 2.*

Unsal, D. F. and Caceres, C. (2011). Sovereign spreads and contagion risks in Asia. *International Monetary Fund, 11.*

Van den End, J. W. (2016). A macroprudential approach to address liquidity risk with the loan-to-deposit ratio. *The European Journal of Finance, 22*(3), 237–253.

https://doi.org/10.1142/9781800614321_0011

Chapter 11

An Empirical Analysis of the Trilemma of Exiting Expansionary Monetary Policy in the Euro Area

Sebastian Lang[*,†,‡] **and Wolfgang Schadner**[*,§]

[*]*University of St. Gallen, St. Gallen, Switzerland*
[†]*Berufliche Hochschule Hamburg, Hamburg, Germany*
[‡]*sebastian_lang@hotmail.com*
[§]*wolfgang.schadner@unisg.ch*

Abstract

This study proposes a theoretic trilemma model for the case of a monetary union and measures it empirically. Accordingly, there exists a trade-off between stabilizing the monetary union, maintaining free capital mobility, and exiting expansionary monetary policy in the euro area. Our results underscore the existence of this trilemma and point out the importance of resolving it without jeopardizing the euro and financial stability in the European Union.

Keywords: European Central Bank (ECB), monetary policy, financial stability, financial crisis, trilemma

1. Introduction

In this chapter, the conflicting goals of (i) stabilizing a monetary union, (ii) maintaining free capital mobility in the union, and (iii) exiting expansionary monetary policy are described as a trilemma, where two of the three objectives can be achieved but not all three of them at the same time. Mundell (1963) already describes the three sides of a trilemma's policy goals for an open economy, namely, monetary independence, exchange rate stability, and financial integration. The result of this article is that, for the case of a monetary union, a new kind of trilemma is proposed. The analytic difference to Mundell's (1963) trilemma lies in the fact that the presented analysis builds on a voting model, which is independent of the assumptions made in IS-LM model types. In addition, the trilemma is induced by monetary policy and not caused by political decisions on the design of the exchange rate regime as in Mundell (1963). Classical trilemma situations in open economies such as Bekaert and Mehl (2019) have been adapted to develop an understanding of modern central bank policies, which often include the task of keeping financial stability. For example, Schoenmaker (2005, 2011) suggests a trilemma situation during the ongoing financial integration in the European Union. Magas (2018) observes different versions of adjustment to external shocks and financial integration for small, open economies in light of the trilemma.

In this context, De Grauwe (2015) finds that the euro crisis that emerged after 2010 was the result of two design failures of the euro currency. First, economic cycles continued to occur at the national levels, leading to large external imbalances of countries within the euro area. Second, the impossibility of national central banks to bail out their home countries allowed liquidity crises to emerge that eventually turned into solvency crises for some euro-area countries. Therefore, De Grauwe and Ji (2015) see the need for intervention by the ECB, when individual countries in the currency union get into debt problems. Steiner *et al.* (2019) argue that the euro area entails an inherent policy trilemma between maintaining financial stability in the common currency area, independent control over the monetary base, and the accommodation of unlimited internal capital flight via the euro-area central banks' so-called "TARGET2-system", the Trans-European Automated Real-time

Gross-settlement Express Transfer system. Also, Canale *et al.* (2018) find a policy trilemma faced by euro-area member countries. They provide empirical evidence on a trade-off between free capital mobility, financial stability, and fiscal policy flexibility by analyzing data for 11 euro-area countries. Lang and Schadner (2021) analyze the trilemma of expansionary monetary policy in the euro area during the COVID-19 crisis. Elnahass *et al.* (2021) find that the COVID-19 pandemic has impacted global banking stability significantly in a negative way. They conclude, based on a large international data sample of banks, that the COVID-19 pandemic has had detrimental impacts both on financial performance and financial stability. Trinh *et al.* (2022) examine the association between bank tail risk and the COVID-19 pandemic by using a large international sample of listed banks. They find that systematic and idiosyncratic components of bank tail risk have increased during the pandemic, but less so for more profitable banks, implying that the COVID-19 pandemic results in a higher possibility of suffering extremely large losses in the stock prices of the global banking sector.

This chapter contributes to the existing literature by focusing on the analysis of the trilemma notion of the monetary policy in a currency union empirically. Since the central bank is the main actor to implement monetary policy, the analysis proposes an explanation of how decisions are made at the European Central Bank in the framework of a voting model. Central bank governors are assumed to be policy-oriented and rational.

In terms of the policy implications of this study, we suggest that a common European fiscal stabilization capacity is necessary to reinforce the euro area in case of a recession, both at the country level and euro-area level. Combining a fiscal stabilization capacity with a stepwise reduction of the ECB's asset purchase programs could give the ECB room to raise interest rates in the medium term to counter inflation and to break free thoroughly of the described trilemma. This chapter proceeds as follows: Section 2 introduces a theoretical model of the trilemma in the European Monetary Union, Section 3 connects the existing trilemma with TARGET2-balances between national European central banks and the ECB. Building on this understanding of the problem, Sections 4 and 5 present empirical evidence on the trilemma and Section 6 concludes this study with an outlook on future research.

2. A Model of the Trilemma in the European Monetary Union

The Governing Council is the ECB's highest decision-making body and responsible for setting interest rates and conducting monetary policy. It consists of six Executive Board members and 19 national central bank governors of the euro-area countries. The accession of Lithuania to the euro area in 2015 triggered a change in the voting rights, as already envisaged by the Governing Council in December 2002. Before January 1st, 2015, the ECB Governing Council had the principle of "one member, one vote". From January 1st, 2015, onward a rotation system of voting rights was put into place, which we briefly summarize.

The rotation helps maintain the Governing Council's ability to take action even as the number of euro-area countries gradually increases and with them the number of members of the Governing Council. Euro-area countries are divided into groups according to the size of their economies and their financial sectors. To determine which national central bank governor belongs to which group, a ranking was established. The governors from countries ranked first to fifth — currently, Germany, France, Italy, Spain, and the Netherlands — share four voting rights. All others (14 since Lithuania joined on January 1st, 2015) share 11 voting rights. The governors take turns using the rights on a monthly rotation. The "one member, one vote" principle applies to those holding a voting right at that time. The ECB's Executive Board members hold permanent voting rights.

All members of the Governing Council attend the meetings and have the right to speak. Since the Governing Council takes most decisions on a consensual basis, in a spirit of cooperation, the decision-making process has not changed. However, the rotation system implies that majorities must be formed and respected in order to attain a broad consensual basis. Hence, in the following model, we abstract from the rotation system of voting rights in the ECB Governing Council because it was put into effect after the major decisions on the ECB's quantitative easing programs in the year 2015. Building on the models of Freixas (2003) and Schoenmaker (2011), we formalize the ECB's trilemma and thereby underscore the importance of solving the problem successively. To do so, we consider the decisions of each country's member in the ECB governing council — the presidents of the national central banks — to vote for an exit or a continuation of the ECB's expansionary monetary policy. Hence, the policy instrument in the model is p, the expansionary monetary policy in the Eurosystem of the central banks of each of the 19 member countries, denoted by sub-index i.

Thus, the governing council members' choice is interpreted as a digital variable $z \in \{0, 1\}$, where $z = 0$ stands for stopping the expansionary monetary policy and $z = 1$ for its continuation. Furthermore, B_i denotes a country's benefit of the expansionary monetary policy and C_i its costs. A president of a national central bank chooses to continue the expansionary monetary policy in the Eurosystem only if the total benefits for his country are larger than the costs, $B_i - C_i > 0$. In a setting with more than one country, the total benefits of the expansionary monetary policy can be split into the benefits for the home country H_i and benefits for a foreign country F_i. The sum of the respective fractions of benefits $\alpha_{h,i}$ for home and $\alpha_{f,i}$ for the foreign country is 1 and sums up to $\alpha_{f,i} = \Sigma_{j \in J} \alpha_j$. Therefore, a majority of votes in the ECB's governing council in favor of the continuation of the expansionary monetary policy can be collected if the respective countries expect sufficient benefits altogether. As in Schoenmaker (2011), this is an example of an improvised cooperation between the countries, since economic and financial dependencies in the euro area may be of multiple natures. The national representatives in the ECB governing council gauge the overall profit or loss of the expansionary monetary policy for their country. If the total amount of policy gains is larger than its cost, the national central bank presidents vote for the continuation of the ECB's expansionary monetary policy measures. Thus, the optimal decision for each country's representative i in the ECB Governing Council is to maximize

$$z^* = (\alpha_i \cdot B_i - p_i) \tag{1}$$

s.t.

$$\begin{cases} z^* = 1 & \text{if } \sum_i p_i - C_i > 0 \\ z^* = 0 & \text{if } \sum_i p_i - C_i < 0 \end{cases} \tag{2}$$

This decision problem has many equilibria, but only one non-cooperative equilibrium leads to a unanimous vote for the full termination of the ECB's expansionary monetary policies. This is the case if no individual country can bear the total cost C by itself so that for no country i we can assert $\alpha_i \cdot B_i - C_i > 0$ and therefore $p_i = 0$, $z^* = 0$. If this non-cooperative equilibrium is selected, the decision to exit expansionary monetary policies completely is inefficient in terms of (i) supporting the monetary union and (ii) maintaining unrestricted capital mobility in the union. This is the case because it would mean a *de facto* limitation of TARGET2-balances and a restriction of credit to peripheral countries in the euro area. The equilibrium occurs only when part of the externalities fall outside the home country. Let us therefore further assume that the country with the highest benefits from expansionary monetary policies is the home country. The home country, however, is not prepared to meet the costs of the expansionary monetary policies entirely.

Proposition: The efficiency of exiting expansionary monetary policies from the perspective of the home country depends on the size of the fraction $\alpha_{h,i}$, where the range of benefits B_i in the home country is $\alpha_{h,i} \in [C_i/B_i, 1]$. If $\alpha_{h,i} < C_i/B_i$, then reducing expansionary monetary policies will be efficient. Vice versa, a home country increases expansionary monetary policies if $\alpha_{h,i} > C_i/B_i$. Therefore, given rational decision-making, a home country will reduce expansionary monetary policies only if the benefits are sufficiently large.

Proof of Proposition: The efficient solution is $z^* = 1 \textit{ if } B_i > C_i$ and $z^* = 0 \textit{ if } B_i < C_i$. Using Equations (1) and (2), the first best solution will be reached in the case of $\alpha_{h,i} = 1$. Given that $\alpha_{h,i} > \alpha_j \forall j \in J$, a continuation of expansionary monetary policies $(z^* = 1)$ will be voted for if the benefits in the home country are larger than the total costs: $\alpha_{h,i} \cdot B - C$. Otherwise, if $\alpha_{h,i} < C/B$, the exit equilibrium $(z^* = 0)$ occurs even if the continuation of expansionary monetary policies is optimal $(B_i > C_i)$.

The proposition states that as soon as measures toward an exit of expansionary monetary policies increase ($\alpha_{f,i} \uparrow$ and $\alpha_{h,i} \downarrow$), they will destabilize the monetary union.

3. The Trilemma and TARGET2-Balances

The trilemma is that upholding free capital mobility and stabilizing the monetary union are compatible only as long as no or very limited reduction of expansionary monetary policies occurs. Sinn and Wollmershäuser (2012) show that TARGET2-balances measure the intra-Euro-area balances of payments. Therefore, they indirectly also reflect international credit given through the Eurosystem in terms of reallocating the ECB's net re-financing credit. If a substantial reduction in the monetary base would take place, the monetary union would be jeopardized, since this leads to capital flight via the TARGET2-system to safe havens within the euro area. This capital flight is perceivable in the rise of the TARGET2-balances of peripheral countries in the euro area. TARGET2-balances are equalized if banks in surplus countries in the euro area grant credit to banks in deficit countries and importers use these loans to pay for imports from surplus countries. With the aggravation of the financial and debt crises, banks in peripheral countries in the euro area started to refinance themselves more and more directly via the ECB, with the effect that capital in the euro inter-banking market also started flowing directly from surplus countries to deficit countries. Inversely, the TARGET2-balances in the euro area built up. For example, the net accounts receivable of the German central bank ("Deutsche Bundesbank") in the TARGET2-system amount to 1,266.65 billion euros as of September 2022, while almost half of the Greek external debt stems from TARGET2-accounts payable. Hence, limiting TARGET2-balances would be equal to restricting the free mobility of capital, which is irreconcilable in a monetary union.

4. Empirical Evidence on the Trilemma

The task of finding empirical evidence on the ECB's trilemma is twofold. First, we define suitable indices for the three dimensions of the trilemma, similar to the research strategy in Canale *et al.* (2018). So the ECB's conflicting goals of (i) stabilizing the monetary union, (ii) maintaining free capital mobility in the union, and (iii) exiting expansionary monetary policy have to be quantified. Second, we test the existence of the trilemma by supposing a trade-off and therefore a linear relationship between these conflicting goals.

The first dimension of stabilizing the monetary union has been at the center of attention since the European debt crisis could only be resolved through the clear and determined intervention of the European Central Bank in the year 2012. To stabilize the European financial system, the ECB then sent the clear message to capital markets that it would do "whatever it takes" to defend the euro. This lifted pressure from the euro and restored financial stability. There are many ways of measuring financial stability, as the definition of the notion is rather wide. In this study, we use the CISS index, the Composite Indicator of Systemic Stress, proposed by Hollo *et al.* (2012) and published by the ECB to measure the stability of the financial system in the euro area.

The CISS is an indicator of contemporaneous stress in the European financial system. It is designed according to definitions of systemic risk and uses portfolio theory to aggregate an additional set of market-specific stress measures.[1] The aggregation takes into account the time-varying cross-correlations between the measures. As a result, the CISS puts relatively more weight on situations in which financial stress prevails in several market segments at the same time, capturing the idea that financial stress easily overspills in the euro area and is thus more dangerous for the European economy as a whole.

In order to measure the inner-euro-area capital mobility, we construct an index focused on TARGET2-balances. Following Sinn

[1]Realized volatility of the 3-month Euribor rate, realized volatility of the German 10-year benchmark government bond index, realized volatility of the Datastream non-financial sector stock market index, CMAX for the Datastream non-financial sector stock market index, stock-bond correlation, realized volatility of the idiosyncratic equity return of the Datastream bank sector stock market index over the total market index, yield spread between A-rated financial and non-financial corporations (7-year maturity), CMAX as defined above interacted with the inverse price-book ratio (book-price ratio) for the financial sector equity market index, and realized volatility of the euro exchange rate vis-à-vis the US Dollar, the Japanese yen, and the British pound.

(2011), we understand TARGET2-balances as real loans, which are secured by countries with positive TARGET2-balances and granted to countries with negative TARGET2-balances to import foreign goods and assets. Behind this stands the idea that current account deficits in the peripheral countries of the euro area are financed by TARGET2-loans, which are granted by countries with current account surpluses.

We construct a TARGET2-index (T2B_t) by adding up the TARGET2-balances retrieved from the ECB Statistical Data Warehouse (ECB, 2020) for the top three countries with positive balances and normalize the result to the numeric space [0;1] according to the following formula:

$$\text{T2B}_t = (\text{T2B}_t - [\text{T2B}_t]_{min})/([\text{T2B}_t]_{max} - [\text{T2B}_t]_{min}) \qquad (3)$$

In the final step, we use the Monetary Conditions Index (MCI) published by the European Commission (2020) to evaluate the ECB's monetary policy. The MCI is an index number calculated from a linear combination of the short-run interest rate and the exchange rate. The weights reflect the relative effects of the respective MCI component on aggregate demand.[2] A dropping index value means that monetary policy is loosened, while a rising index value indicates a tightening of monetary policy conditions by the ECB. This leads to the following set of trilemma indices, which we graph along the timeline from the outbreak of the sub-prime crisis in the USA in the second quarter of 2007 until July 2020, as shown in Figure 1. Accordingly, the summary statistics of the full sample are as shown in Table 1.

Now, it must be demonstrated that there is a trade-off between the policy goals of (i) stabilizing the monetary union, (ii) maintaining free capital mobility in the union, and (iii) exiting expansionary monetary policy in order to be able to suppose the existence of a trilemma. We

[2]The relative weights of the interest rate and the exchange rate components are 6:1, reflecting each variable's relative impact on GDP after two years, and are derived from simulations in the OECD's Interlink model following Richardson (1988). We also normalize the index to the [0;1] space.

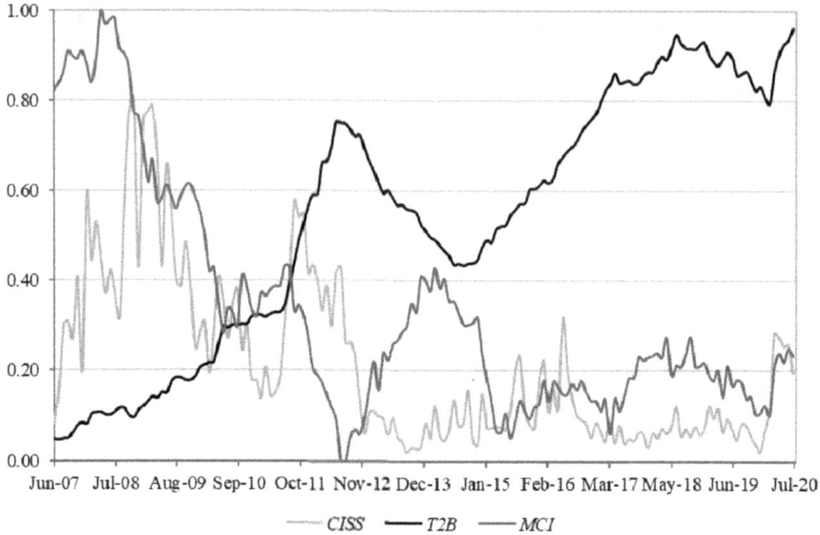

Figure 1. The figure shows the development of the monthly data time series of the three trilemma indices CISS, T2B, and MCI from June 2007 to July 2020.

Table 1. Summary statistics. The table provides the summary statistics of the sample of the three indices CISS, T2B, and MCI.

	CISS	T2B	MCI
Observations	158	158	158
Frequency	monthly	monthly	monthly
Sample start	June 1st 2007	June 1st 2007	June 1st 2007
Sample end	July 31st 2020	July 31st 2020	July 31st 2020
Mean	0.22	0.54	0.34
Standard deviation	0.19	0.28	0.25
Minimum	0.02	0.05	0.00
Maximum	0.80	0.96	1.00

therefore follow Aizenman *et al.* (2008, 2013) and empirically test whether the weighted sum of the three policy variables adds up to the constant 1. This test is carried out by examining the coefficient of determination R^2 of a simple OLS regression. Thereby, the higher the R^2, the stronger the support for the trilemma:

$$1 = \alpha_1 \text{CISS}_t + \alpha_2 \text{T2B}_t + \alpha_3 \text{MCI}_t + \varepsilon_t \tag{4}$$

Alternatively, as in Hsing (2012), we also estimate the logarithmic specification of the model:

$$1 = \beta_1 \text{lnCISS}_t + \beta_2 \text{lnT2B}_t + \beta_3 \text{lnMCI}_t + \mu_t \tag{5}$$

Our first step is to compare the results of the linear specification of regression (4) with the logarithmic specification in regression (5) (see Tables A1 and A2 in the Appendices). We find statistically significant coefficients of similar magnitude in both specifications. Also, the F-tests of both specifications suggest that neither of the models has to be rejected. Hence, comparing the R^2 of the regressions, we find that the logarithmic regression specification (5) has the better fit at $R^2 = 98.41\%$.

Therefore, we can conclude that Equation (5) models the trade-off between the three policy variables in the ECB's trilemma best. If we would find a low goodness of fit and coefficients with negative signs, this would indicate that the theory behind the trilemma was incorrect or econometrically misspecified. Thus, our empirical evidence constitutes that the European Central Bank faces an impossible trinity between stabilizing the monetary union, maintaining free capital mobility, and trying to exit expansionary monetary policy.

Furthermore, it is important to know the contribution that each policy goal has to the trilemma. In order to assess the contributions to each policy goal, we multiply the estimated coefficients of Equation (5) with the actual values of the variables. We do this by multiplying the estimated coefficients with the sample means of each variable reported in the second column of Table 2.

Table 2. Contribution (weights). Drivers of the policy trilemma and their relative contribution to it. Coefficients are estimated from Equation (5). TARGET2-balance (T2B) has the greatest impact, followed by monetary conditions (MCI) and systematic stress (CISS).

	Coefficient	**Sample Mean**	**Contribution (Weight)**
lnCISS	0.4487^{***}	0.1854	0.08
lnT2B	1.3611^{***}	0.4120	0.56
lnMCI	1.2380^{***}	0.2747	0.34

Notes: Sum of contributions (R^2): 98%. ***Significance level at 1%.

Since the approximation is good, we find that the contributions are close to 1 and note that R^2 coincides with the sum of the three calculated weights. The estimated contributions to each policy goal show that the European Central Bank's main focus has been on maintaining free capital mobility with the help of the TARGET2-system. The second most important measure that the ECB has been taking was to constantly loosen monetary policy, culminating in the asset purchase programs as mentioned earlier. Third, calming financial markets and thereby stabilizing the European financial system have been and still are the goals of the ECB, as indicated by the CISS index.

5. Robustness Analysis

The idea behind the concept of cointegration is to analyze a long-run equilibrium between non-stationary economic variables. A long-run relationship between economic variables may exist; however, this relation does not necessarily appear during the observation period. If the observed deviations from the assumed equilibrium relationship are stationary, the variables under examination are deemed cointegrated. Cointegrated variables do not contain independent trends but are driven by common stochastic trends.

Since the presented estimation model has three indexes ranging between zero and one, it is possible that these indexes are non-stationary, and the regression estimation could hence be spurious. Still, if the indexes were non-stationary but cointegrated, the linearity assumption holds. Although our primary focus is not to show any specific long-run equilibrium relationship among the three indexes, we conduct cointegration tests for each of the indexes to show their linearity. Following Johansen's (1991) method, we rank the cointegration relationship among CISS, T2B, and MCI by conducting multiple trace tests, assuming the lag length of 4. Applying this analysis to the dataset, we find that the linear relationship between the three variables holds, as summarized in Table 3.

Table 3. Cointegration tests identify scenarios where the non-stationary time series are integrated together in a way that they cannot deviate from equilibrium in the long term. The linear relationship between all three variables CISS, T2B, and MCI holds.

Included Observations: 153
Series: MCI CISS T2B
Lags Interval: 1 to 4

Selected (0.05 Level*) Number of Cointegrating Relations by Model

Data Trend: Test Type	None No Intercept No Trend	None Intercept No Trend	Linear Intercept No Trend	Linear Intercept Trend	Quadratic Intercept Trend
Trace	1	1	1	0	1
Max-Eig	1	1	1	1	1

Information Criteria by Rank and Model

Data Trend: Rank or No. of CEs	None No Intercept No Trend	None Intercept No Trend	Linear Intercept No Trend	Linear Intercept Trend	Quadratic Intercept Trend
Log Likelihood by Rank (rows) and Model (columns)					
0	1009.496	1009.496	1011.304	1011.304	1011.927
1	1021.773	1022.740	1024.358	1024.520	1025.129
2	1024.178	1026.251	1027.352	1027.977	1028.585
3	1024.866	1028.617	1028.617	1030.687	1030.687
Akaike Information Criteria by Rank (rows) and Model (columns)					
0	−12.72544	−12.72544	−12.70986	−12.70986	−12.67878
1	−12.80749*	−12.80706	−12.80207	−12.79111	−12.77292
2	−12.76049	−12.76146	−12.76277	−12.74480	−12.73968
3	−12.69106	−12.70088	−12.70088	−12.68872	−12.68872
Schwarz Criteria by Rank (rows) and Model (columns)					
0	−12.01240*	−12.01240*	−11.93740	−11.93740	−11.84690
1	−11.97561	−11.95537	−11.91076	−11.87999	−11.82220
2	−11.80977	−11.77112	−11.75262	−11.69504	−11.67011
3	−11.62150	−11.57189	−11.57189	−11.50032	−11.50032

Note: *Critical values based on MacKinnon–Haug–Michelis (1999).

6. Conclusion

The crisis of the European Monetary Union is still not settled to this date and has revealed different flaws in the construction of the euro. National fiscal policies did not build sufficient buffers before the crisis, which forced some countries to tighten the fiscal policy too rapidly during the economic downturn in 2011 to restore market confidence in sovereign borrowing. As the sovereign stress remains high and the banking sector is highly exposed to government bonds, the combination has further weakened the sector. In return, the confidence in fiscal sustainability has undergone even greater damage. As a result, the ECB's monetary policy and emergency measures are the main public supporting instruments. In conclusion in the aftermath of the sovereign debt crisis, euro-area countries agreed on a banking union with a common supervisor to break up the links between banks and their sovereigns.

Since the process of policy normalization was initiated, the ECB governing council has pledged to act against resurgent fragmentation and inflation risks. The COVID-19 pandemic has left lasting vulnerabilities in the euro-area economy, which are contributing to an uneven transmission of the ECB's monetary policy across member states. Based on this assessment, the ECB governing council decided to reinvest redemptions coming due from the pandemic emergency purchase program (PEPP) flexibly in different Euro area jurisdictions, in order to support monetary policy transmission where it is needed. In addition, a new "ECB anti-fragmentation instrument" by the name of "Transmission Protection Instrument (TPI)" was presented in July 2022 by the ECB. The TPI is based on more careful bond-buying programs to reduce possibly rising credit spreads in selected euro-area countries during times of crises.

However, from a practical point of view, further progress is needed in reducing and sharing risks in the euro area in the long run, such as creating a common deposit guarantee scheme and reducing banks' exposures to domestic sovereign bonds. Such progress may not be sufficient though for national fiscal policies and monetary policy to smooth future major crises. Hence, as Stráský and Claveres (2018) underscore, the introduction of common fiscal stabilization capacity is necessary to reinforce the euro area in case of a recession, both at the country and euro-area levels. Combining a fiscal stabilization capacity with a stepwise reduction of the asset purchase programs could give the ECB additional room to raise interest rates in the medium term in order to reduce inflation to the initial target range of two percent. Furthermore, the ECB could break free thoroughly of the trilemma, which we describe in this study. Future research could focus on a deeper understanding of the design and incentive structures of monetary unions and should lead the way to concepts of how to stabilize and consolidate economically heterogenous monetary unions, such as the euro area.

Appendices

Table A1. Linear specification, $1 = \alpha_1 \mathrm{CISS}_t + \alpha_2 \mathrm{T2B}_t + \alpha_3 \mathrm{MCI}_t + \varepsilon_t$.

Regression Statistics — Linear Specification	
Multiple correlation coefficient	0.9864
R^2	0.9730
Adjusted R^2	0.9662
Standard error	0.1659
Observations	158

	Degrees of Freedom (df)	**Square Sums (SS)**	**Mean Squared Sums (MS)**	***F*-value**	***F*-criterion**
Regression	3	153.7318	51.2439	1860.9234	0.0000
Residuals	155	4.2682	0.0275		
Sum	158	158			

	Coefficients	**Standard Errors**	***t*-statistic**	***p*-value**	**Lower 95%**	**Upper 95%**	**Lower 99%**	**Upper 99%**
CISS	0.4123	0.0852	4.8369	0.0000	0.2439	0.5806	0.2439	0.5806
T2B	1.0521	0.0252	41.7442	0.0000	1.0024	1.1019	1.0024	1.1019
MCI	0.9459	0.0580	16.2955	0.0000	0.8313	1.0606	0.8313	1.0606

Table A2. Logarithmic specification, $1 = \beta_1 \ln\text{CISS}_t + \beta_2 \ln T2\text{B}_t + \beta_3 \ln\text{MCI}_t + \mu_t$.

Regression Statistics — Logarithmic Specification	
Multiple correlation coefficient	0.9920
R^2	0.9841
Adjusted R^2	0.9774
Standard error	0.1275
Observations	158

	Degrees of Freedom (df)	Square Sums (SS)	Mean Squared Sums (MS)	*F*-value	*F*-criterion
Regression	3	155.4802	51.8267	3187.9918	0.0000
Residuals	155	2.5198	0.0163		
Sum	158	158			

	Coefficients	Standard Errors	*t*-statistic	*p*-value	Lower 95%	Upper 95%	Lower 99%	Upper 99%
lnCISS	0.4487	0.0856	5.2399	0.0000	0.2796	0.6179	0.2796	0.6179
lnT2B	1.3611	0.0275	49.4301	0.0000	1.3067	1.4155	1.3067	1.4155
lnMCI	1.2380	0.0629	19.6803	0.0000	1.1137	1.3622	1.1137	1.3622

References

Aizenman, J., Chinn, M. D. and Ito, H. (2008). Assessing the emerging global financial architecture: Measuring the trilemma's configurations over time. *NBER Working Paper No. 14533, National Bureau of Economic Research, Inc.*

Aizenman, J., Chinn, M. D. and Ito, H. (2013). The "impossible trinity" hypothesis in an era of global imbalances: Measurement and testing. *Review of International Economics, 21*, 447–458.

Bekaert, G. and Mehl, A. (2019). On the global financial market integration swoosh and the trilemma. *Journal of International Money and Finance, 94*, 227–245.

Canale, R., De Grauwe, P., Foresti, P. and Napolitano, O. (2018). Is there a trade-off between free capital mobility, financial stability and fiscal policy flexibility in the EMU? *Review of World Economics, 154*, 177–201.

De Grauwe, P. (2015). Design failures of the Eurozone. In R. Baldwin and F. Giavazzi (eds.) *The Eurozone Crisis — A Consensus View of the Causes and a Few Possible Solutions*, pp. 99–108. London: Centre for Economic Policy Research.

De Grauwe, P. and Yuemei, J. (2015). Mispricing of sovereign risk and macroeconomic stability in the Eurozone. *Journal of Common Market Studies, 50*, 886–880.

Elnahass, M., Trinh, V. Q. and Li, T. (2021). Global banking stability in the shadow of Covid-19 outbreak. *Journal of International Financial Markets, Institutions and Money, 72*, 101322.

European Central Bank, Statistical Data Warehouse (2020). TARGET balances of Participating NCBs.

European Commission (2020). Monetary conditions index.

Freixas, X. (2003). Crisis management in Europe. In J. Kremers, D. Schoenmaker and P. Wierts (eds.) *Financial Supervision in Europe*. Cheltenham: Edward Elgar.

Hollo, D., Kremer, M. and Lo Duca, M. (2012). CISS — A Composite Indicator of Systemic Stress in the Financial System, ECB Working Paper Series, No 1426.

Hsing, Y. (2012). Impacts of the trilemma policies on inflation, growth and volatility in Greece. *International Journal of Economics and Financial Issues, 2*, 373–378.

Lang, S. and Schadner, W. (2021). The trilemma of expansionary monetary policy in the Euro area during the COVID-19 crisis. *Finance Research Letters, 42*, 102048.

Magas, I. (2018). Financial adjustment in small, open economies in light of the "impossible trinity" trilemma. *Financial and Economic Review, 17*, 5–33.

Mundell, R. (1963). Capital mobility and stabilization policy under fixed and flexible exchange rates. *Canadian Journal of Economics, 29*, 475–485.

Sinn, H. W. and Wollmershäuser, T. (2012). Target loans, current account balances and capital flows: The ECB's rescue facility. *International Tax and Public Finance, 19*, 468–508.

Schoenmaker, D. (2005). Central banks and financial authorities in Europe: What prospects? In D. Masciandaro (ed.) *The Handbook of Central Banking and Financial Authorities in Europe.* Cheltenham: Edward Elgar.

Schoenmaker, D. (2011). The financial trilemma. *Economics Letters, 111*, 57–59.

Stráský, J. and Claveres, G. (2018). Stabilisation policies to strengthen Euro area resilience. *OECD Economics Department Working Papers, No. 1492.* Paris: OECD Publishing.

Steiner, A., Steinkamp, S. and Westermann, F. (2019). Exit strategies, capital flight and speculative attacks: Europe's version of the trilemma. *European Journal of Political Economy, 59*, 83–96.

Trinh, V. Q., Cao, N. D. and Elnahass, M. (2022). Financial stability: A 'vaccine' for tail risk of the global banking sector in the shadow of the pandemic. *The European Journal of Finance*, 1–28.

https://doi.org/10.1142/9781800614321_0012

Chapter 12

Credit-to-GDP Gaps in Real Time: Correcting Indicators for More Reliability in Policy Decision-Making*

Tihana Škrinjarić
Stress Test Strategy Division,
Bank of England, London, UK
tihana.skrinjaric@bankofengland.co.uk

Abstract

Countercyclical capital buffer (CCyB) is an essential instrument of macroprudential policy. Over the last couple of years, many studies have dealt with finding adequate indicators of credit activity monitored for CCyB calibration purposes. The credit-to-GDP gap is widely used and recognized as the leading indicator of credit dynamics for CCyB decision-making. Research and applications in practice regarding the stability of the credit-to-GDP gap are still lacking today. This stability refers to the end-point problems within the statistical filtering part of the analysis and problems with the GDP volatility, especially during crises, such as COVID-19. This chapter focuses on several practical approaches

*The author states that the views presented in this paper are those of the author and do not necessarily represent the institution the author works at. This chapter was written at the time the author was working for Croatian National Bank, Zagreb, Croatia.

to correcting the credit-to-GDP gap as the primary indicator of credit dynamics in real time. Moreover, the chapter deals with possible corrections of the credit-to-GDP gap. The solutions allow for lower volatility of indicators over time so that the decision-maker can use stable signals.

Keywords: Credit-to-GDP gap, out-of-sample forecasts, augmented credit gap, countercyclical capital buffer

1. Introduction

The macroprudential policy has the task of tracking and monitoring the financial cycle, among other relevant tasks regarding the financial system and maintaining its stability. The pro-cyclicality of the financial process has proven to be the origin of the previous Global Financial Cycle (GFC). Thus, the Countercyclical Capital Buffer (CCyB) has been designed and put forward (BCBS, 2011; ESRB, 2014) as a critical macroprudential instrument to help counter some of the mentioned pro-cyclicality of the financial cycle (see Škrinjarić, 2022c). CCyB is an essential instrument of macroprudential policy. Credit institutions could accumulate additional capital in the upward phase of the financial cycle by increasing the CCyB values. When the downward phase occurs, this can help in credit activity facilitation. Calibration of CCyB values depends on the indicator of the financial cycle, i.e., excessive cyclical risk accumulation. Current international financial regulations in BCBS (2010) and ESRB (2014) are standardized estimating the primary indicator. Its usual name is the Basel credit gap. Excess credit dynamics and cyclical risk accumulation are measured with this indicator, and that is why it is a harmonized indicator. It is easy to calculate, interpret, and compare across countries. Some of the main literature that recognize the importance and usefulness of the Basel gap are Galán (2019), Detken *et al.* (2014), Drehmann *et al.* (2010), Borio and Drehmann (2009), and Borio and Lowe (2002). Others (Drehmann *et al.*, 2014; Dell Ariccia *et al.*, 2012; Schularick and Taylor, 2012) find that the Basel gap is a leading indicator of the probability of crises and their severity, and the general findings are that strong credit activity precedes crises (Gourinches and Obstfeld, 2012).

The Basel credit gap is calculated based on the credit-to-GDP ratio, filtered via the Hodrick–Prescott (HP henceforward,

Hodrick and Prescott, 1997) filter. This filter was selected as it was pretty popularized in the research of business cycles. Thus, national authorities, based on the BCBS proposition, utilize the HP filter, where the one-sided approach is made. Only past information alongside the current (last) observation estimates the HP trend and the gap series. The one-sided approach is based on the decision-making process of macroprudential policies, as they have to be made in real time. Thus, the statistical filtering procedure of estimating the trend and consequently the gap is based only on data up to the last point that refer to the current period in the analysis. Due to the optimization process of the HP filter, the last value has a different weight in the trend estimation compared to other series values. This problem is well known in the literature and is called the end-point problem of the HP filter. Other issues can be found in Škrinjarić (2022a), Hamilton (2018), Kamber *et al.* (2018), or Cogley and Nason (1005), but this issue is potentially the biggest one. Reasoning is found in the decision-making process that is based on the last values of a gap series, which are always affected by this problem. The real-time estimates and final revisions of the credit-to-GDP gaps were considered in Edge and Meisenzahl (2011). The authors found that the HP gap estimation approach had extensive *ex post* modifications. Such results are essential for CCyB decision-making in real time and, consequently, on total capital requirements credit institutions face over time.

That is why the last decade has experienced an increase in research that focuses on alternative approaches to credit gap calculation, as well as research on enhancing the original HP gap as described in ESRB (2014). The focus of this chapter is to give a concise overview of one part of the HP gap augmentation with out-of-sample (oos) forecasts. After the overview, the empirical part of this chapter contrasts several alternative approaches of oos augmentations of original credit gaps. As Kaiser and Maravall (1999) and Mise *et al.* (2005) recommend solving the end-point bias problem with oos forecasts, this chapter is going to analyze possibilities of utilizing such approaches for better policy decision-making.

Previous related literature is not as detailed in studying different possibilities of oos forecasting, alongside comparisons of the results. Here, the focus is on researching how to fix the end-point problem of the HP filter to stay within the Basel framework and ESRB (2014) guidance. Finally, this chapter extensively compares the augmented gaps via the oos performance, variability of the indicators, and their revisions to the two-sided gap. This is done for differing values of the length of the forecast horizon.

As this type of result is of great importance for macroprudential policymakers that need to have current credit gap estimates as precise as possible, such detailed analysis provides essential insights into this topic. That is why the rest of this chapter is structured as follows. The second section gives an overview of related literature on credit gap calculation. Afterward, a description of the credit gap estimation and the oos augmentations is provided in the third section. An empirical analysis of the results is given in the fourth section, alongside the discussion regarding the obtained results. The final fifth section concludes the chapter.

2. Literature Review

Based on the BCBS (2010, 2011) guidance, authorities started calculating the credit gap by following the procedure of one-sided HP filtering of the credit-to-GDP ratio. However, literature has been emerging since the early 2010s that focuses on comparisons of different approaches to calculating the credit gap, comparing the results between countries and other crises, and papers dealing with improving the current methodology, due to its many problems. Besides, critiques and general improvements of HP filters in business cycle literature were already available. Credit gap is considered as an early warning indicator of future financial crisis. That is why a lot of research that focuses on signaling properties of this indicator exists. Borio and Lowe (2002) and Borio and Drehmann (2009) are among the first and often cited research on the early warning methodology approach to the signaling of crises so that appropriate indicators can be utilized when making decisions about the CCyB values. Since the credit gap has often been found as the single best predictor in the early warning literature (Drehmann *et al.*, 2010, 2011; Babecký *et al.*, 2014; Bonfim and Monteir, 2013; Behn *et al.*, 2013; Drehmann and Juselius, 2014; Detken *et al.*, 2014), it still presents the main indicator that authorities report and comments on, alongside other information relevant for monitoring cyclical risks. Critiques and enhancements of the primary methodology have focused on different definitions of credit (Baba *et al.*, 2020), using population instead of GDP in the numerator (Richter *et al.*, 2017; Drehmann and Yetman, 2018), using different definitions of the credit gap instead of HP filter approach (Kauko, 2012; Hamilton, 2018), other smoothing parameters in the HP procedure (Drehmann *et al.*, 2010; Galán, 2019; Rünstler and Vlekke, 2016; Wezel, 2019), etc.

The signaling properties of credit gaps could be affected significantly by subsequent revisions of data, especially of GDP, as noted in Edge and Meisenzahl (2011). Adding new data or revising the existing ones can change the HP trend significantly, as seen in Canova (1998) and Pedersen (2001). This has consequences on the policy implementations and decision-making process from one period to another (see Edge and Meisenzahl, 2011; and Alessandri *et al.*, 2015). This is explained in Gerdrup *et al.* (2013) as follows: Due to the HP trend lagging the actual values of the series, the gap values after the turning point of the cycle occurs are greater. This has a consequence of possible phase shift creation in the series. Earlier research (see Kaiser and Maravall, 1999) shows that if oos forecasts are added to the original data, this could reduce revision errors of the last values of the cycle series. This makes it interesting to do such applications in practice. This is why Gerdrup *et al.* (2013) use oos forecasts for the Norwegian credit-to-GDP ratio case. The authors have compared the original Basel gap to the gap series that were augmented with rolling linear forecasts, linear forecasts, and rolling average forecasts. Other relevant series were examined as well: wholesale funding ratio, property prices index, and house prices to income ratio. Some of the used comparison criteria were as follows: the difference between the one- and two-sided gaps for individual series and the early warning signaling approach criteria. A similar study is Valinskytė and Rupeika (2015), who examine Lithuanian data. The study observes four- and eight-quarter moving averages, alongside linear forecasts when comparing oos performance of credit gaps. Final selection criteria of best gaps included having the smallest revisions of one-sided to two-sided gaps as in Gerdrup *et al.* (2013), as well as having the smallest variability of the gap data.

Bank of Portugal (2020), in a publication about the general indicators used for calibrating CCyB values, states that they use an additional credit-to-GDP gap, obtained via oos forecasts based on an autoregressive (AR) integrated model with 28 quarters used of the oos forecast horizon. The optimal lag order for the AR process was obtained recursively for the first part of the sample. For the last part, i.e., the last couple of years, the order was set to 3. Other relevant approaches that were contrasted included the random walk, moving average, linear trend model, moving linear trend, autoregressive integrated moving average (ARIMA), where order q for the MA part was set to zero, and one variant in which both the AR and MA lags were estimated recursively. Geršl and Mitterling (2021) did a study on a panel of countries, including 56 different countries, for an extended period: 1950–2016. The results show that oos forecast augmentations of credit gaps improve the signaling properties of such indicators for the case of emerging markets. Here, the authors focus on the AUROC (area under the receiver operating characteristic curve) values over time to contrast the signaling properties of indicators.

As the results are mixed when dividing the data for developed and emerging markets, individual country studies are also essential. One cannot just copy other practices as given but should test best practices based on data. The oos forecasts can usually flatten the credit gaps compared to the original values. Thus, a question is how helpful is using such type of augmented gaps for signalling purposes. Although they are more stable and have fewer end-point problems, augmented gaps could have lagged reactions when new values indicate a change in the trend. Thus, it is difficult to evaluate these indicators in terms of both signaling properties, alongside the revisions of gaps over time.

Other recent studies incorporating oos augmentation in the filtering process include Jokipii *et al.* (2021), who follow the Alessandri *et al.* (2015) approach but for Swiss data. In contrast, the latter paper developed a correction procedure for the Italian case's difference between the one- and two-sided HP gap. Augmentation of the HP gap in both cases has shown that it enhances the usability of the credit gap itself in terms of greater consistency of the estimates.

As can be seen, the literature on the specific topic of credit gap augmentation via oos forecasts is growing, especially in the last two years. This indicates that the applications in central banks have recognized the need for better usability of the credit gap in practice. Thus, the rest of this chapter gives a detailed methodological approach and estimation results for enhancing the practice of using such an approach.

3. Selected Extensions of the Credit-to-GDP Gap Calculation

3.1. *Introduction of the problem*

This section deals with descriptions of how the credit-to-GDP gap (credit gap henceforward) is calculated, based on the ESRB (2014) guidance, as well as the extensions that this chapter explores. The main takeaway from the credit gap is how much the credit activity exceeds the real activity, i.e., is the credit growth compared to the growth of the rest of the economy justified? The gap is estimated via the Hodrick–Prescott (1997) filter (HP filter and gap afterward), where the primary objective function is as follows:

$$\arg\min_{\{\mu_t\}_{t=0}^{T}} \left[\sum_{t=0}^{T} (y_t - \mu_t)^2 + \lambda \sum_{t=1}^{T-1} ((\mu_{t+1} - \mu_t) - (\mu_t - \mu_{t-1}))^2\right] \tag{1}$$

where the series y_t is the time series to be filtered, μ_t is the trend series, and λ is the smoothing parameter (or the penalization parameter), $t = 1, \ldots, T$. The trend series is estimated such that the deviation from the real series y from the trend series μ is minimized, alongside imposing a penalty in the second part of (1) on changes in the trend's slope. The greater the value of lambda is, the greater the penalty is given to changes in the slope, and the trend resulting from (1) becomes smoother.

For the CCyB decision-making, the HP gap is calculated at every period t, when new data arrive, but on the basis of what is called the recursive gap, i.e., the one-sided filter approach:

$$\arg\min_{\{\mu_t\}_{t=0}^{t'}} \left[\sum_{t=0}^{t'} (y_t - \mu_t)^2 + \lambda \sum_{t=1}^{t'-1} ((\mu_{t+1} - \mu_t) - (\mu_t - \mu_{t-1}))^2\right], \quad t' \leq T \tag{2}$$

This means that at a given period $t' > 0$, the HP gap is calculated as in (1) and the HP gap is calculated as in (1) for all available data up until the point. Then, when new data arrive in $t' + 1$, the optimization problem in (1) is repeated with the additional data point, but the previous values of the gap stay fixed. The new value of the gap series for period $t'+1$ is added to the existing series. When new data arrive again, in $t'+2$, the optimization procedure is done as previously. Still, the gap series with the previous period added gap is fixed, and the only gap from $t'+2$ is added. To put it differently, for the first t' periods, the gap series is set at all times. When additional data become available, the HP filter is applied over the entire series, but only the last value of the gap is added to the existing series. The basis for this is that the macroprudential policymaker has to make decisions based on the available data up to that point in time. The two-sided HP gap assumes that information in the future is available when making the decision itself. Thus, it is a recommendation and common practice to do so.

Now, by observing problem (1) or (2), due to leads and lags of the trend series being different compared to the y series, several μ values are not included in the summation as others. That is to say, values μ_0 and μ_T are included only once, μ_1 and μ_{T-1} twice, whereas all other values occur three times. This means these end values are not penalized as much as other values. Thus, deviations that are more significant are allowed at the end of the series. Since the decision-making process relies on the last value of the credit gap, the end-point problem is relevant in the macroprudential policy. This is especially problematic for the one-sided filtering approach.

3.2. *Out of sample (oos) forecast approaches*

As stated in the related literature review, there are several general approaches to extending the sample of the credit-to-GDP ratio via out-of-sample forecasts when filtering the data so that the trend is stabilized at the end of the sample. We examine several models for oos as follows. First, we do not consider the forecasted values of GDP and credit dynamics based on formal models a central bank uses. This is in line with the literature agreeing that such forecasts are subject to current economic conditions and assumptions. Bias in such results is often found, depending on the phase of the business cycle. For more details, see Bruchez (2003).

Moving averages (MA), denoted with

$$y_{t+h} = \sum_{s=t-n-1}^{t} y_s \tag{3}$$

i.e., MA (n) are observed as a simple way to extend time series. We observe moving averages of the credit-to-GDP ratio values based on the current quarter and previous n quarters for out-of-sample forecasts. For the first oos value $(h = 1)$, the last observed value and previous $n - 1$ are used. As we forecast several oos values $(h = 1, 2, \ldots, H)$, the second, third, etc., values until the last one H are estimated such that previous oos values based on the MA model are included in the calculation of the following moving average. As the procedure is recursive (one-sided filtering), the idea is that for the first fixed window of length x of the credit-to-GDP ratio, the series is extended via MA (n) values. The HP filter is utilized, and the first x values are collected. Then, when the new data become available, the procedure is repeated, and the latest data point is added to the first x fixed values. This is repeated until the end of the current sample of the study. In this way, real-time decision-making is simulated, as with other approaches.

A model of linear trend is estimated in the following way:

$$y_{1:t} = a_{1:t} + b_{1:t} \cdot t \tag{4}$$

in which forecast for horizon h in the current quarter is made based on a constant a and the linear trend t, which are estimated via ordinary least squares (OLS) for all data available upon that point. For the first x series, Model (4) is estimated in the sample, estimates of a and b are collected, and oos forecasts for h horizons are made based on those estimates: $y_{t+h} = a_{1:t} + b_{1:t}(t + h)$. Next, the original series y is extended with oos forecasts, the HP filter is utilized, and the first x gap values are collected. Then, when the new data become available, the estimation of (4) is redone with the additional data point, oos forecasts are made, the HP filter is applied again, and the procedure is repeated until the last data point is available.

Similar to the previous approach, the linear trend model is estimated, but now instead of using the entire sample up to the last point, a moving window model is estimated:

$$y_{(t-q):t} = a_{(t-q):t} + b_{(t-q):t} \cdot t \tag{5}$$

where the sample is now moving from period $t - q$ to t, where $q - 1$ is the desired length of the rolling window; thus, the size of the window is fixed, but the starting and ending points change. When the estimated values of the parameters in (5) are obtained, oos values are calculated and added to the actual series, the HP filter is applied, and the gap series is collected. The procedure is repeated until the end of the sample, with the first x values being fixed again and, one by one, the additional value of the gap series being added throughout.

Most economic time series could be approximated well via a random walk model. Here, we observe the case of a moving window estimation of an RW model:

$$y_{(t-q):t} = a_{(t-q-1):(t-1)} + y_{(t-q-1):(t-1)} \tag{6}$$

where the RW is estimated with a drift that changes for each window, based on the estimated model (6), oos values are forecasted for h horizons. Then, the HP filter is applied over an extended series. Again, as in previous cases, the first x values of the gap series are fixed, h additional values from the RW forecasts are added, and HP filter results are obtained. Then, as we add every new data point, the procedure is repeated, adding the last gap point to the existing series up until the end of the sample.

As credit-to-GDP ratios are non-stationary in practice, we observe a variant in which the ratio is differenced (thus, $d = 1$ in the ARIMA setting). Then, for forecasting, an AR (p) is defined, with p being a small whole number. The window for the estimation is on a rolling basis, as the previous approaches, i.e.,

$$y_{(t-q):t} = a_{(t-q-1):(t-1)} + \sum_{j=1}^{p} \theta_j y_{j,(t-q-1):(t-1)} \tag{7}$$

where the notation j refers to the lag of variable y, up to p, and the rest of the index notations in parentheses refer to the rolling windows. When Model (7) is estimated for the first window of x values, the oos values are forecasted based on the estimates. They are added to the original credit ratio set of x values. The HP filter is applied to such a sample, and gaps are obtained up to the value x. Then, the new data point is added to the initial sample, the model in (7) is re-estimated for the second window, and the procedure is repeated as previously. This is, again, repeated until the end of the entire sample.

3.3. *Evaluating the best approach*

Several approaches can be made to compare different indicators of credit activity, i.e., credit gaps. Usually, the early warning models (EWMs) consist of comparing some usual values such as the actual positive rate, false positive rate, and area under the receiver operating characteristic curve. This is considered in ESRB (2018), Lang *et al.* (2019), or Candelon *et al.* (2012). The problem with Croatian data used in this study is that the results could be biased. The reason for this is having short time series and having one crisis in the sample. This was commented on in Škrinjarić and Bukovšak (2022a, 2022b), where the authors advised caution while taking such results. Moreover, as the oos forecasts tend to smooth out the resulting credit gap series, this affects the resulting values of AUROC and other relevant measures alongside statistical tests. Therefore, although the resulting gaps could be better at predicting a crisis than the original ones (that are not augmented in any way), as the augmented ones are smoothed out, their values could stay positive or negative longer.

That is why the proposition here is to compare all of the approaches by observing the values of each resulting in a one-sided gap to the two-sided final gap, i.e., mean absolute error and root mean squared error of the difference between all augmented gaps for each approach will be calculated such that those values will be compared to the two-sided gap at time T. Here, the idea is that the revisions of augmented gaps are the smallest possible, in line with Gerdrup *et al.* (2013). Written formally, for every indicator i, we calculate the following measure:

$$\text{MAE}_i^{gap} = \frac{1}{T}\sum_{t=1}^{T}\left|1gap_t^i - 2gap_t^i\right| \tag{8}$$

where the *gap* exponent denotes that the mean absolute error (MAE) is calculated for the gap series and $1gap$ and $2gap$ are the resulting one-sided and two-sided gap series at the end of the observed period T, respectively. Moreover, the root mean squared error (MSE) for every indicator i is calculated via formula (9):

$$\text{RMSE}_i^{gap} = \sqrt{\frac{1}{T}\sum_{t=1}^{T}\left(1gap_t^i - 2gap_t^i\right)^2} \tag{9}$$

Besides these measures, the variation of each approach is considered as the variance of each gap estimate at every quarter t such that we collect the gap values in every quarter t for an approach.

Then, at period T, we calculate the variance of the gap value for period $t = 1$ for all recursive estimates. In other words, as the gap series are estimated at every period t, the values for period $t = 1, 2, \ldots$, etc., change in every subsequent estimate. The idea here is that the variation of the gap itself is the smallest possible on average. To calculate the measure representing this, first, we calculate the variance for each gap_t of an indicator i for every period t, as follows:

$$\sigma_{t,i}^{2gap} = \frac{1}{T'} \sum_{t=1}^{T'} \left(2gap_t^i - \overline{2gap^i} \right)^2 \tag{10}$$

where (10) is just the formula for the variance based on observation of the gap value and the average gap value for every period t. Then, all of the variances are used to calculate the average variance of an indicator:

$$\overline{\sigma}_i^2 = \frac{\sum_{i=1}^{T} \sigma_{t,i}^{2gap}}{T} \tag{11}$$

As a final criterion, the MAE and RMSE values of the oos forecasts of credit-to-GDP ratios are going to be compared to the actual values of the mentioned ratios. Previous literature (example is the aforementioned Gerdrup *et al.*, 2013 paper) usually uses this criterion to compare the gap values. But the problem here is that the gap values still have uncertainty and end-point problems, regardless of whether we estimate the one-sided or the two-sided gaps. That is why this study compares the forecasted values of credit-to-GDP ratios to the actual ratios that are observed in the periods that come afterward.

4. Empirical Analysis and Discussion

4.1. *Data description*

For empirical analysis, quarterly data on narrow and broad definitions of credit and GDP values have been collected from the CNB (2022a) website. The period for the analysis ranges from 4Q 1999 to 4Q 2021. The credit-to-GDP ratios were calculated via the following formula:

$$\text{ratio}_t = \frac{\text{credit}_t}{\sum_{k=t-3}^{t} \text{GDP}_k} \cdot 100\% \tag{12}$$

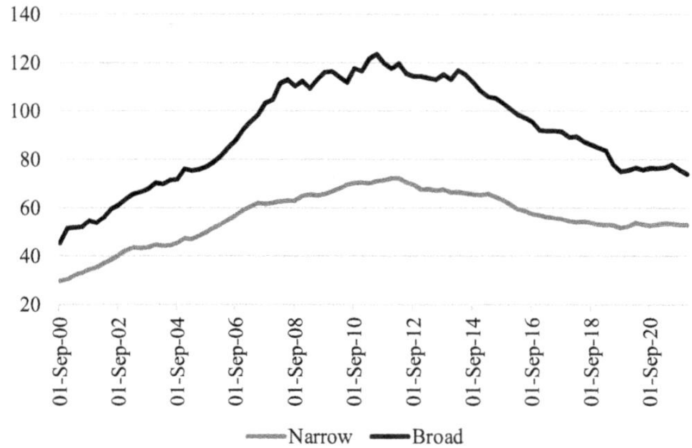

Figure 1. Credit-to-GDP ratios in %.
Source: CNB, author's calculation.

The ratios are shown in Figure 1. Both ratios increased significantly during the 2000s due to financial deepening before the GFC crisis. In the last couple of years, ratios have stagnated, reflecting a subdued recovery after the crisis.

Figure 2 now shows the HP gaps for both credit ratios from Figure 1. These gaps do not have any augmentations yet, and the smoothing parameters are varying from 85.000, over 12.5000, to 400.000. The main differences between the one-sided gaps in panels a and b are in the second part of the sample. Some gap values are closing toward zero value. When looking at the differences between the one- and two-sided gaps (a vs. c and b vs. d panels), one can see that the overall differences are great. This shows the aforementioned problems of the decision-making process in practice. The rest of this section focuses on the augmentation of the gaps that are shown in panels a and b.

4.2. *Main analysis*

We employ forecast horizons of $h = 4, 8$, and 12 quarters for each of the five forecasting approaches. Moreover, for the autoregressive model, values of $p = 1, 2, 3$, and 4 are utilized. Since we observe both narrow and broad credit definitions, for every credit category, in total, 72 different augmented gaps were estimated. Figure 3

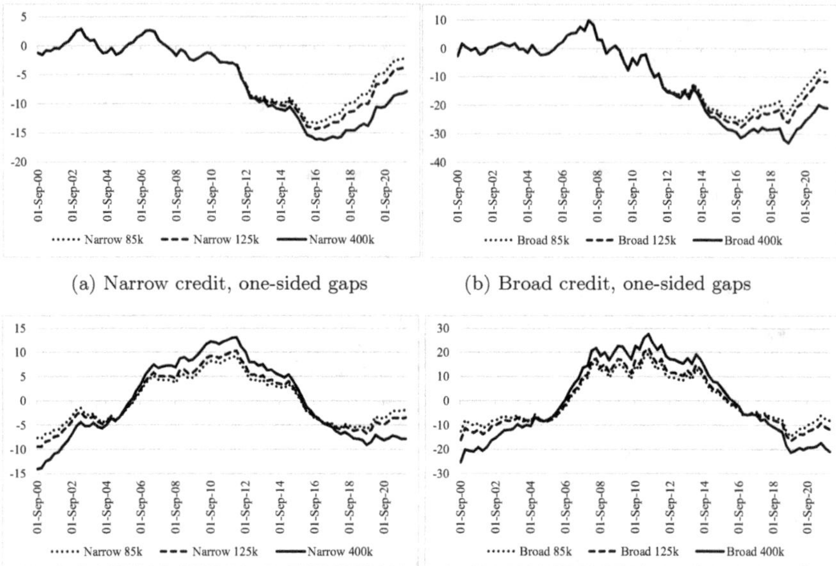

(a) Narrow credit, one-sided gaps (b) Broad credit, one-sided gaps

(c) Narrow credit, two-sided gaps (d) Broad credit, two-sided gaps

Figure 2. One- and two-sided HP gaps for credit ratios in Figure 1 in %.
Note: 85k, 125k, and 400k denote smoothing parameters in values of 85,000, 125,000, and 400,000, respectively.
Source: CNB, author's calculation.

shows the augmented gaps based on every approach for the narrow credit-to-GDP ratio, whereas analogous gaps for the broad credit definition are shown in Figure 4. The initial window for the estimation is 20 quarters long. This is the fixed period for all indicators (i.e., $q = 20$). By observing Figure 3, it is apparent that the worst-performing one is the linear forecast on panel b due to the dynamic being far away from the original indicators without augmentation. Other approaches result in smoothed values of the gaps in the second part of the observed period. This is due to the first part depending on the fixed period of 20 quarters and the upward phase of the credit dynamics before the global financial crisis (GFC).

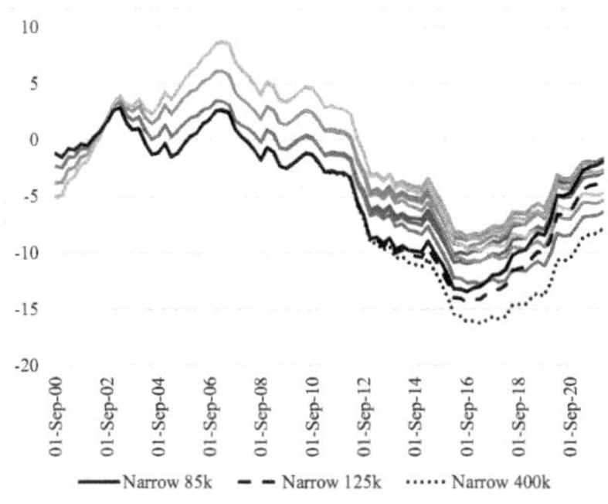

(a) Rolling average

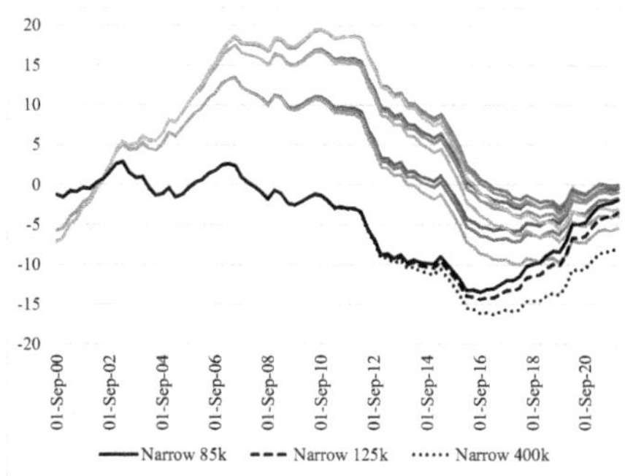

(b) Linear forecast

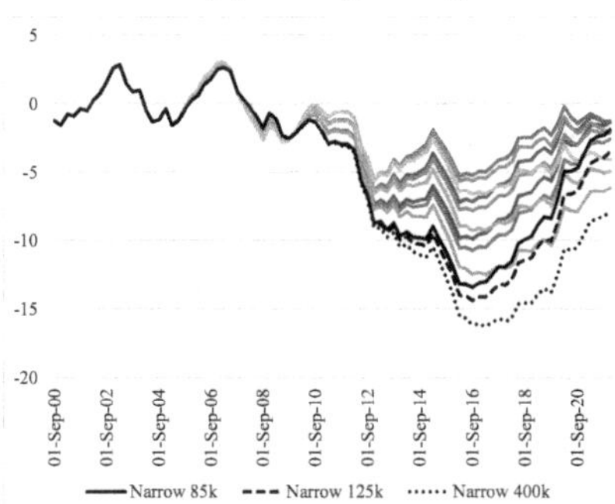

(c) Rolling linear forecast

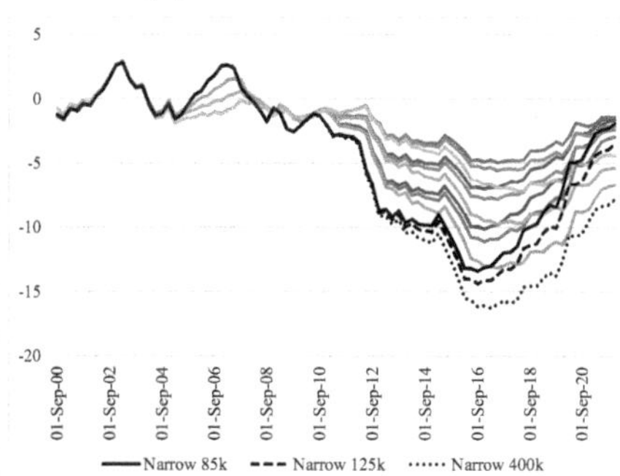

(d) Random walk

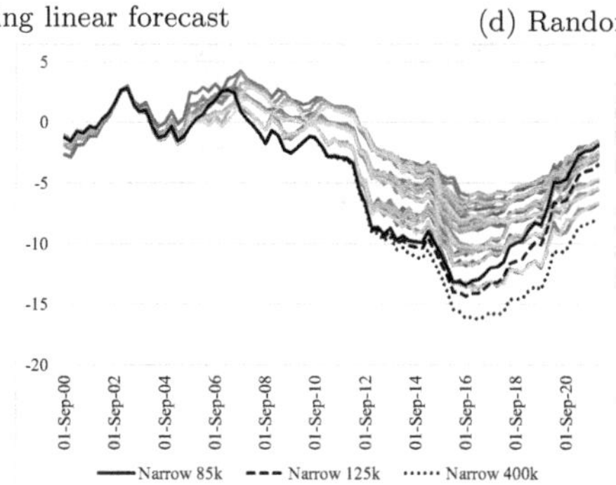

(e) ARIMA

Figure 3. Augmented gaps, narrow credit definition.

Note: Narrow 85k, 125k, and 400k are the credit gaps for smoothing parameters of 85,000, 125,000, and 400,000, respectively, without any oos augmentations.

Source: CNB, author's calculation.

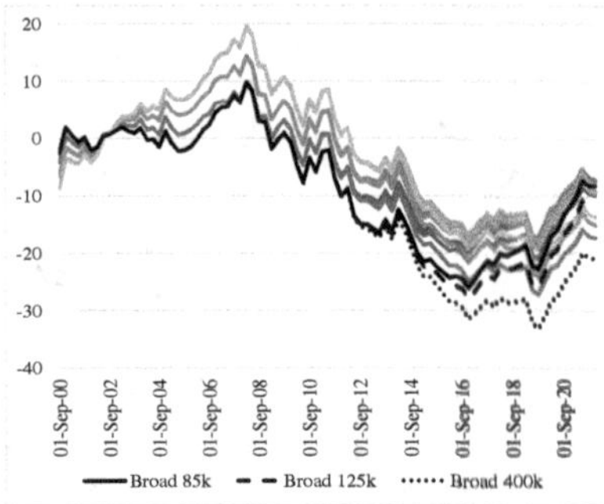

(a) Rolling average

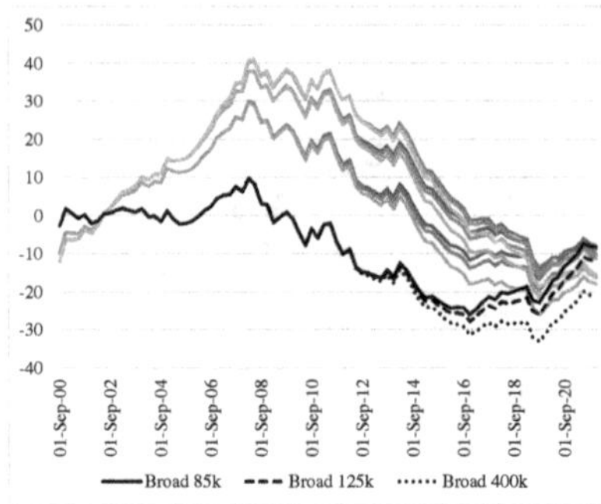

(b) Linear forecast

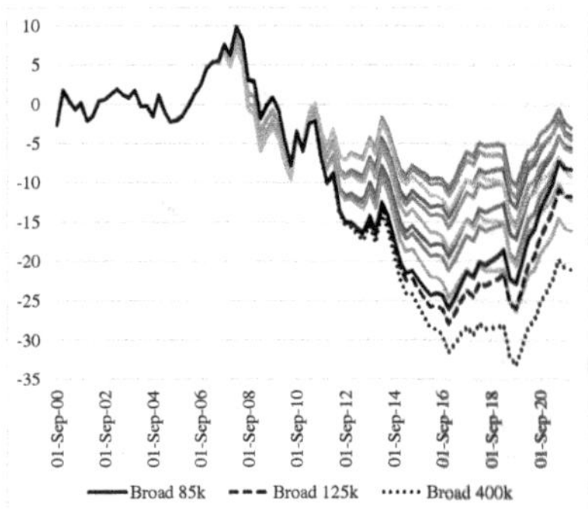

(c) Rolling linear forecast

(d) Random walk

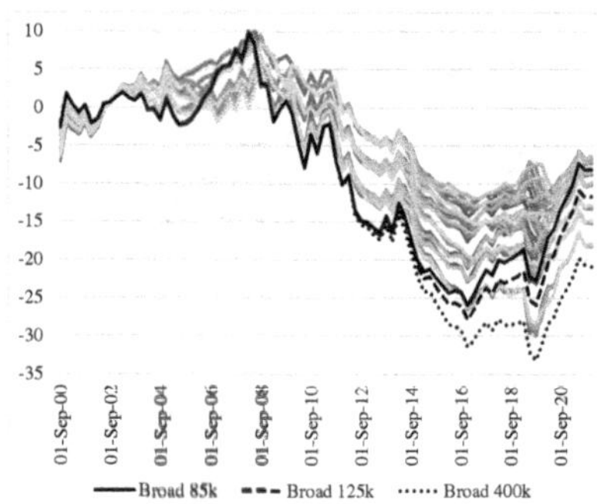

(e) ARIMA

Figure 4. Augmented gaps, broad credit definition.
Note: Broad 85k, 125k, and 400k are the credit gaps for smoothing parameters of 85,000, 125,000, and 400,000, respectively, without any oos augmentations.
Source: CNB, author's calculation.

Most augmented gaps do not have a significant bias to negative values after the GFC period compared to the original gaps without forecasts.

It is hard to make decisions in real time based on these results, as in some cases, the range of the estimated gap values is almost 10 percentage points. The decision could be even harder when the values are close to the threshold one of the CCyB activation. This is true for both the narrow and broad credit definition gap series in Figures 3 and 4. It is also hard to decide which approach is the best for the decision-making process in the mentioned figures. The worst one is, of course, the linear forecast approach. However, the others are hard to distinguish just by looking at the figures. And the used methods are very popular in forecasting, which means that using some more sophisticated approaches could result in even greater problems. This is especially true for the case of some formal models that central banks use. See García and Manzanares (2007) and Charemza and Ladely (2016) for more information.

Next, for each of the five approaches, average values of (8), (9), and (11), and the MAE and RMSE for oos forecasts have been calculated and are shown in Figures 5 and 6. Finally, the concrete values are given in the Appendices in Tables A1 and A2. Again, it is evident that the worst performance is observed for the linear forecast. Although all of the approaches have a relatively comparable performance regarding the average revision from the one- to two-sided gaps (panel a in Figures 5 and 6), the oos performance shows that the autoregression approach has the smallest average error of forecasting. This is true for both narrow and broad credit definitions in Figures 5 and 6.

Dealing with much information at once, especially conflicting, could result in decision-making based on some utility function. For this research, we define a simple utility function as the sum of the values in Figures 5 and 6. The results are shown in Table 1. As the values should be the smallest possible, the smallest value of the utility is considered the best (or one could observe the negative value of the sum, denoted under Optimum 1 in Table 1). To balance the oos forecasting results and more minor revisions toward the possible two-sided gap, we define two other utility functions. One approach is to give a more significant penalty to greater deviations from the two-sided gap (denoted under Optimum 2, where the penalty gives

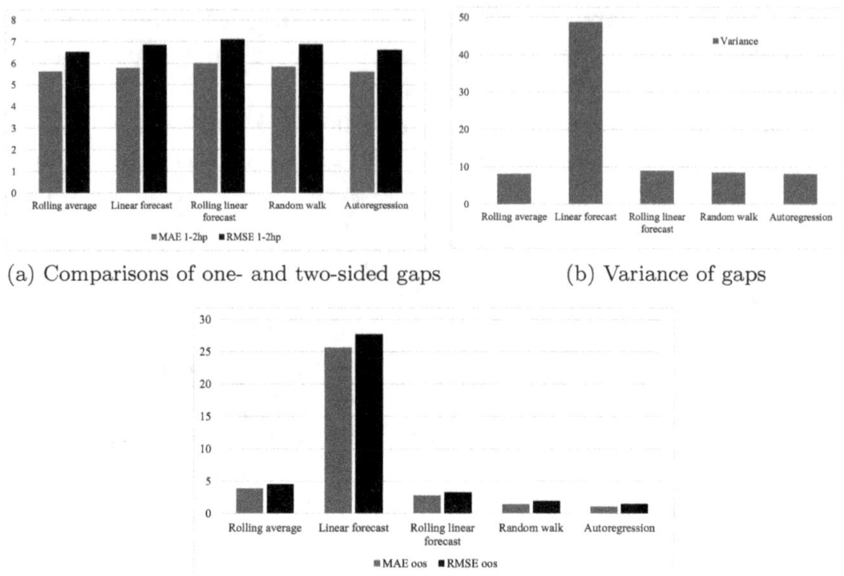

(a) Comparisons of one- and two-sided gaps

(b) Variance of gaps

(c) Oos performance

Figure 5. Average values of comparison criteria, narrow credit definition. *Source*: CNB, author's calculation.

twice the weight to the MAE and RMSE 1–2hp values). The other approach is to provide a greater penalty for the poor oos forecasting of an approach (Optimum 3 in Table 1). Overall, the autoregression approach is the best regardless of the optimum function approach. This indicates the potential usefulness of such an approach for usage, at least as the overall support for decision-making when observing gaps without the oos forecasts' augmentation.

Finally, we compare the overall results of each measure when the forecast horizon varies, depicted in Table 2 for the narrow credit definition and Table A3 in the Appendices for the broad credit definition. A couple of observations could be made when observing the two tables. First, the corrections toward the two-sided gaps are smallest for the case of 12 quarters of oos forecasting horizon length. The reason could be that as the estimated dynamic is prolonged in more periods in the future at each point in time, those values differ more from the one-sided dynamic and go toward the two-sided gaps that

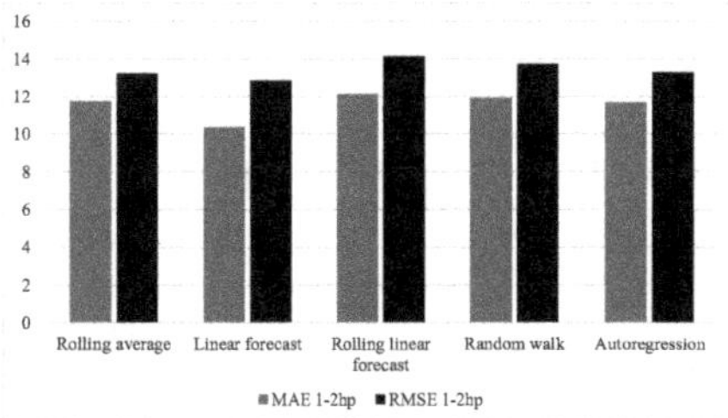

(a) Comparisons of one- and two-sided gaps

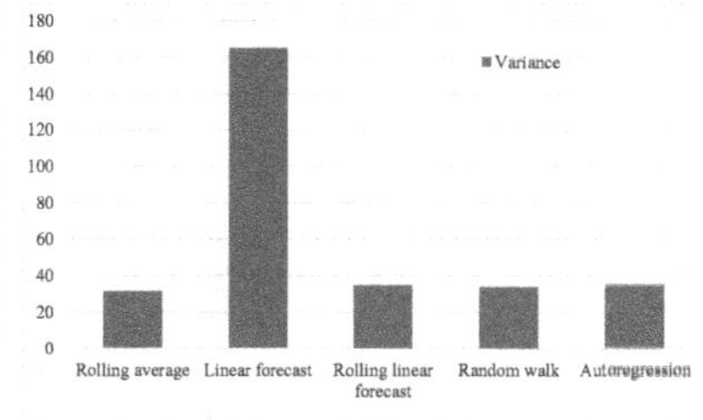

(b) Variance of gaps

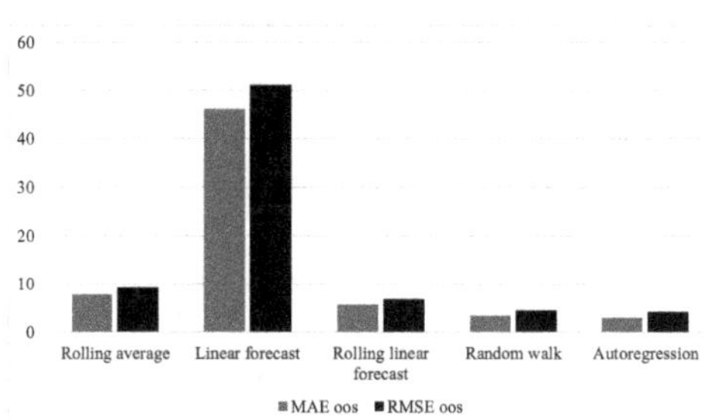

(c) Oos performance

Figure 6. Average values of comparison criteria, broad credit definition.
Source: CNB, author's calculation.

have reasonably different dynamics overall (see Figure 2 panels c and d). The same is true for the variance performance, where again, the $h = 12$ has the best performance, but this is due to such gaps resembling the two-sided gaps that have smaller overall variability. But the decision-maker is also interested in obtaining good forecasts of an approach, measured by comparing the actual credit ratio and the one that was forecasted previously. Therefore, we want the one-sided gap to be as close as possible to the two-sided one, but on the other hand, the decisions are made based on the one-sided ones. Thus, the best horizon regarding the oos RMSE and MAE values for the forecasting part of the estimation procedure is four quarters for most of the results. These conclusions stand both for narrow and broad credit definitions. Now, we see a trade-off here between having the smallest revisions of the one-sided gaps and having minor errors in forecasting. Again, one could use a utility function approach, as

Table 1. Summary of performance measures from Figures 5 and 6.

Group	Narrow Credit Definition			Broad Credit Definition		
	Optimum 1	**Optimum 2**	**Optimum 3**	**Optimum 1**	**Optimum 2**	**Optimum 3**
Rolling average	28.55	40.67	36.89	73.31	98.26	90.41
Linear forecast	114.66	127.29	168.01	285.31	308.49	382.38
Rolling linear forecast	28.06	41.16	34.07	73.34	99.63	85.82
Random walk	24.62	37.34	27.97	67.34	92.98	75.21
Autoregression	**23.01**	**35.20**	**25.59**	**66.41**	**91.41**	**73.45**

Note: Bolded values denote the best performance for each column.
Source: CNB, author's calculation.

Table 2. Comparison criteria based on differing h, narrow credit definition.

	Mean	Max.	Min.	Std. Dev.
MAE 1–2hp				
$h = 4$	6,254	8,145	3,898	1,318
$h = 8$	5,596	7,307	4,271	**1,067**
$h = 12$	**5,248**	**7,427**	**3,512**	1,269
Average	5,699	8,145	3,512	1,277
RMSE 1–2hp				
$h = 4$	7,391	9,482	5,067	1,433
$h = 8$	6,629	8,640	5,155	**1,199**
$h = 12$	**6,141**	**8,469**	**4,282**	1,384
Average	6,720	9,482	4,282	1,421
Variance				
$h = 4$	14,144	56,712	5,854	14,403
$h = 8$	13,757	59,255	5,308	14,965
$h = 12$	**12,282**	**51,916**	**4,643**	**12,804**
Average	13,394	59,255	4,643	13,911
RMSE oos				
$h = 4$	**5,130**	**26,881**	1,427	**8,427**
$h = 8$	5,432	27,710	1,462	8,662
$h = 12$	5,711	28,608	**1,413**	8,965
Average	5,425	28,608	1,413	8,567
MAE oos				
$h = 4$	**4,412**	**24,402**	1,033	**7,745**
$h = 8$	4,749	25,589	1,066	8,102
$h = 12$	5,080	26,869	**1,032**	8,531
Average	4,747	26,869	1,032	8,022

Note: Bolded values denote best performance in each column for each measure.
Source: CNB, author's calculation.

done previously, to sum up the results in one value. This was done in Table 3, where the identical utility functions are used to compare the different horizons of forecasting. Now, the decision could be even harder, as, for most cases, the $h = 8$ length has the best performance, even though it was not the best or worst when commenting on Tables 2 and A.3. This shows that the decision would be challenging when deciding on only just one gap to be the best.

To summarize all of the findings, it can be said that there will be a trade-off between choosing the best oos forecasting approach and the approach with minor corrections toward the two-sided

Table 3. Summary of performance measures from Table 2 and Table A.3.

	Narrow Credit Definition			Broad Credit Definition		
Horizon	**Optimum 1**	**Optimum 2**	**Optimum 3**	**Optimum 1**	**Optimum 2**	**Optimum 3**
$h = 4$	37,33	50,98	46,87	96,54	121,08	116,93
$h = 8$	36,16	**48,39**	46,34	**91,45**	**114,53**	**113,01**
$h = 12$	**34,46**	45,85	**45,25**	95,62	120,62	115,95

Note: Bolded values denote best performance in each column for each measure.
Source: CNB, author's calculation.

gap approach. As the results here are based on a relatively short period that includes one crisis in the sample, the early warning models signaling approach is not considered an excellent strategy to contrast the gaps. This is due to the possible biases of the results, alongside the need to fix a specific initial window for the estimation procedure of the recursive gap estimation. However, as the comparisons were made based on stability and oos forecasting accuracy, the results hold for such findings that focus on these criteria. In general, the findings align with related research in Gerdrup *et al.* (2013) and Valinskytė and Rupeika (2015), where linear projections had smaller variability, and rolling average forecasts were considered better in the performance. This is due to the nature of such approaches, where it is essential to consider that the estimation should be based on a rolling window basis. The estimated forecasting models' coefficients change over time as different phases of the financial cycle occur.

What else is important is the stability of the indicator. This means that it should provide constant signals over time, especially for the case when the decisions about CCyB value have to change. In an ideal setting, an indicator is stationary and reverts to a mean value always. In other words, it should be cyclical and reflect the cyclical nature of the credit dynamics. However, dynamics of original values are rarely stationary, alongside the issues that HP filter has.

5. Conclusion

Although the credit gap measured via the HP estimation procedure is widely used in practice and empirical research, literature critiquing this indicator is almost as broad as the literature that generally deals with credit gaps. Several literature branches try to solve problems regarding the HP gap. This chapter belongs to the strand that deals with the end-point problem via out-of-sample forecasts and augmented gaps. The idea is that adding several data points to the end of an existing series could reduce the estimation bias for the last couple of actual observations, i.e., that are observed. As was seen in the results, there will be a trade-off between the forecast accuracy of an approach and the revision of the gap series toward the two-sided gap, which is considered the "true" one.

A drawback of this study is that only one crisis is included in the sample due to the short period in the analysis. This disables the study of the early warning signaling models, where the future crisis signaling of an indicator can be evaluated. Thus, future work should extend such results via the early warning models' approach to get greater information about the characteristics of each approach to augment the original gap series. However, we did not want to force such an approach here, as the results would be biased.

However, other important aspects were considered. First, as the policymaker has to make decisions in real time (see Škrinjarić, 2022b), the signals provided by the indicator should be as consistent as possible. This is captured via the variability of individual approaches. Next, as the policymaker utilizes out-of-sample forecasts to obtain estimates of the in-sample gap, such forecasts should be as accurate as possible. Instead of observing the errors of trend values, we opted to compare the errors between the forecasted credit ratio series to the true ones that were realized afterward. Although this makes the comparisons retroactive at least we obtain information about past performance to have some fundamental insights into future developments of such approaches. Of course, the results are not straightforward. Some methods give better values of smaller variability over time, whereas others have better out-of-sample forecasting capabilities. The picture is more complicated when observing the indicators in groups based on the forecasting horizon. Naturally, the longer the forecast horizon, the error of forecasting gets greater. But, the decision-maker considers that longer horizons stabilize the trend values at the end of the sample more.

What could be recommended for use in the macroprudential policy's decision-making process to plot the range of specific augmented gaps alongside the original gaps without forecast "corrections"? Based on the preferences toward the variability of the one-sided gap, its mean distance to the two-sided gap, and the forecasting performance of an approach, a choice could be made so that a quasi-interval estimation of the original gap is obtained. Of course, the decision-making process is always based on a range of other relevant criteria, such as the private sector debt burden, external imbalances, overvaluation of property prices, mispricing of risk, general economic conditions, as well as different economic and political events, that could affect the indicators, the decisions, and the overall macroprudential policymaker's choices. Other important factor that could affect the decision-making process in the years to come could be the COVID-19 pandemic (see Elnahass *et al.*, 2021; Trinh *et al.*, 2022; Li *et al.*, 2023).

Appendices

Table A1. Average values of comparison criteria, narrow credit definition.

Group	MAE 1–2hp	RMSE 1–2hp	Variance	MAE oos	RMSE oos
Rolling average	5,609	**6,518**	**8,077**	3,857	4,484
Linear forecast	5,783	6,850	48,669	25,621	27,733
Rolling linear forecast	5,999	7,102	8,940	2,746	3,271
Random walk	5,847	6,878	8,541	1,425	1,929
Autoregression	**5,590**	6,605	8,233	**1,084**	**1,496**

Note: Bolded values denote best performance in each column.
Source: CNB, author's calculation.

Table A2. Average values of comparison criteria, broad credit definition.

Group	MAE 1-2hp	RMSE 1-2hp	Variance	MAE Oos	RMSE Oos
Rolling average	11,716	13,235	**31,268**	7,790	9,303
Linear forecast	**10,343**	**12,837**	165,064	46,062	51,005
Rolling linear forecast	12,152	14,139	34,574	5,683	6,792
Random walk	11,927	13,715	33,823	3,377	4,493
Autoregression	11,712	13,288	34,370	**2,920**	**4,122**

Note: Bolded values denote best performance in each column.
Source: CNB, author's calculation.

Table A3. Comparison criteria based on differing h, broad credit definition.

	Mean	Max.	Min.	Std. Dev.
MAE 1–2hp				
$h = 4$	12,717	16,394	**7,815**	2,571
$h = 8$	11,369	14,803	9,248	2,127
$h = 12$	**10,783**	**14,148**	8,035	**2,060**
Average	11,623	16,394	7,815	2,376
RMSE 1–2hp				
$h = 4$	14,689	18,715	9,976	2,793
$h = 8$	13,171	17,206	10,578	2,307
$h = 12$	**12,294**	**16,401**	**9,124**	**2,407**
Average	13,384	18,715	9,124	2,668
Variance				
$h = 4$	52,407	191,845	22,883	47,258
$h = 8$	51,605	200,777	21,171	49,297
$h = 12$	**46,815**	**176,397**	**19,147**	**42,228**
Average	50,276	200,777	19,147	45,767
RMSE oos				
$h = 4$	**10,426**	4,389	**49,335**	**15,062**
$h = 8$	11,041	4,482	50,951	15,509
$h = 12$	11,562	**4,425**	52,727	16,110
Average	11,010	4,451	52,727	15,352
MAE oos				
$h = 4$	**8,619**	**43,211**	**2,737**	**13,399**
$h = 8$	9,353	45,985	2,857	14,243
$h = 12$	9,998	48,989	2,815	15,252
Average	9,324	48,989	2,737	14,126

Note: Bolded values denote best performance in each column for each measure.
Source: CNB, author's calculation.

References

Alessandri, P., Bologna, P., Fiori, R. and Sette, E. (2015). A note on the implementation of the countercyclical capital buffer in Italy. *Questioni di Economia e Finanza (Occasional Papers)*, No. 278. Banca D'Italia.

Baba, C., Dell'Erba, S., Detragiache, E., Harrison, O., Mineshima, A., Musayev, A. and Shahmoradi, A. (2020). How should credit gaps be measured? — An application to European countries. *IMF Working Paper*, No. 20/6, International Monetary Fund.

Babecký, J., Havránek, T., Matějů, J., Rusnák, M., Šmídková, K. and Vašíček, B. (2014). Banking, debt, and currency crises in developed countries: Stylized facts and early warning indicators. *Journal of Financial Stability*, *15*, 1–17.

Bank of Portugal (2020). The countercyclical capital buffer in Portugal. Available at: https://www.bportugal.pt/sites/default/files/ccb_portugal_en.pdf.

BCBS (2011). Basel III: A global regulatory framework for more resilient banks and banking systems — revised version. Basel Committee on Banking Supervision.

Behn, M., Detken, C., Peltonen, T. and Schudel, W. (2013). Setting countercyclical capital buffers based on early warning models: Would it work? *ECB Working Paper*, No. 1604, European Central Bank.

BIS (2010). Guidance for national authorities operating the countercyclical capital buffer. Bank for International Settlements. Available at: https://www.bis.org/publ/bcbs187.htm.

Bonfim, D. and Monteiro, N. (2013). The implementation of the countercyclical capital buffer: Rules versus discretion. In *Financial Stability Report*, pp. 87–110. Banco de Portugal.

Borio, C. and Drehmann, M. (2009). Assessing the risk of banking crises — revisited. *BIS Quarterly Review*, 29–46. Bank for International Settlements.

Borio, C. and Lowe, P. (2002). Assessing the risk of banking crises. *BIS Quarterly Review*. Bank for International Settlements.

Bruchez, P. A. (2003). A modification of the HP filter aiming at reducing the end-point bias. *Working Paper, Swiss Federal Finance Administration*, Bundesgasse 3, CH-3003 Bern.

Candelon, B., Dumitrescu, E.-I. and Hurlin, C. (2012). How to evaluate an early-warning system: Toward a unified statistical framework for assessing financial crises forecasting methods. *IMF Economic Review*, *60*(1), 75–113.

Canova, F. (1998). Detrending and business cycle facts. *Journal of Monetary Economics*, *41*(3), 475–512.

Charemza, W. and Ladley, D. (2016). Central banks' forecasts and their bias: Evidence, effects and explanation. *International Journal of Forecasting*, *32*(3), 804–817.

CNB (2022a). Croatian National Bank. Data available online at: https://www.hnb.hr/en/statistika/statisticki-podaci/sve-tablice-po-datumu-objave.

CNB (2022b). Macroprudential diagnostics, No 16, Box 2 improvements in the methodology of countercyclical buffer identification and calibration in Croatia, Croatian National Bank. Available at: https://www.hnb.hr/documents/20182/4129930/e-mpd-16-2022.pdf/ca45830d-196a-e18d-6b53-bb8808a8bb0d.

Cogley, T. and Nason, J. M. (1995). Output dynamics in real-business-cycle models. *American Economic Review*, *85*(3), 492–511.

Dell Ariccia, G., Igan, D., Leaven, L. and Tong, H. (2012). Policies for macrofinancial stability: How to deal with credit booms. *IMF Staff Discussion Note. International Monetary Fund.*

Detken, K., Weeken, O., Alessi, L., Bonfim, D., Boucinha, M., Castro, C., Frontczak, S., Giordana, G., Giese, J., Jahn, N., Kakes, J., Klaus, B., Lang, J., Puzanova, N. and Welz, P. (2014). Operationalising the countercyclical capital buffer: Indicator selection, threshold identification and calibration options. *ESRB Occasional Paper*, No. 5, European Systemic Risk Board.

Drehmann, M., Borio, C., Gambacorta, L., Jimenez, G. and Trucharte, C. (2010). Countercyclical capital buffers: Exploring options. *BIS Working Papers, No. 317, Bank for International Settlements.*

Drehmann, M., Borio, C. and Tsatsaronis, K. (2011). Anchoring countercyclical capital buffers: The role of credit aggregates. *International Journal of Central Banking*, *7*(4), 189–240.

Drehmann, M., Borio, C. and Tsatsaronis, K. (2014). The credit-to-GDP gap and countercylical capital buffers: Questions and answers. *BIS Quarterly Review. Bank for International Settlements.*

Drehmann, M. and Juselius, M. (2014). Evaluating early warning indicators of banking crises: Satisfying policy requirements. *International Journal of Forecasting*, *30*(3), 759–780.

Drehmann, M. and Yetman, J. (2018). Why you should use the Hodrick-Prescott filter – at least to generate credit gaps. *BIS Working Papers, No. 744. Bank for International Settlement.*

Edge, R. M. and Meisenzahl, R. R. (2011). The unreliability of credit-to-GDP ratio gaps in real-time: Implications for countercyclical capital buffers. *International Journal of Central Banking*, *7*(4), 261–298.

Elnahass, M., Trinh, V. Q. and Li, T. (2021). Global banking stability in the shadow of Covid-19 outbreak. *Journal of International Financial Markets, Institutions and Money*, *72*, 101322.

ESRB (2014). Recommendation of the European systemic risk board of 18 June 2014, ESRB/2014/1. European Systemic Risk Board. Available at: https://www.esrb.europa.eu/pub/pdf/recommendations/140630_ESRB_Recommendation.en.pdf.

ESRB (2018). *The ESRB Handbook on Operationalising Macroprudential Policy in the Banking Sector*. Frankfurt am Main, Germany: European Systemic Risk Board.

Galán, J. E. (2019). Measuring credit-to-GDP gaps. The Hodrick-Prescott filter revisited. *Documentos de Trabajo, No. 1906, Banco de España.*

García, J. A. and Manzanares, A. (2007). Reporting biases and survey results. Evidence from European professional forecasters. *ECB Working Paper Series, No. 836. European Central Bank.*

Geršl, A. and Mitterling, T. (2021). Forecast-augmented credit-to-GDP gap as an early warning indicator of banking crises. *Finance a úvěr-Czech Journal of Economics and Finance*, *71*(4), 323–351.

Gourinchas, P.-O. and Obstfeld, M. (2012). Stories of the twentieth century for the twenty-first. *American Economic Journal: Macroeconomics*, *4*(1), 226–265.

Hamilton, J. (2018). Why you should never use the Hodrick-Prescott filter. *Review of Economics and Statistics*, *100*(5), 831–843.

Hodrick, R. J. and Prescott, E. C. (1997). Postwar U.S. business cycles: An empirical investigation. *Journal of Money, Credit and Banking*, *29*(1), 1–16.

Jokipii, T., Nyffeler, R. and Riederer, S. (2021). Exploring BIS credit-to-GDP gap critiques: The Swiss case. *Swiss Journal of Economics and Statistics*, *157*(4), 1–19.

Kaiser, R. and Maravall, A. (1999). Estimation of the business cycle: A modified Hodrick-Prescott filter. *Spanish Economic Review*, *1*, 175–206.

Kamber, G., Morley, J. and Wong, B. (2018). Intuitive and reliable estimates of the output gap from a Beveridge-Nelson filter. *Review of Economics and Statistics*, *100*(3), 550–566.

Kauko, K. (2012). Triggers for countercyclical capital buffers. MPRA Paper No. 85692. Available at: https://mpra.ub.uni-muenchen.de/85692/.

Lang, J, H., Izzo, C., Fahr, S. and Ruzicka, J. (2019). Anticipating the bust: A new cyclical systemic risk indicator to assess the likelihood and severity of financial crises. *ECB Occasional Paper Series, No. 219. European Central Bank.*

Li, T., Trinh, V. Q. and Elnahass, M. (2023). Drivers of global banking stability in times of crisis: The role of corporate social responsibility. *British Journal of Management*, *34*(2), 595–622.

Mise, E., Kim, T. H. and Newbold, P. (2005). On suboptimality of the Hodrick-Prescott filter at time series endpoints. *Journal of Macroeconomics*, *27*(1), 53–67.

Pedersen, T. M. (2001). The Hodrick Presscott filter, the Slutzky effect, and the distortionary effect of filters. *Journal of Economic Dynamics and Control*, *25*, 1081–1101.

Richter, B., Schularick, M. and Wachtel, P. (2017). When to lean against the wind. *CEPR Discussion Paper, No. 12188. Centre for Economic Policy Research.*

Rünstler, G. and Vlekke, M. (2016). Business, housing, and credit cycles. *ECB Working Paper Series, No. 1915, European Central Bank.*

Schularick, M. and Taylor, A. M. (2012). Credit booms gone bust: Monetary policy, leverage cycles, and financial crises, 1870–2008. *American Economic Review*, *102*(2), 1029–1061.

Škrinjarić, T. (2022a). Uvođjenje kompozitnog indikatora cikličkog sistemskog rizika u Hrvatskoj: mogućnosti i ograničenja (Introducing a composite indicator of cyclical systemic risk in Croatia: Possibilities and limitations). Research I-70, Croatian National Bank. Available at: https://www.hnb.hr/-/uvodjenje-kompozitnog-indikatora-ciklickog-sistemskog-rizika-u-hrvatskoj-mogucnosti-i-ogranicenja.

Škrinjarić, T. (2022b). Macroeconomic effects of systemic stress: A rolling spillover index approach. *Public Sector Economics*, *46*(1), 109–140.

Škrinjarić, T. (2022c). Do we get cold feet when deciding on countercyclical capital buffer? Ways to deal with uncertainty in estimating credit to GDP gap in real time. *The 28th Dubrovnik Economic Conference Dubrovnik: Croatian National Bank*, pp. 1–40. Available at: https://www.hnb.hr/documents/20182/4135482/skrinjaric.pdf/835451fe-8b80-a287-9f45-795497868ee1?t=1656425985712.

Škrinjarić, T. and Bukovšak, M. (2022a). Novi indikatori kreditnog jaza u Hrvatskoj: unapređenje kalibracije protucikličkog zaštitnog sloja kapitala (New indicators of credit gap in Croatia: Improving the calibration of countercyclical capital buffer). Research I-69, Croatian National Bank. Available at: https://www.hnb.hr/-/novi-indikatori-kreditnog-jaza-u-hrvatskoj-unapredjenje-kalibracije-protuciklickog-zastitnog-sloja-kapitala.

Škrinjarić, T. and Bukovšak, M. (2022b). Novi indikatori kreditnog jaza u Hrvatskoj: unapređenje kalibracije protucikličkog zaštitnog sloja kapitala (New indicators of credit gap in Croatia: improving the calibration of countercyclical capital buffer). Ekonomska misao i praksa: časopis Sveučilista u Dubrovniku (Economic thought and practice: University of Dubrovnik journal), accepted for publication, forthcoming.

Trinh, V. Q., Cao, N. D. and Elnahass, M. (2022). Financial stability: A 'vaccine' for tail risk of the global banking sector in the shadow of the pandemic. *The European Journal of Finance*, *29*(7), 726–753.

Valinskytė, N. and Rupeika, G. (2015). Leading indicators for the countercyclical capital buffer in Lithuania. Available at: https://www.lb.lt/uploads/publications/docs/op_4.pdf.

Wezel, T. (2019). Conceptual issues in calibrating the Basel III countercyclical capital buffer. *IMF Working Paper, No. 19/86. International Monetary Fund.*

https://doi.org/10.1142/9781800614321_0013

Chapter 13

The Ability of Altman's *Z*"-score Model to Detect the Economic Distress of Kazakh Banks

Aigul P. Salina[*,‡], Xin Zhang[†,§], Tong Jiao[†,¶], and Omaima A. G. Hassan[†,||]

[*]*Satbayev University, Almaty, Kazakhstan*
[†]*Aberdeen Business School, Robert Gordon University, Aberdeen, UK*
[‡]*aigulsalina41@gmail.com*
[§]*x.zhang2@rgu.ac.uk*
[¶]*t.jiao@rgu.ac.uk*
[||]*o.hassan@rgu.ac.uk*

Abstract

This study contributes to the literature by evaluating the ability of Altman's *Z*"-score model to predict the economic distress of 12 Kazakh banks over the period 2008–2014. The original *Z*"-score model with a cut-off point implied by Altman (2005) produced a prediction accuracy ratio of 44.05% and correctly classifies 76.19% of the observations as an economically distressed group. This study then re-estimates the model using three approaches, namely, the "leave-one-out", Direct, and Wilks' methods, and identifies new, optimal cut-off points for the re-estimated models. The re-estimated models, together with the new, optimal cut-off points, improved the prediction accuracy ratio to 70% and correctly classified over 90% of the observations originally assigned to the economically distressed group. The results imply that the Kazakh banking regulator and other market participants could use Altman's *Z*"-score model to detect economically distressed banks.

Keywords: Altman's Z"-score model, Kazakhstan, distress, banks, emerging market

1. Introduction

Economic distress refers to vulnerabilities in both the financial health and the business model of a bank. It is broader than the concept of insolvency, which represents the probability that the cash buffer a firm has against variations in cash flows may be insufficient, leaving the firm unable to meet its financial obligations (Beaver, 1966). It is also broader than the concept of financial distress. Altman *et al.* (2019, p. 8) explain the differences between financial and economic distresses. *A firm in financial distress experiences a shortfall in cash flow needed to meet its debt obligations. Its business model does not necessarily have fundamental problems and its products are often attractive. In contrast, firms in economic distress have unsustainable business models and will not be viable without asset restructuring. In practice, many distressed firms suffer from a combination of the two.*

The Z-score model developed by Altman in 1968 is probably the first multivariate failure prediction model. This model has gained wide popularity in the literature, which is evident by a total citation of 22,041 times on Google Scholar as of June 2, 2022. It has several advantages such as simplicity, possibility to work with limited information, comparability of indicators, ability to produce a binary classification of companies into bankrupt and non-bankrupt firms with high predictive accuracy, and reliance on accounting-based measures which enables the application of the model on private companies. In this context, this study evaluates the ability of the original and re-estimated Altman's Z"-score models to predict the economic distress of 12 Kazakh banks over the period 2008–2014.

This study is closely related to studies investigating the original Altman's Z-score model and its variations to predict corporate bankruptcy and financial distress, and assess firms' financial health. Most prior studies use samples from developed countries (e.g., Almamy *et al.*, 2016; Grice and Ingram, 2001; Xu and Zhang, 2009), whereas relatively fewer studies are conducted on emerging markets (e.g., Chouhan *et al.*, 2014; Zhang *et al.*, 2010) and none on Kazakh banks. In this context, this study contributes to the literature by investigating the ability of Altman's models to predict the economic distress of Kazakh banks. It is also closely related to studies that use Altman's Z-score model and its variations in the banking industry to predict bank failure and assess banks' financial soundness (e.g., Al Zaabi, 2011; Ngwa, 2016; Vaziri *et al.*, 2012).

Using data from 12 Kazakh banks over the period 2008–2014, this study further contributes to the literature by assessing the classification performance of Altman's Z"-score model in Kazakhstan. As an emerging market and a post-Soviet state, Kazakhstan provides a unique case to study the economic distress of banks. According to the National Bank of Kazakhstan (NBK), the country experienced a level of non-performing loans of 2.4% at the beginning of 2008, which had dramatically increased to 36% by the beginning of 2014 (NBK, 2015). The World Bank ranked Kazakhstan the first in the world in terms of the percentage of non-performing loans to total gross loans in 2012 (Salina *et al.*, 2021). However, to date, there seem to be scarce international studies of the Kazakhstan banking sector. In addition, following prior studies (e.g., Begley *et al.*, 1996; Moyer, 1977; Nasledov, 2013; Wu *et al.*, 2010), this study re-estimates the original Z"-score model using three approaches, namely, the "leave-one-out", Direct, and Wilks' methods, and calculates new, optimal cut-off points for the re-estimated models. It further examines whether the re-estimated versions of Altman's Z"-score model outperform the original Z"-score model. Using the original Altman's Z"-score model and a cut-off point which is equivalent to the minimum Z"-score of the US firms which have "BBB" ratings, this model correctly classifies 44.05% of the observations into the economically distressed and non-distressed groups. However, it correctly classifies 76.19% of the observations initially assigned to the economically distressed group. The re-estimated models, together with the new, optimal cut-off points, produce prediction accuracy ratios ranging from 52.38% to 70.24% and they correctly classify more than 90% of the observations initially assigned to the economically distressed group.

The results, especially those produced by the re-estimated models, indicate that Altman's Z"-score model is effective in detecting economically distressed Kazakh banks. Therefore, it could be used by the Kazakh banking regulator to monitor the risk of Kazakh banks failing and detect those that may need early intervention. Other financial market participants could also use the model to differentiate economically distressed from non-distressed Kazakh banks, which may help them decide whether to invest in these banks.

The rest of this chapter is organized as follows: Section 2 briefly reviews the history of the Kazakh banking system since Kazakhstan's independence from the USSR. Section 3 reviews related studies. Section 4 describes the dataset and research design of this study. Section 5 presents and discusses the findings. Section 6 concludes this chapter.

2. A Concise History of the Banking System of Kazakhstan

The Republic of Kazakhstan is a post-Soviet state, which gained its independence from the Soviet Union on December 16, 1991. The latest World Economic Situation Prospects classify Kazakhstan as an "economy in transition", which means that the country is still in the process of transforming from a centrally planned economy to a market economy (United Nations, 2022). Upon its independence, Kazakhstan inherited a domestic banking system, which was built during the Soviet era and dominated by a few large state-owned banks.

According to the legislation governing the NBK, the country has a two-tier banking system: the NBK, which is the central bank and forms the top tier of the system, with all the other banks forming the second tier (The Republic of Kazakhstan, 1995). The second-tier banks resemble the commercial banks operating in other countries; they perform financial intermediation and supply credit to the real economy. Salina (2017) documents a series of reforms initiated by the government of Kazakhstan during the period 1991–2007, which aimed to improve the financial stability of its domestic banking system and boost market confidence. For example, a deposit insurance scheme was introduced in November 1999, minimum capital reserve requirements for second-tier banks were introduced in February 2000, initial share capital requirements for opening a new second-tier bank were introduced in June 2001 and tightened in October 2004, a full compliance with the Basel I Standards started in 2000, and the adoption of the International Accounting Standards (IAS) by all second-tier banks for external reporting began in 2002. These reforms and the booming domestic economy during the period 2000–2007 have stimulated fast growth in banks' assets, deposits, and earnings, which all peaked at the end of 2007 (NBK, 2015). During the same period, the Kazakh banking sector became more internationalized; large Kazakh second-tier banks expanded into overseas markets and many foreign banks increased their presence in Kazakhstan. However, the global financial crisis of 2008–2009 triggered a banking crisis in Kazakhstan.

Like their counterparts in many developed economies, several Kazakh banks were heavily exposed to high levels of credit risk, caused by their lending to the domestic real estate and construction sectors, and high levels of liquidity risk, caused by over-reliance on short-term borrowings from the international wholesale funding market (Glass *et al.*, 2013). The bursting of the domestic real estate bubble, which was formed during the economic boom of 2000–2007, resulted in a sharp rise in non-performing loans and a record decline in banks' profits (NBK, 2015). The freezing of international wholesale funding during the global financial crisis has significantly reduced the availability of short-term funding for Kazakh banks and increased their servicing costs. The sale of Kazakh banks' securities by foreign investors and the withdrawal of their deposits exacerbated the liquidity crisis. As a result, three major banks (BTA Bank, Alliance Bank, and Temirbank) were on the brink of collapse. To stabilize the domestic banking system, the government of Kazakhstan decided to provide financial assistance to troubled banks. For example, the National Fund of Kazakhstan (a flagship sovereign wealth fund) injected 3.24 billion USD into four troubled banks (i.e., Kazkommertsbank, Halyk Bank, BTA Bank, and Alliance Bank) and became their major shareholder. Further financial assistance was given to three of them to restructure their non-performing loans. The Chairman of the NBK, Mr Kairat Kelimbetov, claimed that it cost Kazakhstan around six percent of its GDP to assist its banking sector to deal with the negative impact of this banking crisis (Kelimbetov, 2014). Nonetheless, the ratio of the non-performing loans of the whole banking sector went up from 2.7% at the beginning of 2008 to 36% by the beginning of 2014 (NBK, 2015).

The government of Kazakhstan introduced new reforms to address the weaknesses exposed by the crisis and to be able to control the risk within the banking system. For example, Salina (2017) documents that more stringent prudential standards, including higher minimum capital reserve requirements, were introduced on July 1, 2009. Also, the NKB announced the transition to BASEL III standards in 2015 and expected a full compliance by 2022. The Kazakh financial regulators are also taking initiatives to establish effective mechanisms to identify the risk factors in the banking system and to detect deterioration in the financial conditions of banks. In this context, Altman's Z-score model and its variations could help in detecting the economic distress of banks since previous studies show that these models are effective tools for assessing the economic health of banks and predicting bank failure (e.g., Al Zaabi, 2011; Ullah *et al.*, 2021; Vaziri *et al.*, 2012).

3. Literature Review

In this section, we review Altman's Z-score model and its variations. We then justify the use of Altman's Z"-score model in this study and discuss the potential contributions of the study.

3.1. *A review of Altman's models*

Altman's models are a family of Linear Discriminant Functions (LDFs) which use company-level financial ratios as their predictors. A typical LDF can be mathematically expressed as follows:

$$D = \beta_0 + \beta_1 \mathrm{X}_1 + \beta_2 \mathrm{X}_2 + \cdots + \beta_\mathrm{n} \mathrm{X}_\mathrm{n} \tag{1}$$

where D is the discriminant score, β_0 is an estimated intercept, β_n are the estimated coefficients, and X_n are the predictors. LDFs are derived using Multiple Discriminant Analysis (MDA), which enables a classification of observations into distinctive groups based on their discriminant scores.

3.1.1. *Altman's Z-score model*

In 1968, Edward Altman developed the Z-score model to predict corporate bankruptcy using a set of financial ratios. These ratios measure a company's liquidity, profitability, leverage, solvency, and efficiency. A sample of US-listed manufacturing firms, consisting of 33 firms that filed for bankruptcy during the period 1946–1965 and 33 firms that were still in existence in 1966, was used to estimate the LDF that can best classify these firms into bankrupt and non-bankrupt firms. The resulting LDF is as follows:

$$Z = 0.012X_1 + 0.014X_2 + 0.033X_3 + 0.006X_4 + 0.999X_5 \quad (2)$$

where X_1 is the ratio of working capital to total assets, X_2 is the ratio of retained earnings to total assets, X_3 is the ratio of earnings before interest and taxes to total assets, X_4 is the market value of equity deflated by the book value of total liabilities, X_5 is the ratio of sales to total assets, and Z is the discriminant score generated by the LDF (Z-score). When using this model, one should insert absolute percentage values (e.g., 10%) for variables X_1–X_4 and decimals for variable X_5 (e.g., Equation (2)). Altman (2013) suggested a more convenient specification of Equation (2), as described by Equation (3), which has gradually become popular:

$$Z = 1.2X_1 + 1.4X_2 + 3.3X_3 + 0.6X_4 + 1.0X_5 \quad (3)$$

Definitions for all the variables in Equation (3) remain the same. However, when using Equation (3), one can insert decimals for all the predictors. Equations (2) and (3) are commonly referred to as Altman's Z-score model. The five predictors included in this model measure several attributes of a firm that are relevant to bankruptcy. X_1 measures a firm's liquidity scaled by its asset size; a firm which is experiencing consecutive financial losses will have shrinking current assets relative to its total assets. Firms which have high liquidity risk are more likely to go bankrupt. X_2 measures a firm's cumulative profitability and considers both the age and profitability of a firm. Younger and less profitable firms are more likely to go bankrupt. X_3 measures a firm's profitability or the productivity of its assets. More profitable/productive firms are less likely to go bankrupt. X_4 measures how much a firm's assets can decline in value before the liabilities exceed the value of assets. The higher the ratio, the lower the solvency risk. X_5 measures the efficiency of a firm's assets to generate sales revenue. More efficient firms are less likely to fall into financial distress. In summary, variables X_1–X_5 are, in theory, all positively correlated to the Z-score; the higher (lower) the Z-score, the lower (higher) the chance of bankruptcy.

Altman (1968) applied the Z-score model to both the original sample used to estimate this model and new samples to assess its classification performance by using the following three key indicators:

- classification accuracy ratio measured as the number of correct classifications divided by sample size,
- Type I error rate defined as the number of bankrupt firms mistakenly classified by the model as non-bankrupt firms divided by the number of bankrupt firms in the sample,
- Type II error rate defined as the number of non-bankrupt firms incorrectly classified by the model as bankrupt firms divided by the number of non-bankrupt firms in the sample.

The outcome of this assessment shows that the ability of the model to predict bankruptcy with a decent accuracy rate depends on the length of the out-of-sample estimation period. To illustrate, when the prediction of bankruptcy is made one year in advance, the model correctly classified 95% of the 66 sample firms and produced a Type I error rate of 6% and a Type II error rate of 3%. The classification accuracy dropped to 83% when prediction is made two years in advance. In addition, the Type I error rate increased to 28%, while the Type II error rate remained at 6%. Altman (1968) also applied the model to two hold-out samples: one consisting of 25 bankrupt firms and the other consisting of 66 firms that experienced financial losses during 1958–1961 but did not file for bankruptcy. The model correctly classified 24 out of the 25 firms in the first sample (a classification accuracy ratio of 96%); however, it misclassified 14 out of the 66 firms in the second sample (a classification accuracy ratio of 79% and a Type II error rate of 21%).

Altman (1968) also proposed the concepts of "safe zone", "grey zone", and "distress zone". Sample firms with Z-scores greater than 2.99 were all correctly classified by the Z-score model as non-bankrupt firms. This implies that any firm with a Z-score greater than 2.99 could be considered financially safe. Sample firms with Z-scores smaller than 1.81 were all correctly classified by the model as bankrupt firms. This indicates that any firm with a Z-score lower than 1.81 could be considered financially distressed or bankrupt. Sample firms that have Z-scores greater than 1.81 but smaller than 2.99 are prone to misclassifications. Therefore, it is unclear whether firms with Z-scores within this range could be considered financially safe. It is worth noting that the cut-off point used to classify sample firms can be different from the boundary values for the three zones. The cut-off point is a value that often maximizes the classification accuracy and minimizes the sum of Type I and Type II errors. Altman (1968) used a cut-off point of 2.675; firms with Z-scores greater than this value were classified as non-bankrupt firms, whereas firms with Z-scores smaller than this value were classified as bankrupt firms. However, Altman (2002; 2013) also proposed a cut-off point of 1.81, which is the average Z-score of "B"-rated firms included in their samples. This implies that firms with credit ratings lower than a "B" grade are considered in the "distress zone".

3.1.2. *Variations of Altman's Z-score model*

As mentioned above, the Z-score model was originally derived from a sample of US-listed manufacturing firms. Also, the numerator of variable X_4 included in the model is the market value of equity. Therefore, this model cannot be applied to firms whose shares are not listed on a stock exchange, for example, private firms. To accommodate these firms, Altman (1993) substituted the book value of equity for the market value of equity in the definition for X_4 and re-estimated the coefficients by employing the sample used to estimate the coefficients of the original Z-score model. The definitions for X_1, X_2, X_3, and X_5 remain the same as those used in the original Z-score model. The resulting model is the so-called Altman's Z'-score model for private firms:

$$Z' = 0.717X_1 + 0.847X_2 + 3.107X_3 + 0.420X_4 + 0.998X_5 \qquad (4)$$

Altman (2013) reports that when applied to the original sample used to derive the Z-score model, the Z'-score model produced slightly lower classification performance; Type I error rate increased from 6% to 9%, and the classification accuracy declined from 95% to 94%, but Type II error rate did not change. Because the Z'-score model uses a different definition for X_4 and different estimated coefficients for the five predictors, its boundary values for the "safe zone", "grey zone", and "distress zone" also differ from those of the Z-score model. Altman (2013) indicates that a Z'-score greater than 2.90 is in the "safe zone", a Z'-score between 1.23 and 2.90 is in the "grey zone", and a Z'-score lower than 1.23 is in the "distress zone".

To further accommodate non-manufacturing companies, Altman (1993) proposed another variation of the Z-score model, the Z"-score model, which is described as follows:

$$Z\text{''} = 6.56X_1 + 3.26X_2 + 6.72X_3 + 1.05X_4 \quad (5)$$

X_5, the ratio of sales to total assets, was removed because it is industry-sensitive and might introduce a specific industry effect into the *Z*"-score model. The definitions for X_1, X_2, X_3, and X_4 remain the same as those used in the *Z*'-score model. Because the *Z*"-score model is developed from the *Z*'-score model, in theory, it is more versatile than the *Z*'-score model and can be applied to both unlisted and non-manufacturing firms. Altman and Hotchkiss (2006) claim that when tested on US samples comprising both manufacturing and non-manufacturing companies, the *Z*"-score model produced classification performance that is comparable to those produced by the *Z*-score and *Z*'-score models. Because the *Z*"-score model has different coefficients for the predictors, its boundary values for the "safe zone", "grey zone", and "distress zone" also differ from those of the *Z*-score and *Z*'-score models. Altman (2002) indicates that a *Z*"-score smaller than 1.10 is considered in the "distress zone", a *Z*"-score between 1.10 and 2.6 is considered in the "grey zone", and a *Z*"-score greater than 2.6 is considered in the "safe zone".

In addition, another specification of the *Z*"-score model was used by Altman *et al.* (1998) and Altman (2005) to estimate bond ratings equivalent for both US and Mexico companies. Because Mexico is an emerging market, this new specification is often referred to as the emerging market scoring model or the EMS model:

$$Z\text{''} = 6.56X_1 + 3.26X_2 + 6.72X_3 + 1.05X_4 + 3.25 \quad (6)$$

The only difference between Equations (5) and (6) is an intercept of 3.25. Altman *et al.* (1998) introduced this intercept to standardize their analysis so that a *Z*" score of zero or lower is consistent with a default equivalent bond rating (i.e., a "D" rating). Altman *et al.* (1998) and Altman (2005) did not specify clear boundary values for the "safe zone", "grey zone", and "distress zone" for Equation (6); however, these can be derived by adding 3.25 to the boundary values of the original *Z*"-score model (i.e., Equation (5)). For example, the lower bound for the "safe zone" should be 5.85 (2.6+3.25), and the upper bound for the "distress zone" should be 4.35 (1.10+3.25).

Altman *et al.* (2017) used a large international sample of firms to assess the classification performance of the *Z*"-score model and its derivatives in 35 developed and emerging countries. Equation (6) was referred to as the Z"-score model in their study and used as the baseline model.

3.1.3. *Model selection and research contributions*

Following Altman *et al.* (2017), this study employs Altman's Z"-score model, as specified by Equation (6), to predict the economic distress of Kazakh banks. The Z"-score is chosen because it can be applied to non-manufacturing firms from emerging markets (Altman *et al.*, 1998; Altman, 2005; Altman and Hotchkiss, 2006). In addition, this model has been used in prior studies to assess the financial performance of banks from emerging countries and predict bank failure (e.g., Al Zaabi, 2011). This study makes several contributions to the literature.

Firstly, this is the first study to assess the classification performance of Altman's Z"-score model in Kazakhstan. Most prior studies assessing the classification performance of Altman's models used samples from developed countries (e.g., Almamy *et al.*, 2016; Grice and Ingram, 2001; Wu *et al.*, 2010; Xu and Zhang, 2009). Altman and Narayanan (1997) suggest that corporate failure prediction studies conducted for developed markets benefit from several institutional factors which emerging economies might lack, such as data availability, clear bankruptcy laws and well-developed banking infrastructures, strong investor protection regulations, and low likelihood of government intervention if corporate failures occur. Hence, the performance of Altman's models might be uneven between developed and emerging countries. Indeed, using samples from 35 developed and emerging countries, Altman *et al.* (2017) find that the performance of the Z"-score model varies across countries. However, contrary to the conventional wisdom, they find that this model performs well in several emerging economies which have weak institutional environment, such as China and Russia, while they deliver relatively poorer performance for several developed countries which have strong institutional environment, such as Norway, Ireland, Iceland, and Germany. This highlights the importance of advancing our understanding of country-specific classification performance of Altman's models. Although there is a growing literature on using Altman's models to assess firms' financial health and financial distress in emerging markets (e.g., Zhang *et al.*, 2010; Al Zaabi, 2011; Chouhan *et al.*, 2014; Altman *et al.*, 2021; Wu *et al.*, 2022), there are very limited attempts to examine their classification performance (e.g., Zhang *et al.*, 2010). For example, Hájek *et al.* (2017; 2021) calculate the Z- or Z'-scores for two small samples of confectionary companies operating in Kazakhstan and then compare the scores to the boundary values for the "safe", "grey", and "distress" zones to assess the financial performance of these companies. However, these Kazakh studies are conducted for non-financial firms and did not assess the classification performance of Altman's models. In contrast, this study evaluates the classification performance of the Z"-score model, which is more suitable for predicting the economic distress of banks from emerging markets.

Secondly, this study further contributes to the literature by re-estimating Altman's Z"-score model for a sample of Kazakh banks using three approaches, namely, the "leave-one-out", Direct, and Wilks' methods, and identifying new, optimal cut-off points for the re-estimated models. It further examines whether the re-estimated versions of Altman's Z"-score model outperform the original Z"-score model. This is because Altman (2013), Grice and Ingram (2001), and Altman *et al.* (2017) find that the classification performance of Altman's models changes over time and varies across industries and countries. The re-estimation often results in different coefficients for the predictors included in the original versions of Altman's models. To the best of our knowledge, this is the first study to re-estimate the Z"-score model using a Kazakh sample and compare the classification performance of the re-estimated Z"-score model with that of the original Z"-score model.

Thirdly, this study advances knowledge of the ability of Altman's models to predict the economic distress of banks from emerging markets. Prior studies used the Z-scores derived from Altman's models to measure not only the default risk of non-financial firms but also the default risk of banks (Hogan, 2015). In addition, Altman's Z-score model and its variations have been used to assess banks' financial health and predict bank failure for developed markets (e.g., Ngwa, 2016; Vaziri *et al.*, 2012). However, there are relatively fewer attempts at using Altman's models to assess the financial strength of banks or predict bank failure in the context of emerging markets. For example, Al Zaabi (2011) used the Z"-score model to assess the financial health of a sample of Islamic banks from the UAE. To the best of our knowledge, this is the first study to use Altman's Z"-score model to predict the economic distress of Kazakh banks.

4. Data Collection and Research Design

4.1. *Data collection*

This study uses data from twelve Kazakh banks (see Table 1) which can be divided into two groups. The first group consists of six banks that received financial assistance from the Kazakh government, failed to meet their obligations, or/and were forced to merge with other banks to avoid failure after the banking crisis of 2008–2009. These six banks are hence classified as economically distressed banks in this study. The second group consists of six banks, which are comparable to the six economically distressed banks in terms of bank size, business lines, and number of branches. These six banks are not considered in to be economic distress because they did not fail to meet their obligations and were not forced to merge with other banks during the sample period. Financial data at the start of each year of these banks were obtained from the central bank of Kazakhstan and

Table 1. Sample banks.

Distressed Banks		Share of the Total Assets Held by the Banking Sector (%)	Non-distressed Banks		Share of the Total Assets Held by the Banking Sector (%)
1	Kazkommertsbank	16.2	1	Halyk Bank of Kazakhstan	15.8
2	BTA Bank	9.8	2	Bank Centercredit	6.9
3	ATF Bank	5.8	3	SB Sberbank	6.7
4	Alliance Bank	3.6	4	Tsesnabank	6.0
5	Temirbank	2.0	5	Kaspi Bank	5.5
6	Nurbank	1.6	6	Bank RBK	1.4
Total		39.0	Total		42.3
Total share of the two groups					81.3

Note: This table shows that the sample banks control 81.3% of the total assets held by the entire Kazakh banking sector as of January 1, 2014, which form a representative sample.

covered the period January 1, 2008–January 1, 2014. The final sample includes seven annual observations for each bank and eighty-four observations in total. Table 1 shows that the sample banks control 81.3% of the total assets held by the entire Kazakh banking sector as of January 1, 2014, and form a representative sample.

4.2. *Research design*

This study evaluates the ability of the original and re-estimated Altman's Z"-score models to predict the economic distress of 12 Kazakh banks over the period 2008–2014. The data analysis is divided into two parts.

In the first part of the analysis, we use the original Z"-score model (Equation (6)) and the financial ratios of the sample banks to calculate the Z"-scores of these banks. Then, we compare the obtained Z"-scores to the lower bound of the "safe zone", which equals 5.85. We classify any observation with a Z"-score that is lower than 5.85 as economically distressed. This is because it is unclear whether firms, whose Z-scores are in the "grey zone", will be correctly classified either as bankrupt or non-bankrupt firms (Altman, 1968). Furthermore, Altman (2005) showed that the minimum Z"-score of sample firms that have "BBB" ratings is 5.85, which is the same as the lower bound of the "safe zone" for the Z"-score model (Equation (6)). Firms with credit ratings lower than the "BBB" grade are considered vulnerable to default risk and their bonds are "speculative". For example, Fitch Ratings consider firms with the "BB" ratings, one grade below the "BBB" rating, to have "an elevated vulnerability to default risk, particularly in the event of adverse changes in business or economic conditions over time" (Fitch Ratings, 2022). Therefore, our approach of using 5.85 as the cut-off point is also motivated by the credit rating agencies' definition of corporate vulnerability.

In the second part of the analysis, we use three re-estimation methods that are suitable for studies with small samples. Studies applying Altman's models for predicting bankruptcy and financial distress usually use a "training" sample for re-estimation, and a "hold-out" sample for assessing classification performance (e.g., Altman, 1968; Grice and Ingram, 2000). However, this approach might not be possible for studies with relatively small samples. Obtaining a large sample of banks from an emerging market can be challenging because the domestic banking market is likely to be dominated by a few large banks. In addition, even though this study only employs a sample of 12 banks, they control more than 80% of the total assets held by the whole Kazakh banking sector. Also, it is not uncommon for prior studies not to have "held-out" samples. For example, Bellovary *et al.* (2007) reviewed bankruptcy prediction studies published between 1930 and 2007 and found that less than half of these studies used "hold-out" samples.

The first re-estimation method applied is the "leave-one-out" approach proposed by Nasledov (2013). Under this approach, the learning algorithm leaves one selected observation out and uses all the remaining observations as the training set for re-estimation. The re-estimated model is used to make a prediction for the selected observation, i.e., one unique re-estimated model for each selected observation. We further apply two re-estimation approaches proposed by Moyer (1977), namely, the Wilks' and Direct approaches. Wilks' approach adds variables into a discriminant function in a stepwise manner up to the point where Wilks' lambda is minimized. The Direct approach includes all the predictors of the Z"-score model, by default, in the discriminant function. Essentially, each of these two methods generates one unique, re-estimated model and then this model is used to make predictions for the whole sample. When using the three re-estimation methods, we also employ a technique used in Begley *et al.* (1996) and Wu *et al.* (2010) to generate new, optimal cut-off points, which are then used to classify the sample banks.

5. Findings and Discussion

5.1. *Results from the original Altman's Z"-score model*

The application of the original Altman's Z"-score model involves two steps. First, the means and standard deviations of the four predictors included in the model are calculated for each of the two groups of banks. Then, T-test and F-test are used to identify whether the means and standard deviations for the first group are statistically different from those of the second group. Second, financial data of the sample banks are inserted into Altman's Z"-score model

Table 2. A comparison between the means and standard deviations of the four predictors included in the original Altman Z"-score model.

	Non-distressed		Distressed		F-test		T-test	
	Mean	**St. Dev.**	**Mean**	**St. Dev.**	**F value**	**p-value**	**t-value**	**p-value**
X_1	−0.309	0.576	−0.061	0.342	2.834	0.001***	−2.398	0.010***
X_2	0.011	0.014	−0.047	0.313	0.002	0.000***	1.192	0.120
X_3	0.068	0.032	0.033	0.293	0.012	0.000***	0.771	0.223
X_4	0.692	1.767	0.135	0.164	116.73	0.000***	2.031	0.021**

Note: This table shows descriptive statistics of the four predictors in the original Altman Z"-score model. X_1: working capital/total assets; X_2: retained earnings/total assets; X_3: EBIT/total assets; X_4: book value of equity/book value of total liabilities. The sample includes 84 bank-year observations from 12 Kazakh banks and covers the period 1st January 2008–1st January 2014. *,**,***: sig. at 10%, 5%, and 1% level, respectively.

(Equation (6)) to work out the Z-scores. Any observation with a Z"-score lower than 5.85 is classified as economically distressed.

Table 2 presents the means and standard deviations of the four ratios included in Altman's Z"-score model and the T- and F-statistics for testing the between-group differences. The results indicate that observations originally assigned to the economically distressed group have significantly higher liquidity ratio (X_1) and lower solvency ratio (X_4) compared to their counterparts. The result for X_4 is expected, but the result for X_1 may look counterintuitive at first glance because normally one expects higher liquidity to reduce the chances of distress. However, this might be true for non-financial companies but not for banks. Compared to their counterparts, economically distressed banks might have limited access to the money market, which limits their ability to borrow short-term funds. Using less short-term liabilities would lead to better working capital (the numerator of X_1). Thus, the result for X_1 may reflect the unique business model of banks; they use short-term liabilities such as deposits and commercial papers to finance long-term assets such as mortgages and corporate loans (Howells and Bain, 2007). The results on the other two predictors (i.e., X_2 and X_3) are inconclusive.

Table 3 shows the classification result using the cut-off value of 5.85 (the minimum Z"-score to stay in the "safe zone").

Table 3. Application of the Z"-score model with original coefficients to predict the economic distress of Kazakh banks.

Type of Error	Classification Performance				
	No. of Correct Predictions	**% of Correct Predictions**	**No. of Incorrect Predictions**	**% of Incorrect Predictions**	**Obs.**
Type I	32	76.19	10	23.81	42
Type II	5	11.91	37	88.09	42
Total	37	44.05	47	55.95	84

Notes: This table shows the predictive accuracy of Z"-score model. The sample includes 84 bank-year observations from 12 Kazakh banks and covers the period 1st January 2008–1st January 2014. $Z" = 6.56X_1+3.26X_2+6.72X_3+1.05X_4+3.25$. Cut-off point = 5.85.

The results in Table 3 show that 32 out of 42 observations originally assigned to the economically distressed group are correctly classified; the remaining 10 observations are misclassified. In other words, 76.19% of predictions made for the observations originally assigned to the economically distressed group are correct and the remaining 23.81% are incorrect (Type I errors). However, only 5 out of the 42 observations originally assigned to the non-distressed group are correctly classified; the remaining 37 observations in this group are misclassified as economically distressed. In other words, only 11.91% of predictions for the observations originally assigned to non-distressed group are correct and the remaining 88.09% are incorrect (Type II errors). On aggregate, only 37 out of 84 observations in the sample are correctly classified, a prediction accuracy of only 44.05%.

Although the overall prediction accuracy produced using the original Altman's Z"-model and a cut-off point of 5.85 is below 50%, this approach correctly classifies about 80% of the observations originally assigned to the economically distressed group. From a banking regulator's point of view, the costs of not identifying economically distressed banks in advance are much higher than mistakenly identifying non-distressed banks as distressed ones. Therefore, this approach still has value to the banking regulators even though it produces a high Type II error rate and a low overall prediction accuracy ratio.

The low overall prediction accuracy ratio and high Type II error rate might indicate that the cut-off point of 5.85 is too high for our sample. As we have explained in Section 3, Altman (2005) found that the minimum Z"-score of his US sample firms which have "BBB" ratings is 5.85. This indicates that having a "BBB" grade or equivalent rating is potentially a legitimate criterion to assess the economic distress of Kazakh banks. However, the sovereign rating for Kazakhstan never exceeded the "BBB" grade and often carried negative outlooks during the sample period (Tradingeconomics.com, 2022). The "sovereign rating ceiling" rule indicates that the ratings for Kazakh banks were likely to be lower than the "BBB" grade during the sample period.

5.2. *Results from the re-estimated models*

As explained in Section 4, the "leave-one-out" approach will result in one unique re-estimated model for each observation (i.e., 84 models in total); for brevity, we do not present them. Using the Direct and Wilks' methods to re-estimate the original Z"-score model results in two unique re-estimated models for our sample, which are mathematically expressed as follows:

$$Z''_{\mathrm{D}} = -1.960\mathrm{X}_1 + 2.430\mathrm{X}_2 - 1.534\mathrm{X}_3 + 0.670\mathrm{X}_4 + 3.769 \quad (7)$$

$$Z''_{\mathrm{W}} = 2.058\mathrm{X}_1 - 0.728\mathrm{X}_4 + 3.932 \quad (8)$$

The definitions for variables X_1–X_4 are the same as those used in Section 3. Z''_{D} and Z''_{W} are the Z"-scores generated by the two re-estimated models using the Direct and Wilks' methods, respectively. In addition, we employ a technique used by Begley *et al.* (1996) and Wu *et al.* (2010) to identify new, optimal cut-off points. The new cut-off points are then compared to the Z"-scores predicted by the re-estimated models to classify observations into economically distressed and non-distressed groups. This technique assumes that an optimal cut-off point exists between the 25th percentile and 95th percentile of the predicted Z"-scores. At this optimal cut-off point, the sum of Type I and Type II errors is minimized, and the overall prediction accuracy ratio is maximized. Table 4 shows how the optimal cut-off point is determined for the Z"-scores predicted using the "leave-one-out" approach. It shows that the classification accuracy ratio is maximized, and the sum of Type I and II error rate is

Table 4. Finding the optimal cut-off point for the re-estimated Altman Z"-score model using the "leave-one-out" approach.

		Classification Performance			
Ranking of *Z*"-scores (Percentile)	***Z*" Scores**	**Prediction Accuracy (%)**	**Type I Error Rate (%)**	**Type II Error Rate (%)**	**Sum of Type I and II Error Rates (%)**
25th	0.010	36.90	88.10	38.10	126.20
30th	0.573	36.90	83.33	42.86	126.19
35th	1.228	42.86	71.43	42.86	114.29
40th	1.707	42.86	66.67	47.62	114.29
45th	2.716	42.86	61.90	52.38	114.28
50th	2.929	45.24	54.76	54.76	109.52
55th	3.250	47.62	47.62	57.14	104.76
60th	3.457	42.86	47.62	66.67	114.29
65th	3.943	40.48	45.24	73.81	119.05
70th	4.335	39.29	40.48	80.95	121.43
75th	4.942	41.67	33.33	83.33	116.66
80th	5.641	44.05	26.19	85.71	111.90
85th	5.963	46.43	19.05	88.10	107.15
89th	6.574	47.62	14.29	90.48	104.77
90th	6.597	48.81	11.90	90.48	102.38
91st	6.640	50.00	9.52	90.48	100.00
92nd	7.106	51.19	7.14	90.48	97.62
93rd	**7.899**	**52.38**	**4.76**	**90.48**	**95.24**
94th	8.077	51.19	4.76	92.86	97.62
95th	9.938	51.19	4.76	92.86	97.62

Note: This table shows how the optimal cut-off point is identified. The sum of Type I and II error rates is minimized at the 93rd percentile of the predicted *Z*" scores, which indicates that the classification accuracy ratio is maximized. Therefore, 7.899 is used as the optimal cut-off point to classify the sample into the economically distressed and non-distressed groups.

minimized at the 93rd percentile of the predicted *Z*" scores. Therefore, 7.899 is used as the optimal cut-off point to classify the sample into the economically distressed and non-distressed groups. The same approach is used to identify the optimal cut-off points for the re-estimated *Z*"-scores predicted by Equations (7) and (8).

Table 5 presents the classification results produced using the three re-estimation methods, which can be compared to those produced by the original Altman's *Z*"-score model with a cut-off point of 5.85. It

Table 5. A comparison of the classification performance produced by the different approaches.

	Classification Accuracy				
Models	**Full Sample (%)**	**Distressed (%)**	**Non-distressed (%)**	**Type I Error (%)**	**Type II Error (%)**
Z" model (original)[a]	44.05	76.19	11.91	23.81	88.09
Z" model ("leave-one-out")[b]	52.38	95.24	9.52	4.76	90.48
$Z"_{\mathrm{W}}$ model[c]	69.05	90.48	47.62	9.52	52.38
$Z"_{\mathrm{D}}$ model[d]	70.24	95.24	45.24	4.76	54.76

Note: This table compares the classification performance of four models: (a) The original Z"-score model (Equation (6)) with a cut-off point of 5.85; (b) the Z"-score model re-estimated using the "leave-one-out" approach and a cut-off point of 7.899; (c) the $Z"_{\mathrm{W}}$ model re-estimated using the Wilks' method (Equation (8)) and a cut-off point of 2.644; (d) the $Z"_{\mathrm{D}}$ model re-estimated using the Direct method (Equation (7)) and cut-off point of 3.905.

shows that the re-estimation of the original Altman's Z"-score model combined with new, optimal cut-off points significantly improves the classification performance. The re-estimated models correctly classify over 90% of the observations originally assigned to the economically distressed group. This suggests that the re-estimated models combined with new, optimal cut-off points could be used by Kazakh banking regulators to identify economically distressed banks. In addition, re-estimated models using Wilks' and Direct methods produce an overall classification accuracy that is well above 50% for the whole sample. This indicates that using these two methods, combined with the use of optimal-cut-off points, does not result in random predictions of the economic distress classification of the sample banks.

However, our classification results, especially those produced by the re-estimated models, are weaker than those reported by earlier studies, which use Altman's Z-score model and its variations to predict bankruptcy and financial distress for non-financial companies. For example, Altman (1968; 2013) reported that the overall prediction accuracy ratio produced by the original Z-score and Z'-score models is higher than 90%, and over 90% of the bankrupt firms are correctly classified if pre-2000 US samples are used. Grice and Ingram (2001) use a sample over the period 1985–1987 to re-estimate the Z-score model and a hold-out sample over the period 1988–1991 to test the power of the re-estimated model for predicting financial distress. The results show that the re-estimated model has an overall prediction accuracy ratio of 88.1%, and 94.9% of the non-distressed firms are correctly classified; however, only around 55% of the distressed firms are correctly classified. However, our results are largely comparable, if not superior, to the results obtained by relatively recent studies using non-financial samples. This is probably consistent with Grice and Ingram's (2001) finding that Altman's models' predictive power may decline over time. For example, Almamy *et al.* (2016) use a UK sample covering the period 2000–2013 to re-estimate the Z-score model and assess its ability to predict corporate failure. They report an overall prediction accuracy ratio of 54.4%, and 60.6% of failed sample firms are correctly classified by the re-estimated Z-score model. Altman *et al.* (2017) use a sample of firms from 35 countries and cover the period 2007–2010. They find that the Z"-score model estimated using data from all 35 countries produces an average overall prediction accuracy ratio of 49%, and the Z"-score model estimated using country-specific data produces an average overall prediction accuracy ratio of 46.6%.

Our classification results, especially those from re-estimated models, are also largely in line with the findings from a few studies which use Altman's models to predict banks' financial distress. For example, Vaziri *et al.* (2012) use a sample of 100 banks from the US and Europe over the period 2001–2010 to assess Altman's Z"-score model's ability to predict financial distress. They find that the overall prediction accuracy ratio and the prediction accuracy ratio for distressed sample banks vary across years; the former ranges from 59% to 95%, while the latter ranges from 65% to 80%. Ngwa (2016) uses a sample of 6 UK high-street banks and covers the period 2004–2013 to assess Altman's Z-score model's ability to predict financial distress. Ngwa finds that the overall prediction accuracy ratio and prediction accuracy ratio for the distressed sample banks vary across three sample periods: before the financial crisis of 2007–2009, during the crisis, and after the crisis. The overall prediction accuracy ratio ranges between 66.7% and 81%, and the prediction accuracy ratio for the distressed sample banks ranges from 72.2% to 83.3%.

6. Conclusion

This study contributes to the literature by assessing the ability of the original and re-estimated Altman's Z"-score models to predict the economic distress of 12 Kazakh banks over the period 2008–2014.

The study first uses the coefficients of the original Z"-score model and a cut-off point equivalent to the minimum Z"-score of US firms that have "BBB" ratings to classify the sample into economically distressed and non-distressed groups. This approach produces a relatively low overall prediction accuracy ratio of 44.05% but correctly classifies 76.19% of the observations originally assigned to the economically distressed group. Then, we re-estimate the original Z"-score model using three methods, namely, the "leave-one-out", Direct, and Wilks' methods. In addition, new, optimal cut-off points are identified for the re-estimated models using a technique employed in previous studies (e.g., Begley *et al.*, 1996; Wu *et al.*, 2010). Compared to the results produced by the original Z"-score model, the combination of re-estimated models and new, optimal cut-off points delivers improved prediction accuracy. The prediction accuracy ratios produced by the three re-estimated models are all higher than 50% and the ratios produced by the Direct and Wilks' methods are close to 70%, which indicates that these re-estimated models do not produce random predictions for the sample banks' economic distress. In addition, all re-estimated models correctly classify over 90% of the observations originally assigned to the economically distressed group. The results from the re-estimated models are largely consistent with those from relatively recent studies that assess the ability of Altman's models to predict bankruptcy and financial distress.

The results of this study are likely of interest to the banking regulator in Kazakhstan and other financial market participants. The high prediction accuracy for the economically distressed observations indicates that a combination of re-estimated Z"-score models and optimal cut-off points could be an effective tool for the Kazakh banking regulator to detect economically distressed banks. Not being able to detect economically distressed banks before further deterioration of their financial conditions could be costly to a society because these banks may fail or collapse in the future, which often requires large government bailouts and affects market stability. Therefore, the efficacy of the re-estimated Altman's Z"-score models in detecting economically distressed Kazakh banks suggests that they could be used by the Kazakh banking regulator to monitor the risk of Kazakh banks and detect those that may require early or pre-emptive interventions. Other participants in Kazakh financial markets may also use the re-estimated Z"-score models to monitor Kazakh banks' risk and differentiate economically distressed from non-distressed banks. This may help them make informed investment decisions relating to Kazakh banks, such as whether to buy, hold, or sell the securities issued by a Kazakh bank.

This study, however, is not free from limitations; therefore, our findings should be interpreted with caution. First, because we use a relatively small sample, we are not able to test the predictive power of the re-estimated Z"-score model on a "hold-out" sample. Testing the model on the sample used to estimate it may inflate the prediction accuracy, a typical problem for "in-sample" forecasting. Future studies could, for instance, obtain data on more Kazakh banks or cover a longer sample period to create a "hold-out" sample to further test the predictive power of Altman's Z"-score model. Second, the construction of the sample and initial assignment of the observations into economically distressed and non-distressed groups are subjective, which may affect the reliability of the classification results. Future studies may collect credit ratings on Kazakh banks, where available, and use ratings to pre-assign banks into economically distressed and non-distressed groups. Finally, it is debatable whether Altman's models estimated with discriminant analysis are superior to other types of corporate failure prediction models, such as probit/logit models and market-based contingent claim models, for predicting corporate distress and failure (e.g., Hillegeist *et al.*, 2004; Jackson and Wood, 2013). Future studies could, for example, use probit/logit models incorporating more than the five variables included in the Z"-score model and compare the predictive power of these probit/logit models with those of Altman's models.

References

Almamy, J., Aston, J. and Ngwa, L. N. (2016). An evaluation of Altman's Z-score using cash flow ratio to predict corporate failure amid the recent financial crisis: Evidence from the UK. *The Journal of Corporate Finance, 36*, 278–285.

Altman, E. I. (1968). The prediction of corporate bankruptcy: A discriminant analysis. *The Journal of Finance, 23*, 193–194.

Altman, E. I. (1993). *Corporate Financial Distress and Bankruptcy*, 2nd edn. New York: John Wiley and Sons.

Altman, E. I. (2002). Corporate distress prediction models in a turbulent economic and Basel II environment. *NYU Working Paper No. S-CDM-02-11*. NYU Stern School of Business, New York. Available at: https://ssrn.com/abstract=1295810. Accessed 1 July 2022.

Altman, E. I. (2005). An emerging market credit scoring system for corporate bonds. *Emerging Markets Review, 6*, 311–323.

Altman, E. I. (2013). Chapter 17 "Predicting financial distress of companies: Revisiting the Z-score and ZETA®models". In A. R. Bell, C. Brooks, and M. Prokopczuk (eds.) *Handbook of Research Methods and Applications in Empirical Finance*, pp. 428–456. Edward Elgar Publishing.

Altman, E. I., Hartzell, J. and Peck, M. (1998). Chapter 15 "Emerging market corporate bonds — a scoring system". In R. M. Levich (ed.) *Emerging Market Capital Flows*, pp. 391–400. The New York University Salomon Center Series on Financial Markets and Institutions, Boston, MA: Springer.

Altman, E. I. and Hotchkiss, E. (2006). *Corporate Financial Distress and Bankruptcy: Predict and Avoid Bankruptcy, Analyse and Invest in Distressed Debt*, 3rd edn. New York: John Wiley & Sons.

Altman, E. I., Hotchkiss, E. and Wang, W. (2019). Corporate *Financial Distress, Restructuring, and Bankruptcy: Analyze Leveraged Finance, Distressed Debt, and Bankruptcy*, 4th edn. New York: John Wiley & Sons.

Altman, E. I., Hu, X. and Yu, J. (2021). Understanding credit risk for Chinese companies using machine learning: a default-based approach. *European Financial Management Association 2021 Annual Meetings*, June 30–July 03, University of Leeds, Leeds. Available at: https://www.efmaefm.org/0EFMAMEETINGS/EFMA%20ANNUAL%20MEETINGS/2021-Leeds/papers/EFMA%202021_stage-2049_question-Full%20Paper_id-88.pdf. Accessed 15 August 2023.

Altman, E. I., Iwanicz-Drozdowska, M., Laitinen, E. K. and Suvas, A. (2017). Financial distress prediction in an international context: A review and empirical analysis of Altman's Z-score model. *Journal of International Financial Management and Accounting, 28*, 131–171.

Altman, E. I. and Narayanan, P. (1997). An international survey of business failure classification models. *Financial Markets, Institutions & Instruments, 6*, 1–57.

Al Zaabi, O. S. H. (2011). Potential for the application of emerging market Z-score in UAE Islamic banks. *International Journal of Islamic and Middle Eastern Finance and Management, 4*, 158–173.

Beaver, W. H. (1966). Financial ratios as predictors of failure. *The Journal of Accounting Research, 4*, 71–111.

Begley, J., Ming, J. and Watts, S. (1996). Bankruptcy classification errors in the 1980s: An empirical analysis of Altman's and Ohlson's models. *Review of accounting Studies, 1*, 267–284.

Bellovary, J., Giacomino, M. A. and Akers, M. D. (2007). A review of bankruptcy prediction studies: 1930-present. *The Journal of Financial Education, 33*, 1–42.

Chouhan, V., Chandra, B. and Goswami, S. (2014). Predicting financial stability of select BSE companies revisiting Altman Z score. *International Letters of Social and Humanistic Sciences, 26*, 92–105.

Fitch Ratings. (2022). *Rating Definitions.* Available from: https://www.fitchratings.com/products/rating-definitions. Accessed 1 July 2022.

Glass, A., Kenjegalieva, K. and Weyman-Jones, T. G. (2013). Bank performance and the financial crisis: Evidence from Kazakhstan. *Applied Financial Economics, 24*, 121–138.

Grice, J. and Ingram, R. (2001). Tests of the generalizability of Altman's bankruptcy prediction model. *Journal of Business Research, 54*, 53–61.

Hájek, P., Kaňková, E. and Zhunissova, G (2021). Analysis of competitiveness and economic profit of the confectionary sector in Kazakhstan and its comparison with Czech Republic data. *International Food and Agribusiness Management Review, 5*, 263–291.

Hájek, P., Zhunissova, G., Čábelová, T. and Baydildina, A. (2017). Competitiveness analysis of Kazakhstan confectionary sector using financial discriminant models. *CBU International Conference Proceedings.* Available from: https://ojs.journals.cz/index.php/CBUIC/article/view/916. Accessed 1 July 2022.

Hillegeist, S. A., Keating, E. K., Cram, D. P. and Lundstedt, K. G. (2004). Assessing the probability of bankruptcy. *Review of Accounting Studies, 9*, 5–34.

Hogan, T. L. (2015). Capital and risk in commercial banking: A comparison of capital and risk-based capital ratios. *The Quarterly Review of Economics and Finance, 57*, 32–45.

Howells, P. and Bain, K. (2007). *Financial Markets and Institutions*, 5th edn. Harlow: Pearson Education.

Jackson, R. H. G. and Wood, A. (2013). The performance of insolvency prediction and credit risk models in the UK: A comparative study. *The British Accounting Review*, *45*, 183–202.

Kelimbetov, K. (2014). We have become a little smarter. *Forbes*. Available from: http://forbes.kz/finances/finance/kayrat_kelimbetov_myi_stali_nemnojko_umnee. Accessed 1 July 2022. (In Russian).

Moyer, R. C. (1977). Forecasting financial failure: A re-examination. *Financial Management*, *6*, 11–17.

Nasledov, A. (2013). *IBM SPSS Statistics 20 u AMOS: Professional Statistical Analysis*. PiterPeter, Saint Petersburg. (In Russian)

National Bank of Kazakhstan. (2015). Assessment of risks in the financial system of Kazakhstan. Available from: http://www.nationalbank.kz. Accessed 15 June 2016.

Ngwa, L. N. (2016). Impact of financial distress on UK bank performance and customer loyalty: An empirical study. Ph.D. Thesis, University of Wales Trinity Saint David.

Peresetsky, A., Karminsky, A. and Golovan, S. (2011). Probability of default models of Russian banks. *Economic Change and Restructuring*, *44*, 297–334.

Salina, A. P (2017). Financial soundness of Kazakh banks: analysis and prediction. Ph.D. Thesis, Robert Gordon University.

Salina, A. P., Zhang, X. and Hassan, O. A. G. (2021). An assessment of the financial soundness of the Kazakh banks. *The Asian Journal of Accounting*, *6*, 23–37.

The Republic of Kazakhstan. (1995). On the National Bank of the Republic of Kazakhstan. Law of the Republic of Kazakhstan dated 30 March 1995 No. 2155. Available from: https://adilet.zan.kz/eng/docs/Z950002155. Accessed 15 June 2016.

Tradingeconomics.com. (2022). *Kazakhstan – Credit Rating*. Available from: https://tradingeconomics.com/kazakhstan/rating. Accessed 1 July 2022.

United Nations. (2022). *World Economic Situation and Prospects 2022*. Available from: https://www.un.org/development/desa/dpad/publication/world-economic-situation-and-prospects-2022/. Accessed 1 July 2022.

Ullah, H., Abbas, M. G., Zhang, F. and Mahmood, M. R. (2021). Association of financial distress and predicted bankruptcy: The case of Pakistani banking sector. *The Journal of Asian Finance, Economics and Business*, *8*, 573–585.

Vaziri, M., Bhuyan, R. and Manuel, P. A. V. (2012). Comparative predictivity of failure of financial institutions using multiple models. *Investment Management and Financial Innovations*, *9*, 120–127.

Wu, Y., Gaunt, C. and Gray, S. (2010). A comparison of alternative bankruptcy prediction models. *Journal of Contemporary Accounting & Economics*, *6*, 34–45.

Wu, D., Ma, X. and Olson, D. L. (2022). Financial distress prediction using integrated Z-score and multilayer perceptron neural networks. *Decision Support Systems*, *159*, 113814.

Xu, M. and Zhang C. H. (2009). Bankruptcy prediction: The case of Japanese listed companies. *Review of Accounting Studies*, *14*, 534–558.

Zhang, L., Altman, E. I. and Yen, J. (2010). Corporate financial distress diagnosis model and application in credit rating for listing firms in China. *Frontiers of Computer Science*, *4*, 220–236.

https://doi.org/10.1142/9781800614321_0014

Chapter 14

Microfinance During the Global Financial Crisis (2007–2009): Are There Lessons from COVID-19?

Sunil Sangwan[*,‡] **and Md Aslam Mia**[†,§]

[*] *Institute of Rural Management Anand, Anand, Gujarat, India*

[†] *School of Management, Universiti Sains Malaysia, Penang, Malaysia*

[‡] *sunilsangwan07@gmail.com*

[§] *aslammia@usm.my*

Abstract

Although many economic, social, and environmental crises have occurred in the past, the recent novel coronavirus (COVID-19) disease is believed to have generated the most severe impact worldwide. Motivated by the lack of data from the global microfinance sector with respect to COVID-19, we have attempted to understand the effect of the pandemic on the microfinance industries through the lens of the 2007–2009 Global Financial Crisis (GFC). In so doing, global data of 2,995 microfinance institutions (MFIs) from 2000 to 2018 were analyzed, highlighting the effect of the GFC on the outreach and financial objectives of MFIs. Our assessment revealed that the GFC mostly had a negative impact on the dual goals of MFIs. Most importantly, the GFC triggered the transformation of the legal status of MFIs from Non-Governmental Organizations (NGOs) to other types (e.g., non-bank financial institutions). Similar outcomes are expected in the aftermath of the COVID-19 in the microfinance industries.

Keywords: Global financial crisis, microfinance, social outreach, financial sustainability, COVID-19

1. Introduction

The world has sustained many economic, social, and environmental crises in the past (Parker, 2008, 2017; Robinson, 2004) with the most recent and notable being the 2007–2009 Global Financial Crisis (GFC) (Roy and Kemme, 2020). At the time this is written, the world is witnessing another major crisis, the COVID-19 pandemic, which has crippled the economy, environment, and society (Aktar *et al.*, 2021; Borio, 2020; Elnahass *et al.*, 2021; Ozili, 2021; Trinh *et al.*, 2022; van Barneveld *et al.*, 2020). More disturbing is the lack of a specific timeline for abatement of the pandemic, given the re-emergence of deadlier COVID-19 variants from time to time (e.g., Delta and Omicron). Consequently, many have advocated living with COVID-19 by prioritizing mass vaccination rather than social restriction (Li *et al.*, 2022; Phillips, 2021; Skegg *et al.*, 2021).

While some of the economic effects of COVID-19 may be inevitable, adapting the experience from previous crises might reduce the burden. Therefore, this chapter aims to analyze how the GFC of 2007–2009 impacted the microfinance sector and whether lessons can be learnt from the aftermath of COVID-19.[1] This study is particularly important for two main reasons: First, microfinance remains an important channel through which various loan/deposit services are

[1]Specifically, we consider 2007–2009 for the global financial crisis. Between 2010 and 2012, we consider this period as the immediate effect of the GFC. Therefore, the duration between 2007 and 2012 is considered as during the GFC and immediate effect of the GFC.

availed of by poor people in developing countries (Díaz-Martín *et al.*, 2021). Hence, detriment to the microfinance industry due to COVID-19 will directly affect the poor people and the financial inclusion agenda of the sustainable development goals (SDGs). Second, there is no recent organizational data on the actual effect of COVID-19 on the global microfinance industry. Although a few studies have been conducted to investigate the impact of COVID-19 on the microfinance business, they were limited to either conceptual/review (Brickell *et al.*, 2020; Sangwan *et al.*, 2021) or empirical research based on primary data from the clients/staff (Malik *et al.*, 2020; Murshid and Murshid, 2021) and institutional contexts (Zheng and Zhang, 2021). The uniqueness of Zheng and Zhang's (2021) study lies in their use of Asian Development Bank's (ADB) projected impact of COVID-19 on 2018 GDP and other aspects of the economy (going backward). However, their study failed to assess the actual impact of COVID-19 on MFIs' financial and social efficiency due to unavailability of real data. At the time of conducting this study and as per our knowledge, the latest obtainable organizational information on MFIs from one of the world's largest databases, MIX Market, only has data up to the year 2019 and has many missing observations. Considering the data limitations and the severe impact of COVID-19 on the economy, well-planned strategies based on past experiences are needed to cushion the aftermath of COVID-19 on MFIs.

Therefore, we examine the impact of the GFC on different aspects of MFIs, particularly their dual aims of financial sustainability and outreach. In other words, we are interested in exploring how the various aspects of MFIs' objectives fared during the GFC and after the GFC. In particular the five-year period (2007–2009 for GFC and 2010–2012 for post-GFC) will enable us to examine how the global microfinance business struggled and subsequently recovered after a crisis.

We believe that the study's findings will help managers, policymakers, practitioners, and other stakeholders (donors, investors, etc.) understand the potential effect of COVID-19 and subsequently undertake adequate interventions to reduce the impact. Although the scales of the GFC and COVID-19 may differ to a large extent, both crises have repercussions on the financial system, including the microfinance industry.

The organization of the rest of this paper is as follows: Section 2 briefly discusses the method and data used in this study, followed by a detailed discussion of the findings in Section 3. In Section 4, we conclude the findings and provide some recommendations.

2. Method and Data

Considering the study's objectives, we did not employ any sophisticated methods/techniques. Rather, we relied on some descriptive types of analysis based on the secondary data. For example, we studied several aspects of MFIs in this paper, including outreach and financial goals. Then, using trend/graphical analysis, we examined how the GFC of 2007–2009 impacted the various dimensions of MFIs' outreach and financial sustainability goals. The investigated variables are reported in Table 1.

As we are particularly interested in investigating the effect of the GFC on the global microfinance industry to understand the impact of COVID-19, data on MFIs were collected from the World Bank in 2021 (https://datacatalog.worldbank.org/search/dataset/0038647). After cleansing the data, we had a total of 2,995 unique MFIs from about 119 economies in our sample. The dataset spans the period 2000–2018 and is sufficient to examine the effect of the GFC on microfinance. However, the exact number of total observations for each examined variable is reported in Table 2. Generally, less firm-year observations were obtained in the early years than in the recent years (since 2005), and the exact number is presented in the Appendix (Table A1). Furthermore, we have winsorized each continuous variable at 1% and 99% levels to minimize the effect of extreme outliers from our analysis, which is a common practice in the microfinance research.

Table 1. Definition of variables.

Variable	Short Form	Definition
Female borrower	FEMBOT	Total number of female borrowers
Active borrower	ACTBORR	Total number of active borrowers
Revenue	REV	Includes all financial income and other operating revenue which is generated from non-financial services. Operating income also includes net gains (losses) from holding financial assets (changes in their values during the period and foreign exchange differences). Donations or any revenue that unrelated to a financial institution's core business of providing loans and financial services is not considered under this category
Operating expense	OPTEXP	Includes expenses not related to financial and credit loss impairment, such as personnel expenses, depreciation, amortization, and administrative expenses
Cost per loan	CPL	Operating expense/average number of loans outstanding
Cost per borrower	CPB	Operating expense/average number of active borrowers
Portfolio at risk (>30 days)	PAR30	Outstanding balance, portfolio overdue >30 days + renegotiated portfolio/gross loan portfolio
Portfolio at risk (>90 days)	PAR90	Outstanding balance, portfolio overdue > 90 days + renegotiated portfolio/gross loan portfolio
Profit margin	PM	Net operating income/financial revenue
Operational self-sufficiency	OSS	Financial revenue/(financial expense + net impairment loss + operating expense)
Debt-to-equity ratio	DTE	Total liabilities/total equity
Paid in capital	PAIDCAP	Capital paid by shareholders or members at the par value of the shares
Donated equity	DONE	Accumulated donations to a financial institution. Financial institutions use different methods for calculating donated equity. For most, donated equity includes all donations, regardless of their use. For others, donated equity includes only in-kind donations and donations for financing the gross loan portfolio or fixed assets. All donations for operating and non-operating expenses are included in retained earnings. Financial institutions should indicate what donations are included in donated equity and are encouraged to break out donations restricted to a specific use from those which are unrestricted as revenue

(Continued)

Table 1. (*Continued*)

Variable	Short Form	Definition
Retained earnings	RE	The total value of net income from current and prior years, net of any dividends, or transfers to other equity accounts

Source: Authors' compilation from the World Bank field definition.

Table 2. Descriptive statistics.

Variable	Obs.	Mean	Std. Dev.	Min.	Max.
ACTBORR	18,185	53794.79	160048.30	42.00	1214344.00
FEMBOT	14,607	40425.75	127866.00	8.00	987978.00
AVGLOANBAL	17,897	1366.03	2498.48	24.00	16983.00
OSS	17,605	1.14	0.40	0.13	2.87
REV	17,650	10700000.00	30900000.00	2688.00	216000000.00
OPTEXP	17,657	5338560.00	14300000.00	2645.00	99500000.00
PAR30	14,967	0.07	0.10	0.00	0.66
PAR90	12,732	0.05	0.08	0.00	0.55
PM	17,347	−0.04	0.70	−4.69	0.66
ROA	15,060	0.01	0.10	−0.52	0.22
ROE	15,012	0.05	0.46	−2.58	1.63
CPL	10,627	220.32	305.87	6.00	2043.00
CPB	14,073	223.16	336.62	4.00	2310.00
DTE	18,119	4.54	8.41	−14.11	61.82
PAIDCAP	13,788	5564162.00	14800000.00	0.00	99400000.00
DONE	11,423	757536.00	2239257.00	0.00	15200000.00
RE	14,444	2881103.00	10100000.00	−11200000.00	73400000.00
OE	10,398	3864946.00	12800000.00	−298162.00	97500000.00
BANK	19,928	0.11	–	0.00	1.00
CU/C	19,928	0.16	–	0.00	1.00
NBFI	19,928	0.34	–	0.00	1.00
NGO	19,928	0.32	–	0.00	1.00
RB	19,928	0.04	–	0.00	1.00

Source: Authors' compilation based on the World Bank data. Since there are no actual variations related to dummy variables, their standard deviation (Std. Dev.) are not reported here.

3. Results and Discussion

This section discusses the results of trend/graphical analyses depicting the effect of the GFC on the twin objectives of MFIs and tries to understand the impact of the ongoing COVID-19 crisis.

3.1. *Outreach aspects*

First, we examined how the GFC had affected the outreach objective of MFIs. Although many proxies can be used to capture the outreach goal of MFIs, we have resorted to outreach indicators, in line with the existing literature, such as the classical research of Schreiner (2002). Specifically, the provision of loans to borrowers (regardless of gender/entity) is viewed as the breadth of outreach, while loans targeted at the female clients are often considered as the depth of outreach of MFIs (Schreiner, 2002). In light of these two indicators, we drew Figure 1, which highlights that the MFIs' outreach in terms of the number of female borrowers and active members which grew slowly globally during and after the GFC (2007–2012) compared to the pre-GFC period.

One of the convincing reasons for the slower outreach of MFIs to female and active clients is the difficulty of MFI in raising capital from formal financial institutions (banks) during the crisis (Di Bella, 2011; Littlefield and Kneiding, 2009; Llanto and Badiola, 2009). Shortage of funds created the problem of liquidity (Di Bella, 2011;

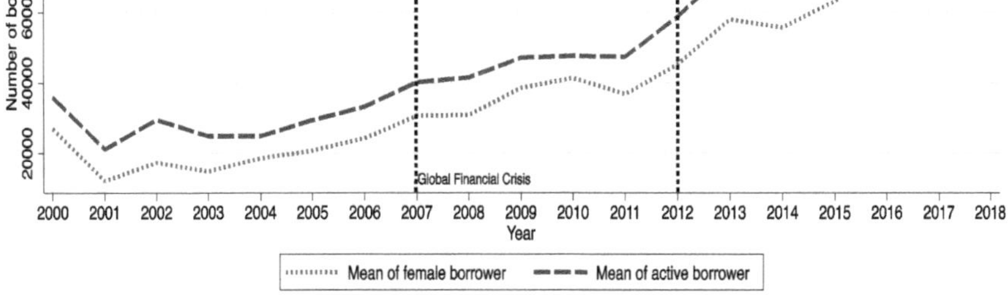

Figure 1. Trend of female and active borrowers in the global microfinance industry.

Source: Authors' compilation based on the World Bank data.

Littlefield and Kneiding, 2009), resulting in the inability of MFIs to disburse new loans to the clients (Garg and Lewin, 2009; Llanto and Badiola, 2009). Among the MFIs, the small- and medium-sized MFIs face more liquidity problems than the larger MFIs (Reille *et al.*, 2009). Consequently, the MFIs resort to managing their scarce financial funds by changing lending strategies, including prioritizing repeat loans over new loans to the borrowers (Littlefield and Kneiding, 2009). Repeat loans are believed to enhance the loan portfolio quality and are also considered a regular income for the MFIs (Di Bella, 2011). Although the adopted strategy enhanced the sustainability of MFIs during financial crises, it resulted in lower outreach, particularly the depth aspect. In a similar fashion, it is expected that COVID-19 will harm the outreach of MFIs. The lower outreach of MFIs can result from liquidity problems or the social restrictions imposed by the government to curb the spread of COVID-19. Since the operation of MFIs, including loan disbursement, primarily involves physical contact between the borrowers and the loan officers, their outreach will be adversely affected by the social restriction order.

Another depth of outreach measure, the average loan balance per borrower, also showed a slower growth from the onset of the GFC in 2007 subsequent to its rapid increase after 2009 (Figure 2). The trend reflects that the MFIs' average loan balance per borrower grew relatively lower during the GFC period than in the pre-GFC period.

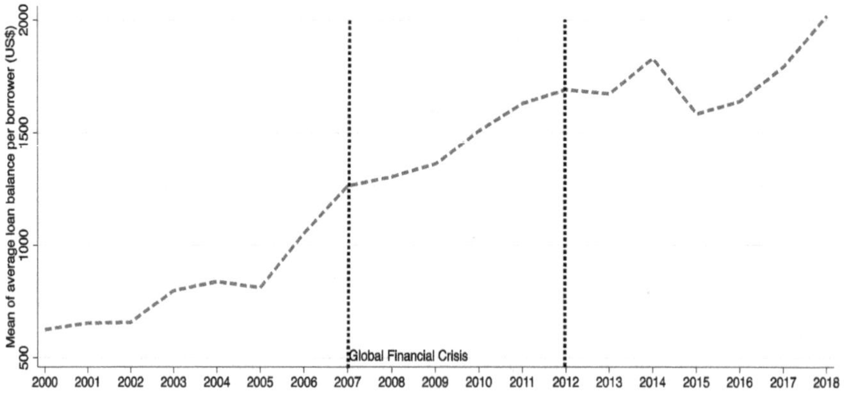

Figure 2. Trend of average loan balance per borrower.
Source: Authors' compilation based on the World Bank data.

As mentioned earlier, MFIs faced a liquidity crisis during the GFC. As a result, they had to slash their average loans per borrower to manage their existing client base with the limited financial capital. However, after the financial crisis, when the economies showed signs of recovery and the formal financial institutions regained their confidence, MFIs availed funds from lenders, resulting in the growth of the average loan balance per borrower after 2009. Ideating similar conditions, it is envisaged that during the COVID-19, MFIs will prefer to reduce their average loan size due to lower funding availability. However, as the economy begins to rebound, there will be increased flow of funds to the microfinance industry, thus raising their average loans per borrower.

3.2. *Financial and cost aspects*

This study has considered different parameters, namely, MFIs' revenues, operating expenses, portfolio at risk, profit margin, return on assets, return on equity, cost per loan, cost per borrower, and operational self-efficiency to capture the effect of the GFC on the financial sustainability of MFIs.

The trend analysis showed that despite the GFC, the MFIs' revenue and cost continued to grow until 2009, followed by a slight decline in 2010 (Figure 3). Overall, the operating expenses are

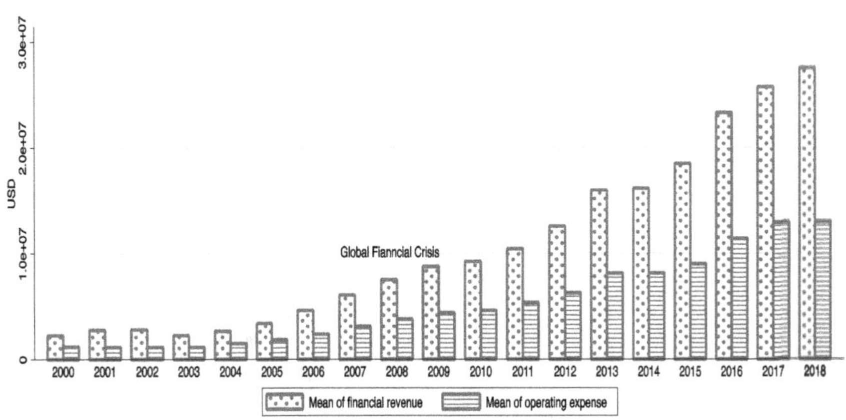

Figure 3. Trend of revenue and expense in the global microfinance industry.
Source: Authors' compilation based on the World Bank data.

comparatively higher (slightly) during the financial crisis than afterward. This may be attributed to higher staff costs and higher costs per loan and borrower during the crisis period (Di Bella, 2011). As mentioned earlier, MFIs' outreach had decreased due to lack of new funding, and the existing funds had been limited to the existing borrowers. Therefore, it is most likely that the MFIs were unable to spread their operating expenses like office rental over a limited number of borrowers. Nevertheless, the scenario changed after the financial crisis, with the proportion of operating expenses to revenues declining.

The higher trend of PAR 30 and PAR 90 indicates that the portfolio loan quality of the MFIs dropped during the GFC (Figure 4). There is an increase in loan delinquency among borrowers during financial crises, which can be attributed to the unfavorable effect of macroeconomic conditions (Di Bella, 2011; Magnoni and Powers, 2009). The adverse macroeconomic conditions due to the GFC resulted in lower confidence of financial institutions in disbursing funds into the market, lower financial investments, and higher unemployment (Llanto and Badiola, 2009). As many borrowers lost their means of livelihood, they struggled to make periodic repayments (Sangwan *et al.*, 2021). On the other hand, MFIs might have had to increase the interest rates due to liquidity shortages (Di Bella,

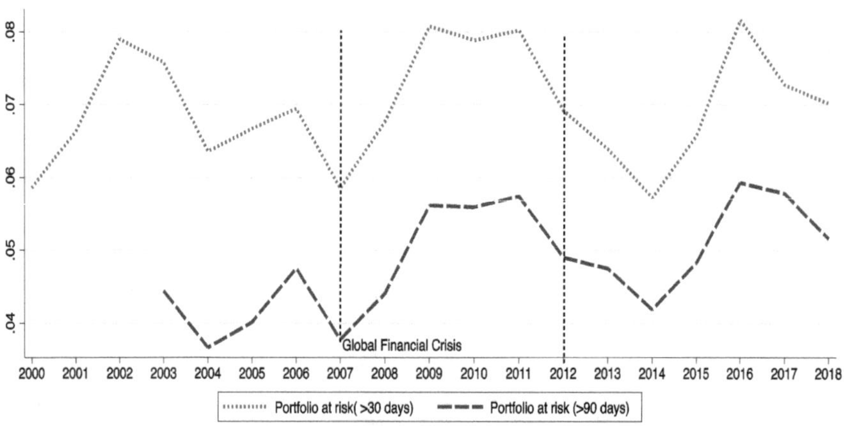

Figure 4. Trend of portfolio at risk (PAR30 and PAR90) in the global microfinance industry.
Source: Authors' compilation based on the World Bank data.

2011). Consequently, the higher cost of borrowing puts the clients on a high-debt burden, leading to their loan delinquency (Sangwan *et al.*, 2020).

During the COVID-19 pandemic, an increase in loan delinquency among the borrowers is expected due to minimal market activities and movement restrictions, all of which disrupted their engagement in economic activities (Sangwan *et al.*, 2021). Moreover, there is a challenge on the part of the loan officers to monitor and supervise the clients during the pandemic. The MFIs' inability to reach and disburse loans to the clients may cause non-availability of financial support to the poor. The limitation of funds and the non-engagement in any economic activity during the pandemic can sink the poor and informal sector workers into a poverty trap (Llanto and Badiola, 2009). Furthermore, the deteriorating portfolio quality may aggravate the problem of moral hazard among the borrowers, threaten MFIs' financial solvency, or prompt MFIs to follow unjustified coercive measures toward ensuring better repayments (CGAP, 2010).

Up until 2007, the overall negative profit margin (average) was approaching 0 (Figure 5). Looking at Figure 5, the negative profit margin was expected to become positive by 2008–2009 but dragged till 2011. The global profit margin only turns positive from the year 2012. The negative profit margin for MFIs can be attributed to the high funding cost, high operating cost (cost per loan and cost per borrower), and low repayment rates (Di Bella, 2011; Llanto and

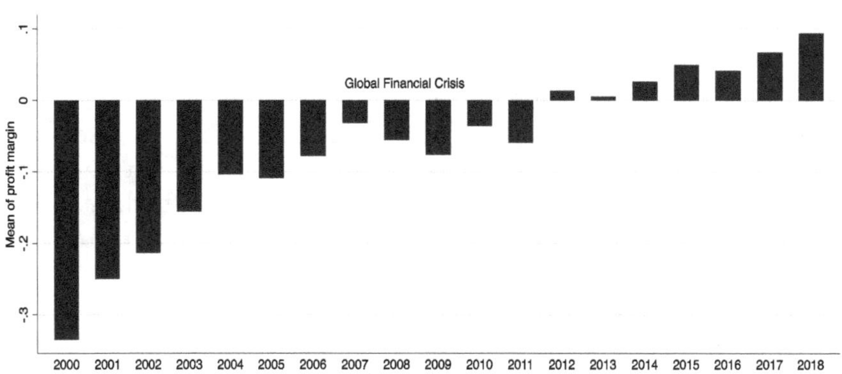

Figure 5. Trend of profit margin in the global microfinance industry.
Source: Authors' compilation based on the World Bank data.

Badiola, 2009). We have observed that during the GFC, the operating expenses incurred by MFIs were relatively higher compared to the non-GFC period. During the crisis, financial institutions held back on their funds to MFIs possibly due to poor investment security in the microfinance market (Littlefield and Kneiding, 2009). Also, the MFIs' portfolio quality deteriorated during the crisis, reducing the confidence of banks/financial institutions in providing funds to the microfinance industry (Magnoni and Powers, 2009). Due to these inherent risks, borrowing from banks/financial institutions at higher interest rates resulted in higher financial costs, thus reducing the interest spread of MFIs (Di Bella, 2011; Llanto and Badiola, 2009). However, if MFIs intend to transfer the financing cost to clients, it may result in a high-debt burden on borrowers and ultimately their low repayments (Sangwan *et al.*, 2021). In the post-GFC period, there is a reduction in MFIs' financing cost and the cost of borrowing to clients, leading to improvements in the repayments of clients. Again, the MFIs' profit margin showed a positive trend after the GFC. The COVID-19 pandemic may also influence the profit margin of MFIs in a similar way as the GFC.

The trend analysis of the financial performance of the MFIs measured in terms of return on equity (ROE) and return on assets (ROA) shows that the financial crisis negatively affected the investors in the microfinance sector, as indicated in the significant drop in ROE during the GFC (Figure 6). The decline may be caused by the low-profit margin in financial services offered by MFIs during and after the GFC (Magnoni and Powers, 2009). The income of MFIs is reduced during the crisis owing to limited outreach, high non-performing assets in loans, and high operating costs (Di Bella, 2011; Llanto and Badiola, 2009). Furthermore, the financial cost of obtaining the funds was also higher during the crisis, thus contracting the debt component, an economical source of funds for MFIs' capital structure (Reille *et al.*, 2009). Ultimately, the credit crunch due to restricted funding access results in the reduced net income of MFIs. The crisis seems to have less effect on ROA than the ROE. A similar scenario may be observed during COVID-19, as MFIs are unable to reach out to clients due to social restrictions and are also devoid of access to funds from formal financial institutions to expand their businesses.

Figure 7 shows that the cost per loan and cost per borrower have increased rapidly during the period of 2007–2008, subsequent to their

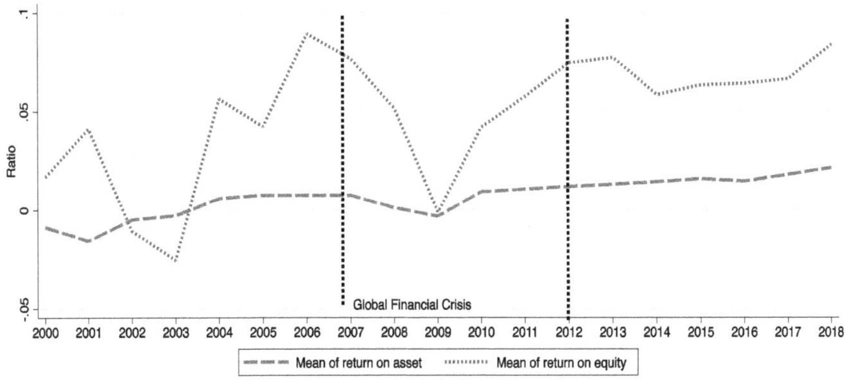

Figure 6. Trend on return on assets and return on equity.
Source: Authors' compilation based on the World Bank data.

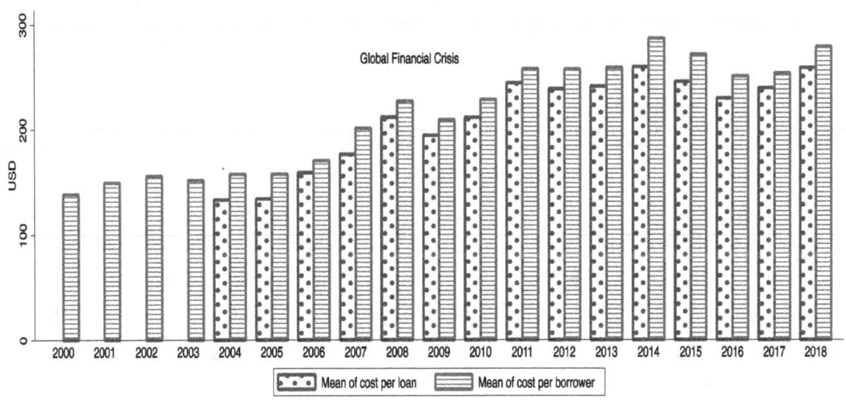

Figure 7. Trend of cost per loan and borrower in the global microfinance industry.
Source: Authors' compilation based on the World Bank data.

slight decline in 2009. The prime contributor to the rise of the cost per loan or cost per borrower is the high operating cost incurred by MFIs during the initial years of the crisis. The high operating cost is related to the administrative expenses, fixed rental, employees' salaries, and loan officers' traveling costs for periodical visits. As there were fewer additions of new loans and borrowers, the operating cost for the MFIs kept increasing (Di Bella, 2011). Furthermore, the rise in non-performing assets also increased the operating expenses for MFIs. During the COVID-19 pandemic, the higher cost per loan

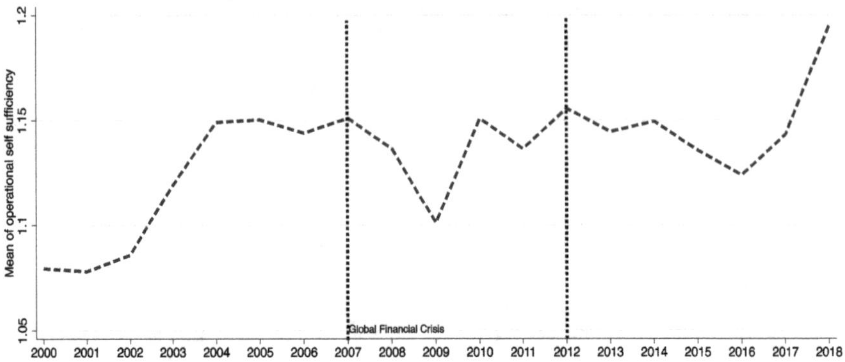

Figure 8. Trend of operational self-sufficiency.
Source: Authors' compilation based on the World Bank data.

and borrower was expected to significantly impact the operation of MFIs. While MFIs might have had to reduce their scale of operation to minimize the costs, it may have resulted in them laying off their staff, consequently damaging the staff–organization relationship (Sangwan *et al.*, 2021). Ultimately, this will lead to rising operational inefficiencies in delivering microfinance services to the poor.

The trend line for MFIs' operational self-sufficiency (OSS) started to decline at the beginning of the GFC, reaching the lowest during the year 2008–2009 (Figure 8), which is the peak of the economic slowdown across the world. This can be attributed to the MFIs' high operating costs, lack of liquidity, low deposits, and limited operational activities (Magnoni and Powers, 2009). However, MFIs seemed to bounce back shortly after the dip (in OSS) in 2009. A similar outcome on OSS is also expected due to COVID-19. Thus, MFIs are advised to undertake proactive actions to reduce the burden of COVID-19 on OSS.

3.3. *Capital structure aspects*

The debt-to-equity graph shows a downward trend, indicating that the MFIs' capital structure largely comprised equity during the GFC period (Figure 9). The debt proportion was reduced because the financial crisis lowered the confidence of financial institutions to disburse funds into the market (Littlefield and Kneiding, 2009; Llanto and Badiola, 2009). The MFIs' mode of operations includes

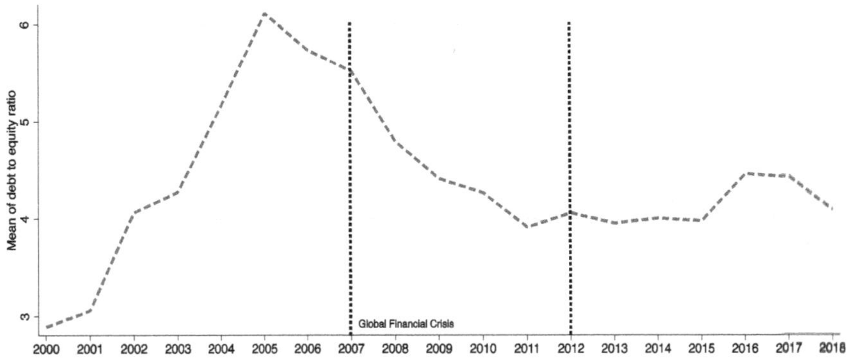

Figure 9. Trend on debt-to-equity ratio.
Source: Authors' compilation based on the World Bank data.

uncollateralized loans to low-income households and suffers from increasing loan delinquency among the borrowers (Di Bella, 2011; Magnoni and Powers, 2009). This affected MFIs' ability to acquire funds from the formal financial institutions, thereby hindering their liquidity position and ultimately their operational efficiencies (Littlefield and Kneiding, 2009). The lower operational activities and subsequent lower income generation had a cascading effect on the MFIs, as they were unable to produce good cash flow statements, which lowered their chances of getting adequate funding support from various lenders (Llanto and Badiola, 2009). Equally, during COVID-19, MFIs may have faced difficulties in raising funds from formal financial institutions. However, big MFIs, equipped with sufficient reserve, can sustain the borrowers' loan delinquency and continue their operation by generating funds from various lenders.

Analyses of MFIs' source of equity indicate that the MFIs' operations were primarily funded using their retained earnings during the GFC (Figure 10), while other types of equities such as donated equity (predominantly from investors) have dried up. The striking decline in the equity contribution during the GFC could be attributed to the donors' poor financial condition mediated by the GFC (Littlefield and Kneiding, 2009; Llanto and Badiola, 2009). In the post-GFC period, the equity graph reflects a return of confidence among the investors, with the proportion of common equity, donation, and other equities increasing relative to the retained earnings. With respect to COVID-19, it can be predicted that MFIs with robust retained

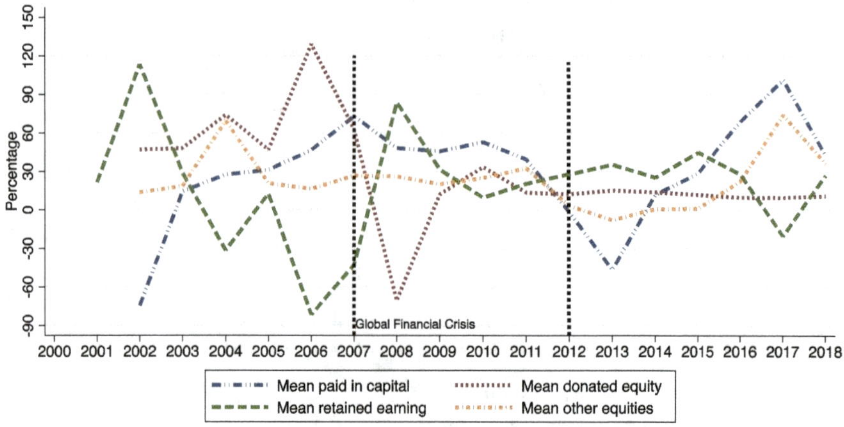

Figure 10. Trend on sources of equities.

Source: Authors' compilation based on the World Bank data.

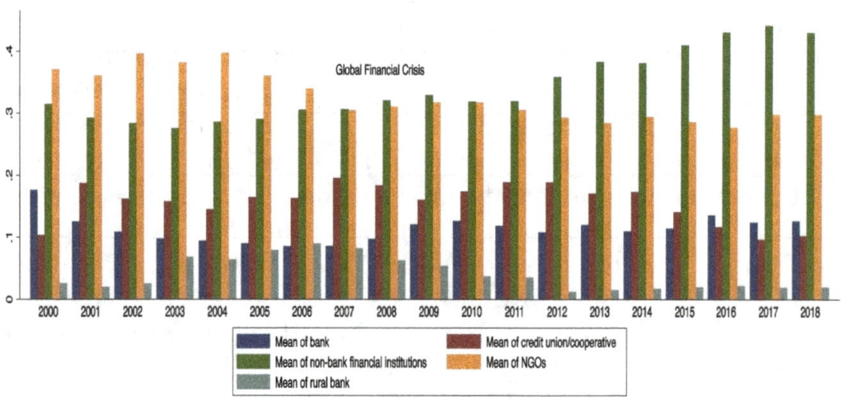

Figure 11. Trend of legal status of MFIs.

Source: Authors' compilation based on the World Bank data.

earnings are less likely to struggle to run their operations even if the sources of equities (common shareholders and donors) become depleted.

3.4. *Legal status*

As per Figure 11, NGOs dominated the worldwide microfinance market until 2006. The growing number of NBFIs in the market coupled with the falling number of NGOs may indicate that the latter has been transitioning into the former since 2007. As previously noted, NGOs frequently convert to shareholder-based financial institutions (e.g., banks and NBFIs) to access local and international capital, mobilize savings, and ensure long-term organizational viability (D'Espallier *et al.*, 2017). Most importantly, the decline in the number of NGOs may be due to diminishing donations/subsidies during the start of the GFC in 2007, causing them to either alter their legal status or quit the market to ensure sufficient liquidity in the aftermath of the GFC. Although some NGOs may have succeeded in restructuring, reorienting, and changing their operations, many have been forced to quit the market owing to poor financial performance and a lack of liquidity to continue operations. As a result, since 2007, NBFIs have dominated the worldwide microfinance market, while the number of rural banks has been declining. Also, the presence of commercial banks was observed to increase after the GFC, while credit unions and cooperatives observed a modest drop only from 2007 to 2009.

Overall, it can be argued that the GFC played a crucial role in reorganizing the overall legal status of the global microfinance industry. A similar effect is expected in aftermath of COVID-19, as small-sized MFIs like NGO–MFI may transform into NBFIs or other types of legal status to enhance their chance of survival through better access to funds from formal institutions. This means that legal entities that face more liquidity issues due to COVID-19 are highly susceptible to organizational transformation, including transformation to other legal entities, such as credit unions/cooperatives or NBFIs. However, such transformations will also depend largely on the legal environment of the country where the MFIs are currently located.

4. Conclusion and Recommendations

Considering the severity of COVID-19 on the global economy and businesses, we have tried to understand the consequences of such a crisis on the global microfinance industry. As institutional data on the actual impact of COVID-19 on the microfinance sector are unavailable, we have envisioned its effect through the lens of the GFC. Our findings revealed that COVID-19 is expected to take its toll on the financial and outreach goals of MFIs, as indicated in the severe impact of the GFC on some of the proxies used in this paper.

Based on the outcome of the GFC, it is anticipated that COVID-19 will primarily cause liquidity problems for the MFIs from both the supply (lenders and financial institutions) and the demand sides (borrowers). Due to the social restrictions imposed by the governments to curb the spread of COVID-19, market operations were limited, resulting in lower engagement of borrowers in income-generating activities. From past experiences, it has been observed that the chances of misappropriation of funds are very high, with a greater proportion of the credit being expended on basic consumptions (food, medicines, or other contingent liabilities) rather than income generation. Such loan utilization behavior affects borrowers' ability to make periodic repayments. Meanwhile, the lenders have also become skeptical toward the microfinance market and imposed more stringent lending conditions due to their envisaged repayment problem of MFIs.

Also, equity investors and donors have shown reluctance in continuously providing financial support to MFIs, thus hampering the financial and social performance of MFIs. For MFIs to maintain liquidity/financial sustainability during COVID-19, they ought to change their lending strategies, as indicated in the GFC experience. The MFIs should stay focused and prioritize the existing customers rather than reaching out to new prospective borrowers. This will help MFIs remain connected and updated on their clients' risk levels, losses, and physical migration. Accordingly, MFIs can develop policies related to refinancing and restructuring the collections from these clients.

In the absence of actual data from the global microfinance industry in reference to the pandemic period (2020–2022), we have attempted to uncover the effect of COVID-19 on MFIs from the standpoint of the GFC. However, the true effect of the pandemic could be more severe than that of the GFC. As per our understanding of the database (World Bank), when organizational data of MFIs for recent years are available, the real impact of COVID-19 on the global microfinance industry can be examined and compared with that of the GFC.

Funding

The corresponding author acknowledges the short-term research grant from Universiti Sains Malaysia, Penang, Malaysia [Grant No: 304/PMGT/6315547].

Declaration/Conflicts of Interest

The authors declare no conflicts of interest related to this study.

Data Availability Statement

The data used in this study can be freely accessed from the following source: https://datacatalog.worldbank.org/search/dataset/0038647.

Appendix

Table A1. Firm-year observations.

Year	Freq.	Percent	Cum.
2000	231	1.16	1.16
2001	351	1.76	2.92
2002	543	2.72	5.65
2003	817	4.1	9.75
2004	997	5	14.75
2005	1,201	6.03	20.77
2006	1,286	6.45	27.23
2007	1,419	7.12	34.35
2008	1,463	7.34	41.69
2009	1,538	7.72	49.41
2010	1,574	7.9	57.31
2011	1,594	8	65.31
2012	1,304	6.54	71.85
2013	1,041	5.22	77.07
2014	1,112	5.58	82.65
2015	1,053	5.28	87.94
2016	822	4.12	92.06
2017	829	4.16	96.22
2018	753	3.78	100
Total	19,928	100	

References

Aktar, M. A., Alam, M. M. and Al-Amin, A. Q. (2021). Global economic crisis, energy use, CO_2 emissions, and policy roadmap amid COVID-19. *Sustainable Production and Consumption*, *26*, 770–781.

Borio, C. (2020). The Covid-19 economic crisis: Dangerously unique. *Business Economics*, *55*(4), 181–190.

Brickell, K., Picchioni, F., Natarajan, N., Guermond, V., Parsons, L., Zanello, G. and Bateman, M. (2020). Compounding crises of social reproduction: Microfinance, over-indebtedness and the COVID-19 pandemic. *World Development*, *136*, 105087.

CGAP (2010). Andhra Pradesh 2010: Global implications of the crisis in Indian microfinance. *CGAP* (November), *144*. Available at: https://www.cgap.org/sites/default/files/CGAP-Focus-Note-Andhra-Pradesh-2010-Global-Implications-of-the-Crisis-in-Indian-Microfinance-Nov-2010.pdf.

Elnahass, M., Trinh, V. Q. and Li, T. (2021). Global banking stability in the shadow of Covid-19 outbreak. *Journal of International Financial Markets, Institutions and Money*, *72*, 101322.

D'Espallier, B., Goedecke, J., Hudon, M. and Mersland, R. (2017). From NGOs to banks: Does institutional transformation alter the business model of microfinance institutions? *World Development*, *89*, 19–33.

Díaz-Martín, S., Feria-Dominguez, J. M. and Naranjo-Gil, D. (2022). Are microfinance institutions' financial performance gender driven? Evidence from Argentina. *Business Strategy & Development*, *5*(3), 197–208. doi: https://doi.org/10.1002/bsd2.190.

Di Bella, C. G. (2011). The impact of the global financial crisis on microfinance and policy implications. *Working Paper* (*WP/11/175*). International Monetary Fund. Available at: https://www.imf.org/external/pubs/ft/wp/2011/wp11175.pdf.

Garg, A. and Lewin, D. (2009). The global financial crisis and Indian microfinance. *Micro Save, India Focus Note 23*. Available at, http://www.microsave.net/files/pdf/IFN_23_Global_Financial_Crisis_and_Indian_Microfinance.pdf.

Li, T., Trinh, V. Q. and Elnahass, M. (2023). Drivers of global banking stability in times of crisis: The role of corporate social responsibility. *British Journal of Management*, *34*(2), 595–622. doi: https://doi.org/10.1111/1467-8551.12631.

Littlefield, E. L. and Kneiding, C. (2009). The global financial crisis and its impact on microfinance (No. 47954, pp. 1–8). The World Bank. Available at: https://www.cgap.org/research/publication/global-financial-crisis-and-its-impact-microfinance.

Llanto, G. M. and Badiola, J. A. R. (2009). The impact of the global financial crisis on rural and microfinance in Asia (No. 2009-24). PIDS Discussion Paper Series. Available at: http://citeseerx.ist.psu.edu/viewdoc/download?doi=10.1.1.615.6460&rep=rep1&type=pdf.

Magnoni, B. and Powers, J. (2009). Will the bottom of the pyramid hit bottom? The effects of the global credit crisis on the microfinance sector. Micro Report, 150. Available at, https://www.findevgateway.org/paper/2009/03/will-bottom-pyramid-hit-bottom-effects-global-credit-crisis-microfinance-sector.

Malik, K., Meki, M., Morduch, J., Ogden, T., Quinn, S. and Said, F. (2020). COVID-19 and the future of microfinance: Evidence and insights from Pakistan. *Oxford Review of Economic Policy, 36*(Supplement_1), S138–S168.

Murshid, N. S. and Murshid, N. (2021). "Innovations" during COVID-19: Microfinance in Bangladesh. *Affiliate*, 08861099211054024.

Ozili, P. K. (2021). COVID-19 pandemic and economic crisis: The Nigerian experience and structural causes. *Journal of Economic and Administrative Sciences*, *37*(4), 401–418.

Parker, G. (2008). Crisis and catastrophe: The global crisis of the seventeenth century reconsidered. *The American Historical Review*, *113*(4), 1053–1079.

Parker, G. (2017). *Global Crisis*. New Haven, CT: Yale University Press.

Phillips, N. (2021). The coronavirus is here to say here's what that means. *Nature*, *590*(7846), 382–384.

Reille, X., Kneiding, C. and Martinez, M. (2009). The impact of the financial crisis on microfinance institutions and their clients-results from CGAP's 2009 opinion survey. CGAP Brief. May. Available at: https://www.cgap.org/sites/default/files/CGAP-Brief-The-Impact-of-the-Financial-Crisis-on-Microfinance-Institutions-and-Their-Clients-May-2009.pdf.

Robinson, W. I. (2004). Global crisis and Latin America. *Bulletin of Latin American Research*, *23*(2), 135–153.

Roy, S. and Kemme, D. M. (2020). The run-up to the global financial crisis: A longer historical view of financial liberalization, capital inflows, and asset bubbles. *International Review of Financial Analysis*, *69*, 101377.

Sangwan, S., Nayak, N. C. and Samanta, D. (2020). Loan repayment behavior among the clients of Indian microfinance institutions: A household-level investigation. *Journal of Human Behavior in the Social Environment*, *30*(4), 474–497.

Sangwan, S., Nayak, N. C., Sangwan, V. and Pradhan, A. K. (2021). Covid-19 pandemic: Challenges and ways forward for the Indian microfinance institutions. *Journal of Public Affairs*, *21*(4), e2667.

Schreiner, M. (2002). Aspects of outreach: A framework for discussion of the social benefits of microfinance. *Journal of International Development*, *14*(5), 591–603.

Skegg, D., Gluckman, P., Boulton, G., Hackmann, H., Karim, S. S. A., Piot, P. and Woopen, C. (2021). Future scenarios for the COVID-19 pandemic. *The Lancet*, *397*(10276), 777–778.

Trinh, V. Q., Cao, N. D. and Elnahass, M. (2022). Financial stability: a 'vaccine' for tail risk of the global banking sector in the shadow of the pandemic. *The European Journal of Finance*, *29*(7), 726–753.

van Barneveld, K., Quinlan, M., Kriesler, P., Junor, A., Baum, F., Chowdhury, A., Junankar, P. R., Clibborn, S., Flanagan, F., Wright, C. F. and Friel, S. (2020). The COVID-19 pandemic: Lessons on building more equal and sustainable societies. *The Economic and Labour Relations Review*, *31*(2), 133–157.

Zheng, C. and Zhang, J. (2021). The impact of COVID-19 on the efficiency of microfinance institutions. *International Review of Economics & Finance*, *71*, 407–423.

https://doi.org/10.1142/9781800614321_0015

Chapter 15

Liquidity Hoarding and Uncertainty for a Small Open Economy

Abdulla Ahmed Albinali
Hamad Bin Khalifa University,
College of Islamic Studies, Doha, Qatar
aalbinali@hbku.edu.qa

Abstract

Using quarterly data on the banking sector covering the period 2002–2020, this chapter assesses the impact of uncertainty on banks' liquidity hoarding in Qatar. To implement this empirically, we utilize the country-specific uncertainty measure and integrate it with a novel measure of bank-specific liquidity hoarding developed in recent research. The findings reveal that banks respond to economic uncertainty by increasing liquidity hoarding, especially on the asset side of their balance sheet, and there is a differential impact for Islamic banks, that too primarily on their asset side. Robustness tests validate these findings.

Keywords: Liquidity hoarding, banking, Islamic, economic policy uncertainty, panel data

1. Introduction

Liquidity creation is integral to banking. Along with risk transformation, modern-day financial intermediation posits this as one of the key functions performed by a bank. In particular, the liquidity creation theory contends that banks create liquidity on the balance sheet by utilizing liquid liabilities to finance illiquid assets. Compared to this, by holding illiquid liabilities (e.g., long-term borrowings) and investing in liquid assets (e.g., cash and tradeable securities), banks destroy liquidity. The interplay of these opposing forces provides a comprehensive assessment of liquidity created by banks (Berger and Bouwman, 2009).

One aspect which has remained virtually unaddressed in the literature is the behavior of banks' liquidity during periods of uncertainty (Berger *et al.*, 2022). This leads to challenges from both the supply and demand sides. Regarding the former, potential default risks, including adverse selection considerations, make banks reluctant to extend credit, and higher liquid asset holding could also be a response to higher expected loan loss provisions or even a decline in the values of other assets owing to higher economic uncertainties. Interbank activity could also get reduced in the face of economic uncertainties, as banks extend less interbank loans during periods of uncertainty.

On the liability side, banks might be inclined to rebalance the composition of their deposits in response to higher levels of economic uncertainty. In particular, they might be inclined to increase their holding of liquid or short-term liabilities so as to increase their liability-side liquidity at the expense of more long-term liabilities. Alternatively, they might raise higher interbank liabilities at the shorter end to cover for potential liquidity risks. While it is possible that higher uncertainties could impel banks to fund their liquid assets through illiquid liabilities, such possibilities are more likely to be implemented by encashing liquid liabilities such as short-term deposits as compared with stickier assets, such as bonds. The overall impact of these factors could be manifest in liquidity hoarding by banks, either on the asset or on the liability sides. As Berger *et al.* (2022) remark, liquidity hoarding[1] is a complement of liquidity creation: it shows how much liquidity is held by the banks, unlike liquidity creation which is the liquidity that is supplied to the market.

[1]Liquidity hoarding refers to an increase in liquidity held by the banks during the periods of crisis.

In this paper, I address four inter-related issues pertaining to liquidity hoarding. First, what does the evidence suggest regarding liquidity hoarding by banks during uncertainty? Second, does liquidity hoarding differ across banking groups? In particular, do Islamic banks hoard liquidity during uncertainty? Third, does such liquidity hoarding occur on the asset side or on the liability side (or both) of banks' balance sheets? And finally, are these findings robust to the instrumental variable approach? We view this as one of the early studies in the Gulf Cooperation Council (GCC) context to examine the banks' liquidity hoarding and its interplay with uncertainty.

These are relevant questions from the standpoint of Qatar for several reasons. First and more generally, the country is a small open economy with an overwhelming dominance of banks: bank asset accounts for over 200 percent of GDP. Second, the country has been buffeted by a series of shocks over the past two decades, some generalized and others more specific to the country. Starting with the global financial crisis of 2008, there were the declines in oil prices during 2014–2015 and subsequently the economic blockade by several neighboring countries in 2017, culminating finally in the COVID-19 pandemic of 2019–2020. In response to these shocks, Qatari banks could have resorted to liquidity hoardings, which is an important channel through which uncertainty may have affected the Qatari economy. Third, the country also has a significant presence of Islamic banks, accounting for around a quarter of financial system assets. It will be interesting to document whether the Islamic banks also resort to liquidity hoarding measures when facing uncertainty. And finally, there is no systematic study available for Qatar which looks at the impact of uncertainty on the banking sector in Qatar and also Islamic banks more specifically, necessitating the need for careful empirical analysis.

Our analysis employs quarterly data on banks' balance sheets covering the period 2002–2020, the most comprehensive time frame for which information on the relevant variables is available. The descriptive statistics reveal that the Qatari banks hoard liquidity during periods of crises, although there is wide dispersion across banks across the liquidity hoarding measures. More specifically, the average level of liquidity hoarding for Islamic banks is 9.7%, which is 4 percentage points lower as compared with their conventional counterparts, suggesting that the former are much more conservative when it comes to managing liquidity. Relatedly, both their asset-side liquidity hoarding (average value of 2.4%) and liability-side liquidity hoarding (average value of 13.4%) are uniformly lower as compared with their conventional counterparts, whose average values are 6% and 16.2% for these ratios, respectively. The empirical analysis which onboards several bank-level controls also suggests that banks in Qatar increase their liquidity hoarding in the face of economic uncertainties, especially on the asset side of their balance sheet. There is also a differential impact on liquidity hoarding for Islamic banks. The evidence concurs with prior research which clearly highlighted that banks hoard liquidity in response to economic uncertainties, both in the US (Berger *et al.*, 2022) and elsewhere (Heider *et al.*, 2015). Earlier, Berrospide (2013) provided evidence in favor of hoarding of liquid assets by U.S. commercial banks during the global financial crisis of 2008.

The findings therefore suggest that policy actions by the government to reduce or eliminate uncertainty can exert positive real effects. In particular, by encouraging banks to extend credit, it can unclog the lending channel and influence economic growth, and the evidence also indicates that it is important to devise policy measures to unlock the flow of credit by Islamic banks since it is this category that is typically prone to hoarding liquidity in response to economic uncertainty.

The remainder of the analysis unfolds as follows: In Section 2, we review the relevant literature and highlight the position of this paper in the field. The data and summary statistics are provided in Section 3. Section 4 provides the empirical strategy. Section 5 presents the results including robustness checks. The final section provides concluding remarks and presents some ideas on the way forward.

2. Extant Literature

The importance of liquidity risk came into prominence only very recently, around the time of the global financial crisis. The limited emphasis on liquidity risk can be gleaned from the fact that the initial Basel Accord had virtually no documentation regarding liquidity risk and possible ways to tackle it. Even banks were not unduly concerned about such risk. Reflecting this consideration, empirical studies regarded liquidity risk as an exogenous variable (Demirguc Kunt and Huizinga, 1999; Pasiouras and Kosmidou, 2007; Athanasoglou *et al.*, 2008; Naceur and Kandil, 2013) and were not concerned about its consequences. Over time, however, although there was a significant change in banks' funding strategy, the role of liquidity and its management remained virtually unaltered.

Since the outbreak of the financial crisis in 2008, liquidity become an integral part of the financial lexicon. Strahan (2008) and Brunnermeier (2009) noted that the asset-backed commercial paper market mostly collapsed while liquidity in the interbank market dried out. Though marginal improvements were observed in the short-term funding market in early 2008, supported by an aggressive policy response by central banks through the injection of enormous liquidity into the banking sector, the failure of Lehman Brothers and its consequent ramifications for wholesale funding markets engendered serious financial market disruptions since late 2008. The liquidity shock during this period which aggravated the global financial crisis also led to studies on the behavior of banks as regards risk-taking. Samet *et al.* (2018) examined whether the crisis has altered the incentives of banks to take more risk. Gorton (2009) and Lucas and Stokey (2011) observed that the financial crisis in 2007–2008 was akin to a run on banks by other financial institutions as against the conventional run on banks by depositors. The repurchase agreement (Repo) market where financial institutions lend short-term funds to other financial intuitions experienced stress when lending banks shied away from the markets by withdrawing their excess funds. Banks having surplus funds refused to roll over their loan agreements as well as increased their repo haircuts. Lown and Morgan (2006) and Berrospide and Edge (2010) provide evidence to suggest that banks tightened their lending standards in the event of an increase in vulnerabilities in funding markets. Sufi (2009) and Huang (2010) noted that financial institutions reduced the availability of credit lines when firms started breaking the financial contracts linked to their credit facilities. Elnahass *et al.* (2021) also examine the impact of various risk factors including illiquidity risk on country-level governance measures and find that illiquidity risk bears a significant and positive relationship with such measures.

In order to remain immune against an increase in vulnerabilities from liquidity drain and provide a forward-looking message to the markets on their solvency as well as to avoid bank runs, financial institutions started hoarding liquidity immediately after a severe liquidity crisis (Ramos, 1996). Consistent with this argument, Berrospide (2012) noted that, during the global financial crisis of 2008, the behavior of banks mostly followed the path they took during the crisis in 1930 by building sufficient liquidity buffers.

The loss-absorbing capacity of the banking sector during periods of vulnerabilities is well known, functioning as a major source for liquidity insurance (Barattieri *et al.*, 2020). There are a number of studies that explore this aspect in some detail. To cite some examples, Acharya and Steffen (2020), Álvarez-Botas *et al.* (2021), and Demirgüç Kunt *et al.* (2021) emphasize the risk-absorbing capacity of banks through liquidity insurance. Boubaker *et al.* (2022) report that the global banking sector needs to maintain and improve the sector's efficiency and productivity to support global economy to recover from long-lasting shocks like the COVID-19 pandemic. In that context, banks have to maintain an optimum level of liquidity to improve their efficiency and productivity. In another study, Boubaker *et al.* (2020) established that multibank holding companies are more efficient as compared to single-bank holding companies given the former takes advantage of the various resources including liquidity of the parent company. Elnahass *et al.* (2022) examined the liquidity risk in the context of terrorism challenges. The study finds that the risk of terrorism as measured by the Global Terrorism Index (GTI) is associated with low liquidity risk for banks, consistent with the fact that the high levels of government bailout helped outweigh the adverse consequences emanating from terrorist attacks.

Theoretical papers have extensively discussed the reasons behind banks holding a large quantum of liquid assets. The evidence in this case is quite compelling. Heider *et al.* (2015) provide evidence in favor of liquidity hoarding by Euro area banks. Ennis and Wolman (2011) observed that banks holding large excess reserves at the Federal Reserve since the outbreak of global financial crises had also increased their exposure to other liquid assets including short-term securities. Allen and Gale (2004) noted that one reason for hoarding liquidity by banks is due to their perception that they will not be able to source funds from the interbank market in case of temporary constraints in liquidity. Diamond and Rajan (2009) claimed that, in anticipation of future forced asset liquidation, banks tend to hoard liquidity. Gale and Yorulmazer (2011) modeled this precautionary hoarding of liquidity by banks. Using an interbank market model, Acharya and Skeie (2011) argued that because of an expectation of a roll-over risk due to counterparty insolvency, banks hoard liquidity. Elucidating on the macrofinancial narrative, Freixas, Martin, and Skeie (2011), Acharya and Merrouche (2013), and Heider, Hoerova, and Holthausen (2015) have argued that a dysfunctional interbank market can lead to hoarding liquid assets by banks.

Considering the impact on the real economy due to idiosyncratic bank shocks as documented by Gabaix (2011) and Amiti and Weinstein (2018), a major aspect recently studied by Helge and Matias (2021) is whether liquidity hoarding can emerge when interbank markets are well functioning with depth and liquidity while there are bank-specific funding constraints. Their study plugs the gap in the literature and establishes a link between liquidity hoarding and funding shocks in interbank markets, while there is no overall liquidity shortage in the funding markets. The study examines whether the bank-specific funding problems lead to cut down of credit to productive sectors to hold more liquid assets and cause any consequences to real economy.

Generating liquidity for supplying to the productive sectors of the economy is one of the core functions of the banking sector (Berger and Bouwman, 2009). In that context, liquidity hoarding can be considered as rescinding from such function (Caballero and Krishnamurthy, 2008). Agénor and Aynaoui (2010) argued that excess liquidity hoarding is negative to the monetary policy transmission mechanism as well as banks' portfolio returns. At times, excess liquidity hoarding increases systemic vulnerabilities through spillover effects as noted by Diamond and Rajan (2011) since stressed banks' behavior of liquidity hoarding and fire sale of assets may trigger other banks to do so.

Uncertainties may force banks to hoard liquidity in both on- and off-balance sheets through multiple routes. Elnahass *et al.* (2022) examined the liquidity risk in the context of risk of terrorism. The study shows the risk of terrorism measured through Global Terrorism Index (GTI) which is associated with low liquidity risk for banks. The rationale attached to lower liquidity risk was on account of considerable bailouts done by the governments to support the economies to weather the negative consequence from terrorist attacks. Banks may hoard liquidity as cash and securities in the on-balance sheet and/or through a higher derivative contract, which functions as a liquid asset in the off-balance sheet. Factoring uncertainty, Allen and Gale (2004) observed that banks tend to hoard more liquid assets as a precautionary approach to protect against future liquidity tightening. Bernanke (1983) viewed that increased uncertainty could hurt bank borrower's financials and therefore banks may reduce the credit provided to them and thereby store more liquidity. Bloom *et al.* (2013) noted that banks hoard liquidity through postponing prospective investments and spending for certain duration. On the other hand, on the liability side, banks may source more deposits since during uncertainty periods, depositors consider banks as the safest option as compared to other investments and spending. The existence of deposit insurance schemes also provided more confidence in the banking system for the depositors during the period of increased uncertainties (Gatev and Strahan, 2006). Thus, banks eventually procure more deposits to build up liquidity buffers during periods of amplified uncertainty.

Empirical studies on uncertainty and its impact on banks' liquidity are limited. Recently, Berger *et al.* (2020) and Ashraf (2020), examining the impact of uncertainty, documented that economic policy uncertainty leads to higher hoarding of liquidity by banks. Developing an indicator to measure bank liquidity hoarding for US banks, Berger *et al.* (2022) studied the link between economic policy uncertainty and liquidity hoarding. They observed that liquidity hoarding is strengthened for banks having low liquidity, which augmented peer bank spillover effects. Based on cross-national banking data, Ashraf (2020) established that the impact of economic policy uncertainty on hoarding of liquidity was more prominent in banks with higher expected loan losses. Others have studied the factors leading to liquidity creation by banks (Sahyouni and Wang, 2018; Chen *et al.*, 2018).

3. Data

Three types of data are collected for purposes of empirical analysis. The first is the bank-level balance sheet data. The second is published data reported by Qatar Central Bank in its monthly and quarterly publications. The third type includes the macroeconomic variables such as real GDP growth obtained from the Planning and Statistics Authority, the statistical agency in the country responsible for collating and reporting macroeconomic statistics.

Bank-level data: The key database is the bankwise balance sheet and profit and loss data statements obtained from the data dump at the Qatar Central Bank. Using this data dump, we carefully filter the data and apply validation checks — based on quarterly and half-yearly information provided by the respective banks to Qatar Central Bank — and build a longitudinal bank-level database on a quarterly basis. The data are comparable across banks because the central bank, as the regulator, requires banks to submit information on a regular basis for most of the broad heads of balance sheet and income–expenditure items. In addition, several banks became operative at different time points in the sample or alternately, there were several mergers during the period, which we suitably account for in the data. After this filtering and adjustments, we have data on a maximum of 17 banks, including 6 conventional banks, 4 Islamic banks, and the remaining foreign banks. The data begin in 2002:Q1 (the first quarter for which consistent data are available) and end in 2020:Q4. Given the high degree of outliers, we winsorize all bank-specific variables at 1% at both ends of the sample.

Other banking data: Using various quarterly and monthly publications from the QCB website, we extract information on other variables such as QCB Deposit and Lending Rates as well as the share of each bank in total banking asset, using which we compute a Herfindahl index of banking concentration. The concentration–fragility hypothesis states that greater concentration exerts a destabilizing effect because banks exploit their monopoly power in the loan market and create a moral hazard, raising overall borrower riskiness (Boyd and De Nicolo, 2005; De Hannan and Poghosyan, 2012). In contrast, the concentration–stability hypothesis contends that banks tend to be more prudent in terms of their approach toward risk-taking and as a result greater concentration exerts a salutary impact (Keeley, 1990; Berger and Bouwman, 2013).

Macroeconomic variables: Using the website of the Planning and Statistics Authority, the official statistical agency in the country, we extract information on macroeconomic variables, such as real GDP growth during the year.

Our key independent variable is the World Uncertainty Index for Qatar (WUIQ). The World Uncertainty Index is a new measure that tracks uncertainty across the globe by text mining the country reports of the Economist Intelligence Unit. The index is available for 143 countries including Qatar and it is computed by counting the percent of word "uncertain" (or its variant) in the Economist Intelligence Unit country reports (Ahir *et al.*, 2022).

Our measure of liquidity hoarding follows from Berger *et al.* (2022) who construct a comprehensive measure of liquidity hoarding for US banks, taking on board all major items on their balance sheet, including off-balance-sheet items. We compute this measure for Qatari banks and arrive at a measure of total liquidity hoarding (*LHTotal*), including those on the liability (*LHLiab*) and asset (*LHAsset*) sides, and we disaggregate the asset- and liability-side liquidity hoarding into its liquid and illiquid components and integrate it with uncertainty, after controlling for bank-specific and macroeconomic factors. A detailed description is provided in Table 1.

Table 2 provides a snapshot of the data on key variables. Asset-side liquidity hoarding (LH) (Asset/GTA) has a mean of 0.085, suggesting that banks hoard liquidity of 8.5% of gross total assets, on average. This hoarding appears to be provided by liability-side liquidity hoarding (average of 16.8%), although there is a decumulation with respect to off-balance-sheet (OBS) items, suggesting that there are more loan commitments. Reflecting this balance, overall liquidity hoarding is mildly negative, averaging (−)2.6% for the entire period. However, there is wide dispersion across banks for all the liquidity hoarding measures, which can be seen from the values at the 25th and 75th percentile.

Prior to the empirical framework, Table 3 shows the correlation matrix of the key variables. On average, uncertainty appears to be weakly correlated with off-balance-sheet items and relatedly, with total liquidity hoarding, although its correlation with asset- and liability-side items is not significant. The raw correlations do not control the business cycle or the economic environment. Therefore, we resort to an econometric framework to analyze the interlinkage in a systematic manner.

Table 1. Bank liquidity hoarding measures.

Asset		**Liabilities**		**Off-balance Sheet**	
Liquid (Weight = 0.5)	**Illiquid (Weight = −0.5)**	**Liquid (Weight = 0.5)**	**Illiquid (Weight = −0.5)**	**Liquid (Weight = 0.5)**	**Illiquid (Weight = −0.5)**
Cash in hand and balances with RBI	Debentures and bonds	Demand deposits	Subordinated debt	Forward exchange contracts	Guarantees
Money at call and short notice	Subsidiary and joint ventures	Savings and term deposits	Other liabilities		Acceptance, endorsements
All securities (regardless of maturity)	Others	Borrowings			Others (includes claims against bank not acknowledged as debt, liability for partly paid investment, bills rediscounted, and letters of credit)
	Loans				
	Fixed assets				
	Other assets				

Source: Author calculations based on Berger *et al.* (2022).

Table 2. Summary statistics for uncertainty and bank liquidity hoarding.

Variable	Mean	SD	p. 25	Median	p. 75	N
Dependent						
LH(Asset)/GTA	0.085	0.103	0.014	0.069	0.145	1,172
LH(Liab)/GTA	0.168	0.068	0.118	0.155	0.198	1,172
LH(OBS)/GTA	−0.279	0.398	−0.412	−0.133	−0.055	1,161
LH(Total)/GTA	−0.026	0.355	−0.117	0.063	0.179	1,161
Independent						
Qatar Uncertainty Index (WUIQ)	0.06	0.08	0	0	0.098	1,172
Log (GTA)	16.273	1.763	14.92	16.473	17.662	1,172
Capital Ratio	0.151	0.09	0.107	0.128	0.17	1,172
IntIncAsset						
Three-bank Concentration	0.641	0.026	0.625	0.636	0.665	1,172
Real GDP Growth	8.436	7.958	3.064	5.334	16.732	1,172

Note: The table shows the summary statistics of key variables employed, including mean and standard deviation (SD) as well as values at the 25th (p.25) and 75th (p. 75) percentiles. LH is the liquidity hoarding, GTA is the gross total assets, Liab is the liabilities, and OBS is the off-balance-sheet items.

Table 3. Correlation matrix of key variables.

Variables	(1)	(2)	(3)	(4)	(5)
(1) LHasset_GTA	1.000				
(2) LHliability_GTA	0.455	1.000			
	(0.000)				
(3) LHOBS_GTA	−0.431	−0.352	1.000		
	(0.000)	(0.000)			
(4) LHTotal_GTA	−0.104	−0.070	0.930	1.000	
	(0.000)	(0.016)	(0.000)		
(5) WUIQAT	−0.039	−0.046	0.066	0.054	1.000
	(0.182)	(0.113)	(0.025)	(0.066)	

Note: *p*-values are given in brackets.

4. Empirical Strategy

To analyze the impact of uncertainty on bank liquidity hoarding behavior, we seek to estimate the following specification (and its variants) for bank i at time t accordingly as follows:

$$y_{it} = \alpha + \beta WUIQ_t + \gamma \boldsymbol{X}_{\mathrm{i,t-1}} + \delta \boldsymbol{M}_{\mathrm{t}} + \theta_i + \eta_t + \varepsilon_{it} \qquad (1)$$

In (1), y is the outcome variable, which is either overall bank liquidity hoarding or its components (such as asset- or liability-side liquidity hoarding, or including off-balance-sheet items).

The independent variables are classified as bank-specific (X) and banking industry-specific (M) variables, the former being included with a lag to account for endogeneity concerns. θ are bank-fixed effects to account for bank-level unobservables, η are quarter-fixed effects to account for changes in the economic environment during the quarter, and ε is the idiosyncratic error.

The coefficient of interest is β: It shows how banks' liquidity hoarding responds to uncertainties in the economic environment. To the extent that higher uncertainty exerts a discernible impact on liquidity hoarding, the coefficient would be statistically significant. Throughout, the reported standard errors are clustered by banks.

5. Results and Discussion

5.1. *Main findings*

The results of the estimation exercise are set out in Table 4. We first estimate the model without the control variables and subsequently incorporate bank-specific and industry controls. In column 1, the coefficient of WUIQ is 0.25 and, therefore, a one standard deviation increase in economic uncertainty raises liquidity hoarding by 2% (or 78% relative to the sample mean). In contrast, evidence for the US suggests that economic uncertainty exerts a much smaller impact on liquidity hoarding, equal to 14% relative to the sample mean. This could occur because of the thinness of the banking market in the country, given the overwhelming high levels of bank concentration, as a result of which liquidity hoarding by one bank (or few major ones) could exert an overall impact on bank liquidity.

Across columns, as we include additional controls, the coefficient gradually loses its significance, suggesting that the liquidity hoarding is not sufficiently compelling. Our most preferred specification is M5, where the coefficient on WUIQ is positive but not statistically significant.

Column 6 shows the *differential impact* of uncertainty on Islamic banks. More specifically, in addition to the terms already included,

Table 4. The effects of World Uncertainty Index for Qatar on total liquidity hoarding.

	(1) M1	(2) M2	(3) M3	(4) M4	(5) M5	(6) M6
WUIQ	.253***	.28***	.28***	.108	.117	.155
	(.075)	(.076)	(.076)	(.081)	(.08)	(.096)
ln_GTA		−.024***	−.021***	−.029***	−.054***	−.054***
		(.006)	(.006)	(.006)	(.008)	(.008)
Capital_ratio			.226**	.221**	.157	.152
			(.092)	(.09)	(.098)	(.098)
IntIncAsset					−3.35***	−3.319***
					(.62)	(.621)
Concentration_bk3					.594**	.595**
					(.275)	(.275)
Islamic*WUIQ						−.183*
						(.109)
Intercept	−.046***	.345***	.253**	−.384**	.609***	.596***
	(.014)	(.092)	(.105)	(.181)	(.229)	(.23)
Observations	1,161	1,161	1,161	1,161	1,161	1,161
R-squared	.617	.619	.621	.627	.641	.641
Bank FE	Yes	Yes	Yes	Yes	Yes	Yes
Quarterly FE	Yes	Yes	Yes	Yes	Yes	Yes

Note: Robust standard errors (clustered by bank) in parentheses $^{***}p < .01$, $^{**}p < .05$, $^{*}p < .1$.

we include the interaction of WUIQ*Islamic. The coefficient on this term is negative and statistically significant with a point estimate of −0.18. To understand its statistical significance, consider an increase in uncertainty from zero to 0.098 or an increase from the 25th to the 75th percentile as in Rajan and Zingales (1998). Based on the point estimates, we can infer that such an increase in uncertainty increases liquidity hoarding for Islamic banks by 68%.[2] Our results add to the literature which highlights the differential liquidity behavior of banks in countries with dual banking systems.

From an economic standpoint, Islamic banks' lending strategy is either asset-backed or asset-based. In the event of the absence of adequate liquidity-hedging instruments, in response to uncertainties

[2]This is calculated as $0.678 = -0.18 * (0.098 - 0)/(-0.026)$.

in the economic environment, they hoard much higher levels of liquidity, suggesting an outsized response in order to cover for their low liquidity levels.

The signs on the control variables indicate the following. Smaller banks hoard higher levels of liquidity, whereas well-capitalized banks hoard higher liquidity (Affinito *et al.*, 2019; Berger *et al.*, 2022). Banks with higher fee income have multiple sources of income generation and therefore are less inclined to hoard liquidity. Higher competition leads to an increase in liquidity hoarding, indicating lower levels of competition for lending.

Collectively, the findings indicate higher liquidity hoarding by banks in response to economic uncertainties. In addition, there exist differential levels of liquidity hoarding for Islamic banks.

5.2. *Robustness checks*

We undertake several robustness checks. First, we check whether liquidity hoarding occurs on the asset or the liability side (or both). Second, given the significant interlinkages of Qatar with other GCC countries, we compute a relative uncertainty index where we weigh the uncertainty of each country by its nominal GDP and calculate the ratio of uncertainty for Qatar relative to other GCC countries. Finally, we assess the robustness of the findings using instrumental variable (IV) analysis.

5.2.1. *Liquidity hoarding — Asset versus liability sides*

We present the results of the liquidity hoarding separately on the assets (Table 5) and liabilities (Table 6) sides.

In Table 5, we find that the coefficient on WUIQ equals −0.05 and therefore uncertainty lowers asset-side liquidity hoarding. The decline in asset-side liquidity hoarding is consistent with Berger *et al.* (2022) who report a decline in loan and loan commitments in response to higher levels of economic uncertainty. The point estimates in M1 indicate a 5.4% decline in asset-side liquidity hoarding, the magnitudes being broadly comparable to evidence obtained for the US

Table 5. The effects of World Uncertainty Index for Qatar on Asset-side liquidity hoarding.

	(1) M1	(2) M2	(3) M3	(4) M4	(5) M5	(6) M6
WUIQ	$-.054^{**}$	$-.027$	$-.026$	$-.012$	$-.01$	$-.059^{*}$
	(.028)	(.027)	(.025)	(.027)	(.027)	(.032)
ln_GTA		$-.024^{***}$	$-.019^{***}$	$-.018^{***}$	$-.023^{***}$	$-.025^{***}$
		(.003)	(.003)	(.003)	(.003)	(.003)
Capital_ratio			$.324^{***}$	$.324^{***}$	$.309^{***}$	$.316^{***}$
			(.041)	(.041)	(.043)	(.042)
Concentration_bk3				$-.099$	$-.228^{**}$	$-.232^{**}$
				(.101)	(.11)	(.109)
IntIncAsset					$-.72^{***}$	$-.767^{***}$
					(.233)	(.236)
Islamic*WUIQ						$.23^{***}$
						(.049)
Intercept	$.093^{***}$	$.482^{***}$	$.35^{***}$	$.4^{***}$	$.607^{***}$	$.629^{***}$
	(.005)	(.05)	(.043)	(.067)	(.097)	(.097)
Observations	1,172	1,172	1,172	1,172	1,172	1,172
R-squared	.437	.468	.519	.52	.527	.533
Bank FE	Yes	Yes	Yes	Yes	Yes	Yes
Quarterly FE	Yes	Yes	Yes	Yes	Yes	Yes

Note: Robust standard errors (clustered by bank) in parentheses $^{***}p < .01$, $^{**}p < .05$, $^{*}p < .1$.

(Berger *et al.*, 2022) who report a 7% decline in lending and 5% fall in lending commitments in response to higher uncertainty. Column 6 shows the different impact and shows that the overall response of economic uncertainty on Islamic banks is 0.17 (=−0.06 + 0.23), indicating that Islamic banks increase asset-side liquidity hoarding by nearly 17% in response to higher economic uncertainty. This follows from the business strategy of Islamic banks who tend to hold back lending (which is typically collateralized) in response to higher uncertainty levels.

The response on the liability side is set out in Table 6. In column 1, the coefficient on WUIQ is negative and statistically significant. In other words, banks decumulate liquidity in response to higher uncertainties, especially on the liability side. Based on the

Table 6. The effects of World Uncertainty Index for Qatar on Liability-side liquidity hoarding.

	(1) M1	(2) M2	(3) M3	(4) M4	(5) M5	(6) M6
WUIQAT	$-.038^{***}$	$-.052^{***}$	$-.052^{***}$	$-.023$	$-.022$	$-.019$
	(.014)	(.013)	(.013)	(.015)	(.015)	(.016)
ln_GTA		$.012^{***}$	$.012^{***}$	$.014^{***}$	$.011^{***}$	$.011^{***}$
		(.002)	(.002)	(.002)	(.002)	(.002)
Capital_ratio			.01	.011	.002	.002
			(.03)	(.03)	(.031)	(.031)
Concentration_bk3				$-.202^{***}$	$-.275^{***}$	$-.274^{***}$
				(.054)	(.058)	(.058)
IntIncAsset					$-.406^{***}$	$-.402^{***}$
					(.113)	(.114)
Islamic*WUIQ						$-.017$
						(.031)
Intercept	$.167^{***}$	$-.03$	$-.034$	$.07^{*}$	$.186^{***}$	$.185^{***}$
	(.003)	(.031)	(.029)	(.038)	(.051)	(.052)
Observations	1,172	1,172	1,172	1,172	1,172	1,172
R-squared	.641	.66	.66	.665	.67	.67
Bank FE	Yes	Yes	Yes	Yes	Yes	Yes
Quarterly FE	Yes	Yes	Yes	Yes	Yes	Yes

Note: Robust standard errors are in parentheses $^{***}p < .01$, $^{**}p < .05$, $^{*}p < .1$.

point estimate, we can infer that there is a 4% decline in liquidity hoarding. As we include additional controls, the coefficient loses its significance, suggesting that liability-side liquidity hoarding is not very compelling. There is also no differential impact of uncertainty on the liquidity hoarding behavior of Islamic banks.

5.2.2. *Liquidity hoarding — Impact of relative uncertainty*

Given the significant interlinkages among GCC nations, it might also be relevant to ascertain the importance of *relative uncertainty* (WUIQR) as opposed to *absolute uncertainty*. To implement this, we use annual data on nominal GDP for GCC countries (reported for Kuwait, Oman, Qatar, Saudi Arabia, and the United Arab Emirates) from the IMF website and integrate it with information on bank-level variables for Qatar, as earlier. The analysis in this case is based on

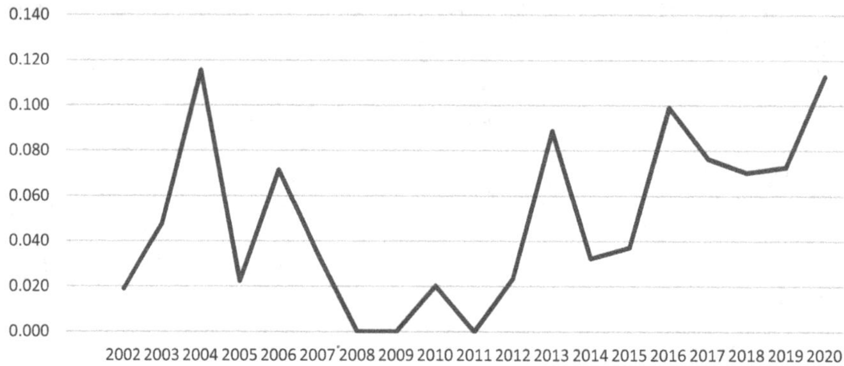

Figure 1. QATAR (Relative EPU).

annual data for the period 2002–2020. Figure 1 shows the WUIQR for the sample period.

In essence, this variable measures the importance of Qatar in the overall economic uncertainty for the GCC region. The variable has a mean value of 0.05, suggesting that Qatar on average contributes 5% to the economic uncertainty of the GCC region. The correlation between *relative uncertainty and* WUIQ is −0.15 and therefore an increase in uncertainty in Qatar lowers relative uncertainty, presumably because the GCC uncertainty levels increase at a much faster rate. In the regressions, we employ WUIQR as a key variable. Results are set out in Table 7.

The results indicate that relative uncertainty increases overall liquidity hoarding, although the magnitudes are lower as compared with the baseline findings. Based on the point estimates in column 1, a one standard deviation increase in relative uncertainty raises liquidity hoarding by 1.2%. There is however no differential impact of relative uncertainty on the liquidity hoarding behavior of Islamic banks.

5.2.3. *Addressing endogeneity*

Endogeneity concerns could be a major issue that could contaminate the findings. To address this challenge, we use an instrumental variable (IV) approach. Such an approach requires the use of an appropriate variable (instrument) that is correlated with uncertainty but

Table 7. The effects of Relative World Uncertainty Index for Qatar on total liquidity hoarding.

	(1) M1	(2) M2	(3) M3	(4) M4	(5) M5	(6) M6
WUIQR	.149***	.118***	.093*	0.108	0.086	.144**
	(.070)	(.055)	(.056)	(.077)	(0.063)	(.053)
Islamic*WUIQR						−.061
						(.052)
Controls	Yes	Yes	Yes	Yes	Yes	Yes
Observations	266	266	266	266	266	266
R-squared	.617	.619	.621	.627	.641	.641
Bank FE	Yes	Yes	Yes	Yes	Yes	Yes
Quarterly FE	Yes	Yes	Yes	Yes	Yes	Yes

Note: Robust standard errors (clustered by bank) in parentheses $^{***}p < .01$, $^{**}p < .05$, $^{*}p < .1$.

does not directly impact the dependent variable other than via the endogenous variable.

In our case, we use a dummy variable which equals one for the period June 2017–December 2020. This period coincided with the sudden imposition of economic blockade on Qatar by several neighboring nations. This instrument satisfies the twin conditions of relevance and exclusion (Roberts and Whited, 2013). It is a relevant instrument since the economic blockade is likely to directly aggravate economic uncertainty in Qatar. At the same time, an economic blockade is less likely to directly affect liquidity hoarding other than the impact on economic uncertainty, reiterating its usefulness for the exclusion criteria.

In Table 8, the first-stage regressions highlight a positive and statistically significant impact of the economic blockade on economic uncertainty. In the second stage, economic uncertainty is observed to positively and significantly impact the overall liquidity hoarding.

The diagnostics show that the F-statistic for the joint significance of the instruments excluded from the model is higher than 10, compared to the rule-of-thumb value of 10 (Cameron and Trivedi, 2010). Thus, a blockade is not a weak instrument. The Kleibergen–Paap LM statistics rejects the null hypothesis of under-identification, supporting the fact that the model is identified.

Table 8. Regression results: IV estimation.

	First Stage	Second Stage
	WUIQ	LHTotal
WUIQ		0.121**
		(0.058)
Blockade	0.024***	
	(0.005)	
Controls	Y	Y
Bank FE	N	Y
Quarter FE	Y	Y
Observations	1,161	1,161
R-squared		0.066
F-test (p-Val.)	10.22(0.00)	
Kleiberger-Paap LM statistics		45.40(0.00)

Note: Standard errors in parentheses $^{***}p < .01$, $^{**}p < .05$, $^{*}p < .1$.

6. Concluding Remarks

Using an extended database on Qatari banks, we assess the impact of economic uncertainty on banks' liquidity hoarding. The findings reveal an increase in the overall liquidity hoarding and primarily on the asset side. In addition, there is also a differential impact on liquidity hoarding for Islamic banks. Further analysis reveals that the impact is lower when relative uncertainty is considered as compared with overall uncertainty. The results are robust after accounting for potential endogeneity concerns.

Several policy implications follow from the analysis. First and foremost, policy measures by the government to reduce or eliminate uncertainty can help improve real economic activity. Given the strong and positive impact of bank credit on the real economy (Berger *et al.*, 2020), it can help unclog the lending channel. Second, the challenges of liquidity management are much more acute for Islamic banks as compared with their conventional counterparts. As a result, these banks exhibit an outsized response by hoarding excessive liquidity during periods of economic uncertainties. This calls for instruments that can help them better manage their liquidity. And finally, while relative uncertainty is important for Qatar, its impact on the banking sector and especially domestic banks is not so compelling. This follows from the relatively insulated nature of their banking system and their limited presence across GCC nations.

It is possible to extend the debate in several directions. First, one can examine which items on the asset and liability sides — liquid versus illiquid assets or liquid versus illiquid liabilities — are most impacted by such uncertainties. Second, whether such behavior differs across bank size and capital remains to be explored. In addition, whether and to what extent liquidity hoarding impacts banks with high versus low levels of such hoarding remains to be analyzed. Addressing these issues will facilitate a more holistic assessment of the liquidity debate, in turn, allowing for more comprehensive policy formulation around these issues.

Acknowledgments

I would like to thank, without implicating, Prof. Marwa Elnahass (Co-Editor of the volume) for the incisive comments and suggestions which greatly improved the analysis. Needless to state, the views expressed and the approach pursued in this paper are strictly personal.

References

Acharya, V. V. and Merrouche, O. (2013). Precautionary hoarding of liquidity and interbank markets: Evidence from the subprime crisis. *Review of Finance*, *17*, 107–160.

Acharya, V. V. and Skeie, D. (2011). A model of liquidity hoarding and term premia in interbank markets. *Staff Report No. 498. Federal Reserve Bank of New York: NY.*

Acharya, V. V. and Steffen, S. (2020). The risk of being a fallen angel and the corporate dash for cash in the midst of COVID. *Review of Corporate Finance Studies*, *9*(3), 430–471.

Affinito, M., Albareto, G. and Santioni, R. (2019). Purchases of sovereign debt securities by banks during the crisis: The role of balance sheet conditions. *Journal of Banking and Finance*, *138*, 105575.

Agénor, P. R. and Aynaoui, K. E. (2010). Excess liquidity, bank pricing rules, and monetary policy. *Journal of Banking and Finance*, *34*, 923–933.

Ahir, H., Bloom, N. and Furceri, D. (2022). The world uncertainty index. *NBER Working Paper No. 29763. Cambridge: MA.*

Allen, F. and Gale, D. (2004). Competition and financial stability. *Journal of Money, Credit, and Banking, 36*, 453–480.

Álvarez-Botas, C., Fernández-Méndez, C. and González, V. M. (2021). Large bank shareholders and terms of bank loans during the global financial crisis. *Journal of International Financial Management & Accounting, 33*, 107–133.

Amiti, M. and Weinstein, D. E. (2018). How much do idiosyncratic bank shocks affect investment? Evidence from matched bank-firm loan data. *Journal of Political Economy, 126*, 525–587.

Ashraf, B. N. (2020). Policy uncertainty and bank liquidity hoarding: International evidence. *SSRN Electronic Journal No. 3574193.*

Barattieri, A., Eden, M. and Stevanovic, D. (2020). Risk sharing, efficiency of capital allocation, and the connection between banks and the real economy. *Journal of Corporate Finance, 60*, 101538.

Berger, A. and Bouwman, C. (2009). Bank liquidity creation. *Review of financial Studies, 22*, 3779–3837.

Berger, A. N. and Bouwman, C. H. S. (2009). Bank liquidity creation. *Review of Financial Studies, 22*, 3779–3837

Berger, A. N., Guedhami, O., Kim, H. H. and Li, X. (2020). Economic policy uncertainty and bank liquidity hoarding. *Journal of Financial Intermediation, 49*, 100893.

Berger, A. N., Molyneux, P. and Wilson, J. (2020). Banks and the real economy: An assessment of the research. *Journal of Corporate Finance, 62*, 101513.

Bernanke, B. S. (1983). Irreversibility, uncertainty, and cyclical investment. *Quarterly Journal of Economics, 98*, 85–106.

Berrospide, J. (2013). Bank liquidity hoarding and the financial crisis: An empirical analysis. *Finance and Economics Discussion Series, No 3. Federal Reserve Board, Washington, DC.*

Berrospide, J. and Edge, R. (2010). The effects of bank capital on lending: What do we know, and what does it mean? *International Journal of Central Banking*, 6, 5–54.

Bloom, N., Kose, M. A. and Terrones, M. E. (2013). Held back by uncertainty. *Finance and Development, 50*, 38–41.

Boubaker, S., Do, D. T., Hammami, H. and Ly, K. C. (2022). The role of bank affiliation in bank efficiency: A fuzzy multi-objective data envelopment analysis approach. *Annals of Operations Research*, 311, 611–639.

Boubaker, S., Le, T. D. and Ngo, T. (2022). Managing bank performance under COVID-19: A novel inverse DEA efficiency approach. *International Transactions in Operational Research.* Advance online publication, 10.1111/itor.13132.

Brunnermeier, M. (2009). Deciphering the 2007-08 liquidity and credit crunch. *Journal of Economic Perspectives, 23*, 77–100.

Caballero, R. J. and Krishnamurthy, A. (2008). Collective risk management in a flight to quality episode. *Journal of Finance, 63*, 2195–2230.

Chen, Y. K., Shen, C. H., Kao, L. and Yeh, C. Y. (2018). Bank liquidity risk and performance, *Review of Pacific Basin Financial Markets and Policies, 21*, 1–40.

Demirgüç-Kunt, A., Pedraza, A. and Ruiz-Ortega, C. (2021). Banking sector performance during the COVID-19 crisis. *Journal of Banking & Finance, 133*, 10630.

Diamond, D. W. and Rajan, R. G. (2011). Fear of fire sales, illiquidity seeking, and credit freezes. *Quarterly Journal of Economics, 126*, 557–591.

Elnahass, M., Marie, M. and Elgammal, M. (2022). Terrorist attacks and bank financial stability: Evidence from MENA economies. *Review of Quantitative Finance and Accounting, 59*, 383–427.

Elnahass, M., Trinh, V. Q. and Li, T. (2021). Global banking stability in the shadow of Covid-19 outbreak. *Journal of International Financial Markets, Institutions and Money, 72*, 101322.

Ennis, H. and Wolman, A. (2015). Large excess reserves in the U.S.: A view from the cross-section of banks. *International Journal of Central Banking, 7*, 252–289.

Freixas, X., Martin, A. and Skeie, D. (2011). Bank liquidity, interbank markets, and monetary policy. *Review of Financial Studies, 24*, 2656–2692.

Gabaix, X. (2011). The granular origins of aggregate fluctuations. *Econometrica, 79*, 733–772.

Gale, D. and Yorulmazer, T. (2011). Liquidity hoarding. *Staff Report No. 488. Federal Reserve Bank of New York: NY.*

Gatev, E. and Strahan, P. E. (2006). Banks' advantage in hedging liquidity risk: Theory and evidence from the commercial paper market. *Journal of Finance, 61*, 867–892.

Gorton, G. (2009). Information, liquidity, and the (ongoing) panic of 2007. *American Economic Review: Papers and Proceedings, 99*, 567–572.

Heider, F., Hoerova, M. and Holthausen, C. (2015). Liquidity hoarding and interbank market spreads: The role of counterparty risk. *Journal of Financial Economics, 118*, 336–354.

Helge C. N. L. and Busch, M. O. (2021). Banks fearing the drought? Liquidity hoarding as a response to idiosyncratic interbank funding dry-ups. *Journal of International Money and Finance*, *119*, 102474.

Huang, R. (2010). How committed are bank lines of credit? Experiences in the subprime mortgage crisis. *Working Paper No. 25. Federal Reserve Bank of Philadelphia: PA.*

Lown, C. and Morgan, D. (2006). The credit cycle and the business cycle: New findings using the loan officer opinion survey. *Journal of Money, Credit and Banking*, *38*, 1575–1597.

Lucas, R. and Stokey, N (2011). Liquidity crisis: Understanding sources and limiting consequences: A theoretical Framework. *Economic Policy Paper No. 3. Federal Reserve Bank of Minneapolis: MN.*

Ramos, A. (1996). Deposit insurance, bank capital structures and the demand for liquidity. *Working Paper No. 8. Federal Reserve Bank of Chicago: IL.*

Roberts, M. R. and Whited, T. M. (2013). Endogeneity in empirical corporate finance. In G. M. Constantinides, M. Harris and R. M. Stulz (eds.) *Handbook of the Economics of Finance*, pp. 493–572. North Holland: Elsevier.

Sahyouni, A. and Wang, M. (2018). The determinants of bank profitability: Does liquidity creation matter? *Journal of Economics and Financial Analysis*, *2*, 61–85.

Samet, A., Boubakri, N. and Boubaker, S. (2018). Does public–private status affect bank risk taking? Worldwide evidence. *Journal of International Financial Markets, Institutions and Money*, *53*, 287–306.

Strahan, P. (2008). Liquidity production in 21st century banking. *NBER Working Paper No 13798. Cambridge: MA.*

Sufi, A. (2009). Banks lines of credit in corporate finance: An empirical analysis. *Review of Financial Studies*, *22*, 1057–1088.

https://doi.org/10.1142/9781800614321_bmatter

Index

R

S

T

U

V

W

Z

www.ingramcontent.com/pod-product-compliance
Lightning Source LLC
LaVergne TN
LVHW010328220926
848484LV00004BB/855
* 9 7 8 1 8 0 0 6 1 4 3 1 4 *